# Contemporary Issues in Green and Ethical Marketing

In recognising the realms of eco-marketing, sustainable marketing, social marketing and ethical consumption, this collection provides an accessible overview of the multi-faceted and challenging nature of green and ethical issues. In revealing that there are many ways to explore the consumption activities of green and ethical consumers, the contributors point to some of the weaknesses identified in previous marketing research. The book also considers fundamental ways in which marketing academics and marketing practitioners can gain a more holistic understanding of the demographic, psychological and socio-cultural influences upon the green and ethical consumer. The contributors offer insights underpinned by holistic and cross-cultural perspectives. As a result, this collection will advance marketing theory as well as offer valuable implications and recommendations for managers, practitioners and policymakers, the joint efforts of which are needed to ensure a more 'green', ethical and sustainable marketplace.

This book was originally published as a special issue of the *Journal of Marketing Management*.

**Morven G. McEachern** is a Reader in Marketing at the University of Salford, UK, and is also Director of The Centre for Social Business at the University of Salford. Her research interests lie primarily in the area of ethical consumption and corporate social responsibility. She has published in a wide range of academic journals such as the *Journal of Agricultural & Environmental Ethics*, *Journal of Marketing Management* and *Consumption, Markets and Culture*.

**Marylyn Carrigan** is Professor of Marketing in the Faculty of Business, Environment & Society at Coventry University, UK, and is also the Co-Director of The Centre for Trust and Ethical Behaviour (CETEB) at Coventry University. Her research interests include corporate social responsibility, marketing ethics, social marketing, and ethical consumption. She has published her work in several journals, including the *Journal of Business Ethics*, *Psychology and Marketing*, *European Journal of Marketing*, and *International Marketing Review*.

# Key Issues in Marketing Management

The *Journal of Marketing Management* was founded in 1985 by Michael J. Baker to provide a forum for the exchange of the latest research ideas and best practice in the field of marketing as a whole, in an accessible way.

Currently edited by Mark Tadajewski and Paul Hewer, the *Journal of Marketing Management* is the official Journal of the Academy of Marketing and has an international reputation for publishing influential and original contributions which blend the best of theory and practice. It is concerned with all aspects of the management of marketing, and seeks to meet the needs of a wide but sophisticated audience comprising senior marketing executives and their advisors, senior line managers, teachers and researchers in marketing, and undergraduate and postgraduate students of the subject.

The *Key Issues in Marketing Management* book series contains a wide range of the journal's special issues. These special issues are an important contribution to the work of the journal, where leading theoreticians and practitioners bring together articles dedicated to a key topic in the industry. Through publishing these special issues as a series of books, Westburn Publishers and Taylor & Francis hope to allow a wider audience of scholars, students and professionals to engage with the work of the *Journal of Marketing Management*.

## Titles in the series include:

**The Marketing/Accounting Interface**
*Edited by Robin Roslender and Richard M. S. Wilson*

**New Horizons in Arts, Heritage, Nonprofit and Social Marketing**
*Edited by Roger Bennett, Finola Kerrigan and Daragh O'Reilly*

**New Developments in Online Marketing**
*Edited by Stephen Tagg, Alan Stevenson and Tiziano Vescovi*

**Multicultural Perspectives in Customer Behaviour**
*Edited by Maria G. Piacentini and Charles C. Cui*

**Expanding Disciplinary Space: On the Potential of Critical Marketing**
*Edited by Douglas Brownlie, Paul Hewer and Mark Tadajewski*

**Contemporary Issues in Green and Ethical Marketing**
*Edited by Morven G. McEachern and Marylyn Carrigan*

**On the Marketisation and Marketing of Higher Education**
*Edited by Anthony Lowrie and Jane Hemsley-Brown*

**Historical Research in Marketing Management**
*Edited by Mark Tadajewski and D.G. Brian Jones*

# Contemporary Issues in Green and Ethical Marketing

*Edited by*
Morven G. McEachern and Marylyn Carrigan

First published 2014
by Routledge
2 Park Square, Milton Park, Abingdon, Oxfordshire OX14 4RN

and by Routledge
711 Third Avenue, New York, NY 10017

First issued in paperback 2015

*Routledge is an imprint of the Taylor & Francis Group, an informa business*

© 2014 Westburn Publishers Ltd.

All rights reserved. No part of this book may be reprinted or reproduced or utilised in any form or by any electronic, mechanical, or other means, now known or hereafter invented, including photocopying and recording, or in any information storage or retrieval system, without permission in writing from the publishers.

*Trademark notice*: Product or corporate names may be trademarks or registered trademarks, and are used only for identification and explanation without intent to infringe.

*British Library Cataloguing in Publication Data*
A catalogue record for this book is available from the British Library

ISBN 13: 978-1-138-94828-0 (pbk)
ISBN 13: 978-0-415-72382-4 (hbk)

Typeset in Garamond
by Taylor & Francis Books

**Publisher's Note**
The publisher accepts responsibility for any inconsistencies that may have arisen during the conversion of this book from journal articles to book chapters, namely the possible inclusion of journal terminology.

**Disclaimer**
Every effort has been made to contact copyright holders for their permission to reprint material in this book. The publishers would be grateful to hear from any copyright holder who is not here acknowledged and will undertake to rectify any errors or omissions in future editions of this book.

# Contents

| | |
|---|---|
| *Citation Information* | ix |
| *Notes on Contributors* | xiii |

1. Revisiting contemporary issues in green/ethical marketing:
An introduction
*Morven G. McEachern and Marylyn Carrigan*      1

2. Emotions as determinants of electric car usage intention
*Ingrid Moons and Patrick De Pelsmacker*      7

3. The impact of general and carbon-related environmental
knowledge on attitudes and behaviour of US consumers
*Michael Jay Polonsky, Andrea Vocino, Stacy Landreth Grau,
Romana Garma and Ahmed Shahriar Ferdous*      49

4. Understanding local food shopping: Unpacking the ethical
dimension
*Phil Megicks, Juliet Memery and Robert J. Angell*      74

5. A cross-cultural analysis of pro-environmental consumer
behaviour among seniors
*Lynn Sudbury Riley, Florian Kohlbacher and Agnes Hofmeister*      100

6. Chinese consumers' adoption of a 'green' innovation –
The case of organic food
*John Thøgersen and Yanfeng Zhou*      122

7. Consumer attitudes towards sustainability aspects of food
production: Insights from three continents
*Athanasios Krystallis, Klaus G. Grunert, Marcia D. de Barcellos,
Toula Perrea and Wim Verbeke*      143

8. Individual values and motivational complexities in ethical
clothing consumption: A means-end approach
*Thomas Jägel, Kathy Keeling, Alexander Reppel and
Thorsten Gruber*      181

9. Barriers to downward carbon emission: Exploring sustainable
consumption in the face of the glass floor
*Hélène Cherrier, Mathilde Szuba and Nil Özçaglar-Toulouse*      204

## CONTENTS

10. Normalising green behaviours: A new approach to sustainability marketing
*Ruth Rettie, Kevin Burchell and Debra Riley*     226

11. Individual strategies for sustainable consumption
*Seonaidh McDonald, Caroline J. Oates, Panayiota J. Alevizou, C. William Young and Kumju Hwang*     250

12. Environmentally responsible behaviour in the workplace: An internal social marketing approach
*Anne M. Smith and Terry O'Sullivan*     273

13. Heterotopian space and the utopics of ethical and green consumption
*Andreas Chatzidakis, Pauline Maclaran and Alan Bradshaw*     297

*Index*     319

# Citation Information

The chapters in this book were originally published in the *Journal of Marketing Management*, volume 28, issue 3–4 (March 2012). When citing this material, please use the original page numbering for each article, as follows:

**Chapter 1**
*Revisiting contemporary issues in green/ethical marketing: An introduction to the special issue*
Morven G. McEachern and Marylyn Carrigan
*Journal of Marketing Management*, volume 28, issue 3–4
(March 2012) pp. 189–194

**Chapter 2**
*Emotions as determinants of electric car usage intention*
Ingrid Moons and Patrick De Pelsmacker
*Journal of Marketing Management*, volume 28, issue 3–4
(March 2012) pp. 195–237

**Chapter 3**
*The impact of general and carbon-related environmental knowledge on attitudes and behaviour of US consumers*
Michael Jay Polonsky, Andrea Vocino, Stacy Landreth Grau, Romana Garma and Ahmed Shahriar Ferdous
*Journal of Marketing Management*, volume 28, issue 3–4
(March 2012) pp. 238–263

**Chapter 4**
*Understanding local food shopping: Unpacking the ethical dimension*
Phil Megicks, Juliet Memery and Robert J. Angell
*Journal of Marketing Management*, volume 28, issue 3–4
(March 2012) pp. 264–289

# CITATION INFORMATION

**Chapter 5**
*A cross-cultural analysis of pro-environmental consumer behaviour among seniors*
Lynn Sudbury Riley, Florian Kohlbacher and Agnes Hofmeister
*Journal of Marketing Management*, volume 28, issue 3–4 (March 2012) pp. 290–312

**Chapter 6**
*Chinese consumers' adoption of a 'green' innovation – The case of organic food*
John Thøgersen and Yanfeng Zhou
*Journal of Marketing Management*, volume 28, issue 3–4 (March 2012) pp. 313–333

**Chapter 7**
*Consumer attitudes towards sustainability aspects of food production: Insights from three continents*
Athanasios Krystallis, Klaus G. Grunert, Marcia D. de Barcellos, Toula Perrea and Wim Verbeke
*Journal of Marketing Management*, volume 28, issue 3–4 (March 2012) pp. 334–372

**Chapter 8**
*Individual values and motivational complexities in ethical clothing consumption: A means-end approach*
Thomas Jägel, Kathy Keeling, Alexander Reppel and Thorsten Gruber
*Journal of Marketing Management*, volume 28, issue 3–4 (March 2012) pp. 373–396

**Chapter 9**
*Barriers to downward carbon emission: Exploring sustainable consumption in the face of the glass floor*
Hélène Cherrier, Mathilde Szuba and Nil Özçağlar-Toulouse
*Journal of Marketing Management*, volume 28, issue 3–4 (March 2012) pp. 397–419

**Chapter 10**
*Normalising green behaviours: A new approach to sustainability marketing*
Ruth Rettie, Kevin Burchell and Debra Riley
*Journal of Marketing Management*, volume 28, issue 3–4 (March 2012) pp. 420–444

## Chapter 11

*Individual strategies for sustainable consumption*
Seonaidh McDonald, Caroline J. Oates, Panayiota J. Alevizou,
C. William Young and Kumju Hwang
*Journal of Marketing Management*, volume 28, issue 3–4
(March 2012) pp. 445–468

## Chapter 12

*Environmentally responsible behaviour in the workplace:*
*An internal social marketing approach*
Anne M. Smith and Terry O'Sullivan
*Journal of Marketing Management*, volume 28, issue 3–4
(March 2012) pp. 469–493

## Chapter 13

*Heterotopian space and the utopics of ethical and green*
*consumption*
Andreas Chatzidakis, Pauline Maclaran and Alan Bradshaw
*Journal of Marketing Management*, volume 28, issue 3–4
(March 2012) pp. 494–515

Please direct any queries you may have about the citations to
clsuk.permissions@cengage.com

# Notes on Contributors

**Panayiota J. Alevizou,** after following a career in Marketing has recently completed her doctorate at the Management School, University of Sheffield, UK, on sustainability claims on FMCGs – consumers' perceptions and company practice in the UK and in Greece. This was an investigation of how the labels on product packaging are generated by manufacturers and understood by consumers. Following this, she was a research fellow on an ESRC project, which was part of their Sustainable Technologies Programme, and she now teaches at the Management School, University of Sheffield.

**Robert J. Angell** is Lecturer in marketing at the University of Plymouth, UK, specialising in marketing, consumer psychology, and research methods. His professional background is in market research where he worked with both qualitative and quantitative methods for several international organisations. His specific research interests are in customer satisfaction, segmentation, gerontology, and the philosophy of marketing science.

**Marcia D. de Barcellos** is Associate Professor at the Management School of the Federal University of Rio Grande do Sul (UFRGS), Brazil, and is affiliated with the MAPP Centre. She holds an MSc and a PhD in Agribusiness, both from the Federal University of Rio Grande do Sul. She was a Guest PhD student at Wageningen University in the Netherlands and at the University of New England in Australia. Her research interests include food marketing and innovation, consumer behaviour, applied market research, sustainability, branding, and agri-food supply-chain management.

**Alan Bradshaw** is Senior Lecturer in marketing at Royal Holloway, University of London, UK, and co-director of the Centre for Consumption Studies. His research is concerned with how we mediate our lives, imaginations, identities, experiences, and cultures with the consumer society. His work can be found in numerous journals including *Consumption, Markets and Culture*, *Marketing Theory*, the *European Journal of Marketing*, *Journal of Macromarketing*, and the *Journal of Marketing Management*.

**Kevin Burchell** is a Senior Research fellow at Kingston University, UK. He is the Co-Investigator on Smart Communities (ESRC), a community action project on energy consumption reduction (http://business.kingston.ac.uk/smartcommunities). Previously, he was the senior researcher on CHARM (EPSRC), a social norm intervention project on sustainability issues (http://www.projectcharm.info/). He has recently worked on the UK Department of Energy and Climate Change's *Low Carbon Community Challenge* and

NOTES ON CONTRIBUTORS

*Green Deal* initiatives. He has research interests in sustainability, energy consumption, community action, practice theory, social learning theory, the social norm approach, social marketing, green marketing, public engagement, and science and society issues. He has a PhD in science, society, and sustainability issues.

**Marylyn Carrigan** is Professor of Marketing in the Faculty of Business, Environment & Society at Coventry University, UK, and is also the Co-Director of The Centre for Trust and Ethical Behaviour (CETEB) at Coventry University. Her research interests include corporate social responsibility, marketing ethics, social marketing, and ethical consumption. She has published her work in several journals, including the *Journal of Business Ethics, Psychology and Marketing, European Journal of Marketing*, and *International Marketing Review*.

**Andreas Chatzidakis** is Senior Lecturer in marketing at the School of Management, Royal Holloway University of London, UK. He received his PhD from Nottingham Business School in 2007. His main research interests include anti-consumption, consumer resistance, and ethical and altruistic behaviour. He has published in *Journal of Business Ethics, Advances in Consumer Research, Journal of Marketing Management*, and *Journal of Consumer Behaviour*.

**Hélène Cherrier** is Senior Lecturer at Griffith University, Brisbane, Australia. Her research interests embrace radical changes in consumption lifestyles, social and environmental activism, appropriation and reconfiguration of consumer meanings, symbols, and usage, identity politics, and the role of disposal in identity construction. She has published her work in several conference proceedings and in refereed academic journals including the *Journal of Business Research*, the *Journal of Qualitative Market Research, Marketing Education Review, Advances in Consumer Research*, the *Journal of Research for Consumers, Consumption, Markets and Culture*, the *Journal of Consumer Behavior*, the *European Journal of Marketing*, the *Journal of Marketing Management*, the *International Journal of Consumer Studies, World Management Review*. She has contributed to Harrison, Newholm, and Shaw's edited book, *The Ethical Consumer*, and she also co-edited a book on the theories and practices of simple living.

**Ahmed Shahriar Ferdous** is Senior Lecturer in the School of Business, North South University, Bangladesh. He is presently pursuing his PhD in the area of internal marketing at Deakin University, Australia. His research interest is in the area of internal marketing, sustainable marketing, service dominant logic, Theory of Planned Behaviour, and structural equation modelling. He has published in journals such as *Marketing Intelligence and Planning, The Marketing Review, Journal of Asia Business Studies*, and *Journal of International Consumer Marketing*.

**Romana Garma** is Senior Lecturer in marketing at Victoria University, Australia. Her research interests are in the areas of customer citizenship behaviour, service and relationship marketing, and social and non-profit marketing. She has published in the *Journal of Strategic Marketing, Journal of Marketing Theory and Practice, Asia-Pacific Journal in Marketing and Logistics, European Business Review, Journal of Non-Profit and Public Sector Marketing*, and *Australasian Marketing Journal*.

xiv

## NOTES ON CONTRIBUTORS

**Stacy Landreth Grau** is an Associate Professor of professional practice in marketing at Texas Christian University, USA. Her research interests are in the areas of corporate social responsibilities, non-profit branding, and social media marketing. She has published in the *Journal of Retailing*, *Journal of Advertising*, *International Journal of Advertising*, *Journal of Nonprofit and Public Sector Marketing*, and *Journal of Macromarketing*.

**Thorsten Gruber** is Professor of marketing and service management at Loughborough University, UK. Prior to that, he was a Senior Lecturer (Associate Professor) in marketing at Manchester Business School, University of Manchester, UK. He received his PhD and MBA from the University of Birmingham, UK. His research interests include consumer complaining behaviour, services marketing and the development of qualitative online research methods. His work has been published in journals such as *Journal of the Academy of Marketing Science*, *Journal of Product Innovation Management*, *Journal of Business Research*, *Journal of Service Management*, and *Industrial Marketing Management*.

**Klaus G. Grunert** is Professor of marketing at the Department of Business Administration, School of Business and Social Sciences, Aarhus University, Denmark, and is the founder and director of the MAPP Centre for Research on Customer Relations in the Food Sector. His scientific interests focus on consumer behaviour (acceptance of new foods, attitudes, decision making, lifestyle, and segmentation), society and politics (everyday life, regulation and control, health, food, and nutrition), and marketing strategy (market-oriented product development, user-driven innovation).

**Agnes Hofmeister-Toth** is the Dean of the Faulty of Business Administration of the Corvinus University of Budapest, Hungary. She received her PhD in Marketing from Budapest University of Economic Sciences. She spent periods as visiting professor at several universities abroad, for example Haas School University of Berkeley, Hosei University Tokyo, Northwestern University, London Business School, and University of Passau. She is teaching consumer behaviour and negotiation for undergraduate and graduate students. She also supervises several PhD students. Her research interests are cultural differences, transition of consumer behaviour, changing consumer values, the silver generation, sustainable consumption, and symbolic consumption. She is author of three books as well as of a great deal of research studies published at national and international journals.

**Kumju Hwang** is Associate Professor of marketing in School of Business Administration at Chung-Ang University, South Korea. Her main research interests lie in the field of sustainable marketing, consumer decision making, science and technology management, and corporate social responsibility. Her research has appeared in the *Journal of Marketing Communications*, *Science, Technology and Human Values*, *Science Communication*, *Sustainable Development*, and *Psychology and Marketing*, among others.

**Thomas Jägel** worked as a research project assistant for Manchester Business School (MBS), University of Manchester, UK. Prior to that, he completed his masters in marketing at MBS. He received his bachelor degree in Communication Science and Political Science from the University of Muenster, Germany. His research interest focuses on ethical consumption and marketing and on qualitative online research methods. Further interests centre on advertising and consumer behaviour in the context of new media. He has interned in international advertising and PR agencies and is now media sales consultant at Google, Germany.

**Kathy Keeling** is currently Senior Lecturer in research methods and data analysis at Manchester Business School, University of Manchester, UK. With a PhD investigating and modelling user acceptance of e-banking services and an MSc in Applied Psychology from the University of Manchester as well as a BSc in Psychology, she researches cross disciplinary areas and applies psychological models of behaviour.

**Florian Kohlbacher** is Senior Research fellow at the German Institute for Japanese Studies (DIJ), Tokyo. He holds both a master's degree and a doctorate from the Vienna University of Economics and Business (WU Vienna). His research focuses on the business implications of demographic change, particularly from a marketing and innovation management perspective. He has presented papers on this topic at marketing, management, and gerontology conferences around the globe, and published papers in *Ageing International*, *Sex Roles: A Journal of Research*, and *International Journal of Human Resources Development and Management*, among others. Dr. Kohlbacher is a fellow of the World Demographic & Ageing Forum and an adviser to the International Mature Marketing Network (IMMN). He is author of *International Marketing in the Network Economy: A Knowledge-Based Approach* (2007) and co-editor of *The Silver Market Phenomenon: Marketing and Innovation in the Aging Society*, 2nd ed. (2011).

**Athanasios Krystallis** is Associate Professor of marketing at the Department of Business Administration, School of Business and Social Sciences, Aarhus University, Denmark, and is co-responsible for consumer research at the MAPP Centre. He holds an MSc degree in food marketing and a PhD in consumer behaviour (both from the University of Newcastle upon Tyne, UK). His scientific interests focus on food consumer behaviour with emphasis on perceived extrinsic sustainability attributes and marketing strategy.

**Pauline Maclaran** is Professor of marketing and consumer research at Royal Holloway, University of London, UK. Her publications have been in internationally recognised journals such as the *Journal of Consumer Research*, *Psychology and Marketing*, *Journal of Advertising*, *Journal of Business Research*, and *Consumption, Markets and Culture*. She has co-edited various books including *The Sage Handbook of Marketing Theory*, *Marketing and Feminism: Critical Issues and Research*, and *Critical Marketing: Defining the Field*. She is also editor in chief of *Marketing Theory*, a journal that promotes alternative and critical perspectives in marketing and consumer behaviour.

**Seonaidh McDonald** is Reader in sustainable behaviours at Aberdeen Business School, Robert Gordon University, UK. Her research interests centre on sustainable consumption, and she has investigated consumer behaviour and consumer decision making across a wide range of issues, including waste, travel, domestic appliances, food, household goods, and energy. She also has a strong interest in qualitative research methods and how these are used within organisational research.

**Morven G. McEachern** is a Reader in Marketing at the University of Salford, UK, and is also Director of The Centre for Social Business at the University of Salford. Her

NOTES ON CONTRIBUTORS

research interests lie primarily in the area of ethical consumption and corporate social responsibility. She has published in a wide range of academic journals such as the *Journal of Agricultural & Environmental Ethics*, *Journal of Marketing Management* and *Consumption, Markets and Culture*.

**Phil Megicks** is Professor of marketing and strategy at the University of Plymouth, UK, and Head of the School of Management. He undertakes research and teaches in the fields of marketing strategy and consumer behaviour. His specific research interests cover small service businesses and consumer behaviour in these contexts. Recent work focuses on ethical and sustainability issues in retailing, including strategies for the survival of the small shop and socially responsible shopping behaviour.

**Juliet Memery** is Associate Professor in marketing at the University of Plymouth, UK. Before coming to Plymouth, she worked in design for companies based in both Europe and Africa. Her PhD thesis investigated the role of ethical and social responsibility issues in food and grocery shopping decisions. Research interests include ethical shopping, consumer behaviour, decision making in relation to consumer choice, and product design.

**Ingrid Moons** holds a master's degree in psychology. She teaches consumer behaviour, marketing and marketing management at the Department of Design Sciences at the Artesis University College Antwerp, Belgium, and is working on a PhD on the role of emotions in the adoption process of electric cars. Her research interests are consumer behaviour, adoption processes of new products, and the role of emotions in product design.

**Caroline J. Oates** is Senior Lecturer in marketing at the University of Sheffield Management School. She was awarded her PhD in 1997, and since then has been teaching marketing communications and researching environmental marketing issues and marketing to children. Her main interests lie in the area of consumer behaviour, both in terms of 'green' consumption, and children as consumers of marketing communications. She has published many articles in international journals such as *Psychology and Marketing*, *Sociology*, *Journal of Consumer Behaviour*, *Sustainable Development*, and *Journal of Marketing Communications*, and has co-authored two books. She is on the editorial board of the journal *Young Consumers*.

**Terry O'Sullivan** is Senior Lecturer in management at the Open University Business School, UK, and a member of ISM-Open, the Institute of Social Marketing at the Open University in collaboration with the University of Stirling. As well as researching social marketing topics in the areas of environmental behaviour and advertising to children, he has published in the area of arts marketing (particularly audience experience of classical music) and is a joint author of *Creative Arts Marketing*, the leading UK text in the field of arts marketing education. His work has appeared in the *Journal of Marketing Management*, *Consumption, Markets and Culture*, *Qualitative Market Research: An International Journal*, *The International Journal of Arts Management*, the *International Journal of Culture, Tourism and Hospitality Research*, and the *International Journal of Non-profit and Voluntary Sector Marketing*.

xvii

# NOTES ON CONTRIBUTORS

**Nil Özçağlar-Toulouse** is Professor of marketing at Univ Lille North of France and at SKEMA Business School. She primarily carries out research in the field of consumption, including analysing consumer ethics, immigration, sustainable development, or promising niche markets such as Fairtrade. Her work has been published in *Décisions Marketing, Recherche et Applications Marketing, Journal of Business Research, Journal of Macromarketing, Journal of Business Ethics, International Journal of Consumer Studies, Advances in Consumer Research*, amongst others. She is also co-author of several books. She has presented her research findings at international marketing conferences (ACR, EACR, CCT, AFM, AM, etc.). Nil is a co-founder of FairNESS (Network on Exchanges in Social Sciences) and a member of the Association of Consumer Research and French Marketing Association.

**Patrick De Pelsmacker** holds a PhD in economics and is Professor of marketing at the Faculty of Applied Economics of the University of Antwerp, Belgium. He teaches marketing communications, marketing research, and consumer behaviour. His research interests are advertising effectiveness, marketing communications in interactive media (interactive television, consumer-generated content), new communication formats such as product placement, branding strategy, health communication, cross-cultural advertising, and ethical consumer behaviour and social marketing.

**Toula Perrea** is a PhD candidate at the Department of Business Administration, School of Business and Social Sciences, Aarhus University, Denmark, and is affiliated with the MAPP Centre. She holds an MSc in Agricultural and Food Marketing from the University of Newcastle upon Tyne, UK. Her research interests deal with food consumer behaviour with emphasis on sustainable/green foods.

**Michael Jay Polonsky** is the Chair in marketing within the School of Management and Marketing at Deakin University. He has been researching environmental marketing issues for more than 20 years, as well as researching a range of other issues including social issues in marketing, non-profit issues, health issues, international marketing, and marketing education. He has published a number of previous papers in the *Journal of Marketing Management*, as well as recent works in the *Journal of Business Research, International Journal of Public Opinion Research, Asia Pacific Journal of Marketing and Logistics, Corporate Social Responsibility and Environmental Management Journal, Australasian Marketing Journal, European Business Review, International Journal of Nonprofit and Voluntary Sector Marketing, Psychology and Health, Social Science and Medicine, Transfusion*, and *International Journal of Hospitality Management*.

**Alexander Reppel** is Reader in marketing at Royal Holloway, University of London, UK. His main research interests are in relationship marketing in consumer markets, marketing ethics, and consumer data management practices. Alexander is also involved in the development of innovative online research methods, such as interviewer- and non-interviewer-based online laddering techniques.

**Ruth Rettie's** background is interdisciplinary, combining philosophy, marketing, and sociology. After 10 years as a brand manager for Cadbury, Kraft, and Unilever, Professor Rettie joined Kingston University where she is a Professor in social marketing. Her research applies social marketing and sociological perspectives to the adoption of

## NOTES ON CONTRIBUTORS

sustainable behaviours. She is principal investigator of two major pro-environmental behaviour-change research projects, CHARM (http://www.projectcharm.info) and Smart Communities. She has recently worked on the UK Department of Energy and Climate Change's *Low Carbon Community Challenge* and *Green Deal* initiatives.

**Debra Riley** is a Researcher at Kingston Business School, UK. Her research focuses on marketing strategy, new product development and innovation. She has extensive experience in industrial sales and marketing in both the United States and the UK.

**Lynn Sudbury Riley** is Lecturer in marketing at the University of Liverpool, UK. Her PhD focused on senior consumers, and she has presented papers on this topic at marketing and gerontology conferences in the UK, Europe, and the United States. She has also published papers in the *Journal of Marketing Management*, *Psychology and Marketing*, the *Journal of Consumer Marketing*, the *Journal of Consumer Behaviour*, the *International Journal of Advertising*, and *Advances in Consumer Research*, as well as in the gerontology literature. She has received several prizes and awards for her work, including two Emerald Literati Network awards.

**Anne M. Smith** is Reader in marketing at the Open University Business School. Her main research interests focus on services marketing and the principles and practice of social marketing. Studies have examined how consumers evaluate health services, the ways in which service design and service quality impact on evaluation and behaviour, and how this differs across cultures. Further research focuses on the nature and determinants of ERBs and how an IM approach can promote such behaviour within organisations. Her work has been published in a number of international journals including the *Journal of Service Research*, the *European Journal of Marketing*, the *Journal of Business Research*, the *International Marketing Review*, the *Journal of Marketing Management*, the *Service Industries Journal*, and *Long Range Planning*.

**Mathilde Szuba** is a PhD student in sociology at the University of Paris 1, Panthéon-Sorbonne, France. Her supervisor is Professor Alain Gras from the CETCOPRA: Technology, Knowledge and Practices Research Centre. She received a research grant from the French Agency for the Environment and Energy Management (ADEME). Her research interests focus on energy and climate policies, voluntary and mandatory energy consumption contraction, personal carbon quotas, energy sufficiency, and the cultural meanings of energy consumption. Her work has recently been published in *Sociologies Pratiques* and in Séverine Frère and Helga-Jane Scarwell's edited book, *Ecofiscalité et Transport Durable: Entre Prime et Taxe?* She is part of the editorial board for *Entropia* and *Développement Durable et Territoires*. She is currently involved in 'Sobriétés', a research program on sufficiency.

**John Thøgersen** is Professor of economic psychology at the Department of Business Administration, School of Business and Social Sciences, Aarhus University, Denmark. His current research interests include social norms in the environmental field; promoting energy conservation in households; consumer acceptance of organic food products in China, Brazil, and Europe; and intergenerational transfer of environmental concern. He has published extensively on 'green' issues in consumer behaviour in international journals.

# NOTES ON CONTRIBUTORS

**Wim Verbeke** is Professor in agro-food marketing and consumer behaviour, affiliated with the Department of Agricultural Economics at Ghent University, Belgium. He holds an MSc degree in bio-science engineering, an MBA in marketing management, and a PhD in applied biological sciences. His research deals with consumer perception, attitudes, and acceptance of technologies in relation to food production, processing, and food products, with specific attention to the role of individual difference variables and communication.

**Andrea Vocino** is a Lecturer in marketing at the School of Management and Marketing at Deakin University, Australia. His areas of research include consumer behaviour, branding, retailing, and quantitative research methods. Andrea has published in the *Journal of Business Ethics*, *International Journal of Public Opinion Research*, *Marketing Intelligence and Planning*, *Asia Pacific Journal of Marketing and Logistics*, among others.

**C. William Young** is Senior Lecturer in environment and business and heads the Business and Organisations for Sustainable Societies research group (BOSS) at the Sustainability Research Institute, University of Leeds, UK. He is a leading authority on behaviour change towards sustainability for consumers, householders, and employees. William's expertise also includes evaluating companies' sustainability performance, developing routes to sustainable entrepreneurship, and implementing education for sustainable development. He is one of the founders of the Corporate Responsibility Research Conference.

**Yanfeng Zhou** is Associate Professor and head of the marketing department at the Business School of Sun Yat-Sen University, China. Her current research interests include social marketing and 'green' and ethical issues in consumer behaviour.

# Revisiting contemporary issues in green/ethical marketing: An introduction

The *Journal of Marketing Management* was one of the first marketing journals to feature a specially themed issue on 'Green marketing: The fad that won't slip slide away' in the late 1990s. Therefore, it is fitting that the journal facilitates our return to this domain of marketing inquiry and builds on Andrea Prothero's (1998) special issue published 14 years earlier. As Prothero (1998) predicted, the field of green/ethical marketing shows no sign of diminishing and has since generated numerous special issues in marketing journals on related topics such as anti-consumption and sustainable consumption over the last decade. The enormous response to our call for papers for this special issue indicates that trend being set to continue, and it was with regret that we were unable to include several other interesting green/ethical studies taking place around the globe. Notwithstanding the sustained attention from academics, the uptake of green/ethical research from policymakers and marketing practitioners has been somewhat tokenistic. This is despite statistics suggesting that an entire planet is needed to sustain prevailing consumption trends beyond the next 25 years or so, confirming that 'business as usual' is no longer an option (Soron, 2010). As marketing continues to be criticised for stimulating unsustainable levels of consumption, we would argue that the more attention our discipline gives to green/ethical marketing, the better it could be for societal well-being in the long term. Therein lies the justification for revisiting the field of green/ethical marketing both from a theoretical and practice-based perspective.

Since Prothero's (1998) special issue, the green marketing literature has become intertwined with the realms of eco-marketing, sustainable marketing, social marketing, and ethical consumption. This is evident in the following collection of papers whose titles all refer to a variety of these terms. While we acknowledge the narrow distinctions between each term, we argue that the objective of shedding light on such complex behaviours is a common goal amongst them all. Moreover, to ensure green/ethical concerns underpin the prevailing mode of marketing in the future, we believe that there is a strong need for our discipline to give some thought to the multifaceted and challenging nature of green/ethical consumption, as well as demonstrate how policymakers, managers, and social marketers can embed green/ethical strategies within their everyday marketing practices. We envisage that the following papers go some way to contributing successfully to this endeavour.

From an international pool of 78 papers, 12 papers were selected from 11 countries, thus helping to develop new insights from around the world. As hoped by Prothero in 1998, another trend identified from our selected papers is the rising number of researchers working across different disciplines. Although collaborations with management academics was identified as being the most common, other collaborations involved academics from agricultural economics, Japanese studies, design science, and environmental disciplines. Another strength identified amongst the selected papers is the rich variety of methodological tools used to gain such insights. This included survey research (online, telephone, and face-to-face), structural equation modelling, interviews, ethnography, focus groups, and netnography. While each of those methods point towards significant strengths in their own right, we believe that all of the aforementioned aspects taken together help to provide innovative and valuable insights relating to green/ethical practices around the world.

The first paper to initiate our special issue is written by Patrick de Pelsmacker and Ingrid Moons. In contrast to the traditional cognitive constructs usually explored within the Theory of Planned Behaviour, their paper looks at the understudied influence of emotions underpinning consumers' adoption decision-making processes of the electric car. Using an online survey with more than 1200 Belgian participants, they identify emotions and attitudes as being the strongest determinants of both early and late adopters of the electric car. The authors conclude that their findings offer marketing managers valuable information to aid segmentation, targeting, and positioning of electric cars. However, they acknowledge that further exploration of the role of emotions may be needed and that a method that focuses on actual behaviour rather than behavioural intention may prove even more revealing for future researchers. Indeed, many of the papers in this special issue refer to the limitations of previous green/ethical research and the subsequently revealed attitude–behaviour gaps that have been identified as a result of focusing on behavioural intention rather than actual behaviour.

Our next paper is written by Michael Jay Polonsky (who interestingly also published in the original special issue), Andrea Vocino, Stacy Landreth Grau, Romana Garma, and Ahmed Shahriar Ferdous. Their paper takes on de Pelsmacker and Moon's recommendations in closing the research gap regarding consumer knowledge and behaviour by looking at the impact of knowledge upon American consumers' actual pro-environmental behaviours rather than behavioural intentions. Using an online survey with just under 400 US consumers, the authors conclude that a strong relationship exists between general and carbon-offset knowledge and attitudes, and that general and specific environmental behaviours are driven by attitudes towards the environment. Also acknowledged here is the difficulty that consumers have of knowing which messages to believe and/or adhere to. Therefore, in taking the field further forward, the authors suggest that marketing managers' communications need to reflect more accurately the environmental impact of certain consumption behaviours in a way that is not only accurate but also meaningful and relevant to their consumption. In unpacking the ethical dimensions of local food purchasing, Phil Megicks, Juliet Memery, and Robert J. Angell's paper also responds to de Pelsmacker and Moon's recommendations by analysing the stimulatory and detracting factors upon intentions to purchase and actual purchasing of local food. Via a mixed-methods approach, the authors reveal that the sustainability aspects related to this type of purchasing behaviour are not first and foremost in consumers' minds when attempting to buy such products. Instead, the most influential motivation of consumers is for provenance and to support local producers. Similar to Polonsky et al., the authors' implications of their findings are directed towards marketing communications managers and call for such research to be replicated in other countries.

Lynn Sudbury Riley, Agnes Hofmeister, and Florian Kohlbacher respond to calls for a greater cross-cultural approach when looking at pro-environmental behaviours amongst older consumers. As the ageing of the world population is expected to grow even more rapidly in the twenty-first century, the authors argue that marketers cannot afford to ignore the views of the older consumer concerning pro-environmental behaviours. Their questionnaire was completed by more than 1200 respondents from Japan, Hungary, Germany, and the UK, and was based on an adapted Ecologically Conscious Consumer Behaviour (ECCB) scale. Not only do the authors argue that the adapted ECCB scale can now help marketers to comprehend a wide variety of ethical behaviours, but also that it provides greater validity and reliability as a result of its testing in a cross-cultural context. Interestingly, the authors hint at the complexity of exploring such behaviours, as UK consumers demonstrated higher levels of awareness regarding ethical product choices compared to other countries but subsequently scored lower on the ECCB scale compared to German and Japanese consumers. They conclude their paper by criticising marketers for underrepresenting the older consumer in their marketing campaigns, and argue that there is substantial market potential for green/ethical product manufacturers and retailers to increase this consumer segment's awareness of the ethical choices they have.

Our fifth and sixth papers by John Thøgersen and Yanfeng Zhou and Athanasios Krystallis, Klaus Grunert, Marcia de Barcellos, Toula Perrea, and Wim Verbeke respectively also respond to suggestions for a more global approach, examining eight different countries between them. Due to the significant role that food production plays in providing a sustainable food chain, both papers focus on the benefits to policymakers of taking a cross-cultural approach to understanding motivations and attitudes towards sustainability aspects of food production and consumption. Using a mall-intercept survey with more than 700 Chinese consumers, Thøgersen and Zhou examine the underpinning motivations of early adopters of organic food, and found very few differences between those identified in Europe. As expected perhaps given the early nature of the organic market in China, availability of organic products proved to be the main limiting factor impinging on consumers' adoption of organic food. Via an online survey with more than 2800 respondents from the EU, Brazil, and China, Krystallis et al. revealed attitudes to have a limited influence on purchasing behaviour despite consumers from all three continents possessing moderately strong attitudes towards nature and the environment. However, one important difference identified between both studies concerns the issue of normative influences. While Krystallis et al. speculate that the moderately strong attitudes held towards the environment may help minimise societal criticism, Thøgersen and Zhou identify a non-existent role for normative influences upon organic food purchases.

It is these complexities and barriers to green/ethical consumption that are then examined by our next two papers. Thomas Jägel, Kathy Keeling, Alexander Reppel, and Thorsten Gruber's paper examines the values and motivational complexities underpinning ethical clothing consumption. As well as focusing on actual clothing purchases rather than intended purchases, the authors argue that by using a means-end approach, they are able to reconcile the motivational and cognitive schools of consumer research. Their study identifies five dominant perceptual patterns relating to environmental and altruistic concerns, but also reveals individual motives of value for money, personal image, and well-being. Consequently, they identify trade-offs between competing values in food and clothing, suggesting that consumer internal conflicts can be expected across product categories. In the context of reducing greenhouse gas emissions (GHG), Hélène Cherrier, Mathilde Szuba, and Nil Özçağlar-Toulouse's ethnographic study of French and British consumers argues that marketers need to acknowledge that consumers are not free, autonomous agents that are able to incorporate reduced or alternative consumption into their lifestyles, and therefore call for a re-conceptualisation of alternative and reduced consumption. They identify that consumers' green consumption is being constrained by social and cultural forces (i.e. the glass floor), and go on to explain that although consumers are aware and highly motivated towards green living, they must have a high capacity for resistance and willingness to make sacrifices. As the media and academics are both identified here as playing a central role in maintaining consumption as the dominant norm and in marginalising downward consumption, the authors conclude by calling for green marketers to de-normalise needs for consumption beyond necessities and to normalise practices of green/ethical consumption.

In their paper on normalising green behaviours, Ruth Rettie, Kevin Birchell, and Debra Lynne Riley's paper also work on the premise that some sustainable behaviours are not adopted because they are seen not to be 'normal', and that some unsustainable behaviours persist because they are seen to be normal. Via a telephone survey of 1000 consumers, they found that there was some consensus about which activities were green and which ones were not. They also found that perceptions about their normality was often polarised, demonstrating the potential for segmentation, targeting, and positioning on the basis of conceptions of normality. The authors conclude by arguing that there is no point in segmenting according to consumers' self-perception of being green because most consumers see themselves as being green. Similar to Cherrier et al., the authors call for marketing practitioners to place more promotional emphasis on normalising substitute activities.

Seonaidh McDonald, Caroline J. Oates, Panayiota J. Alevizou, C. William Young, and Kumju Hwang's paper on strategies for sustainable consumption also pick up on Cherrier et al.'s and Rettie et al.'s observations regarding the difficulty of changing the everyday behaviour of individuals. Via in-depth interviews and focus groups, the authors argue that in order to build a richer picture of the green consumer, researchers should take a more holistic view of consumption activities. In so doing, the authors conclude that there is no such thing as a 'green consumer' and that it is more accurate to describe them as greening rather than green. Consequently, they identify three groups: Translators who are open to change, though they do not deliberately seek change; Exceptors who are the most committed, and attempt to achieve a low environmental impact but still have one aspect of their lives where they live as grey consumers; and Selectors who act as green in just one aspect of their lives but grey in all others. For marketing practitioners, the study acknowledges the particular relevance of the 'Selector' group, which may account for attitude–behaviour inconsistencies recorded in the past.

Responding to McDonald et al.'s criticism of previous studies looking at individuals in isolation of any extended networks, Anne M. Smith and Terry O'Sullivan's paper looks at environmentally responsible behaviour in the workplace. Given that organisations account for a far greater environmental impact, the authors argue that marketers can reduce this impact by harnessing the citizenship behaviours of their employees. Via 14 focus groups with employees from five large UK organisations, they found instead that the lack of environmental leadership and environmentally friendly facilities in the workplace was a barrier to performing what they refer to as environmentally responsible organisational citizenship behaviours despite carrying them out in the home. Thus participants often experienced tension or conflict between their role as an employee and that of a citizen. The authors conclude by urging organisations to adopt more of an internal social marketing approach, and in so doing identify a number of benefits such as making cost reductions, achieving environmental targets, and employee motivation.

Similar to Cherrier et al.'s and McDonald et al.'s criticisms of marketing researchers' focusing too much on the individual consumer, our final paper by Andreas Chatzidakis, Pauline Maclaran, and Alan Bradshaw looks at how ethical consumer discourses, micro-cultures, and identities are constructed in the marketplace. Using ethnographic and photographic methods, the authors suggest that much of the literature on the green/ethical consumer has become de-politicised, and that in actual practice, consumers' defy marketplace ideologies and in some cases go as far as to perform illegal acts to promote citizen liberation, thus confirming that consumption activity is essentially spatialised and that it has political repercussions. The authors conclude by calling for more research into the (anti)consumption of public space/place and a deeper understanding of the dialogical relationship between space/place and various public/private consumption settings.

Overall, the above 12 papers clearly show that there are many ways to explore the consumption activities of green/ethical consumers, as well as characterise and depict the green/ethical consumer. Although many of the above authors point to some of the weaknesses identified in previous marketing research, they also collectively point to fundamental ways in which marketing academics and marketing practitioners can gain a more holistic understanding of the demographic, psychological, and sociocultural influences upon the green/ethical consumer. The first proposition offered here is to incorporate more emphasis on what consumers actually do rather than plan to do, thus helping to avoid the common attitude–behaviour pitfalls identified in many previous studies. Second, many papers illustrate the advantages of taking more of a holistic approach to investigating consumption activities. Here, many of the above papers propose that researchers by all means should incorporate the context of the individual but simultaneously acknowledge the irrationality often underpinning such consumption decisions. However, they also point to the many benefits of widening the focus beyond the individual, thus incorporating data about their green/ethical roles within their households and extended networks such as the workplace. Given the insightful advantages of the cross-cultural perspective taken in many of the above papers, we strongly believe that the above articles help to advance marketing theory, as well as offer valuable implications and recommendations for managers, practitioners, and policymakers, the joint efforts of which are needed to ensure a more 'green', ethical, and/or sustainable marketplace.

Finally, we would like to thank Susan Hart for granting us the opportunity to run with our idea for this special issue, and the current editors of the *Journal of Marketing Management* for granting us the additional space required to publish all 12 papers. For their efficiency, expert assistance, and guidance throughout the whole editorial process, a special thanks also goes to Fiona Lees and Anne Foy at Westburn Publishers Ltd. Obviously, our thanks go to all 40 authors for their commendable and thought-provoking contributions, as well as their acquiescent cooperation throughout the publication process. This special issue would not have seen the light of day without the time and effort of the many academics from around the globe who reviewed papers for us – so, a big, heartfelt thanks to you all.

Morven G McEachern
Lancaster University Management School,
Dept. of Marketing,
Charles Carter Building,
Lancaster University,
Lancaster, LA1 4YX

Marylyn Carrigan
Birmingham Business School
Dept. of Marketing,
University House,
University of Birmingham,
Edgbaston Park Road,
Birmingham, B15 2TY

## References

Prothero, A. (1998). Green marketing: The 'fad' that won't slip slide away. *Journal of Marketing Management*, *14*, 507–512.
Soron, D. (2010). Sustainability, self-identity and the sociology of consumption, *Sustainable Development*, *18*, 172–181.

# Emotions as determinants of electric car usage intention

Ingrid Moons, *Artesis Hogeschool Antwerpen, Belgium*
Patrick De Pelsmacker, *University of Antwerp, Belgium*

---

**Abstract** In a sample of 1202 Belgians, the determining factors of the usage intention of an electric car and the differences between early and late usage intention segments are investigated. The Theory of Planned Behaviour (TPB) framework is extended with emotional reactions towards the electric car and car driving in general. Emotions and the attitude towards the electric car are the strongest determinants of usage intention, followed by the subjective norm. Reflective emotions towards car driving and perceived behavioural control factors also play a significant role. Differences in the relative importance of the determinants of usage intention between subgroups based on environmental concern and behaviour and social values are also studied. In general, people in segments that are more inclined to use the electric car are less driven by emotions towards the electric car and more by reflective emotions towards car driving, and take more perceived behavioural concerns into account.

---

## Sustainable product usage intention and the role of emotions

The development and the successful introduction of new products are important for companies, as they are aware that this is a key factor for their existence and future success (Bayus, Erickson, & Jacobson, 2003). Nowadays, product innovations are often triggered by growing concerns about the changing resources needed to produce and use products (sustainable product development). Ehrenfeld (2008) and Manzini (2009) argue that a sustainable future is not reached by diminishing 'unsustainability'. In recent years, there is consensus about the large potential for achieving environmental benefits, from altering users' behaviour and the way they interact with products (Sitarz, 1994). The present study focuses on the factors affecting the usage intention of electric vehicles, a newly developed product that can lead to a fundamental change in sustainable mobility behaviour (Smith, 2008). What will make or break the successful introduction of electric mobility in the real world is consumer acceptance (Feitelson & Salomon, 2000; Verhoef, Bliemer, Steg, & Van Wee, 2008). Therefore, insights into the motivations and barriers of this acceptance, especially by early adopter market segments, are important for a successful introduction of the electric car.

What are the determinants of the usage intention of an electric car? Some argue that the emotional side of a new product may be more critical to a product's success than its rational or practical elements (McLean, 1990; Norman, 2004). Emotions are an important component of consumer response (Richins, 1997). However, the role of affect in the adoption decision process of this type of product has rarely been investigated. As Loewenstein (1996) states: 'With all its cleverness, however, decision theory is somewhat crippled emotionally, and thus detached from the emotional and visceral richness of life' (p. 289). The single utilitarian (cognitive) viewpoint of most consumer decision-making models may be traced to the traditional economic perspective of products as objects. One contribution of this study is that it explicitly integrates emotions towards car driving and electric cars in the Theory of Planned Behaviour (TPB) framework and that it investigates the relative importance of these emotional factors compared to the traditional cognitive dimensions in the TPB.

Typically, market penetration starts with a small segment consisting of customers with particular characteristics, needs, or wants (A. Gärling & Thøgersen, 2001). It is therefore important to study the particular decision-making process of these early adopter groups that may be different from that of late usage intention segments. In their overview article of the Technology Acceptance Model (TAM), Sun and Zhang (2005) state that the inclusion of moderators leads to enhancing a model's explanatory power. Also Leonidou, Leonidou, and Kvasova (2010) suggest more research into psychographic factors as moderators of the decision-making process. A second contribution of this study is that it develops insights into the specific motivators for those segments that might become the early adopters of the electric car compared to those who would adopt this innovation at a later stage. More specifically, and following suggestions by Jansson (2011), Kilbourne and Beckmann (1998), and Kilbourne and Pickett (2008), the difference in the decision-making process between individuals with high and low environmental concern and behaviour, and individuals with different personal value orientations is studied.

Identifying the sociodemographic characteristics of early adoption or usage segments is very important for marketing new products. However, several authors concluded that the explanatory effect of sociodemographic variables on adoption is generally found to be low (Jansson, 2011; Kilbourne & Beckmann, 1998; Leonidou et al., 2010). Results on the usage intention of new products may be mixed because their effect may be different for different types of products or issues. More specifically, their relevance in a high-involvement ecological consumer decision such as the usage of an electric car has seldom been studied. Therefore, sociodemographic factors are added as control variables in our model of the usage intention of the electric car.

The study was carried out on a sample of Belgians and contributes to both theory and practice. The main theoretical contribution is the study of the role of emotions in the usage intention decision process of a new and more sustainable high-involvement and environmentally friendly durable consumer product, and differences in motivations to use these new products depending on environmental concern and behaviour and on personal values perceived as important. The contribution to practice is that it provides marketers of sustainable products such as the electric car with both a deeper insight into the main determinants of early and late usage intention groups. This should enable them to better fine-tune segmenting, targeting, and positioning their persuasive efforts in marketing electric vehicles.

First, the role of emotions in the consumer decision process and in traditional models such as the TPB is discussed. Next, potentially relevant consumer characteristics that could moderate this process are highlighted, and sociodemographic variables that have been shown to drive environmentally friendly behaviour in other contexts are described. Subsequently, the method and results are discussed, and implications for theory and practice are highlighted.

## Models of new product and behaviour adoption

In the context of the adoption (intention) of innovations and (new) behaviour, two conceptual frameworks have been extensively studied. In the TAM, the attitude towards and the adoption or continuous use (intention) of an innovation is determined by three antecedents: perceived ease of use (PEOU), perceived usefulness (PU), and compatibility (Taylor & Todd, 1995). PEOU is the degree to which a person believes that using the system will be effortless (Davis, 1989). PU is the degree to which a person believes that using a particular technology will enhance his/her job performance (Davis, 1989). Compatibility is the degree to which the innovation fits with the potential adopter's existing values, previous experiences, and current needs (Rogers, 1995).

The TPB is a second conceptual framework that has often been used for analysing and predicting a variety of intentions and behaviours. The TPB predicts behavioural intention which, in turn, is assumed to be a predictor of actual behaviour (Ajzen, 1991; Ajzen & Fishbein, 1980). Behavioural intention is explained by three general dimensions: the *attitude* towards the behaviour, the *social influence* (*subjective norm*) on the behaviour, and the *perceived behavioural control* in conducting the behaviour. Attitudes are evaluative responses to the behaviour. The subjective norm stands for perceived social pressure by significant others or different reference groups to perform or not to perform a certain behaviour. A reference group is a group that serves as a comparison point and the opinion of which is perceived as important for the individual (Kim, Chan, & Chan, 2007). Perceived behavioural control over performing the behaviour is a person's perception about whether different aspects of the behaviour are in his or her control or are easy or difficult. It is related to the perceived ability and the external source constraints and facilitators of the behaviour (Ajzen, 1991; Ajzen & Fishbein, 1980; Bandura, 1986; Taylor & Todd, 1995). The TPB has been applied to a variety of contexts, and has often been used to describe environmentally related behaviours (Bamberg & Schmidt, 2003; Cheung, Chang, & Wong, 1999; Goldenhar & Connell, 1992; Kaiser, Woefling, & Fuhrer, 1999; Lam, 1999). The TPB, as a general model of consumer behaviour, has been shown to be equally or even more relevant for predicting intentions than more ad hoc models (e.g. De Cannière, De Pelsmacker, & Geuens, 2009), and has therefore required the status of a general consumer behaviour model that is applicable in a variety of situations. We therefore concentrate on this model as the conceptual framework for the present study.

## The role of emotions in consumer decision making

Notwithstanding the overwhelming evidence of the role of affective reactions in consumer decision making, conceptual models and empirical research on the adoption (intention) of innovations or (new) behaviour have largely ignored the role of emotions (Bagozzi, Gopinath & Nyer, 1999; Kim et al., 2007; Perlusz, 2011; Richins, 1997). Visceral states, emotions, and cravings can have a disproportionate effect on behaviour (Loewenstein, 1996). However, the connection between emotions and behaviour may be stronger and more direct than between attitude and behaviour (Bagozzi, Gurhan-Canli, & Priester, 2002), and in certain situations, spontaneously evoked affective reactions rather than cognitions tend to have a greater impact on choice (Shiv & Fedorikhin, 1999). In fact, two conceptual systems tend to operate in parallel: affective and rational (Shiv & and Fedorikhin, 1999). This is explicitly recognised in dual processing models, such as the Elaboration Likelihood Model (ELM; Petty & Cacioppo, 1986). Standard expectations of the ELM imply that in high-involvement situations, people would centrally and predominantly cognitively process stimuli or messages, while in low-involvement situations, peripheral processing would take place, and peripheral cues such as affective reactions to the stimulus would determine responses.

However, emotions can also be a strong determinant of consumer behaviour in high-involvement situations. For instance, Pham (1998) found that emotions strongly determine behaviour, provided they are relevant and diagnostic. Forgas's (1995) Affect Infusion Model (AIM) posits that there are two underlying mechanisms of affect infusion: affect as information and affect priming. The affect-as-information theory suggests that rather than forming a judgement based on features of a target, individuals may ask themselves, 'How do I feel about it?' and in doing so, may be guided by their feelings to judge a message or a stimulus. In the affect-priming theory, affect can indirectly inform judgements by facilitating access to related cognitive categories (Bower, 1981; Isen, 1987). Within the AIM model, it is implied that it is in the course of substantive, constructive processing that affect is most likely to play a significant role in what is perceived and how a stimulus is interpreted (Forgas, 1995). The AIM also implies that judgements about more complex stimuli (substantive processing context), requiring more elaborate processing and made without the benefit of objective evidence, should show greater affective effects. Previous research (e.g. Petty, Schumann, Richman, & Strathman, 1993) reported that positive affect produces more positive judgements in both high- and low-elaboration conditions. Geuens, De Pelsmacker, and Faseur (2011) also concluded that affective reactions to advertising stimuli were important determinants of brand attitudes for different product categories, varying both in product category involvement and buying motivation (hedonic or utilitarian). For instance, in the context of car purchase and use, a relatively high-involvement decision about a complex product for most people, it is well recognised by both academics and practitioners that emotions play an important role in consumers' decision making (Carsalesprofessional.com, 2011; Sheller, 2004; Steg, Vlek, & Slotegraaf, 2001). Also in the context of car advertising, Morris, Woo, Geason, and Kim (2002) concluded that the affective reaction had more explanatory power for purchase intention than cognitive attitude.

People also have feelings about (new) technology and innovations (Perlusz, 2011). Venkatesh (2000), studied the effect of computer anxiety on the adoption intention of new information technology, and found it a very relevant factor. Also

Chaudhuri, Aboulnasr, and Ligas (2010) argue that the innovation literature has often overlooked emotions as a cause of successful diffusion. They argue that the role of emotions is particularly eminent in the context of new products that represent radical innovations. One of the examples they give is the adoption of hybrid cars. They develop a model of information processing for initial exposure to radical innovations that includes consumers' emotional responses. The results illustrate the importance of emotions in the process of innovation diffusion and evaluation.

In conclusion, affect plays an important role as a determinant of intentions to use (new) products or to adopt (new) behaviour in both high-involvement and low-involvement contexts.

## Emotions in the Theory of Planned Behaviour

Although the TPB has been widely used to predict behaviour(al intentions), various authors question its completeness. For instance, Perugini and Bagozzi (2001) argue that 'although there is little question that the TPB offers a parsimonious account of purposive behaviour, its sufficiency can be questioned' (p. 81). Bagozzi (2007) states that the TPB has seemingly seduced researchers into overlooking the fallacy of simplicity. Therefore, various authors suggest extending the TPB with other factors (e.g. Pavlou & Fygenson, 2006). One of the most often suggested improvements is extending the TPB with measures of emotional responses to the product or the issue for which the intention to use is predicted. In the TPB, emotions are only a background factor without direct effect on intention and behaviour (Mazzon, 2011). However, the anticipation of emotions or stimulus-induced affect is important in the elicitation of behavioural intentions (Bagozzi, Baumgartner, & Pieters, 1999; Shiv & Fedorikhin, 1999). According to Wood and Moreau (2006), the affective influence is often stronger and more far-reaching than previously considered, and the addition of emotional responses benefits traditional models of diffusion. Therefore, many authors argued for integrating feelings into extant decision models (Hirschman & Holbrook, 1982; Holbrook & Hirschman, 1982; Parker, Manstead, & Stradling, 1995; Peterson, Hoyer, & Wilson, 1986; Pham, 2004; Richard, van der Pligt, & de Vries, 1995). One could argue that integrating emotional factors into the TPB conceptually alters the nature of the model in that emotions are not compatible with 'planned behaviour'. On the other hand, emotions can a determinant factor of planning behaviour too.

How should emotions be integrated in the TPB? In this respect, there are two distinct conceptual questions: are emotions different from attitudes, and how should emotions be modelled in the classical TPB framework? First, emotions are a distinct construct from general attitudes or affective attitude (Bagozzi, 2007; Wang, 2011). An attitude is an evaluative judgement of a stimulus that can contain both cognitive and affective elements (Kim et al., 2007; Schepers & Wetzels, 2007). Affect (feelings) are valenced affective reactions to emotion-eliciting objects/states being processed by the individual, a valenced affective reaction to perceptions of situations (Dolan, 2002; Kim et al., 2007; Richins, 1997). Bagozzi et al. (1999) state that research based on the reaction to a single stimulus frequently finds that emotions often cluster in only a limited number of dimensions. Bagozzi (2007) also concludes that when emotions are modelled in the TAM, they measure affect towards use (e.g. joy–sadness) and/or affect as liking for a particular behaviour. Since in the present study we measure emotions towards a new product that is in its very early stage of introduction, in line with this, it is assumed that consumers can only express their affective reactions in general valenced feeling terms, and we measure the emotional response to using the electric car accordingly. However, we also measure emotions towards car driving. Since all consumers in our sample drive a car, they can be expected to have more specific emotional reactions to the car-driving experience. Therefore, for the emotions towards car driving in general, we measure a number of specific emotions.

How should emotions be integrated in the TPB? Some authors argue that emotions are antecedents of TPB components (e.g. Doll, Mentz, & Orth, 1991; Perugini & Bagozzi, 2001). However, most authors argue that emotions are an extra factor in the TPB and thus a direct driver of intentions (Bagozzi, 2007). Allen, Machleit, and Kleine (1992) and Morris et al. (2002) claim that emotions can have a direct influence on behaviour that is not captured or summed up by attitude judgement. Affect is not necessarily dependent on or related to cognitive variables (Machleit & Wilson, 1983). Emotional appraisal and more cognitive attribute analysis independently determine intentions, preference, and choice (Kim et al., 2007; Kwortnik & Ross, 2007). Perugini and Bagozzi (2001) and Wang (2011) model emotion as a determinant of intentions at the same level and as a parallel predictor as the other TPB constructs. Therefore, we model emotional reactions to the electric car and car driving in general as an independent determinant of usage intentions alongside the traditional cognitive variables of the TPB model.

## Emotions as a relevant addition to the TPB in different decision contexts

Are emotional responses to a (new) product or behaviour equally relevant in all situations? Emotions have been added to the TPB for various products and issues, and have consistently been found to be highly relevant for predicting behavioural intentions and continuance behaviour. For instance, Hsu, Yen, Chiu, and Chang (2006) found that continuance intention of online shopping could be predicted by TPB components enriched with feelings of disconfirmation and satisfaction. Kim et al. (2007) integrated pleasure and arousal as main dimensions of feelings in their model. They found that affective dimensions as well as cognitive (rational) components had a positive effect on the intention to continue using mobile Internet services. Wang (2011) predicted physical activity intentions by means of TPB components and anticipated negative emotions. Negative emotions explained behavioural intentions over and above TPB variables, especially for people with low physical activity.

In spite of the many examples of the added value of emotional factors to the more cognitive TPB model, the evidence for their relevance in case of a relatively high-involvement environmentally friendly new durable consumer product in the early stage of its introduction (such as an electric car) is circumstantial. However, this circumstantial evidence suggests that emotions may also be an important factor in these situations. First, various studies on the role of emotions in the TPB relate to issues or behaviours that are relatively *highly involving*. Bae (2008) found that emotions enhance the explanatory power of the TPB in predicting intentions to cornea donations. Hynie, MacDonald, and Marques (2006) found that self-conscious emotions like shame and guilt had a significant effect on condom use, above and beyond the TPB variables. Perugini and Bagozzi (2001) established that anticipated emotions appeared to be highly significant in explaining body-weight regulation and studying effort.

Electric car usage intention reflects *environmentally friendly behavioural* intention. In the area of mobility decisions, for instance, Duran, Alzate, Lopez, and Sabucedo (2011) extended the TPB with emotional aspects to predict low vehicle use behaviour. The anger emotion appeared to be more important to predict behaviour than, for instance, perceived behavioural control. In the domain of car use, previous studies have explicitly established the role of affect in explaining environmental behaviour (Gatersleben & Appleton, 2007). Emotional factors have also been shown to be very important in the context of sustainable mobility (www.trendy-travel. eu/emotions/start.phtml?link=project, 2011). There appears to be support for the idea of including emotional factors in predicting the behaviour with regard to relatively highly involving and environmentally friendly products or issues.

Is it particularly relevant to include emotions in a model of *early stage usage* intention for a technological innovation such as the electric car? Wood and Moreau (2006) claim that emotional influences are the greatest during the early learning stages of product usage. Moreover, they argue that the emotional (anticipation of) experience is more influential for technological or functional innovations (e.g. computer programs, GPS) than for simple experiential or aesthetic products. Also Kwortnik and Ross (2007) state that emotions are particularly important early in the decision process. The pleasure of consumption can begin before the act of consuming. Emotions are motivators that influence goal-directed behaviour. Consequently, there also seems to be a case for including emotional reactions to the anticipated use of a new technological product in the early stages of its introduction.

Besides electric-car-specific emotions, more product-category-related emotions can also be relevant for decision making. Richins (1997) states that emotions that result from consumption of the product category itself are an important research focus. A. Gärling and Thøgersen (2001) argue that for a new product, benefits are compared to the benefits of other products within the individual's evoked set. For instance, they argue that car drivers who prefer prestigious, sporty, or off-road cars are less likely to perceive an electric vehicle as a satisfactory substitute and that many car lovers do not like the electric vehicle idea. On the other hand, people who feel bad about the negative environmental impact of their car use are more likely to perceive that there exists a social norm about changing to the electric vehicle. Joireman, Van Lange, and Van Vugt (2004) argue that the consideration of future consequences of using a product can have a significant effect on the choice between travel modes. Therefore, besides specific emotional responses to the idea of using an electric car, we also include various dimensions of emotional responses towards car driving into the TPB. In that respect, three specific emotional processing levels can be distinguished: visceral, behavioural, and reflective (McLean, 1990; Norman, 2004). The first level, *visceral affect*, is perception-based and relates to visceral aspects that are related to product appearance. The second level, *behavioural emotion*, is expectation-based and corresponds with behavioural aspects that have to do with the pleasure and effectiveness of use. The third level, *reflective emotion* is intellectually based and corresponds with reflective dimensions that are concerned with self-image, personal satisfaction, and memories.

Finally, in his study on the use of alternative fuel vehicles in Sweden, Jansson (2011) argues that the study of consumer behaviour of purchasing high-involvement products that are marketed as being environmentally responsible received far less attention than the study of reducing negative environmental impact. This is an additional argument to study the usage intention process of electric cars. Overall, there is a strong case for studying the role of emotions in the early adoption stage of a technological innovation for a high-involvement environmentally friendly consumer durable such as the electric car.

It can be expected that positive attitudes, the subjective norm, and perceived behavioural control, as well as positive affective reactions towards the electric car will all have a positive effect on the usage intention of the electric vehicle. For instance, Oliver and Rosen (2010) in their study in the United States showed the impact of social factors (neighbours) on purchasing hybrid electric vehicles. They also concluded that environmental self-efficacy is an important factor for predicting environmental behaviour. However, the effects of emotional reactions associated with current car driving are less clear. Reflective emotions towards car driving may make people more critical towards the (environmental) consequences of car driving, and may therefore have a positive effect on the intention to use the electric car that could alleviate these consequences. However, depending upon the perception of electric cars, strong positive visceral and behavioural emotions towards current car driving may lead people to dislike the electric car as a less satisfying alternative to their current vehicle. Since there is no formal conceptual framework to formulate directional hypotheses with respect to the effect of car-driving emotions, and no clear guidance as to the relative importance of the determinants of adoption intention, we formulate the following research question:

> *RQ1: To what extent are the attitude towards the electric car, the subjective norm, perceived behavioural control factors, emotions towards the electric car, and the visceral, behavioural, and reflective emotions towards car driving significant determinants of the usage intention of the electric car?*

## Sociodemographic characteristics and electric car usage intention

Many studies conclude that sociodemographic factors have no or an inconclusive effect on consumer behaviour in general and on environmentally friendly behaviour in particular (Wang, 2011). Jansson (2011) concludes that attitudinal factors explain consumer behaviour to a much higher degree than sociodemographics. Leonidou et al. (2010) state that the use of traditional sociodemographic factors, even though important, was characterised as inappropriate for identifying green consumers because of contradictory and inconclusive findings. Also Kilbourne and Beckmann (1998) state that the literature on 'who is the green consumer' is frequently inconclusive and sometimes contradictory.

Nevertheless, links between social and demographic characteristics and environmental concern and behaviour have been explored by several researchers. A. Gärling and Thøgersen (2001) conclude that early adopters of electric vehicles are generally *high in social status* and *better educated*. *Age* has shown positive (Clark, Kotchen, & Moore, 2003; Rice, 2006; Roberts, 1996), negative (Moon, Florkowski, Braäuckner, & Schonhof, 2002), or no impact (Loureiro, McCluskey, &

Mittelhammer, 2001). Also *gender* could play a role. Most studies report that women express greater concern about environment than men (Hunter, Hatch, & Johnson, 2004; Mohai, 1992; Schahn & Holzer, 1990) and behave in a more ecologically conscious way than men (Johnston, Wessels, Donath, & Asche, 2001; Loureiro et al., 2001; Zelezny, Chua, & Aldrich, 2000). The *level of education* has been found to have positive (Blend & van Ravenwaay, 1999), negative (Johnston et al., 2001), or no effect (Moon et al., 2002).

Additionally, for the electric car adoption, *the place where one lives* may be important. Living in a city can be an opportunity for electric car driving, as driving in the city often implies short trips, which reduces the problem of the small distance autonomy of an electric car. But on the other hand, citizens may have restricted charging facilities at home. Another reason for taking this variable into account is the fact that urban residents are more likely to be environmentally concerned than rural residents (Arcury & Christianson, 1990; Buttel & Flinn, 1974; Howell & Laska, 1992; Tremblay & Dunlap, 1978). The *car one drives* could be a differentiating characteristic, as electric cars nowadays are most typically smaller family cars. Finally, the longer one has had a driving licence, the more car driving may become a habit or the more one has positive and negative experiences with car driving. So the *period of time one has a driving license* might be a relevant determinant of usage intention.

The conclusions discussed in the previous findings were obtained for various types of environmentally friendly behaviour in different contexts. It may well be that in a specific context and with respect to a specific usage situation or products, some sociodemographics are relevant. Therefore, although several studies have found that these factors are poor predictors of green consumer behaviour, they are often used as control variables. For that reason, we add a number of potentially relevant sociodemographic variables as control variables to our model.

## Different determinants of usage intention for different consumer segments?

In their study of marketing of electric vehicles, A. Gärling and Thøgersen (2001) argue that it is very important to identify early adopters correctly. Equally important is to find out to what extent their decision-making process is different from late adoption intention groups. The processes that drive the usage intention of a new environmentally friendly or sustainable product may be different for different consumer segments (Urban & Hauser, 1993). In their overview study of 55 TAM studies on the acceptance of technology systems, Sun and Zhang (2005) conclude that the inclusion of moderators leads to enhancing a model's explanatory power. Also Kilbourne and Beckmann (1998) and Leonidou et al. (2010) argue that there is more need for the study of psychographic factors as moderators of the decision-making process. Many potential moderators can be envisaged. In the context of the present study, the most important criterion to select a moderator is the extent to which it is related to differences in usage intention of the electric car. Subsequently, differences in the decision-making process between consumer segments scoring differently on this dimension can be explored. In this study, environmental concern, environmental behaviour, opinion leadership with respect to cars, and personal values are considered.

### Environmental concern

Environmental concern is the evaluative response towards environmental issues (Eagly & Chaiken, 1998; Fransson & Gärling, 1999; Schultz, 2001). Bamberg (2003) and Bamberg and Möser (2007) showed that the degree of environmental concern can have a direct and strong impact on people's behaviour in specific environmentally related domains like recycling, energy savings, buying environmentally friendly products, and travel-mode choices. A. Gärling and Thøgersen (2001) found that environment-friendliness is highly important for people in favour of electric cars. Oliver and Rosen (2010) in their study on hybrid vehicles state that environmental values have been in previous research very predictive of environmental behaviour.

### Environmental behaviour

Thøgersen (1999) demonstrates the relevance of general environmental behaviour. He concluded that environmentally friendly behaviours are not independent. When people start to act in an environmentally friendly way in one area, this behaviour tends to spill over into other areas. On the other hand, Leonidou et al. (2010) make the distinction between green purchasing behaviour and general environmental behaviour. They found that inward eco-attitudes are predictive of green purchasing behaviour, while outward eco-attitudes are predictive of green behaviour in general. This demonstrates the potential moderating role of (different types of) environmental behaviour.

### Opinion leadership with respect to cars

Opinion leadership refers to the inclination of individuals to be 'lead users', core consumers at the forefront who drive an innovation forward. They are often the first ones to adopt an innovation and, having information and having used the product, they articulate the link between their need and the technology. Opinion leaders are often innovators and adopt the innovation first (Chaudhuri et al., 2010; A. Gärling & Thøgerson, 2001; Gatignon & Robertson, 1991; Jansson, 2011; Rogers, 1995). In the context of the adoption of hybrids, Oliver and Rosen (2010) also identified opinion leadership as a relevant variable to describe segments.

### Personal values

Personal values are guiding principles that are important in a person's life (Rohan, 2000; Rokeach, 1973; Schwartz, 1992). Similar personal values are referred to as value types. Value orientations are defined as clusters of compatible values or value types. Personal value orientations have often been referred to as determinants of pro-environmental behaviour or moderators of the decision-making process (Jansson, 2011; Jansson, Marell, & Nordlund, 2011; Kilbourne & Beckmann, 1998). For instance, Schwartz's (1992) self-transcendence value types universalism and benevolence have been found to be positively related to pro-environmental attitudes and behaviour (Thøgersen, 1996). The self-enhancing achievement and power value types have been shown to be negatively related to pro-environmental attitudes and behaviour (T. Gärling, Fujii, A. Gärling, & Jacobsson, 2003; Kilbourne & Pickett, 2008; Leonidou et al., 2010).

The second research question of the present study explores the potentially different relative importance of the determining factors of the usage intention process of electric cars for different consumer segments:

> RQ2: To what extent does the relative importance of the determinants of the usage intention of the electric car differ between low and high environmentally concerned individuals, between individuals with weak and strong environmental behaviour, between weak and strong opinion leaders and between individuals in different social value type groups?

## Method

### Procedure and respondents

After an exploratory qualitative study (Moons, De Pelsmacker, De Bont, & Standaert, 2010), between 20 November and 20 December 2009 an online survey was sent out to investigate the usage intention decision process of the electric car. Data were gathered via the snowball method. Sixty students were mailed and asked to complete the questionnaire and also to forward the link to their friends, parents, and neighbours. The latter were invited to mail the survey again to their friends and colleagues. The survey was also placed on an Internet forum about car driving. In total, the responses of 1202 participants are used in this study. The respondents all have a driving licence: 37.1% has held one for three years or less, 35.5% for more than three and up to 20 years, and 27.4% more than 20 years. A total of 57.3% are male. The sample over-represents younger and higher-educated people: 53.9% are aged between 18 and 25 years; 21.5% between 26 and 45 years, and 24.6% are 46 or older. A total of 32.7% have a high school diploma or less, 67.3% have a higher education diploma. The place of living of the sample more or less reflects the Belgian situation: 39.3% lives on the countryside, 38.6% in the suburbs, and 22.1% in the city centre. In terms of car use, 33.7% drives a small car, 36.6% a large one, and 29.7% a special one.

### Measures

The *intention to use an electric car* was the dependent variable in the regression models in which a number of variables were included as independents. An overview of the definition of these variables, alphas, and references is given in Appendix 1. The independent variables in the model are: the attitude towards the electric car, emotions towards the electric car, subjective norm peers (interpersonal), and subjective norm media (external; following Bhattacherjee, 2000, and Hsu et al., 2006). Ten perceived behavioural control (PBC) items were generated in the exploratory qualitative study. Cheung et al. (1999) and Terry and O'Leary (1995) identified two conceptually different PCB constructs: difficulty (personal ability) and control (perceived external constraints). The 10 items generated in the qualitative study reflect both dimensions. A factor analysis on the 10 items did not generate a meaningful reduction into a more limited number of PBC dimensions. Therefore, it was decided to enter all 10 PBC items separately into the regression analyses. The PBC factor analysis results are shown in Appendix 2. The three levels related to car-driving emotions were measured by means of 17 items based on the qualitative study. We asked respondents to what extent 17 different car features contributed to positive emotions towards car driving. Principal component analysis reveals that these 17 affective reactions represent the three process levels proposed by Norman (2004): visceral, behavioural, and reflective. The details of this factor analysis are given in Appendix 3. The item scores of each construct were averaged, and these mean scores were used in further analysis.

For the moderator analysis, environmental concern, environmental behaviour, and opinion leadership were measured as shown in Appendix 1. With respect to environmental behaviour, initially we measured the number of behaviours people indicated they conducted for environmental reasons. We then summed the number of behaviours one conducts. However, these behaviours relate to various domains: some of them are purchase-related, others are general, and some of them are reduction-oriented, others promotion-oriented. We defined four different sets of behaviours consistent with these four types of behaviours, and calculated the correlation between the overall behavioural variable and the four variables related to subtypes of behaviour. These correlations were very strong: overall environmentally friendly behaviour versus purchase-oriented ($r = .933$, $p < .001$), general ($r = .904$, $p < .001$), reduction-oriented ($r = .930$, $p < .001$), and promotion-oriented ($r = .858$, $p < .001$). Therefore, we decided to proceed with the overall environmentally friendly behaviour variable.

Schwartz's (1992) 15-item value scale was used to compose value orientation groups. A factor analysis revealed four relevant factors: *idealism, altruism, achievement*, and *power*. The scores on the items loading on each factor were averaged and the mean scores were used in a k-means cluster analysis, leading to three meaningful clusters: the self- transcendent universalist (CL1), the benevolent (CL2), and the self-enhancing power-seeking achiever (CL3). Details on this factor and cluster analysis are given in Appendix 4. Finally, a number of sociodemographic variables were also measured: age, gender, level of education, place of living, number of years the respondent had a driving licence, and type of car.

# Results

### Predictors of usage intention

By means of regression analysis, the effect of the attitude towards electric cars, the subjective norm peers, the subjective norm media, the 10 perceived behavioural control items, emotions towards the electric car, visceral, behavioural, and reflective emotions towards car driving, and a number of sociodemographic variables on the intention to use an electric car is estimated. The descriptives of the variables used are shown in Table 1a and b. Correlations between the variables in the model are given in Table 2. The results of the regression analysis are shown in Table 3.

The beta-coefficients show that emotions and the attitude towards the electric car are the strongest predictors of usage intention. The subjective norm of both reference groups (peers and media) is significant as well, but of secondary importance. Reflective emotions evoked by current car driving also determine the usage intention of the electric car. All these variables have a significantly positive effect on usage intention. Having sufficient budget (personal ability), not being able to load the car

## CONTEMPORARY ISSUES IN GREEN AND ETHICAL MARKETING

**Table 1**(a) Descriptives of metric variables used in regression analyses.

| Variable | Mean | Standard deviation | N |
|---|---|---|---|
| Intention to use an electric car | 2.865 | .982 | 1200 |
| Attitude towards the electric car | 4.860 | .278 | 1200 |
| Subjective norm peers | 2.992 | .500 | 1200 |
| Subjective norm media | 2.728 | .794 | 1200 |
| Emotion towards the electric car | 3.090 | .801 | 1200 |
| Visceral emotion towards car driving | 2.988 | .957 | 1200 |
| Reflective emotion towards car driving | 2.870 | 1.076 | 1200 |
| Behavioural emotion towards car driving | 3.465 | .940 | 1199 |
| My budget is sufficient to buy an electric car | 2.531 | 1.103 | 1199 |
| Charging an electric car is possible with an ordinary electric socket | 3.372 | 1.004 | 1199 |
| Cars with a combustion engine will soon not be allowed to enter the city | 3.201 | 1.015 | 1199 |
| You can drive a long distance with an electric car | 2.764 | .959 | 1199 |
| I will not be able to charge an electric car at home | 3.092 | .980 | 1199 |
| Our society offers the necessary means and instruments to use an electric car | 2.643 | .938 | 1199 |
| The costs of using an electric car are acceptable | 3.023 | .742 | 1199 |
| The maintenance of an electric car is well organised | 2.872 | .625 | 1199 |
| I will not be allowed to charge my electric car with energy I have produced myself | 3.225 | .874 | 1199 |
| The battery of an electric car cannot be charged underway | 2.675 | .900 | 1199 |

(b) Descriptives of sociodemographic variables used in the full-sample regression analysis.

| Dummy | Definition |
|---|---|
| Gender | 0 = male, 1 = female |
| Education level | 1 = higher education, 0 = until high school |
| City centre | 1 = city centre, 0 = countryside or suburbs |
| Suburbs | 1 = suburbs, 0 = countryside or city centre |
| Age middle | 1 = 26–45, 0 = other |
| Age old | 1 > 45, 0 = other |
| Driving licence 1 | 1 = 3–20 years, 0 = other |
| Driving licence 2 | 1 > 20 years, 0 = other |
| Car type 1 | 1 = special car (SUV, two-seater, etc.), 0 = other |
| Car type 2 | 1 = small car, 0 = other |

**Table 2** Correlation between metric variables in the full sample regression analysis (correlation coefficient (p-value)).

| | PBC1 | PBC2 | PBC3 | PBC4 | PBC5 | PBC6 | PBC7 | PBC8 | PBC9 | PBC10 |
|---|---|---|---|---|---|---|---|---|---|---|
| Intention to use | .012 | .158 | .295 | .136 | .022 | .029 | .160 | .126 | .064 | −.121 |
| | (.341) | (<.001) | (<.001) | (<.001) | (.220) | (.104) | (<.001) | (<.001) | (.013) | (<.001) |
| Attitude | −.089 | .075 | .248 | .223 | .007 | .107 | .159 | .149 | .110 | −.092 |
| | (.002) | (.005) | (<.001) | (<.001) | (.199) | (<.001) | (<.001) | (<.001) | (.001) | (<.001) |
| SN peers | −.031 | .103 | .281 | .193 | .004 | .100 | .196 | .160 | .108 | −.100 |
| | (.145) | (<.001) | (<.001) | (<.001) | (.440) | (<.001) | (<.001) | (<.001) | (<.001) | (<.001) |
| SN media | .012 | .086 | .261 | .139 | .071 | .094 | .177 | .120 | .098 | −.022 |
| | (.341) | (.001) | (<.001) | (<.001) | <.001) | (<.001) | (<.001) | (<.001) | (<.001) | (.223) |
| Emotion selec. car | −.053 | .108 | .293 | .200 | .012 | .084 | .167 | .124 | .120 | −.173 |
| | (.034) | (<.001) | (<.001) | (<.001) | (.334) | (.002) | (<.001) | (<.001) | (<.001) | (<.001) |
| Visceral em. car use | .026 | .123 | −.019 | −.092 | .049 | −.038 | −.025 | −.049 | −.045 | −.051 |
| | (.185) | (<.001) | (.255) | (<.001) | (.045) | (.094) | .193) | (.044) | (.059) | (.034) |
| Reflective em. car use | −.085 | .038 | .177 | .103 | −.033 | .042 | .063 | .071 | −.008 | −.012 |
| | (.001) | (.092) | (<.001) | (<.001) | (.126) | (.073) | (.014) | (.007) | (.396) | (.340) |
| Behavioural em. car use | .001 | .035 | −.021 | −.040 | −.042 | −.032 | −.007 | −.034 | −.060 | .003 |
| | (.481) | (.111) | .237) | (.82) | (.071) | (.136) | (.404) | (.121) | (.018) | (.458) |
| PBC1 | 1 | .104 | .041 | −.026 | .023 | .053 | .154 | .012 | .016 | −.014 |
| | | (<.001) | (.072) | (.182) | (.208) | (.034) | (<.001) | (.333) | (.294) | (.318) |
| PBC2 | | 1 | .165 | .010 | .360 | .048 | .143 | .062 | .076 | −.057 |
| | | | (<.001) | (<.001) | (.364) | (<.001) | (.047) | (<.001) | (.004) | (.024) |

| | PBC3 | PBC4 | PBC5 | PBC6 | PBC7 | PBC8 | PBC9 | PBC10 |
|---|---|---|---|---|---|---|---|---|
| PBC3 | 1 | | | | | | | |
| PBC4 | .171 [<.001] | 1 | | | | | | |
| PBC5 | .011 [.351] | .054 [.031] | 1 | | | | | |
| PBC6 | .041 [.080] | .248 [<.001] | .051 [.037] | 1 | | | | |
| PBC7 | .126 [<.001] | .181 [<.001] | .080 [.003] | .287 [<.001] | 1 | | | |
| PBC8 | .101 [<.001] | .202 [<.001] | .056 [.025] | .364 [<.001] | .389 [<.001] | 1 | | |
| PBC9 | .012 [.343] | .092 [<.001] | .107 [<.001] | .056 [<.001] | .103 [<.001] | .025 [.190] | 1 | |
| PBC10 | −.047 [.052] | −.066 [.011] | −.074 [.005] | −.003 [.412] | .006 [.411] | −.002 [.476] | −.144 [<.001] | 1 |

**Table 2** Correlation between metric variables in the full sample regression analysis (continued).

| | Intention to use | Attitude | SN peers | SN media | Emotions elec. car | Visceral emotion car use | Reflective emotion car use | Behavioural emotion car use |
|---|---|---|---|---|---|---|---|---|
| Intention to use | 1 | −.560 | .510 | .404 | .597 | −.041 | .283 | .003 |
| | | (<.001) | (<.001) | (<.001) | (<.001) | (.077) | (<.001) | (.454) |
| Attitude | | 1 | .487 | .384 | .644 | −.193 | .235 | −.014 |
| | | | (<.001) | (<.001) | (<.001) | (<.001) | (<.001) | .313) |
| SN peers | | | 1 | .402 | .596 | −.145 | .258 | .005 |
| | | | | (<.001) | (<.001) | (<.001) | (<.001) | (<.001) |
| SN media | | | | 1 | .390 | −.022 | .169 | .009 |
| | | | | | (<.001) | (.224) | (<.001) | (.371) |
| Emotions elec. car | | | | | 1 | −.205 | .309 | −.034 |
| | | | | | | (<.001) | (<.001) | (.121) |
| Visceral em. car use | | | | | | 1 | .074 | .336 |
| | | | | | | | (.005) | (<.001) |
| Reflective em. car use | | | | | | | 1 | .216 |
| | | | | | | | | (<.001) |
| Behavioural em. car use | | | | | | | | 1 |

PBC1-10 are the Perceived Behaviour Control variables listed in Table 1a. Cells are correlation coefficients; one-tailed significance levels in brackets. $N = 1199$.

**Table 3** Regression results: Full sample. Dependent: Intention to use an electric car

| Variable | B | St. error | Beta | $t$-value | Sig. |
|---|---|---|---|---|---|
| Intercept | 1.572 | .341 | | 4.605 | <.001 |
| Attitude towards the electric car | .932 | .103 | .263 | 9.071 | <.001 |
| Subjective norm peers | .299 | .054 | .152 | 5.512 | <.001 |
| Subjective norm media | .137 | .030 | .111 | 4.564 | <.001 |
| Emotion towards the electric car | .337 | .039 | .275 | 8.562 | <.001 |
| Visceral emotion towards car driving | .050 | .026 | .049 | 1.941 | .052 |
| Reflective emotion towards car driving | .081 | .021 | .089 | 3.774 | <.001 |
| Behavioural emotion towards car driving | −.035 | .024 | −.034 | −1.461 | .144 |
| My budget is sufficient to buy an electric car | .058 | .021 | .066 | 2.757 | .006 |
| Charging an electric car is possible with an ordinary electric socket | .048 | .023 | .049 | 2.060 | .040 |
| Cars with a combustion engine will soon not be allowed to enter the city | .055 | .022 | .057 | 2.452 | .014 |
| You can drive a long distance with an electric car | −.022 | .024 | −.021 | −.917 | .359 |
| I will not be able to charge an electric car at home | −.014 | .023 | −.014 | −.592 | .554 |
| Our society offers the necessary means and instruments to use an electric car | −.057 | .025 | −.054 | −2.296 | .022 |
| The costs of using an electric car are acceptable | .000 | .032 | .000 | .0140 | .989 |
| The maintenance of an electric car is well organised | .043 | .038 | .027 | 1.140 | .255 |
| I will not be allowed to charge my electric car with energy I have produced myself | −.028 | .024 | −.025 | −.137 | .256 |
| The battery of an electric car cannot be charged underway | −.029 | .024 | −.026 | −1.186 | .236 |
| Gender | .135 | .048 | .068 | 2.829 | .005 |
| Education level | −.052 | .046 | −.025 | −1.155 | .248 |
| City centre | −.007 | .056 | −.003 | −.122 | .903 |
| Suburbs | −.044 | .047 | −.022 | −.937 | .349 |
| Age middle | −.212 | .110 | −.089 | −1.932 | .054 |
| Age old | −.080 | .069 | −.035 | −1.161 | .246 |
| Driver's licence 1 | .051 | .107 | .023 | .474 | .635 |
| Driver's licence 2 | −.018 | .061 | −.009 | −.292 | .770 |
| Car type 1 | .003 | .052 | .002 | .063 | .950 |
| Car type 2 | −.024 | .052 | −.012 | −.463 | .644 |

$R^2 = .484$; $R^2_{adj} = .472$; $F_{(27, 1171)} = 40.617$, $p < .001$. Multicollinearity diagnostics: all VIF < 2.

in a normal socket (functional source constraint), and not being allowed to enter the city centre with a car with a combustion engine (regulatory source constraint) are also significantly predictors of usage intention, but of lesser importance. A counter-intuitive but small effect is the negative effect of society offering the necessary means and instruments to use an electric car on usage intentions. Behavioural and visceral emotions towards car driving do not have a significant effect on the adoption intention. Of all the sociodemographic variables, only gender has a small significant effect on usage intention: women are more inclined to use the electric car than men.

### *Determinants of usage intention for subgroups*

Before exploring the differences in usage intention decision processes between subgroups of respondents differing in environmental concern, environmental behaviour, and opinion leadership, first a correlation analysis was carried out to test whether there is a significant correlation between these variables and electric car usage intention. The correlation between intention and environmental concern is $r = .307$ ($p < .001$) and between intention and environmental behaviour $r = .300$ ($p < .001$). The correlation between intention and opinion leadership is $r = -.028$ ($p = .334$). In order to test the difference in usage intention between the three personal value clusters, a one-way analysis of variance (ANOVA) was carried out. The three value clusters are significantly different in terms of usage intention ($F(2, 1194) = 16.527$, $p < .001$). Cluster 1 ($M = 2.976$) is not significantly different from cluster 2 ($M = 2.966$), but both show a significantly stronger intention to use the electric car than cluster 3 ($M = 2.622$; $p < .001$). Based on this analysis, it does not make sense to study the decision-making process for individuals who are low and high in opinion leadership separately, because this variable does not correlate with usage intention. For the other moderating variables, the regression model was estimated for subsamples of respondents. For environmental concern and environmental behaviour, the 33% lowest-scoring respondents and the 33% highest-scoring ones were compared. For value orientation, the three clusters were compared. In these regression models, for parsimony reasons the sociodemographic were not included, since in the general model most of them did not contribute meaningfully to the prediction of adoption intention. The results of these regression analyses are given in Tables 4–6.

In general, attitudes and emotions towards the electric car remain the most important determinants of usage intention in all subgroups. However, there are remarkable differences between the groups. In the low environmental concern groups and the self-enhancing power-seeking achiever segment, emotions towards the electric car are relatively more important determinants of usage intention than in the high environmental concern and the universalist and benevolent groups. This pattern does not emerge in the environmental behaviour groups. With respect to the subjective norm, the results are mixed. Peer pressure is a significant determinant of usage intention in most groups, especially in the achiever social segment, and, generally speaking, media pressure is somewhat less important. A very outspoken pattern is that reflective emotions towards car driving in general are a significant determinant in the highly environmentally concerned, the high environmental behaviour, and the universalist and benevolent groups, but are not significant in the lowly concerned, low environmental behaviour, and achiever segments. Visceral emotions towards car driving seem to affect the achievers, but not the other personal

**Table 4** Regression results: Low and high environmental concern groups. Dependent: Intention to use an electric car.

| Variable | Low environmental concern | | | High environmental concern | | |
|---|---|---|---|---|---|---|
| | Beta | $t$-value | Sig. | Beta | $t$-value | Sig. |
| Attitude towards the electric car | .337 | 6.158 | <.001 | .296 | 5.721 | <.001 |
| Subjective norm peers | .129 | 2.622 | .009 | .132 | 2.566 | .011 |
| Subjective norm media | .078 | 1.691 | .092 | .140 | 3.107 | .002 |
| Emotion towards the electric car | .278 | 4.682 | <.001 | .193 | 3.517 | <.001 |
| Visceral emotion towards car driving | .053 | 1.184 | .237 | .071 | 1.569 | .118 |
| Reflective emotion towards car driving | .038 | .887 | .376 | .088 | 2.000 | .046 |
| Behavioural emotion towards car driving | −.004 | −.099 | .921 | −.047 | −1.013 | .312 |
| My budget is sufficient to buy an electric car | −.008 | −.203 | .839 | .107 | 2.423 | .016 |
| Charging an electric car is possible with an ordinary electric socket | .092 | 2.143 | .033 | .110 | 2.371 | .018 |
| Cars with a combustion engine will soon not be allowed to enter the city | −.018 | −.428 | .669 | .031 | .712 | .477 |
| You can drive a long distance with an electric car | −.098 | −2.279 | .023 | −.054 | −1.251 | .212 |
| I will not be able to charge an electric car at home | −.060 | −1.441 | .150 | −.030 | −.657 | .511 |
| Our society offers the necessary means and instruments to use an electric car | −.052 | −1.123 | .262 | −.020 | −.459 | .646 |
| The costs of using an electric car are acceptable | .022 | .480 | .631 | −.037 | −.789 | .431 |
| The maintenance of an electric car is well organized | .044 | .931 | .351 | .049 | 1.078 | .282 |
| I will not be allowed to charge my electric car with energy I have produced myself | .035 | .858 | .392 | −.073 | −1.743 | .082 |
| The battery of an electric car cannot be charged underway | .051 | 1.231 | .219 | −.097 | −2.268 | .024 |
| | $R^2 = .447, R^2_{adj} = .421$ | | | $R^2 = .415, R^2_{adj} = .387$ | | |
| | $F(17, 361) = 17.173, p < .001$ | | | $F(17, 354) = 14.750, p < .001$ | | |

**Table 5** Regression results: Low and high environmental behaviour groups. Dependent: Intention to use an electric car.

| Variable | Low environmental behaviour | | | High environmental behaviour | | |
|---|---|---|---|---|---|---|
| | **Beta** | *t*-value | **Sig.** | **Beta** | *t*-value | **Sig.** |
| Attitude towards the electric car | .272 | 6.447 | <.001 | .248 | 6.596 | <.001 |
| Subjective norm peers | .167 | 4.046 | <.001 | .141 | 3.864 | <.001 |
| Subjective norm media | .110 | 3.007 | .003 | .118 | 3.637 | <.001 |
| Emotion towards the electric car | .237 | 5.167 | <.001 | .275 | 6.863 | <.001 |
| Visceral emotion towards car driving | .099 | 2.762 | .006 | .109 | 3.452 | .001 |
| Reflective emotion towards car driving | .031 | .870 | .385 | .061 | 1.964 | .050 |
| Behavioural emotion towards car driving | −.026 | −.718 | .473 | −.039 | −1.235 | .217 |
| My budget is sufficient to buy an electric car | .052 | 1.535 | .126 | .068 | 2.263 | .024 |
| Charging an electric car is possible with an ordinary electric socket | .089 | 2.431 | .015 | .063 | 1.929 | .054 |
| Cars with a combustion engine will soon not be allowed to enter the city | .095 | 2.665 | .008 | .084 | 2.706 | .007 |
| You can drive a long distance with an electric car | .002 | .057 | .955 | −.018 | −.596 | .552 |
| I will not be able to charge an electric car at home | .012 | .329 | .742 | −.006 | −.184 | .854 |
| Our society offers the necessary means and instruments to use an electric car | −.054 | 1.463 | .144 | −.078 | −2.482 | .013 |
| The costs of using an electric car are acceptable | −.058 | −1.524 | .128 | −.010 | −.298 | .766 |
| The maintenance of an electric car is well organised | .034 | .911 | .363 | .032 | 1.004 | .316 |
| I will not be allowed to charge my electric car with energy I have produced myself | −.038 | −1.123 | .262 | −.064 | −2.153 | .032 |
| The battery of an electric car cannot be charged underway | −.079 | −.2304 | .022 | −.070 | −2.364 | .018 |
| | $R^2 = .473$, $R^2_{adj} = .455$ | | | $R^2 = .469$, $R^2_{adj} = .469$ | | |
| | $F(17, 367) = 26.537$, $p < .001$ | | | $F(17, 365) = 33.286$, $p < .001$ | | |

**Table 6** Regression results: Three personal value type groups. Dependent: Intention to use an electric car.

| Variable | Self-transcendent universalist | | | Benevolent | | | Self-enhancing and Power seeking achiever | | |
|---|---|---|---|---|---|---|---|---|---|
| | Beta | $t$-value | Sig. | Beta | $t$-value | Sig. | Beta | $t$-value | Sig. |
| Attitude towards the electric car | .249 | 5.092 | <.001 | .301 | 6.235 | <.001 | .190 | 3.586 | <.001 |
| Subjective norm peers | .081 | 1.658 | .098 | .142 | 2.985 | .003 | .234 | 4.819 | <.001 |
| Subjective norm media | .159 | 3.723 | <.001 | .079 | 1.912 | .056 | .091 | 1.994 | .047 |
| Emotion towards the electric car | .267 | 4.911 | <.001 | .221 | 4.127 | <.001 | .305 | 5.315 | <.001 |
| Visceral emotion towards car driving | .067 | 1.710 | .088 | .034 | .847 | .397 | .118 | 2.865 | .004 |
| Reflective emotion towards car driving | .086 | 2.006 | .046 | .102 | 2.546 | .011 | .054 | 1.211 | .197 |
| Behavioural emotion towards car driving | .084 | 1.976 | .049 | −.040 | −1.000 | .318 | −.030 | −.740 | .460 |
| My budget is sufficient to buy an electric car | −.028 | −.695 | .488 | .076 | 1.987 | .048 | −.011 | −.273 | .785 |
| Charging an electric car is possible with an ordinary electric socket | .014 | .354 | .723 | .035 | .849 | .396 | .053 | 1.287 | .199 |
| Cars with a combustion engine will soon not be allowed to enter the city | −.084 | −2.066 | .040 | .017 | .438 | .662 | .075 | 1.831 | .068 |
| You can drive a long distance with an electric car | −.029 | .660 | .509 | .027 | .673 | .501 | −.054 | −1.333 | .183 |
| I will not be able to charge an electric car at home | .014 | .327 | .744 | −.011 | −.269 | .788 | −.054 | −1.337 | .182 |
| Our society offers the necessary means and instruments to use an electric car | −.048 | −1.241 | .215 | −.094 | −2.293 | .022 | .001 | .012 | .990 |

(Continued)

**Table 6** (Continued).

| Variable | Self-transcendent universalist | | | Benevolent | | | Self-enhancing and Power seeking achiever | | |
|---|---|---|---|---|---|---|---|---|---|
| | Beta | $t$-value | Sig. | Beta | $t$-value | Sig. | Beta | $t$-value | Sig. |
| The costs of using an electric car are acceptable | −.111 | −2.802 | .005 | .013 | .310 | .757 | .040 | .424 | .356 |
| The maintenance of an electric car is well organised | .089 | 2.096 | .037 | .067 | 1.625 | .105 | −.005 | −.111 | .912 |
| I will not be allowed to charge my electric car with energy I have produced myself | .079 | 1.897 | .059 | −.033 | −.886 | .376 | .017 | .429 | .668 |
| The battery of an electric car cannot be charged underway | −.022 | −.540 | .590 | <.001 | .003 | .998 | .037 | .935 | .350 |
| | $R^2 = .498$, $R^2_{adj} = .474$ $F(17, 365) = 21.274$, $p < .001$ | | | $R^2 = .436$, $R^2_{adj} = .413$ $F(17, 429) = 19.490$, $p < .001$ | | | $R^2 = .511$, $R^2_{adj} = .487$ $F(17, 348) = 21.372$, $p < .001$ | | |

value types. Finally, perceived behavioural control factors appear to play a much more prominent role in highly environmentally concerned, high environmental behaviour, and universalist and benevolent segments. Various personal ability and technical and regulatory constraints appear to determine usage intention significantly, while this is far less the case for lowly concerned, low environmental behaviour, and achiever groups.

The fact that these different segments show meaningful differences in their usage intention formation makes it meaningful to explore the sociodemographic characteristics of the groups (detailed figures available from the authors). Women are more highly environmentally concerned, as well as people with a higher educational level. The longer people have their driving licence, the more environmentally friendly behaviours they report. The older people are, the more environmentally friendly they seem to behave. Women behave in a more environmentally friendly way than men and so do more highly educated individuals compared to lower educated ones. Individuals who only recently got their driving licence are more often in the self-enhancing and power-seeking value segment; people who have held their driving licence for 3–20 years in the benevolent value group, and the majority of people who have held their driving licence for more than 20 years are in the self-transcendent universalists group. A similar pattern emerges for young versus older people. Individuals with special vehicles are most often in the benevolent group. Large car owners are less often in the achiever group, while the opposite is true for small car owners. Males are most often in the achiever group, while only a minority of females is part of this value cluster. Highly educated people are most often in the benevolent group, while lowly educated people are most often found in the self-transcendent universalist segment.

Although the evidence is mixed and sometimes inconsistent, individuals who are in groups that are most inclined to use the electric car (high environmental concern, strong environmental behaviour, universalists, and benevolents) appear to be more often female, higher educated, and older, and consequently have held their driving licence for a longer time. The type of car people currently drive does not seem to be of importance. Also the place people live does not directly or indirectly relate to their electric car usage intention. Belgium is so densely populated that the distinction between city centre, suburbs, and countryside is probably not relevant.

## Discussion and conclusions

Adding affective components to the TPB appears to be highly relevant for predicting the usage intention of electric cars. Both in the general model and in all models for subgroups, emotions towards the electric car are the most or the second most important factor that determine electric car usage intention. This is in line with an overwhelming amount of earlier behavioural and TPB research in different contexts. The unique contribution of the present study is to show that in a high-involvement environmentally friendly durable consumer product context, emotional factors are important determinants of usage intention. Also all traditional cognitive TPB are significant factors. A positive attitude towards the electric car is very important, and is the first or second most important determinant of usage intention in all models. One or both subjective norm factors are mostly in third place as determinants of intention, but substantially less important than attitude and emotion towards the electric car. This is consistent with the findings of Munnukka and Järvi (2011) that consumers are more influenced by personal considerations while social factors have a more of a background effect on perceptions. In general, peer pressure is somewhat more important than media pressure. Behavioural control factors are generally less important than the previous factors, but both personal ability and control variables are still relevant. Emotions towards current car driving are generally of minor importance. If they are a significant determinant of intentions at all, mostly reflective (and thus cognitively oriented) emotions seem to be important. The results confirm the claims of, amongst others, Bagozzi et al. (1999), Bagozzi et al. (2002), Chaudhuri et al. (2010), Kim et al. (2007), and Richins (1977) that emotional reactions to (innovative) products and (new) behaviour, also in the context of environmentally friendly consumer durables, are at least as important as cognitive considerations in the usage intention formation process.

Highly environmentally concerned people, people already showing strong environmental behaviour, universalists, and benevolents are segments of the population that are more strongly inclined to use the electric car once it becomes widely available. This is in line with Bamberg (2003), Jansson (2011), Kilbourne and Beckmann (1998), and Thogerson (1999) who also identified these personal characteristics as important factors in pro-environmental behaviour. Somewhat surprisingly, opinion leadership with respect to cars is not correlated with usage intention of the electric car. Apparently, opinion leaders for cars are not the ones that are at this point of time inclined to adopt the electric car. The reason for this could be that these opinion leaders may well be at the forefront of adopting new car models and technology, but at present they do not see the electric car as a particularly appealing way to express this opinion leadership. They may perceive the electric-car technology to date as not innovative and appealing enough with respect to the car characteristics they perceive as important. Earlier research (Grewal, Metha, & Kardes, 2000) demonstrated the importance of the social identity function of a product for opinion leaders. Their desired social identity is contingent upon owning the product. Public access also pictures the owner as well informed. In the case of the electric car, it is too early to get public access to the product. This may explain why opinion leadership and electric-car adoption are not related in this study.

In terms of their decision-making process, these groups are different from less interested groups in a number of ways. First, although still highly significant, emotions towards the electric car seem to be a somewhat less important determinant of usage intention than for less interested groups. This is consistent with both the ELM and the AIM. Environmentally concerned people and universalist and benevolent individuals can be considered to be more involved in environmental socially responsible issues. According to the ELM (Petty & Cacioppo, 1986), stronger involvement leads to more cognitive, central processing of information, and peripheral cues such as affective reactions could be less important. Conversely, lower environmentally concerned people and achievers are less involved with environmental issues. In their case, peripheral cues such as affective reactions towards the electric car could be relatively more important. However, the results also support the principles of the AIM (Forgas, 1995). Even for the highly environmentally involved individuals, emotions towards using the electric car are still important and relevant, and are therefore significant determinants of usage intentions.

Another remarkable difference between subgroups is that reflective emotions towards car driving play a significant role in usage intention formation in environmentally concerned, strong environmental behaviour, and universalist and benevolent segments, but not in those groups that exhibit a lower intention to use the electric car. This type of emotions originates in reflecting upon the consequences of car driving on society in general and the environment in particular. It is not surprising that these emotions play a significant role in more environment- and society-oriented groups. The role of visceral and behavioural emotions towards car driving is ambiguous and not very important. If these emotions are significant at all, their effect is positive (e.g. in the achiever and the universalist groups). Probably, in these groups, the electric car is seen as a product that, because of its new technology and special features, will enhance their visceral and behavioural driving experience. Maybe they are thrilled by the electric car as the latest 'toy'. Jansson et al. (2011) also remark that there is a segment of the population that exhibits both green norms and interest for innovative products simultaneously.

Finally, there is a remarkable difference between the groups with respect to the importance of perceived behavioural control factors in their decision process. Environmentally concerned, strong environmentally behaviour, and universalist and benevolent groups appear to take more behaviour control elements into account than segments of the population that are less inclined to use the electric car. These concerns relate to both personal ability (e.g. being able to afford the car, the cost of the car) and control factors (e.g. being able to charge the car, use it in city centres, maintaining it). This is again in line with the ELM. The high-intention-to-use groups are generally more involved in environmental and societal factors in general, and in the electric car in particular. They are therefore expected to take more and more rational and cognitive factors into account when considering their usage intention.

As in previous studies, the role of sociodemographic factors is somewhat inconsistent, although certain patterns emerge. Women have a significantly higher intention to use the electric car, and in those subgroups that have a higher intention of using it, women, highly educated, and older individuals are over-represented. This confirms the findings of, amongst others, Clark et al. (2003), Hunter et al. (2004), Moon et al. (2002), Rice (2006), and Shen and Saijo (2008).

The insights of the present study can be used by designers, marketers, public policymakers, and advocates of the electric car. First, in terms of target-group definition, there are indications that a somewhat older, female, and higher educated public is most susceptible to using the electric car. Psychographically, the electric car will not so much have to appeal to opinion leaders in cars, but to people who have a high environmental concern and adhere to values such as idealism and altruism (the universalists and the benevolents). In terms of behavioural segmentation criteria, people who are already acting in an environmentally friendly way are also most inclined to adopt the additional environmentally friendly behaviour of electric car driving. One of the most important insights of this study is that designers and marketers will have to develop and advertise the electric car in such a way that it is emotionally appealing. Apart from all the rational considerations that people take into consideration, a positive emotional response to the idea of electric car driving is vital for its success. This is not just a matter of designing the car in such a way that it evokes pleasurable emotions, but also of positioning the electric car as a product to love and that friends and neighbours will envy you for. Also stressing the fact that electric cars will make you feel good about your impact on society and the environment (reflective emotions) will support these groups in their electric car usage intentions. At the same time, high-intention groups have a lot of control concerns. Not only marketers but also public policy actors and advocacy groups should take the necessary measures to remove the constraints that potential users of electric cars are concerned about by developing clear legislation and regulation concerning (electric) car use, providing the right infrastructure to charge the car regularly and conveniently, and by disseminating the right information to counter misperceptions and take away concerns, for instance with respect to driving and charging regulations.

The present study has a number of limitations and also offers opportunities for further research. The study was carried out using an online snowball sample that is sociodemographically not entirely representative of the Belgian population. Snowball sampling is uncontrolled and non-probabilistic and has its limitations in terms of representativeness. Although about 70% of the Belgian population regularly uses the Internet, the representativeness of online surveys may suffer from the fact that certain segments of the population, such as older people and digitally not very experienced groups, may be under-represented. However, this does not necessarily jeopardise the validity of our findings. Many studies that aim at testing theory or conceptual models use non-probability or non-representative samples of student or Internet populations and are nevertheless considered as useful (Basil, Brown, & Bocarnea, 2002). Moreover, since hardly any sociodemographic factor has a direct impact on electric car usage intention and the model is controlled for sociodemographic variables, this non-representativeness will probably not have affected our conclusions.

One obvious limitation of almost all empirical studies using the TPB as a conceptual framework is that it predicts intentions and not actual behaviour. Bagozzi (2007) states that the intention–behaviour linkage is probably the most uncritically accepted assumption in social science research. Behavioural intentions do not evidently translate into objectively measured buying behaviour. Therefore, the usefulness of the TPB to predict real buying behaviour has been questioned (for an overview, see De Cannière et al., 2009; Foxall, 2005). Nevertheless, for instance, Sheppard, Hartwick, and Warshaw (1988) in their meta-analysis of 87 studies found a correlation of .53 between intention and behaviour. Consequently, intentions can be expected to be relevant for predicting actual behaviour. Nevertheless, testing the model to predict actual adoption of electric cars at a later stage would enhance the validity of our findings.

Future research could explore more in depth to what extent opinion leadership with respect to environmentally positioned products in general and eco-friendly cars in particular is related to usage intention of electric cars. Building upon the results of the present study, in further research, the determinants of the attitude towards the electric car, such as complexity, availability, compatibility, and relative advantage (Taylor & Todd, 1995), will be studied and the role of emotions in the adoption process will be explored more extensively. The determinants of the emotions towards the electric car will be investigated in more depth by means of setting up experiments to explore product and design features that evoke positive and negative emotional responses to different types of electric cars and how persuasive different advertising strategies for electric cars are for different market segments. Also the relationship with existing brands is important. Car models, as any other brand on the market, have a certain personality and are associated with certain typical experiences. An interesting question is how the addition of an electric vehicle to the product line will influence this personality and experience, and which type of brand personality will most benefit from which type of emotional positioning focus (visceral, behavioural, reflective) that is used to design and promote the electric model.

## References

Ajzen, I. (1991). The Theory of Planned Behavior. *Organizational Behavior and Human decision processes*, 50, 179–221.

Ajzen, I., & Fishbein, M. (1980). *Understanding attitudes and predicting social behaviour.* Englewood Cliffs, NJ: Prentice-Hall.

Allen, C.T., Machleit, K.A., & Kleine, A. (1992). A comparison of attitudes and emotions as predictors of behavior at diverse levels of behavioral experience. *Journal of Consumer Research*, 18(4), 493–504.

Arcury, T.A., & Christianson, E.H. (1990). Environmental worldview in response to environmental problems: Kentucky 1984 and 1988 compared. *Environment and Behavior*, 22, 387–407.

Bae, H.-S. (2008). Entertainment-education and recruitment of cornea donors: The role of emotion and issue involvement. *Journal of Health Communication*, 13, 20–36.

Bagozzi, R.P. (2007). The legacy of the technology acceptance model and a proposal for a paradigm shift. *Journal of the Association for Information Systems*, 8(4), 244–254.

Bagozzi, R.P., Baumgartner, H., & Pieters, R. (1998). Goal-directed emotions. *Cognition and Emotion*, 12, 1–26.

Bagozzi, R.P., Gopinath, M., & Nyer, P.U. (1999). The role of emotions in marketing. *Journal of the Academy of Marketing Science*, 27(2), 184–206.

Bagozzi, R.P., Gurhan-Canli, Z., & Priester, J.R. (2002). *The social psychology of consumer behaviour*. Milton Keynes, UK: Open University Press.

Bamberg, S. (2003). How does environmental concern influence specific environmentally related behaviors? A new answer to an old question. *Journal of Environmental Psychology*, 23, 21–32.

Bamberg, S., & Möser, G. (2007). Twenty years after Hines, Hungerford and Tomera: A new meta-analysis of psycho-social determinants of pro-environmental behaviour. *Journal of Environmental Psychology*, 27, 14–25.

Bamberg, S., & Schmidt, S. (2003). Incentives, morality or habit? Predicting students' car use for university routes with the models of Ajzen, Schwartz and Triandis. *Environment and Behavior*, 35(2), 264–285.

Bandura, A. (1986). *Social foundations of thought and action*. Englewood Cliff, NJ: Prentice Hall.

Basil, M.D., Brown, W.J., & Borcarnea, M.C. (2002). Differences in univariate values versus multivariate relationships: Findings from a study of Diana, Princess of Wales. *Human Communication Research*, 28, 501–514.

Bayus, B.L., Erickson G., & Jacobson, R. (2003). The financial rewards of new product introductions in the personal computer industry. *Management Science*, 49(2), 197–210.

Bhattacherjee, A. (2000). Acceptance of internet application services: The case of electronic brokerages. *IEEE Transactions on Systems, Man and Cybernetics – Part A: Systems and Humans*, 30(4), 411–420.

Blend, J.R., & van Ravenwaay, E.O. (1999). Measuring consumer demand for eco-labeled apples. *American Journal of Agricultural Economics*, 81(5), 1072–1077.

Bower, G.H. (1981). Mood and memory. *American Psychologist*, 36, 129–148.

Buttel, F.H., & Flinn, W.L. (1974). The structure of support for the environmental movement. *Rural Sociology*, 39, 56–69.

Carsalesprofessional.com/the-car-buyers-emotions/, Retrieved July 1, 2011.

Cauberghe, V., & De Pelsmacker, P. (2011). Adoption of digital TV by advertising professionals: A longitudinal extension of the theory of planned behaviour. *Journal of Interactive Advertising, 11*(2).

Chaudhuri, A., Aboulnasr, K., & Ligas, M. (2010). Emotional responses on initial exposure to a hedonic or utilitarian description of a radical innovation. *Journal of Marketing Theory and Practice, 18*(4), 339–359.

Cheung, S.F., Chang, D.K.-S., & Wong, Z.S.-Y. (1999). Re-examining the Theory of Planned Behaviour in understanding wastepaper recycling. *Environment and Behavior, 31*(5), 587–612.

Clark, C.F., Kotchen, M.J., & Moore, M.R. (2003). Internal and external influences on pro-environmental behavior. Participation in a green electricity program. *Journal of Environmental Psychology, 23*, 237–246.

Davis, F.D. (1989). Perceived usefulness, perceived ease of use, and user acceptance of information technology. *MIS Quarterly, 13*(3), 319–339.

De Cannière, M.H., De Pelsmacker, P., & Geuens M. (2009). Relationship quality and the Theory of Planned Behavior models of behavioral intentions and purchase behavior. *Journal of Business Research, 62*(1), 82–92.

Dolan, R.J. (2002). Emotion, cognition and behaviour. *Science, 298*, 1191–1194.

Doll, J., Mentz, M., & Orth, B. (1991). The prediction of goal-directed behavior: Attitude, subjective estimations of competence, and emotions. *Zeitschrift für Experimentelle und Angewandte Psychologie, 38*, 539–559.

Duran, M., Alzate, M., Lopez, W., & Sabucedo, M. (2011). Emotions and pro-environmental behavior. *Revista Latinoamericana de Psicología, 39*(2), 287–296.

Eagly, A.H., & Chaiken, S. (1998). Attitude structure and function. In D.T. Gilbert, S.T. Fiske, & G. Lindzey (Eds.), *Handbook of social psychology* (pp. 269–322). Englewood Cliffs, NJ: McGraw-Hill.

Ehrenfeld, J.R. (2008). *Sustainability by design*. New Haven, CT: Yale University Press.

Feitelson, E., & Salomon, I. (2000). The implications of differential network flexibility for spatial structures. *Transportation Research, Part A: Policy and Practice, 34*, 459–479.

Forgas, J.P. (1995). Mood and judgment: The Affect Infusion Model (AIM). *Psychological Bulletin, 117*(1), 39–66.

Foxall, G.R. (2005) Understanding Consumer Choice. Basingstoke: Palgrave Macmillan.

Fransson, N., & Gärling, T. (1999). Environmental concern: Conceptual definitions, measurement methods and research findings. *Journal of Environmental Psychology, 19*, 369–382.

Gärling, A., & Thøgersen, J. (2001). Marketing of electric vehicles. *Business Strategy and the Environment, 10*, 53–65.

Gärling, T., Fujii, S., Gärling, A., & Jacobsson, C. (2003). Moderating effects of social value orientation on determinants of proenvironmental behavior intention. *Journal of Environmental Psychology, 23*, 1–9.

Gatersleben, B., & Appleton, K. (2007). Contemplating cycling to work: Attitudes and perceptions in different stages of change. *Transportation Research Part A: Policy and Practice, 41*(4), 302–312.

Gatignon, H., & Robertson, T.S. (1991). Innovative decision processes. In T.S. Robertson & H.H. Kassarjian (Eds.), *Handbook of consumer behavior*. Englewood Cliffs, NJ: Prentice-Hall.

Geuens, M., De Pelsmacker, P., & Faseur, T. (2011). Emotional advertising: Revisiting the role of product category. *Journal of Business Research, 64*(4), 418–426.

Goldenhar, L.M., & Connell, C.M. (1992). Understanding and predicting recycling behaviour: An application of the theory of reasoned action. *Journal of Environmental Systems, 22*, 91–103.

Grewal, R., Metha, R., & Kardes, F.R. (2000). The role of the social identity function of attitudes in consumer innovativeness and opinion leadership. *Journal of Economic Psychology*, *21*, 233–252.

Hansla, A., Gamble, A., Juliusson, A., & Gärling, T. (2008). The relationship between awareness of consequences, environmental concern and value orientation. *Journal of Environmental Psychology*, *28*, 1–9.

Haustein, S., Klöckner, C.A., & Blöbaum, A. (2009). Car use of young adults: The role of travel socialization. *Transportation Research Part F: Traffic Psychology and Behaviour*, *12*(2), 168–178.

Hirschman, E.C., & Holbrook, M.B. (1982). Hedonic consumption: Emerging concepts, methods and propositions. *Journal of Marketing*, *46*, 92–101.

Holbrook, M.B., & Hirschman, E.C. (1982). The experiential aspects of consumption: Consumer fantasies, feelings and fun. *Journal of Consumer Research*, *9*(2), 132–140.

Howell, S.E., & Laska, S.B. (1992). The changing face of the environmental coalition: A research note. *Environment and Behavior*, *24*, 134–144.

Hsu, M.-H., Yen, C.-H., Chiu, C.-M., & Chang, C.-M. (2006). A longitudinal investigation of continued online shopping behavior/An extension of the Theory of Planned Behavior. *International Journal of Human–Computer Studies*, *64*, 889–904.

Hunter, L.M., Hatch, A., & Johnson, A. (2004). Cross-national gender variation in environmental behaviors. *Social Science Quarterly*, *85*, 677–694.

Hynie, M., MacDonald, T.K., & Marques, S. (2006). Self-conscious emotions and self-regulation in the promotion of condom use. *Personality and Social Psychology Bulletin*, *32*, 1072–1084.

Isen, A. (1987). Positive affect, cognitive processes and social behaviour. In L. Berkowitz (Ed.), *Advances in experimental social psychology* (Vol. 20, pp. 203–253). San Diego, CA: Academic Press.

Jansson, J. (2011). Consumer eco-innovation adoption: Assessing attitudinal factors and perceived product characteristics. *Business Strategy and the Environment*, *20*, 192–210.

Jansson, J., Marell, A., & Nordlund, A. (2011). Green consumer behaviour: Determinants of curtailment and eco-innovation adoption. *Journal of Consumer Marketing*, *27*(4), 358–370.

Johnston, R.J., Wessels, C.R., Donath, A., & Assche, F. (2001). Measuring consumer preferences for eco-labeled seafood: An international comparison. *Journal of Agricultural and Resource Economics*, *26*(1), 20–39.

Joireman, J.A., Van Lange, P.A.M., & Van Vugt, M. (2004). Who cares about the environmental impact of cars? Those with an eye toward the future. *Environment and Behavior*, *36*(2), 187–206.

Kaiser, F.G., Woefling, S., & Fuhrer, U. (1999). Environmental attitude and ecological behaviour. *Journal of Environmental Psychology*, *19*, 1–19.

Kilbourne, W.E., & Beckmann, S.C. (1998). Review and critical assessment of research on marketing and the environment. *Journal of Marketing Management*, *14*, 513–532.

Kilbourne, W.E., & Pickett, G. (2008). How materialism affects environmental beliefs, concerns, and environmental responsible behaviour. *Journal of Business Research*, *61*, 885–893.

Kim, H.W., Chan, H.C., & Chan, Y.P. (2007). A balanced thinking-feelings model of information systems continuance. *International Journal of Human Computer Studies*, *65*, 511–525.

Kwortnik, R.J., & Ross, W.T. (2007). The role of positive emotions in experiential decisions. *International Journal of Research in Marketing*, *24*, 324–335.

Lam, S.P. (1999). Predicting intentions to conserve water from the theory of planned behaviour, perceived moral obligation, and perceived water right. *Journal of Applied Social Psychology*, *29*, 1058–1071.

Leonidou, L.C., Leonidou, C.N., & Kvasova, O. (2010). Antecedents and outcomes of consumer environmentally friendly attitudes and behaviour. *Journal of Marketing Management*, 26(13–14), 1319–1344.

Loewenstein, G.F. (1996). Out of control: Visceral influences on behaviour. *Organizational Behavior and Human Decision Processes*, 65, 272–292.

Loureiro, M.L., McCluskey, J.J., & Mittelhammer, R.C. (2001). Assessing consumer preferences on organic, eco-labeled, and normal apples. *Journal of Agricultural and Resource Economics*, 26(2), 209–227.

Machleit, K., & Wilson, R.D. (1983). Emotional feelings and attitude towards the advertisement: The roles of brand familiarity and repetition. *Journal of Advertising*, 17(3), 27–35.

Manzini, E. (2009). New design knowledge. *Design Studies*, 30, 4–12.

Mazzon, J.A. (2011). *What are you afraid of? The role of emotions in social marketing.* Proceedings of the 2nd World Social Marketing Conference. Retrieved 15 August 2011 from http://wsmconference.com/2011/downloads/12S9SS1%20Jose%20 Afonso%20Mazzon.pdf.

McLean, P. (1990). *The triune brain in evolution.* New York: Plenum.

Mohai, P. (1992). Men, women and the environment: An examination of the gender gap in environmental concern activism. *Society and Natural Resources*, 5, 1–19.

Moon, W., Florkowski, W.J., Braäuckner, B., & Schonhof, I. (2002). Willingness to pay for environmental practices: Implications for eco-labeling. *Land and Economics*, 78(1), 88–102.

Moons, I., De Pelsmacker, P., De Bont, C., & Standaert, A. (2010). *The extended decomposed Theory of Planned Behaviour. A framework for investigating the adoption process of electric cars.* Proceedings of the 39th Annual Conference of the European Marketing Academy, Copenhagen, Denmark.

Morris, J.D., Woo, C., Geason, J.A., & Kim, J. (2002). The power of affect: Predicting intention. *Journal of Advertising Research*, 42(3), 7–17.

Munnukka, J., & Järvi, P. (2011). The value drivers of high-tech consumer products. *Journal of Marketing Management*, 27(5–6), 582–601.

Norman, D.A. (2004). *Emotional design.* New York: Basic Books.

Oliver, J.D., & Rosen, D.E. (2010). Applying the environmental propensity framework: A segmented approach to hybrid electric vehicle marketing strategies. *Journal of Marketing Theory and Practice*, 18(4), 377–393.

Parker, D., Manstead, A.S.R., & Stradling, S.G. (1995). Extending the theory of planned behaviour: The role of personal norm. *British Journal of Social Psychology*, 34, 127–137.

Pavlou, P.A., & Fygenson, M. (2006). Understanding and predicting electronic commerce adoption: An extension of the theory of planned behaviour. *MIS Quarterly*, 30(1), 115–143.

Perlusz, S. (2011). Emotions and technology acceptance. Development and validation of a technology affect scale. 2004 IEEE International Engineering Management Conference (CD), Singapore.

Perugini, M., & Bagozzi, R.P. (2001). The role of desires and anticipated emotions in goal-directed behaviours/Broadening and deepening the Theory of Planned Behaviour. *British Journal of Social Psychology*, 40, 79–98.

Peterson, R.E., Hoyer, W.D., & Wilson, W.R. (1986). *The role of affect in consumer behaviour: Emerging theories and applications.* Lexington, MA: D.C. Heath.

Petty, R.E., & Cacioppo, J.T. (1986). *Communication and persuasion: Central and peripheral routes to attitude change.* New York: Springer-Verlag.

Petty, R.E., Schumann, D.W., Richman, S.A., & Strathman, A.J. (1993). Positive mood and persuasion: Different roles for affect under high and low elaboration conditions. *Journal of Personality and Social Psychology*, 64(1), 5–20.

Pham, M.T. (1998). Representativeness, relevance, and the use of feelings in decision making. *Journal of Consumer Research*, 25(2), 144–159.

Pham, M.T. (2004). The logic of feeling. *Journal of Consumer Psychology*, 14(4), 360–369.

Preisendorfer, P. (1998). *Umweltbewusstsein in Deutschland. Ergebnisse einer repäsentativen Bevölkungsumfrage*. Bonn: Bundesministerium für Umwelt, Naturschutz und Reaktorsicherheit.

Rice, G. (2006). Pro-environmental behavior in Egypt. Is there a role for Islamic environmental ethics? *Journal of Business Ethics*, 65, 373–390.

Richard, R., van der Pligt, J., & de Vries, N. (1995). Anticipated affective reactions and prevention of AIDS. *British Journal of Social Psychology*, 34, 9–21.

Richins, M.L. (1997). Measuring emotions in the consumption experience. *Journal of Consumer Research*, 24(2), 127–146.

Roberts, J.A. (1996). Green consumers in the 1990s: Profile and implications for advertising. *Journal of Business Research*, 36(3), 217–231.

Rogers, E.M. (1995). *Diffusion of innovations*. New York: Free Press.

Rohan, M.J. (2000). A rose by any name? The values construct. *Personality and Social Psychology Review*, 4, 255–277.

Rokeach, M. (1973). *The nature of human values*. New York: Free Press.

Schahn, J., & Holzer, E. (1990). Studies of individual environmental concern: The role of knowledge, gender and background variables. *Environment and Behavior*, 22, 767–786.

Schepers, J., & Wetzels, M. (2007). A meta-analysis of the technology acceptance model: Investigating subjective norm and moderation effects. *Information and Management*, 44, 90–103.

Schultz, P.W. (2001). The structure of environmental concern: Concern for self, other people, and the biosphere. *Journal of Environmental Psychology*, 21, 327–339.

Schwartz, S.H. (1992). Universals in the content and structure of values: Theoretical advances and empirical tests in 20 countries. In M. Zanna (Ed.), *Advances in experimental social psychology* (pp. 1–65). Orlando, FL: Academic Press.

Sheller, M. (2004). Automotive emotions. Feeling the car. *Theory, culture and society*, 21(4/5), 221–242.

Shen, J., & Saijo, T. (2008). Reexamining the relations between socio-demographic characteristics and individual environmental concern: Evidence from Shanghai data. *Journal of Environmental Psychology*, 28, 42–50

Sheppard, B.H., Hartwick, J., & Warshaw, P. (1988). The theory of reasoned action: A meta-analysis of past research with recommendations for modifications and future research. *Journal of Consumer Research*, 15(3), 325–343.

Shiv, B., & Fedorikhin, A. (1999). Heart and mind in conflict: The interplay of affect and cognition in consumer decision making. *Journal of Consumer Research*, 26, 278–292.

Sitarz, D. (Ed.). (1994). *Agenda 21: The earth summit strategy to save our planet*. Boulder, CO: EarthPress. Worldwatch Environmental Alert Series.

Smith, R.A. (2008). Enabling technologies for demand management: Transport, *Energy Policy*, 36, 4444–4448.

Steg, L., Vlek, C., & Slotegraaf, G. (2001). Instrumental-reasoned and symbolic affective motives for using a motor car. *Transport Research, Part F*, 4, 151–169.

Sun, H, & Zhang, P. (2005). The role of moderating factors in user technology acceptance. *International Journal of Human–Computer Studies*, 64, 53–78.

Taylor, S., & Todd, P. (1995). Understanding information technology usage: A test of competing models. *Information Systems Research*, 6, 144–176.

Terry, D.J., & O'Leary, J.E. (1995). The theory of planned behaviour: The effects of perceived behavioural control and self-efficacy. *British Journal of Social Psychology*, 34, 199–220.

Thøgersen, J. (1996). Recycling and morality. A critical review of the literature. *Environment and Behavior*, 28, 536–558.

Thøgersen, J. (1999). Spill-over processes in the development of a sustainable consumption pattern. *Journal of Economic Psychology*, 20, 53–81.

Tremblay, K.R., & Dunlap, R.E. (1978). Rural-urban residence and concern with environmental quality: A replication and extension. *Rural Sociology*, 43, 474–491.

Trendy-travel.eu/emotions/start.phtml?link=project. Retrieved 1 July 2011.

Urban, G.L., & Hauser, J.R. (1993). *Design and marketing of new products*. Englewood Cliffs, NJ: Prentice Hall.

Venkatesh, V. (2000). Determinants of perceived ease of use: integrating control, intrinsic motivation, and emotion into the technology acceptance model. *Information Systems Research*, 11(4), 342–365.

Verhoef, E., Bliemer, M., Steg, L., & Van Wee, B. (2008). *Pricing in road transport: A multidisciplinary perspective*. Cheltenham, UK: Edward Elgar.

Wang, X. (2011). The role of anticipated negative emotions and past behaviour in individuals' physical activity intentions and behaviours. *Psychology of Sport and Exercise*, 12, 300–305.

Whitmarsh, L. (2009). Behavioural responses to climate change: Asymmetry of intentions and impacts. *Journal of Environmental Psychology*, 29(1), 13–23.

Wood, S.L., & Moreau, C.P. (2006). From fear to loathing? How emotion influences the evaluation and early use of innovations. *Journal of Marketing*, 70, 44–57.

Zelezny, L.C., Chua, P., & Aldrich, C. (2000). Elaborating on gender differences in environmentalism. *Journal of Social Issues*, 56(3), 443–457.

## Appendix 1. Variables used in the analyses – Items, scale definition, source of scale, factor structure, and alphas

| Variables and items | Type of scale and labels | Alpha |
| --- | --- | --- |
| *Intention to use electric car* | Five-category Likert scale | |
| I have the intention to drive an electric car in the near future | Labels: 1 = 'fully disagree'; 5 = 'fully agree' | $\alpha = .875$ |
| I will recommend the use of the electric car to other people | | |
| I expect that I will be driving an electric car in the near future | Cauberghe and De Pelsmacker (2011) | |
| *Attitude towards electric car* good–bad | Sum of positive choices made on six | Not applicable |
| like–don't like | dichotomous items (0–6) | |
| clever–stupid | | |
| nice–not nice | | |
| useful–useless | Cauberghe and De Pelsmacker (2011) | |
| suitable–not suitable | | |
| *Subjective norm peers* | Five-category Likert scale | |
| People driving an electric car are making a fool of themselves (r) | Labels: 1 = 'fully disagree'; 5 = 'fully agree' | $\alpha = .616$ |
| Driving an electric car is cool | | |
| My friends will find it weird that I'm driving an electric car (r) | | |
| My family will raise objections against driving an electric car (r) | Haustein, Klöckner, and Blöbaum (2009) and exploratory qualitative study | |

(*Continued*)

## CONTEMPORARY ISSUES IN GREEN AND ETHICAL MARKETING

**Appendix 1.** (Continued).

| Variables and items | Type of scale and labels | Alpha |
|---|---|---|
| People who are important to me will support me when I should drive an electric car | | |
| People who are important to me tell me that I should consider driving an electric car | | |
| People who are important to me try to convince me to drive an electric car | | |
| *Subjective norm media* | Five-category Likert scale | |
| The media gave me a good feeling about using an electric car | Labels: 1 = 'fully disagree'; 5 = 'fully agree' | $\alpha = .731$ |
| Articles in the media influenced me to use an electric car | Cauberghe and De Pelsmacker (2011) | |
| *Emotion towards electric car* | Five-category Likert scale | |
| I will like driving an electric car | Labels: 1 = 'fully disagree'; 5 = 'fully agree' | $\alpha = .795$ |
| I look forward to drive an electric car | | |
| Driving an electric car could frustrate me (r) | Cauberghe and De Pelsmacker (2011); Kim et al. (2007) | |
| *Perceived behavioural control* | Five-category Likert scale | No useable factor structure. |
| My budget is sufficient to buy an electric car | Labels: 1 = 'fully disagree'; 5 = 'fully agree' | |
| Charging an electric car is possible with an ordinary electric socket | | Single items used |
| Cars with a combustion engine will soon not be allowed to enter the city | Exploratory qualitative study | |
| You can drive a long distance with an electric car | | |
| I will not be able to charge an electric car at home | | |
| Our society offers the necessary means and instruments to use an electric car | | |
| The costs of using an electric car are acceptable | | |
| The maintenance of an electric car is well organised | | |
| I will not be allowed to charge my electric car with energy I have produced myself | | |
| The battery of an electric car cannot be charged underway | | |

(*Continued*)

## Appendix 1. (Continued).

| Variables and items | Type of scale and labels | Alpha |
|---|---|---|
| *Visceral emotions towards car driving* | 'To what extent do the following aspects contribute to you experiencing positive emotions when driving a car:' 1 = 'not at all'–5 = 'a lot' | $\alpha = .880$ |
| Throb of the engine | | |
| Rapid acceleration | | |
| Information on the dashboard | | |
| Beauty of the interior | | |
| Looks of the car | Norman (2004) and exploratory qualitative study | |
| High speed possibility | | |
| Technological sophistication | | |
| *Behavioural emotions towards car driving* | 'To what extent do the following aspects contribute to you experiencing positive emotions when driving a car:' 1 = 'not at all'–5 = 'a lot' | $\alpha = .738$ |
| Enjoying the environment while driving | | |
| Getting relaxed while driving | | |
| | Norman (2004) and exploratory qualitative study | |
| *Reflective emotions towards car driving* | 'To what extent do the following aspects contribute to you experiencing positive emotions when driving a car:' 1 = 'not at all'–5 = 'a lot' | $\alpha = .856$ |
| Low cost of the car | | |
| Environmentally friendly car | | |
| Economic fuel consumption of the car | | |
| | Norman (2004) and exploratory qualitative study | |
| *Environmental concern* | Five-category Likert scale | |
| The major part of the population does not act in an environmentally conscious way | Labels: 1 = 'fully disagree'; 5 = 'fully agree' | $\alpha = .778$ |
| Limits of economic growth have been crossed or will be reached very soon | | |
| Environmental protection measures should be carried out even if this costs jobs | Preisendorfer (1998) | |
| I am concerned about the environmental conditions our children will have to live in | | |
| Newspaper articles or TV reports about environmental problems make me angry | | |

(*Continued*)

**Appendix 1.** (Continued).

| Variables and items | Type of scale and labels | Alpha |
|---|---|---|
| If we continue as before, we are heading towards an environmentally catastrophe | | |
| Politicians do far too little for environmental protection | | |
| For the benefit of the environment, we should be ready to restrict our style of living | | |
| *Environmental behaviour* | Respondents could choose between: no, because I had to, because it saves money, because everyone else does it, because it is better for the environment | Not applicable |
| I use energy-saving bulbs | | |
| I use biological soap | | |
| I selectively collect garbage | | |
| Installed a renewable energy system | | |
| Member of an environmentalist organisation | | |
| Use rainwater or well water | | |
| Switched to green energy | Scale is sum of behaviours (0–15) that respondent indicate to conduct for environmental reasons (last category) | |
| Avoid needless packaging | | |
| Always take a quick shower in order not to waste too much water | | |
| Installed a low flush toilet | | |
| Often talk with others about a more environmentally friendly way of living | Whitmarsh (2009) and exploratory qualitative study | |
| Clothes are made in an environmentally friendly way | | |
| Installed insulation in house | | |
| Installed a heat pump | | |
| Whenever possible, don't use the car | | |
| *Opinion leadership with respect to cars* | Five-category Likert scale | |
| Compared to your circle of friends, how likely are you to be asked about cars? | Items 1–3: Labels: 1 = 'very seldom'; 5 = 'very often' | $\alpha = .721$ |
| Overall, in all of your discussions with friends and neighbours, are you used as a source of information? | Item 4: labels: 1 = 'fully disagree'; 5 = 'fully agree' | |

41

(*Continued*)

## CONTEMPORARY ISSUES IN GREEN AND ETHICAL MARKETING

**Appendix 1.** (Continued).

| Variables and items | Type of scale and labels | Alpha |
|---|---|---|
| Are you the first in your circle of friends to buy a new model of car when it appears on the market? | Grewal et al. (2000) | |
| In general, can you tell a lot about a person by seeing which car he drives? | | |
| *Value dimension idealism* | Five-category Likert scale | |
| Equality | 'To what extent are the following values a guideline in your life?' | $\alpha = 0.810$ |
| Social justice | | |
| World peace | Labels: 1 = 'very weak guideline'; 5 = 'very strong guideline' | |
| | Hansla, Gamble, Juliusson, & Gärling (2008); Schwartz (1992) | |
| *Value dimension altruism* | Five-category Likert scale | |
| Helpfulness | 'To what extent are the following values a guideline in your life?' | $\alpha = .758$ |
| Forgivingness | | |
| Loyalty | | |
| Responsibility | Labels: 1 = 'very weak guideline'; 5 = 'very strong guideline' | |
| | Hansla et al. (2008); Schwartz (1992) | |
| *Value dimension achievement* | Five-category Likert scale | |
| Ambition | 'To what extent are the following values a guideline in your life?' | $\alpha = .797$ |
| Efficiency | Labels: 1 = 'very weak guideline'; 5 = 'very strong guideline' | |
| | Success | |
| | Hansla et al. (2008); Schwartz (1992) | |
| *Value dimension power* | Five-category Likert scale | |
| Social power | 'To what extent are the following values a guideline in your life?' | $\alpha = .814$ |
| Authority | Labels: 1 = 'very weak guideline'; 5 = 'very strong guideline' | |
| | Influence | |
| | Hansla et al. (2008); Schwartz (1992) | |

All items of each scale load on one factor, unless mentioned otherwise.

## Appendix 2. Exploratory factor analysis output for the 10 perceived behavioural control items

*Total variance explained.*

| Component | Initial eigenvalues | | | Extraction sums of squared loadings | | | Rotation sums of squared loadings | | |
|---|---|---|---|---|---|---|---|---|---|
| | Total | % of variance | Cumulative % | Total | % of variance | Cumulative % | Total | % of variance | Cumulative % |
| Dimension 0 | | | | | | | | | |
| 1 | 2.028 | 20.278 | 20.278 | 2.028 | 20.278 | 20.278 | 1.822 | 18.224 | 18.224 |
| 2 | 1.370 | 13.698 | 33.977 | 1.370 | 13.698 | 33.977 | 1.369 | 13.686 | 31.911 |
| 3 | 1.120 | 11.197 | 45.174 | 1.120 | 11.197 | 45.174 | 1.170 | 11.701 | 43.612 |
| 4 | 1.021 | 10.211 | 55.385 | 1.021 | 10.211 | 55.385 | 1.117 | 11.174 | 54.787 |
| 5 | 1.005 | 10.054 | 65.439 | 1.005 | 10.054 | 65.439 | 1.065 | 10.653 | 65.439 |
| 6 | .850 | 8.499 | 73.938 | | | | | | |
| 7 | .795 | 7.946 | 81.884 | | | | | | |
| 8 | .665 | 6.653 | 88.537 | | | | | | |
| 9 | .593 | 5.933 | 94.470 | | | | | | |
| 10 | .553 | 5.530 | 100.000 | | | | | | |

Extraction method: Principal component analysis.

*Rotated component matrix[a].*

| | Component | | | | |
|---|---|---|---|---|---|
| | 1 | 2 | 3 | 4 | 5 |
| My budget is sufficient to buy an electric car | .065 | .013 | .050 | .025 | .922 |
| Charging an electric car is possible with an ordinary electric socket | .028 | .802 | .000 | .198 | .153 |
| Cars with a combustion engine will soon not be allowed to enter the city | .030 | .088 | −.026 | .911 | .071 |
| You can drive a long distance with an electric car | .452 | −.072 | .234 | .423 | −.286 |
| I will not be able to charge an electric car at home | .068 | .827 | .113 | −.107 | −.108 |
| Our society offers the necessary means and instruments to use an electric car | .741 | −.002 | .034 | −.044 | −.035 |
| The costs of using an electric car are acceptable | .676 | .119 | .022 | .088 | .299 |
| The maintenance of an electric car is well organised | .761 | .041 | −.062 | .054 | −.031 |
| I will not be allowed to charge my electric car with energy I have produced myself | .115 | .106 | .733 | −.138 | .025 |
| The battery of an electric car cannot be charged underway | .096 | −.003 | −.746 | −.159 | −.014 |

Extraction method: Principal component analysis. Rotation method: Varimax with Kaiser normalisation.

[a]Rotation converged in five iterations.

## Appendix 3. Exploratory factor analysis output for the 17 car-driving emotions items

*Total variance explained.*

| Component | Initial eigenvalues | | | Extraction sums of squared loadings | | | Rotation sums of squared loadings | | |
|---|---|---|---|---|---|---|---|---|---|
| | Total | % of variance | Cumulative % | Total | % of variance | Cumulative % | Total | % of variance | Cumulative % |
| Dimension 0 | | | | | | | | | |
| 1 | 5.413 | 31.840 | 31.840 | 5.413 | 31.840 | 31.840 | 4.615 | 27.147 | 27.147 |
| 2 | 2.699 | 15.877 | 47.717 | 2.699 | 15.877 | 47.717 | 2.538 | 14.928 | 42.075 |
| 3 | 1.338 | 7.871 | 55.588 | 1.338 | 7.871 | 55.588 | 2.297 | 13.513 | 55.588 |
| 4 | 1.156 | 6.802 | 62.390 | | | | | | |
| 5 | .898 | 5.283 | 67.673 | | | | | | |
| 6 | .774 | 4.555 | 72.228 | | | | | | |
| 7 | .727 | 4.277 | 76.505 | | | | | | |
| 8 | .618 | 3.633 | 80.138 | | | | | | |
| 9 | .599 | 3.523 | 83.661 | | | | | | |
| 10 | .530 | 3.116 | 86.777 | | | | | | |
| 11 | .426 | 2.505 | 89.282 | | | | | | |
| 12 | .415 | 2.441 | 91.723 | | | | | | |
| 13 | .391 | 2.301 | 94.024 | | | | | | |
| 14 | .364 | 2.139 | 96.163 | | | | | | |
| 15 | .237 | 1.396 | 97.560 | | | | | | |
| 16 | .230 | 1.355 | 98.915 | | | | | | |
| 17 | .184 | 1.085 | 100.000 | | | | | | |

Extraction method: Principal component analysis.

## CONTEMPORARY ISSUES IN GREEN AND ETHICAL MARKETING

*Rotated component matrix[a].*

| | Component | | |
|---|---|---|---|
| | **1** | **2** | **3** |
| Throb of the engine | .674 | −.180 | .159 |
| Rapid acceleration | .766 | −.178 | .102 |
| Information on the dashboard | .654 | .169 | .143 |
| The beauty of the interior | .761 | .176 | .111 |
| High speed possibility | .814 | .065 | .119 |
| High speed possibility | .779 | −.148 | .107 |
| Technological sophistication | .768 | .142 | .090 |
| The other things I can do while driving | .411 | .102 | .250 |
| The personalisation of my car | .496 | .081 | .183 |
| On the road with friends | .239 | .129 | .356 |
| Realising my car is environmentally friendly | .077 | .833 | .116 |
| The low cost of my car | −.023 | .833 | .153 |
| The economic fuel efficiency of my car | .055 | .882 | .173 |
| The flexibility of my journey | .012 | .310 | .564 |
| Car handling | .409 | .228 | .522 |
| Enjoying the environment while driving | .108 | .121 | .823 |
| Getting relaxed while driving | .216 | −.075 | .798 |

Extraction method: Principal component analysis.
Rotation method: Varimax with Kaiser normalisation.
[a]Rotation converged in five iterations.

## Appendix 4. Factor and cluster analysis results for the personal value types

*Total variance explained.*

| Component | Initial eigenvalues | | | Extraction sums of squared loadings | | | Rotation sums of squared loadings | | |
|---|---|---|---|---|---|---|---|---|---|
| | Total | % of variance | Cumulative % | Total | % of variance | Cumulative % | Total | % of variance | Cumulative % |
| Dimension 0 | | | | | | | | | |
| 1 | 4.060 | 27.068 | 27.068 | 4.060 | 27.068 | 27.068 | 2.589 | 17.263 | 17.263 |
| 2 | 3.581 | 23.871 | 50.939 | 3.581 | 23.871 | 50.939 | 2.562 | 17.081 | 34.344 |
| 3 | 1.452 | 9.679 | 60.619 | 1.452 | 9.679 | 60.619 | 2.498 | 16.653 | 50.997 |
| 4 | .923 | 6.157 | 66.775 | .923 | 6.157 | 66.775 | 2.367 | 15.778 | 66.775 |
| 5 | .755 | 5.031 | 71.806 | | | | | | |
| 6 | .649 | 4.328 | 76.134 | | | | | | |
| 7 | .620 | 4.132 | 80.266 | | | | | | |
| 8 | .495 | 3.303 | 83.569 | | | | | | |
| 9 | .449 | 2.995 | 86.564 | | | | | | |
| 10 | .425 | 2.835 | 89.400 | | | | | | |
| 11 | .420 | 2.802 | 92.201 | | | | | | |
| 12 | .359 | 2.391 | 94.592 | | | | | | |
| 13 | .291 | 1.943 | 96.535 | | | | | | |
| 14 | .283 | 1.887 | 98.422 | | | | | | |
| 15 | .237 | 1.578 | 100.000 | | | | | | |

Extraction method: Principal component analysis.

## CONTEMPORARY ISSUES IN GREEN AND ETHICAL MARKETING

*Rotated component matrix*[a]

|                | Component | | | |
|----------------|--------|--------|--------|--------|
|                | **1**  | **2**  | **3**  | **4**  |
| Social control | −.105  | −.042  | .083   | .870   |
| Authority      | −.092  | −.003  | .250   | .830   |
| Prosperity     | −.242  | −.021  | .525   | .402   |
| Ambition       | −.061  | .043   | .783   | .277   |
| Competence     | .082   | .270   | .770   | .088   |
| Success        | .013   | .137   | .825   | .180   |
| Influence      | .071   | .051   | .271   | .747   |
| Helpfulness    | .329   | .631   | .075   | .184   |
| Forgivingness  | .316   | .676   | −.103  | .077   |
| Loyalty        | .035   | .824   | .172   | −.076  |
| Responsibility | .121   | .742   | .344   | −.104  |
| Tolerance      | .526   | .508   | .141   | −.115  |
| Equality       | .815   | .238   | .017   | −.118  |
| Social justice | .850   | .243   | −.068  | −.051  |
| World peace    | .781   | .078   | −.065  | .003   |

Extraction method: Principal component analysis.
Rotation method: Varimax with Kaiser normalisation.
[a] Rotation converged in six iterations.
Factor 1: Idealism: equality. social justice. world peace.
Factor 2: Altruism: Helpfulness, forgivingness, loyalty, responsibility.
Factor 3: Achievement: Ambition, competence, success.
Factor 4: Power: Social control, authority, influence.

*Mean scores of the four value factors per cluster (value type).*

|             | Cluster | | |
|-------------|---------|---|---|
|             | **1 Self-transcendent universalist (32.0%)** | **2 Benevolent (37.3%)** | **3 Self-enhancingpower seeking achiever (30.7%)** |
| Idealism    | 3.74 | 4.12 | 2.57 |
| Altruism    | 3.89 | 4.30 | 3.68 |
| Achievement | 3.10 | 4.19 | 3.97 |
| Power       | 1.86 | 2.92 | 3.23 |

# The impact of general and carbon-related environmental knowledge on attitudes and behaviour of US consumers

Michael Jay Polonsky, *Deakin University, Australia*
Andrea Vocino, *Deakin University, Australia*
Stacy Landreth Grau, *Texas Christian University, USA*
Romana Garma, *Victoria University, Australia*
Ahmed Shahriar Ferdous, *Deakin University, Australia*

**Abstract** Global warming and carbon emissions have gained international attention. However, it would appear that consumers are still unclear about what it encompasses and how it relates to their individual behaviour. Using the Theory of Reasoned Action (TRA) as a guiding framework, this study presents a structural equation model that tests the relationships between carbon and environmental knowledge, environmental attitude and behaviour using a sample of US consumers. The findings of the research suggest that a positive relationship was found between general and carbon-specific knowledge, attitude towards the environment, and general and carbon-specific behaviours. Therefore, general and carbon-specific environmental behaviours are related and may be driven by general attitudes and knowledge (i.e. both carbon-specific and general environmental knowledge). The implications of the study would suggest that marketers, working in tandem with government policymakers, need to focus efforts on developing consumers' knowledge about specific sub-issues, such as global warming. However, additional research needs to be undertaken to develop marketing communication that accurately reflects the environmental impact of consumption behaviour, thereby allowing for considered consumption.

## Introduction

Global warming is acknowledged as a direct and significant consequence of climate change (Shi, Wang, & Yang, 2010). It is widely recognised that global warming is an international problem but, to date, national and multinational attempts like the Copenhagen Climate Conference to restrict carbon production have failed to address this pressing issue (Dyer, Harvey, Kazmin, & Wheatley, 2009). Much of the focus attempts to address the issue of large emitters of carbon dioxide ($CO_2$), namely, corporations (Onishi, 2007). While firms can reduce the amount of carbon they produce, they can also offset their production of carbon voluntarily by purchasing savings in other areas (Ristino, 2008). For example, corporations in developed countries may purchase emission reductions that are associated with projects in the developing or emerging countries that create carbon sinks, that is, carbon produced elsewhere by the firm is offset. Companies can also offset their energy use by purchasing carbon credits that are generated by projects that include a range of activities such as developing renewable energy or biofuels (Bumpus & Liverman, 2008). Carbon offset activities are defined as programs that implement a 'measurable avoidance, reduction or sequestration of [carbon or greenhouse gases]' (Ramseur, 2007, p. 1), where one carbon offset represents a reduction of one tonne of carbon dioxide. Offsets are purchased through carbon offset retail providers who then contract with the developers of the carbon offsetting projects. The retail providers vary in terms of their offerings, pricing, and understanding of carbon offset programs and offset quality (Kollmuss, Zink, & Polycaro, 2008). For example, within the aviation industry, individuals have the option to offset their $CO_2$ travel emissions by voluntarily adding the cost to their travel bill. The offset payments are provided by firms providing offset services, all with different offset project creation, prices, and policies (Offset Offerings, 2007). The variability in approaches means that the quality of retail carbon offset programs is inconsistent (Ristino, 2008).

This study is set in the United States, as it is one of the largest contributors of $CO_2$ gas emissions in the world (Onishi, 2007), with some authors arguing any US reduction of $CO_2$ would, on its own, have a significant impact on global climatic change (Heinzerling, 2010). On a positive note, Ristino (2008) argues that the recent growth of the US carbon market reflects a genuine desire by US firms and consumers to address climate change. However, recent consumer polls in the United States have shown a declining trend in adult consumers' 'green' attitudes and engagement in various environmentally friendly activities (Harris Interactive, 2010). This might be caused partly by ongoing debate about the causes of climate change, and by consumer confusion associated with attempting to integrate carbon-specific issues into their green purchasing behaviour, which has been found to be problematic elsewhere (Bulkeley, 2000).

Given the complexity of carbon issues and variations in the quality of offset programs, it is no surprise that consumers become confused or even misled while trying to integrate carbon issues into their consumption and decision making because of incorrect understanding of the intricacy of carbon claims and offset programs (Bulkeley, 2000; Majoras, 2008). For example, consumers may believe that a firm investing in planting trees will reduce the carbon it produces today, whereas, in reality, carbon savings will *only* occur in the future, *assuming* the trees grow to maturity. This raises an interesting question of whether consumer behaviour in relation to carbon offsets and the environment, in general, is influenced by consumer knowledge of the issue. Therefore, more investigation is needed into the underlying process of how various types of environmental knowledge (i.e. general and carbon-specific) shape consumers' environmental attitudes, and, in turn, how knowledge influences their general environmentally related behaviours. Consumer environmental knowledge and attitudes have been researched for almost 40 years in an attempt to provide understanding and insight into pro-environmental behaviour (Leonidou & Leonidou, 2011; Maloney & Ward, 1973). However, researchers have generally not focused on whether or not knowledge related to specific aspects of the environmental debate has an impact on different pro-environmental behaviours. This study has, therefore, focused its attention on investigating the relationship between general and carbon-specific knowledge, attitudes towards the environment, and the general and carbon-specific behaviours of a sample of consumers in the United States. In this way, the study aims to close the gap in the research regarding consumers' knowledge and behaviour, specifically regarding this new "product" – carbon offsets.

The theory underpinning this research is the Theory of Reasoned Action (TRA), which has previously found clear links between environmental attitudes and behaviours (Abdul-Muhmin, 2007; Kaiser, Wolfing, & Fuhrer, 1999) and therefore adds to the ongoing theoretical debate about the efficacy of the TRA and other similar models in predicting responsible consumer behaviour (Rokka & Uusitalo, 2008). Our extended model integrates both general and specific knowledge, as well as making links to reported behaviour (general and specific) rather than behavioural intentions alone. The research uses a structural equation modelling (SEM) approach, and the results suggest general and carbon-specific knowledge drive overall environmental attitudes and that those attitudes, in turn, drive both carbon and general environmental behaviours.

The article is organised in the following way. First, there is an overview of the literature on environmental knowledge, attitudes, and behaviours, which is followed by a discussion of the research method and results, discussion, implications, and directions for future research.


## Literature review and hypotheses development

The issue of environmental behaviour has been the topic of many research articles over the past few years. According to Abdul-Muhmin (2007), much of the past environmental work can be organised into three streams of research. First, there are descriptive studies of consumers' knowledge, concerns, attitudes, and behaviours (see Beck-Larsen, 1996; Chan, 1999; Daniere & Takahashi, 1999). Second, there are studies that develop measures of these constructs (see Bohlen, Schlegelmilch, & Diamantopoulas, 1993; Schlegelmilch, Bohlen, & Diamantopoulos, 1996; Van Liere & Dunlap, 1981). Third, there are models that have been developed using several theories, with much of the research on environmental behaviour basing its premise on different variations of Ajzen and Fishbein's (1980) TRA or Ajzen's (1985) modification of that model – the Theory of Planned Behaviour (TBP). Generally, the models propose that for an attitude to be formed, individual factual knowledge about the issue is a precondition (Flamm, 2009; Kaiser et al., 1999; Stutzman & Green, 1982). Behaviour is then a function of intention, which, in turn, is a function of attitude and subjective norms. Although in its purest form, researchers seek to predict behavioural intentions rather than behaviours (Ajzen & Fishbein, 1980). Some researchers (e.g. Davies et al., 2002) have suggested that the connection between intentions and behaviours may not be as strong as the model proposed. Thus it is potentially more prudent to integrate self-reported actual behaviour into the models, because that is the ultimate concern, rather than intentions (Rokka & Uusitalo, 2008).

The TRA model has been tested in a number of countries, and links have been explored in a range of contexts over the years (Ferrell & Gresham, 1985) including environmental knowledge, attitudes, and intentions (Arcury, 1990; Bang, Ellinger, Hadjimarcou, & Traichal, 2000; Barber, Taylor, & Strick, 2009; Diamantopoulos, Schlegelmilch, Sinkovics, & Bohlen, 2003; Flamm, 2009; Fraj-Andres & Martinez-Salinas, 2007; Goldenhar & Connell, 1993; Ivy, Geok-Chin, Kim-Eng, & Chuan, 1998; Jones, 1990; Kaiser et al., 1999; Maloney, Ward, & Braucht, 1975; Oreg & Katz-Gerro, 2006; Schlegelmilch et al., 1996; Taylor & Todd, 1995). For example, using TRA, Arcury (1990) found US consumers' environmental knowledge was positively related to their general environmental attitudes and general behavioural intentions. Others such as Bang et al. (2000) used the TRA as a theoretical framework, and found that there was a positive relationship between environmental knowledge and environmental attitudes and consumers' willingness to pay more for renewable energy. Given the impact of the results for general environmental knowledge on behavioural intentions, the relationships between specific knowledge and behaviours – in this case, for carbon offsets and general environmental knowledge on actual behaviour – were explored. This research draws on measures of environmental knowledge, environmental attitudes, and purchasing behaviour (Bohlen et al., 1993; Diamantopoulos et al., 2003; Ivy et al., 1998) and adapts them for carbon offsets, with the TRA as a theoretical foundation.

Given the extensive research suggesting that the TRA has validity in pro-environmental behaviours contexts in different countries (Oreg & Katz-Gerro, 2006), this study builds on the theory to suggest that knowledge influences attitudes, which, in turn, influence behaviour (rather than behavioural intentions). In this paper, we have examined general environmental issues and behaviours, as well as knowledge and behaviours related specifically to carbon (as shown in Figure 1), recognising that consumers assess environmental issues differently, that is, some are more important than others (Rokka & Uusitalo, 2008; Thøgersen, 2004). Thus we propose that different types of knowledge shape overall environmental attitudes (Barber et al., 2009), which then shape both generic and specific behaviours. The four hypothesised associations between the constructs of the model are identified and are presented in the following sections.

**Figure 1** Hypothesised model of knowledge, attitudes, and behaviours.

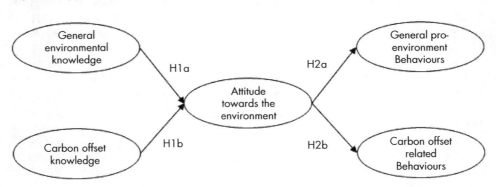

## Environmental attitudes

The central core of the model is the role of attitudes towards the environment. Allport (1935) stated that 'an attitude is a mental and neutral state of readiness, organised through experience, exerting a directive or dynamic influence on an individual's response to all objects and situations with which it is related' (p. 810). Within the environmental domain, general attitude has been viewed as 'cognitive and affective evaluation of the object of environmental protection' (Bamberg, 2003, p. 21). Past studies have established attitudes as one of the strong determinants affecting behaviour (Ballantyne & Packer, 2005; Kotchen & Reiling, 2000), and in these models environmental attitudes generally include respondents' views on a range of environmental issues. Studies related to pro-environmental behaviour (and behavioural intentions) have introduced attitudes as a central variable between environmental knowledge and behaviour (Barber et al., 2009; Davies et al., 2002; Flamm, 2009). Environmental knowledge has been found to be a precondition to one's environmental attitude, while attitude towards the environment has been commonly found to be an antecedent to pro-environmental behaviour (Flamm, 2009; Kaiser et al., 1999; Lynne & Rola, 1988; Oreg & Katz-Gerro, 2006). For example, Barber et al. (2009) found that attitudes influenced behavioural intentions, where generic attitudes were shaped by different types of knowledge, although they focused on objective and subjective rather than different objective knowledge types. The issues of global warming and the impacts of carbon have not been studied as much, although Howell (2011) finds that increasing positive perceptions about one's attitude towards the consequences of global warming have also been found to increase intentions to behave in more pro-environmental ways.

The primary contribution of this research is that we are examining the role of two types of knowledge – general environmental knowledge and carbon offset knowledge – and what impacts they have on environmental attitudes, which, in turn, affects two types of behaviour – general environmental behaviour and carbon offset behaviour. This also focuses on self-reported actual behaviour, rather than behavioural intentions, which may be a better indicator of actual behaviour (Rokka & Uusitalo, 2008).

## Environmental knowledge

It has been argued that knowledge about the environment must be present for environmentally responsible consumer behaviour to occur (Barber et al., 2009; Hines, Hungerford, & Tomera, 1986; Maloney & Ward, 1973; Schlegelmilch et al., 1996). Environmental knowledge is defined as 'general knowledge of facts, concepts, and relationships concerning the natural environment and its major ecosystems' (Fryxell & Lo, 2003, p. 48). Therefore, environmental knowledge involves what people know about the environment and the key relationships leading to environmental impacts (Mostafa, 2007). Environmental knowledge can be general in nature, such as awareness of environmentally friendly products, or more specific knowledge on issues such as recycling or carbon offset programs (Schahn & Holzer, 1990). However, the complexity of the science means that consumers may not fully understand environmental warming or how it relates to their actions (Bulkeley, 2000).

Different measures have been used empirically to assess consumers' environmental knowledge. Some research has attempted to measure factual environmental knowledge, where consumers undertake factual tests to determine their knowledge level (Barber et al., 2009; Maloney et al., 1975; Tanner & Kast, 2003). Other researchers measure consumers' perception of environmental issues or the impacts of action-related knowledge (Tanner & Kast, 2003) but do not consider factual knowledge (Diamantopoulos et al., 2003; Schlegelmilch et al., 1996). However, if beliefs about environmental knowledge are inaccurate, consumers would behave in inappropriate ways (i.e. behaviours do not address the underlying environmental issues). The third approach used has considered broader attitudinal responses to define environmental knowledge, for example, 'It's no use worrying about environmental issues; I can't do anything about them anyway' (Stone, Barnes, & Montgomery, 1995, p. 608). This would again mean that people might act because they believe an action will be effective, even if their belief is incorrect. This study focuses on consumers' factual knowledge to identify what consumers actually know about the environment (Maloney et al., 1975) both generally and, specifically, about carbon offsets, rather than their more general beliefs about actions. Having factual knowledge enables consumers to make effective decisions, that is, to modify their behaviour to reduce their environmental footprint. Thus this study proposes that specific environmental information can be related to specific decisions (Thøgersen, 2006), making factual environmental knowledge the most appropriate for measuring consumers' knowledge levels.

Past research indicates that consumers who have greater environmental knowledge are more likely to act in a positive way (Flamm, 2009; Gram-Hanssen, 2010; Hines et al., 1986; Mostafa, 2007; Pickett-Baker & Ozaki, 2008; Thøgersen, 2006). Indeed, knowledge plays a central role in many theoretical models of attitude–behaviour relations, such as TRA (see Ajzen & Fishbein, 1977, 1980) because it is hypothesised to influence behaviour through the intermediary of attitudes (Barber et al., 2009). Within the field of pro-environmental behaviour, attitudes are assumed to be changed by increased knowledge, and both environmental knowledge and attitudes are assumed to influence environmental purchase behaviour (Arcury, 1990; Barber et al., 2009; Flamm, 2009). For instance, Arcury (1990) reveals that environmental knowledge has a positive impact on shaping the environmental attitudes of consumers, and Flamm (2009) finds significant relationships between environmental knowledge, attitudes, and behaviour in the context of consumers' vehicle ownership. Barber et al. (2009) test for the relationship between general environmental knowledge and wine-specific environmental knowledge on environmental attitudes, and, consequently, on consumers' willingness to buy wine that is environmentally friendly. Barber et al. (2009) report that only consumers' wine-specific knowledge significantly affects their environmental attitudes, that is, their general knowledge was less important. This, in turn, affects their intention to buy environmentally friendly wines. This article proposes that both general and specific environmental knowledge should be considered when testing for consumers' factual environmental knowledge, especially if the knowledge is linked to different types of behaviours (i.e. general and specific), with many past studies being very context specific. For example, Flamm (2009) found that consumers with more environmental knowledge were more likely to use fuel efficient vehicles. We, therefore, postulate that both general environmental and specific carbon offset knowledge have a positive impact on consumers' environmental attitudes. Based on the past research using the TRA framework, we propose:

> H1a: General environmental knowledge is positively related to attitudes towards the environment.

> H1b: Carbon offset knowledge is positively related to attitudes towards the environment.

## Environmental behaviour

Steg and Vleka (2009) define pro-environmental behaviour as 'those behaviours that harm the environment as little as possible, or even benefit the environment' (p. 309). Environmental behaviour has also been viewed as psychological elements that reflect a person's sensitivity to environmental issues, such as energy savings, keeping places clean, and avoiding waste (Kilbourne & Pickett, 2008). Consumer environmental behaviour has been known to stem from their pro-environmental attitudes (Best & Kneip, 2011; Flamm, 2009; Kaiser et al., 1999; Oreg & Katz-Gerro, 2006). Bamberg (2003) suggests that people use general environmental attitudes as an accessible heuristic, which indirectly guides their consequent behaviour. Though an indirect link between general attitudes and specific environmental behaviour has been argued, past studies have, however, linked environmental attitudes with specific environmental behaviour such as the purchase of green products (Mostafa, 2007), use of fuel-efficient vehicles (Flamm, 2009), household recycling (Best & Kneip, in press), and voluntary reduction of travel-related $CO_2$ footprints (McKercher, Prideaux, Cheung, & Law, 2010). Other studies have also tested the effect of environmental attitudes on generalised environmental behaviours (GEB) (Fraj-Andres & Martinez-Salinas, 2007; Kaiser et al., 1999) or specific environmental behaviours (Barber et al., 2009; Oreg & Katz-Gerro, 2006). Within much of the environmental focused research using the TRA framework (Abdul-Muhmin, 2007; Bang et al., 2000; Barber et al., 2009), researchers have tended to focus on intentions rather than actual behaviours, with the assumption that intentions determine behaviours, although in the case of recycling, Davies et al. (2002) suggests that intentions might not translate in to actual recycling behaviour. To address this potential inconsistency, some environmental marketing researchers have examined behaviour rather than intentions (Leonidou, Leonidou, & Kvasova, 2010). Thus, as suggested by Rokka and Uusitalo (2008), focusing on behaviours would possibly be more appropriate and thus, in this study, reported behaviour was modelled as being endogenous. However, relying on self-reported behaviours has its own limitations of respondents possibly exaggerating positive social behaviours (Podsakoff & Organ, 1986).

Environmentally focused consumers can be motivated by a range of factors (Stone et al., 1995), and someone who supports one type of environmental behaviour may not necessarily participate in others (Kahn, 2007). For example, Thøgersen and Ölander (2006) find consumers' recycling behaviour does not necessarily relate to their use of alternative 'green' transportation. McKercher et al. (2010) find that while international tourists in Hong Kong expressed intentions to behave in pro-environmental ways, they are less willing to alter their behaviour when it comes to cutting air travel to reduce their carbon footprints. Oreg and Katz-Gerro (2006) find that, across 27 countries, environmental attitudes influenced recycling, reduced driving, and environmental stewardship differently. Leonidou et al. (2010) investigate the link between consumers' inward and outward pro-environmental attitudes and their environmental behaviours. The authors find inward pro-environmental attitudes (i.e. attitudes towards taking drastic measures to protect the environment) are related to consumers' ecologically friendly purchasing behaviour, whilst outward environmental attitudes (i.e. attitudes towards more public involvement of an individual with the society and its problems) are related to consumers' general environmental behaviour. While some consumers have positive attitudes – even preferences – toward environmentally friendly products, there is a lack of consistency between attitudes and behaviour measures (Alwitt & Pitts, 1996; Moisander, 2007; Thøgersen, 1999; Uusitalo, 1989, 1990a).

Given the varying results in past studies related to consumers' environmentally responsible behaviour, it is important to examine both general as well as carbon-specific behaviour to identify if attitudes impact on both. Further, from the earlier discussion linking knowledge and general attitudes, it is posited that consumers' environmental behaviours (i.e. general and specific) are influenced by the types of knowledge consumers hold (i.e. general as well as specific environmental knowledge). The link between knowledge and behaviour is usually interceded by environmental attitudes according to the TRA (Barber et al., 2009; Kaiser et al., 1999).

However, the link between environmental attitudes and environmental behaviour is not without its problems. First, a general criticism of the TRA is the free-rider problem where, although consumers have consumer knowledge and positive attitudes toward environmentally friendly products, they typically do not purchase them, primarily because they believe other people will act to solve the problem or that their contribution will not make a difference (Ellen, Wiener, & Cobb-Walgren, 1991; Uusitalo, 1989, 1990b). Additionally, some researchers have found inconsistencies in other areas of environmental attitudes and behaviours (e.g. Alwitt & Pitts, 1996; Moisander, 2007; Thøgersen, 1999; Thøgersen & Ölander, 2006). For example, Alwitt and Pitts (1996) found that consumers' environmental attitudes have an indirect effect on purchase intentions for environmentally related products and that this relationship is mediated by product-specific attitudes about consequences of using the environmentally related product and the product's environmental attributes.

Second, it has been suggested that general environmental attitudes will not necessarily spill over into other environmentally specific domains (Thøgersen, 2004; Thøgersen & Ölander, 2003). For example, Thøgersen and Ölander (2003) investigate whether environmentally friendly behaviours spread to more areas of consumption, and find that while there are cases of some spillover effects, they are few with modest effects. Thus concern in one area does not affect others. Oreg and Katz-Gerro (2006) also find that, across 27 countries, environmental attitudes have varying impacts on a variety of environmentally oriented behaviours (recycling, reduced driving, and environmental stewardship); the strongest impact was found in regard to the most generalised behaviour – environmental stewardship. This is further supported theoretically by Schwartz's (1973) Norm Activation Theory, which focuses on cases in which the costs associated with behaviour to benefit others is too high, and people tend not to do it even though they know they should. People also tend to do things that are relatively easy, such as recycling, in order to assuage guilt about not doing harder things such as biking to work (Green-Demers, Pelletier, &

Ménard, 1997). We, therefore, investigate whether or not there are links between general knowledge and actions, as well as between specific knowledge and behaviour (i.e. carbon related), using general environmental attitude as a central variable, which if successful can then be applied to other specific contexts. We propose:

> H2a: Attitude towards the environment is positively related to general pro-environment behaviours.

> H2b: Attitude towards the environment is positively related to carbon offset-related behaviours.

## Methodology

An online survey was administered to a random sample of US consumers, using a commercial consumer panel. Online panels are increasingly used in marketing research, and it is suggested that more than 50% of all empirical research in the United States uses online panels (uStamp, 2010). The target sample was 350 respondents; 395 responses were received, as the online process sometimes provides extra responses depending on how closely the cut-off rates are managed. Of the responses, 352 were deemed usable. Calculating overall response rates is very difficult for online panels (Callegaro & DiSogra, 2008). A range of metrics can be used, such as the number of people who responded to the survey as a percentage of those who were invited, the number who completed as a portion of those who started the survey (i.e. dropout rates or the traditional number of usable responses from completed received). Unfortunately, the numbers of total invitations or dropouts are unknown. Thus the 89.1% of usable responses is relied upon (i.e. 352 complete surveys from the 395 responses received).

The relationships of observed (measured) and latent (unobserved) variables are investigated, making use of SEM which allows estimating simultaneously the measurement and structural model, rather than testing the effect of one variable at a time as in regression analyses (Bollen, 1989). Such a method also allows researchers to account for measurement error, and is increasingly being used in marketing (Babin, Hair, & Boles, 2008). In addition, SEM has been used in examining environmental behaviour when testing the TRA (e.g. Barber et al., 2009; Chan & Lau, 2000; Fransson & Garling, 1999; Kaiser et al., 1999).

The research company was asked to source a nationally representative sample, as occurs in much research using online panels (Baker et al., 2010), and location was not included as a demographic question (see Table 1 for respondent demographics). While there may be regional differences in views regarding the environment, such differences were not included as part of the study's design, and further research could be undertaken to examine whether regional differences exist.

Eight items measuring factual environmental knowledge drew on Maloney et al.'s (1975) scale, which has been used by other researchers in the environmental area (e.g. Fraj-Andres & Martinez-Salinas, 2007; Ivy et al., 1998). Eight additional items were developed to investigate consumers' knowledge of carbon offsets, as knowledge about carbon has not been investigated previously in regard to environmental knowledge, attitudes, or behaviours. The questions were crafted taking into account issues raised by Ramseur (2007) in a briefing paper written for the US Congress, as well as

# CONTEMPORARY ISSUES IN GREEN AND ETHICAL MARKETING

**Table 1** Respondent demographics.

|  | $n = 352$ |
| --- | --- |
| Age | |
| 18–24 | 17.0% |
| 25–34 | 19.9% |
| 35–44 | 27.0% |
| 45–54 | 13.1% |
| 55–65 | 9.4% |
| 65+ | 12.8% |
| Gender | |
| Male | 50.3% |
| Female | 48.6% |
| Marital status | |
| Single | 38.9% |
| Married | 52.0% |
| Other | 9.1% |
| Children living at home: | |
| Yes | 40.9% |
| No | 50.0% |
| Not specified | 9.1% |
| Employed | |
| Full-time (35+ hours) | 50.3% |
| Part-time (<35 hours) | 15.3% |
| Not working | 34.3% |
| Education | |
| High school/less | 20.8% |
| Diploma/some college or professional degree | 41.9% |
| University degree | 25.6% |
| Postgraduate | 10.8% |

US investigations into the use of carbon offsets by the Federal Trade Commission (Majoras, 2008).

Past researchers have extensively examined a range of environmental behaviours which have, in many cases, investigated behavioural intentions rather than actual/self-report behaviour (Schlegelmilch et al., 1996; Stone et al., 1995), with some questioning the link between environmental intentions and behaviour (Davies et al., 2002). As our focus was on self-report behaviour, the degree to which consumers undertook activities in regard to general environmental issues was examined (Fraj-Andres & Martinez-Salinas, 2007; GfK Roper Consulting, 2007), rather than behavioural intentions. Matching items on specific activities related to general environmental behaviour and carbon offsets were used to compare activities directly. The three behavioural items asked how often people undertook the following activities (1 = 'never'; 7 = 'always'): (1) I investigate the specific details of firms' environmental claims or behaviour (or the carbon offset programs offered by firms); (2) I switch brands to ones that are less environmentally harmful (or offer carbon offsets); and (3) I choose to pay more for products because they are less environmentally harmful (or they offer carbon offsets). Attitude to the environment was measured using a seven-point Likert-type scale developed by Bohlen et al. (1993) and Diamantopoulos et al. (2003), with 1 = 'strongly disagree' through to 7 = 'strongly agree'. The items used in the questionnaire are reported in Table 2, and the knowledge items are in Appendix 1.

## Data analysis

First, the descriptive statistics and the level of normality were examined at the univariate level, as shown in Table 2. Next, the reliability and internal consistency of the scales were examined. The reliability test endorsed that the items conceived to gauge a construct are satisfactorily associated and can be reliably (e.g. low on measurement error) regarded as a set of items (Cronbach, 1951). To test reliability, Cronbach's alpha coefficient was used, as well as the inter-item correlations and corrected item-to-total correlations. The *mean* of the inter-item correlation was used as a guide to items' homogeneity in a unidimensional scale. The corrected item-to-total correlation was used to determine whether any particular items had low correlations with any of the items in the scale, by correlating the item being evaluated with all other scale items. Corrected item-to-total correlations of less than .50 were deemed candidates for deletion (Churchill, 1979). The Cronbach's alpha values for the constructs were .88 for general pro-enviroment behaviour (three items), .94 for carbon offset-related behaviour (three items), .93 for attitude towards the environment (16 items), all of which were acceptable (Cronbach, 1951). Carbon offset knowledge and general environmental knowledge were both summations of eight-item true–false scales and, thus, no Cronbach's alpha was calculated, as they assessed people's levels of factual knowledge (Fraj-Andres & Martinez-Salinas, 2007; Maloney et al., 1975).

Confirmatory factor analysis (CFA) was run to examine the measurement model and to assess convergent and discriminant validity. In the CFA model, we allowed to co-vary the error terms of the items 6.4 with 6.10, 6.3 with 6.80, and 6.9 with 6.20, as they have the same wording type (see Table 2 for wording of items). The fit of the first CFA showed insufficient support to validate the congeneric measurement model as $SB\chi^2_{(df=241)}$ 1466.07 ($p = 0.000$), root mean square error of approximation (RMSEA) .11, comparative fit index (CFI) .77, Tucker–Lewis index (TLI) .73, standardised root mean square residual (SRMR) .12. However, after checking the model diagnostics, another model was produced wherein the construct attitude towards the environment (ATE) was structured with a second-order configuration having three sub-dimensions (ATE1, ATE2, and ATE3). The subsequent model produced $SB\chi^2_{(df=238)}$ 474.59 ($p = 0.000$), RMSEA .05, CFI .96, TLI .95, and SRMR .07. Such fit ratios were deemed acceptable.

Further, convergent validity was appraised, as suggested by Fornell and Larker (1981) and Anderson and Gerbing (1988), by looking at the lambda coefficients (should be $\geq$.70), the average variance explained (should be $\geq$.50), and composite reliability (should be $\geq$ 0.70). All such test results are reported in Table 3. The lambdas of items 4.80, 4.90, and 4.20 performed slightly under the recommended guidelines. However, given the marginal discrepancy, such items were deemed to be kept in order to yield a more parsimonious model.

**Table 2** Descriptive statistics.

| Construct | ID | Item | Mean | SD | Skewness | Kurtotis |
|---|---|---|---|---|---|---|
| ATE1 | | | | | | |
| | 4.16 | Everyone is personally responsible for protecting the environment in their everyday life | 5.55 | 1.25 | −.70 | .72 |
| | 4.18 | If all of us, individually, made a contribution to environmental protection, it would have a significant effect | 5.41 | 1.38 | −.77 | .41 |
| | 4.19 | Each of us, as individuals, can make a contribution to environmental protection | 5.52 | 1.27 | −.78 | .84 |
| ATE2 | | | | | | |
| | 4.1 | The environment is one of the most important issues facing society today | 5.11 | 1.57 | −.79 | .21 |
| | 4.2 | We should pay a considerable amount of money to preserve our environment | 4.71 | 1.50 | −.55 | .09 |
| | 4.3 | Strict global measures must be taken immediately to halt environmental decline | 5.01 | 1.50 | −.72 | .38 |
| | 4.4 | A substantial amount of money should be devoted to environmental protection | 4.91 | 1.44 | −.68 | .51 |
| | 4.14 | The government should take responsibility for environmental protection | 4.80 | 1.55 | −.57 | .01 |
| ATE3 | | | | | | |
| | 4.6 | The benefits of protecting the environment do not justify the expense involved | 4.77 | 1.59 | −.32 | −.60 |
| | 4.8 | Green issues should not be a main consideration when deciding what we do in the future | 4.43 | 1.63 | −.17 | −.61 |
| | 4.9 | Personally, I cannot help to slow down environmental deterioration | 4.93 | 1.547 | −.45 | −.34 |
| | 4.10 | The importance of the environment is frequently exaggerated | 4.60 | 1.72 | −.25 | −.72 |
| | 4.11 | The benefits of overcoming environmental deterioration are not sufficient to warrant the expense involved | 4.74 | 1.52 | −.23 | −.44 |

(Continued)

**Table 2** (Continued).

| Construct | ID | Item | Mean | SD | Skewness | Kurtotis |
|---|---|---|---|---|---|---|
| | 4.12 | Even if each of us contributed towards environmental protection, the combined effect would be negligible | 4.72 | 1.55 | −.42 | −.20 |
| | 4.13 | Too much fuss is made about environmental issues | 4.02 | 1.73 | .44 | .69 |
| | 4.20 | Firms should always put profitability before environmental protection | 5.03 | 1.72 | −.54 | −.61 |
| CARB_BEH | | | | | | |
| | 6.8 | I investigate the specific details of the carbon offset programs offered by firms | 2.94 | 1.65 | .43 | −.58 |
| | 6.9 | I switch brands to ones that offer carbon offsets | 3.11 | 1.71 | .32 | −.74 |
| | 6.10 | I choose to pay more for products because they offer carbon offsets | 3.07 | 1.71 | .37 | −.70 |
| GEN_BEH | | | | | | |
| | 6.2 | I switch brands to ones that are less environmentally harmful | 4.32 | 1.36 | −.16 | .17 |
| | 6.3 | I investigate the specific details of firms' environmental claims or behaviour | 3.34 | 1.61 | .27 | −.50 |
| | 6.4 | I choose to pay more for products because they are less environmentally harmful | 3.75 | 1.60 | .07 | −.36 |

*Note*: CARBON_K = carbon offset knowledge; GENERAL_K = general environmental knowledge, measured on a seven-point scale with 1 = 'never' through to 7 = 'always'. ATE [1, 2, and 3] = attitude towards the environment; GEN_BEH = general pro-environment behaviours; CARB_BEH = carbon offset-related behaviours, measured on a seven-point Likert scale with 1 = 'strongly disagree' through to 7 = 'strongly agree'.

## CONTEMPORARY ISSUES IN GREEN AND ETHICAL MARKETING

**Table 3** Convergent validity assessment.

| Construct | Parameter | | SE | *t*-value | *p*-value | CR | AVE |
|---|---|---|---|---|---|---|---|
| | Items | estimate | | | | | |
| ATE1 | | | | | | .92 | .80 |
| | 4.16 | .85 | .02 | 44.49 | .000 | | |
| | 4.18 | .89 | .02 | 47.30 | .000 | | |
| | 4.19 | .94 | .01 | 76.40 | .000 | | |
| ATE2 | | | | | | .93 | .72 |
| | 4.10 | .86 | .02 | 53.27 | .000 | | |
| | 4.20 | .87 | .02 | 47.06 | .000 | | |
| | 4.30 | .92 | .02 | 51.87 | .000 | | |
| | 4.40 | .91 | .02 | 52.92 | .000 | | |
| | 4.14 | .67 | .04 | 15.59 | .000 | | |
| ATE3 | | | | | | .89 | .52 |
| | 4.11 | .86 | .02 | 39.61 | .000 | | |
| | 4.60 | .80 | .02 | 33.09 | .000 | | |
| | 4.10 | .80 | .03 | 32.11 | .000 | | |
| | 4.12 | .63 | .05 | 12.63 | .000 | | |
| | 4.13 | .80 | .03 | 26.98 | .000 | | |
| | 4.90 | .62 | .04 | 16.50 | .000 | | |
| | 4.80 | .63 | .05 | 13.83 | .000 | | |
| | 4.20 | .56 | .04 | 12.95 | .000 | | |
| CARB_BEH | | | | | | .94 | .84 |
| | 6.80 | .87 | .02 | 53.59 | .000 | | |
| | 6.90 | .97 | .01 | 72.25 | .000 | | |
| | 6.10 | .91 | .02 | 50.57 | .000 | | |
| GEN_BEH | | | | | | .88 | .72 |
| | 6.20 | .87 | .02 | 49.65 | .000 | | |
| | 6.30 | .84 | .02 | 42.46 | .000 | | |
| | 6.40 | .83 | .03 | 24.56 | .000 | | |

*Note*: Complete standardised coefficients. K = carbon offset knowledge; GENERAL_K = general environmental knowledge; ATE [1, 2, and 3] = attitude towards the environment; GEN_BEH = general pro-environment behaviours; CARB_BEH = carbon offset-related behaviours.

Discriminant validity was tested, as suggested by Bagozzi, Yi, and Phillips (1991), by comparing the unconstrained ($\varphi$ freely estimated) and constrained ($\varphi$ set to 1) correlations between pairs of latents. The results of this test are reported in Table 4. Notably, it can be observed that some $\Delta SB\chi^2$ were negative, which is an improper value for a $\chi^2$ variate. Thus we also estimated Wald test statistics for the nested model, as suggested by Satorra (2000), indicating that discriminant validity was achieved.

## Analysis

While we did not have any hypotheses related to knowledge levels, it is important to understand the respondents' level of general environmental knowledge and carbon knowledge. To do this, consumers' with more than half of the items correct were

**Table 4** Discriminant validity assessment.

| Pair comparison | Unconstrained model | | Constrained model | | $\Delta SB\chi^2_{(df=1)}$ | $p$ | $\Delta$ Wald test$_{(df=1)}$ | $p$ |
|---|---|---|---|---|---|---|---|---|
| | $\chi^2 - SB\chi^2$ | df | $\chi^2 - SB\chi^2$ | df | | | | |
| CARB_BEH ⟷ GEN_BEH | 39.16 − 21.13 | 5 | 186.88 − 106.71 | 6 | 119.09 | .000 | 1678.09 | .000 |
| CARB_BEH ⟷ ATE | 376.71 − 300.73 | 148 | 690.73 − 556.6 | 149 | −649.18 | n/a | 45.08 | .000 |
| CARB_BEH ⟷ CARB_K | 504.84 − 24.30 | 3 | 1491.06 − 93.99 | 4 | 872.65 | .000 | 100.95 | .000 |
| CARB_BEH ⟷ GEN_K | 923.26 − 1024.38 | 3 | 1912.89 − 1920.59 | 4 | 773.09 | .000 | 466.37 | .000 |
| GEN_BEH ⟷ ATE | 415.15 − 332.07 | 148 | 646.04 − 520.98 | 149 | −883.55 | n/a | 125.84 | .000 |
| GEN_BEH ⟷ CARB_K | 501.60 − 24.21 | 3 | 1076.26 − 67.47 | 4 | 347.01 | .000 | 240.47 | .000 |
| GEN_BEH ⟷ GEN_K | 934.00 − 860.08 | 3 | 1505.45 − 1411.71 | 4 | 567.04 | .000 | 1489.87 | .000 |
| ATE ⟷ CARB_K | 807.59 − 459.15 | 117 | 1141.07 − 658.77 | 118 | −238.54 | n/a | 344.37 | .000 |
| ATE ⟷ GEN_K | 1228.51 − 963.49 | 117 | 1539.29 − 1203.91 | 118 | 183.92 | .000 | 7007.35 | .000 |
| CARB_K ⟷ GEN_K | 968.09 − 31.46 | 2 | 4608.24 − 221.64 | 3 | 4351.83 | .000 | 146,553.02 | .000 |

*Note*: CARBON_K = carbon offset knowledge; GENERAL_K = general environmental knowledge; ATE = attitude towards the environment; GEN_BEH = general pro-environment behaviours; CARB_BEH = carbon offset-related behaviours.

classified as being knowledgeable (i.e. they knew more than they did not know), and those with 50% or less correct were classified as having low knowledge. This resulted in 71.8% of the consumers being classified as having high levels of knowledge about general environmental issues, but only 39.8% were classified as having high levels of knowledge about carbon offsets. There were 29.2% of respondents who had both high general environmental knowledge and high carbon offset knowledge, and 48.3% of the sample had high general knowledge but low carbon offset knowledge. Thus there appears to be a limited relationship between knowledge types.

The hypotheses were tested using SEM, keeping the measurement configuration which resulted from the previous CFA. SEM has frequently been used in examining TRA and related models examining environmental knowledge, attitudes, and behaviour/behavioural intentions (e.g. Barber et al., 2009; Oreg & Katz-Gerro, 2006). The model converged to a proper solution with an acceptable fit: $SB\chi^2_{(df=242)}$ 478.94 ($p = .000$), RMSEA .05, CFI .96, TLI .95, and SRMR .07. The endogenous structural residuals of the latents, general pro-environment behaviour and carbon offset-related behaviour, were correlated in order to avoid a problem with endogeneity and, in so doing, to enable the model to gain greater efficiency (Cole, Ciesla, & Steiger, 2007; Zellner & Theil, 1962). Such a method also allows for the possibility to co-vary errors terms (Fornell & Larker, 1981). The completely standardised coefficients are referred to in Table 5 reporting the correlation matrix, and Table 6 reporting the standardised parameter estimates.

**Table 5** Factors' correlations matrix.

|  | CARB_BEH | GEN_BEH | BEA | CARB_K | GEN_K |
|---|---|---|---|---|---|
| RB_BEH | — |  |  |  |  |
| GEN_BEH | .84 (41.72) | — |  |  |  |
| ATE | .35 (6.88) | .55 (10.49) | — |  |  |
| CARB_K | −.08 (−1.55) | −.12 (−2.92) | −.13 (−3.61) | — |  |
| GEN_K | .05 (0.92) | .13 (2.42) | .27 (5.23) | −.13 (−3.66) | — |

*Note*: Completely standardised estimates. *t*-values in parentheses. CARBON_K = carbon offset knowledge; GENERAL_K = general environmental knowledge; ATE = attitude towards the environment; GEN_BEH = general pro-environment behaviours; CARB_BEH = carbon offset-related behaviours.

**Table 6** Structural coefficients.

|  | $\varphi$ | $\gamma$ | $\beta$ | $\zeta$ |
|---|---|---|---|---|
| CARB_K $\longleftrightarrow$ GEN_K | −.13 (−3.60) |  |  |  |
| CARB_K $\rightarrow$ ATE |  | −.10 (−2.93) |  |  |
| GEN_K $\rightarrow$ ATE |  | .25 (5.09) |  |  |
| ATE $\rightarrow$ CARB_BEH |  |  | .35 (6.78) |  |
| ATE $\rightarrow$ GEN_BEH |  |  | .55 (10.47) |  |
| CARB_BEH $\longleftrightarrow$ GEN_BEH |  |  |  | .83 (37.15) |

*Note*: All coefficients are completely standardised and significant at $p = .000$. *t*-values in parentheses. CARBON_K = carbon offset knowledge; GENERAL_K = general environmental knowledge; ATE = attitude towards the environment; GEN_BEH = general pro-environment behaviours; CARB_BEH = carbon offset-related behaviours.

The results of the structural equations suggest that having a general understanding of environmental knowledge is positively related to one's general attitude towards the environment. Thus H1a is supported. Having a higher level of carbon offset knowledge is also found to be positively related to one's general attitude towards the environment, and H1b is also supported. As a result, general environmental knowledge appears to be related to attitudes, as is specific knowledge about offsets.

By examining how attitudes relate to behaviour, attitude was found to affect both general behaviour (i.e. H2a is accepted) and carbon-related knowledge (i.e. H2b is accepted). This suggests that both general and specific behaviours are driven by consumers' overall attitudes towards the environment.

## Conclusions and implications

The aim of this paper was to examine the relationship between general environmental and carbon offset knowledge and the respective consumer behaviours. The findings of the research suggest that general environmental knowledge, as well as specific carbon offset knowledge, appear to be related to attitudes, and both general and specific behaviours are driven by attitudes towards the environment. The overall results suggest that consumers are integrating new knowledge about the environment into their general attitudes. One would, therefore, anticipate that as consumers become more knowledgeable about specific environmental issues, they, in turn, modify their attitudes and behaviours. This suggests that more information about global warming may result in consumer action, where they modify their behaviour to have a smaller environmental impact, that is, they become more mindful consumers (Seth, Sethia, & Srinivas, 2011).

First, the research finds that both general and specific carbon knowledge are related to generalised environmental attitudes. This is consistent with past research that has found different types of knowledge contribute to consumers' attitudes (e.g. Arcury, 1990; Barber et al., 2009; Schahn & Holzer, 1990). This finding is extremely important, as it suggests that, as environmental issues arise, consumers integrate those issues into their attitudes. However, the fact that those consumers generally had low levels of carbon environmental knowledge does raise potential concerns, and suggests that consumers are responding to information that they may or may not understand. Therefore, the 'hype' around global warming and carbon indicates that, potentially, consumers realise they are important issues without necessarily understanding the complexities of the associated issues. Global warming impacts on a diverse range of environmental outcomes (Shi et al., 2010) and also relates to almost all consumption behaviour (ACCC, 2008). It may be that the extensive promotion of this issue in recent times has resulted in carbon and carbon offsetting having higher salience than other issues such as the reduction of biodiversity or the use of palm oil, as these other environmental issues are less widely promoted, even though these other environmental issues are equally important and linked directly to consumers and their behaviour.

Second, we find that generalised attitudes drive both general and specific environmental behaviours, which is consistent with other research that has found generalised attitudes drive multiple types of behaviours (Flamm, 2009; Fraj-Andres & Martinez-Salinas, 2007; Thøgersen, 2004). However, if changes in behaviour are to be effective, consumers need to adopt activities that truly reduce their environmental impact. If they do not understand the complexities of the information on which they have to make decisions, they might change behaviour but not reduce their environmental impact (Bulkeley, 2000). There is not clear agreement as to how one determines the environmental impact of a good over its lifecycle (i.e. production, use, and disposal). As such, communicating environmental information to consumers is difficult, and even if there were scientific agreement on lifecycle assessments, would consumers be able to interpret the complex environmental information that would need to be reported? For example, will consumers know how much carbon their consumption produces or what is the environmental impact of reducing their consumption in some way (i.e. if I drive 10% less, what is the environmental impact)? This will result in consumers having difficulty in assessing the environmental impacts of alternative consumption decisions.

For researchers using the TRA, this study suggests that there should be more integration of issue-specific types of knowledge and behaviours. Some research in the environmental area has started to explore multiple types of consumer outcomes (see, e.g., Thøgersen, 2004). Research to date has not examined how alternative types of knowledge shape attitudes and associated behaviours. The complexity of environmental information and associated behaviours would seem to suggest that the TRA needs to have broader inclusion of predictive facts, as well as take into consideration relationships that might result in spillover effects (Uusitalo, 1990a). This is in addition to examining the interconnections in terms of knowledge and behavioural actions (Barber et al., 2009; Rokka & Uusitalo, 2008).

From a regulatory perspective, uninformed consumer decision making would result in some type of market failure. Therefore, there is a need to integrate carbon issues into environmental marketing regulations, since consumers are being asked to make decisions around complex carbon-related claims and issues (MacKerron, Egerton, Gaskill, Parpia, & Mourato, 2009) that they may not fully understand. This may be why the US Federal Trade Commission has become so interested in carbon offsets and regards them as requiring consumer protection regulations (ACCC, 2008; Majoras, 2008). It may be that the alternatives, and the information provided about alternatives, are, in fact, not as responsible as marketers propose. Appropriate metrics, similar to 'Energy Star' ratings found on new electrical appliances, could also be developed in order to help consumers to make a more informed decision so that their behaviour that may have a substantive environmental impact. Such actions, however, require collaboration across regulatory spheres, that is, the science of measuring impact and the marketing communication of this information.

Without information clarity, consumers may believe information is misleading, which could result in increased levels of scepticism about green claims (Mohr, Eroglu, & Ellen, 1998). Such an outcome could mean that consumers would not change their behaviour, and would possibly also discount environmental information in the future if they cannot verify the accuracy of the claims and information. This outcome would make it difficult to change consumers' environmental behaviour to a more positive direction, both for marketers and policymakers seeking to reduce society's impact on the natural environment. However, it is still unclear as to how marketers provide this complex information in a meaningful way, as consumers may in fact not necessarily interpret environmental information as it is intended by marketers. For example, Polonsky, Carlson, Prothero, and Kapelianis (2002) found that consumers potentially misinterpreted a range of 'environmental' information provided on packaging, even when this was not intended to communicate environmental information. (e.g.

'safe on your hands'). However, providing meaningful environmental information is important, especially as consumers seek to make more mindful consumption decisions (Seth et al., 2011). Marketers have long integrated environmental issues into a range of marketing actions, including pricing, logistics, advertising, and design (Polonsky & Rosenberger, 2001). This will continue to be important as sustainability issues become more focal to the marketing concept (Kotler, 2011). Carbon issues are already being used in marketing. For example, MacKerron et al. (2009) examined how consumers respond to different types of carbon programs, and Vanclay et al. (2011) have identified that consumers respond to different types of carbon information for grocery products. However, for the most part, research has not examined how behaviour varies based on consumer knowledge levels, which our work suggests is an important avenue for consideration.

Overall, this research, therefore, has made a number of contributions to the literature by identifying the role of general and specific environmental knowledge on environmental attitudes, and by examining the effects on general and specific behaviours. It has also addressed concerns with research focused on behavioural intentions (e.g. Davies et al., 2002) and has sought to examine how general and specific knowledge and attitudes impact on actual behaviours (both general and specific).

## Future research

There are multiple areas available for future research. This study could be replicated in other countries to see whether these relationships hold. There is also an opportunity to explore whether the relationships hold across regions within countries, or whether they differ across segments of consumers (whether they are defined by demographics, psychographics, or other measures). It appears that green marketing has moved from a niche strategy to one with wider appeal (GfK Roper Consulting, 2007), but segmentation may still be important. In focusing on types of information, one might also look at whether integrating other new information has similar impacts on attitudes and behaviours. As suggested earlier, carbon and global warming can be linked to almost all human activity and, thus, might have more salience than other environmental issues. Future research could also look at what types of information could be used to modify consumers' knowledge levels and, in turn, their attitudes. This latter point is essential if we want consumers to undertake behaviour change that brings about positive environmental impacts.

It would also be possible to examine whether the incorporation of more specific attitudes would have an impact on the model. Might consumer views vary based on the environmental issue being considered? That is, may they perceive some issues to be more pressing or salient to them? Thus while carbon is highly extensively discussed in the popular press and public policy, it is also important to examine consumers' knowledge and responses to other environmental issues such as biodiversity, over-fishing, or other more specific issues. The fact that attitudes have been found to have varying degrees of predictive ability in regard to alternative environmental behaviours (e.g. Thøgersen, 2004) would potentially mean that attitudes towards the specific underlying environmental issues and specific behaviours would therefore also differ. For example, if consumers have strong attitudes about animal rights issues, they might possibly be more concerned about biodiversity than land salinity issues, suggesting that there may in fact be sub-segments within the green consumer market that could be explored in the future. From a marketing practice perspective, research is needed to examine how information can be provided for integration to allow consumers to act on new complex information regarding carbon issues, as well as other environment-related issues, given the limited research into consumer responses suggests the type of information provided impacts consumers behaviour (MacKerron et al., 2009; Vanclay et al., 2011).

Future research also needs to examine whether or not there are mediating or moderating variables in the relationship, as research suggests that other factors (e.g. issue involvement, social norms, self-efficacy, etc.) may also influence the relationship between knowledge, attitudes, and behaviour (Cialdini, Petty, & Cacioppo, 1981; Hines et al., 1986). The fact that purported behaviour was looked at rather than an objective measure of behaviour is also a potential issue that needs to be explored in future research, especially as there may be social desirability bias when exploring issues about the environment (i.e. people report more positive responses). While measures of different types of behaviours were included, additional carbon-related products could also be examined, such as individuals personally purchasing offsets for their consumption, rather than looking at offsets as a component of other purchases. When such environmentally focused goods increasingly become available, research on consumer behaviour in relation to their purchase will present a future avenue for research.

## References

Abdul-Muhmin, A.G. (2007). Explaining consumers' willingness to be environmentally friendly. *International Journal of Consumer Studies*, *31*, 237–247.

Ajzen, I. (1985). From intentions to actions: a theory of planned behavior. In J. Kuhl & J. Beckman (Eds.), *Action-control: From cognition to behavior* (pp. 11–39). Heidelberg, Germany: Springer.

Ajzen, I. (1991). The Theory of Planned Behavior. *Organizational Behaviour and Human Decision Processes*, *50*, 179–211.

Ajzen, I., & Fishbein, M. (1977). Attitude–behaviour relations: A theoretical analysis and review of empirical research. *Psychological Bulletin*, *84*, 888–918.

Ajzen, I., & Fishbein, M. (1980). *Understanding attitudes and predicting social behavior*. Englewood Cliffs, NJ: Prentice-Hall.

Allport, G. (1935). Attitudes. In C. Murchison (Ed.), *Handbook of social psychology series*. Worchester, MA: Clark University Press.

Alwitt, L.F., & Pitts, R.E. (1996). Predicting purchase intentions for an environmentally sensitive product. *Journal of Consumer Psychology*, *5*, 49–64.

Anderson, J.C., & Gerbing, D.W. (1988). Structural modeling in practice: A review and recommended two-step approach. *Psychological Bulletin*, *103*, 411–423.

Arcury, T.A. (1990). Environmental attitude and environmental knowledge. *Human Organization*, *49*, 300–304.

Australian Compensation and Consumer Commission (ACCC). (2008). *Carbon offset claims – Issues paper*. Retrieved 17 April 2009 from http://www.accc.gov.au/content/item. phtml?itemId=808255&nodeId=7fb158e03286f64038540c9146d08742&fn=ACCC% 20Issues%20paper%E2%80%94carbon%20offset%20claims.pdf

Babin, B.J., Hair, J.F., & Boles, J.S. (2008). Publishing research in marketing journals using structural equation modeling. *Journal of Marketing Theory and Practice*, *16*(4), 279–286.

Bagozzi, R.P., Yi, Y., & Phillips. L.W. (1991). Assessing construct validity in organizational research. *Administrative Science Quarterly, 36*, 421–458.

Baker, R., Blumberg, S., Brick, J M., Couper, M.P., Courtright, M., Dennis, M., et al. (2010). AAPOR report on online panels. *Public Opinion Quarterly, 74*(4), 711–781.

Ballantyne, R., & Packer, J. (2005). Promoting environmentally sustainable attitudes and behavior through free-choice learning experiences: What is the state of the game? *Environmental Education Research, 11*, 281–295.

Bamberg, S. (2003). How does environmental concern influence specific environmentally-related behaviors? A new answer to an old question. *Journal of Environmental Psychology, 23*(1), 21–32.

Bang, H.K., Ellinger, A., Hadjimarcou, J., & Traichal, P. (2000). Consumer concern, knowledge, belief, and attitude toward renewable energy: An application of the reasoned action theory. *Psychology and Marketing, 17*(6), 449–468.

Barber, N., Taylor, C., & Strick, S. (2009). Wine consumers' environmental knowledge and attitudes: Influence on willingness to purchase. *International Journal of Wine Research, 1*(1), 59–72.

Beck-Larsen, T. (1996). Danish consumers' attitudes to the functional and environmental characteristics of food packaging. *Journal of Consumer Policy, 19*, 339–363.

Best, H., & Kneip, T. (2011). The impact of attitudes and behavioral costs on environmental behavior: A natural experiment on household waste recycling. *Social Science Research, 40*, 917–930.

Bohlen, G., Schlegelmilch, B.B., & Diamantopoulos, A. (1993). Measuring ecological concern: A multi-construct perspective. *Journal of Marketing Management, 9*, 415–430.

Bollen, K.A. (1989). *Structural equations with latent variables.* New York: John Wiley.

Bulkeley, H. (2000). Common knowledge? Public understanding of climate change in Newcastle, Australia. *Public Understanding of Science, 9*, 313–334.

Bumpus, A.G., & Liverman, D.M. (2008). Accumulation by decarbonization and the governance of carbon offsets. *Economic Geography, 84*(2), 127–155.

Callegaro, M., & DiSogra, C. (2008). Computing response metrics for online panels. *Public Opinion Quarterly, 72*, 1008–1032.

Chan, R.Y.K. (1999). Enviornmental attitudes and behaviors of consumes in China: Survey findings and implications. *Journal of International Consumer Marketing, 11*, 25–52.

Chan, R.Y.K., & Lau, L.B.Y. (2000). Antecedents of green purchases: A survey in China. *Journal of Consumer Marketing, 17*, 338–357.

Churchill, G.A., Jr. (1979). Paradigm for developing measures of marketing constructs. *Journal of Marketing Research, 16*(1), 64–73.

Cialdini, R.B., Petty, R.E., & Cacioppo, J.T. (1981). Attitude and attitude change. *Annual Review of Psychology, 32*, 357–404.

Cole, D.A., Ciesla, J.A., & Steiger, J.H. (2007). The insidious effects of failing to include design-driven correlated residuals in latent-variable covariance structure analysis. *Psychological Methods, 12*, 331–398.

Cronbach, L. (1951). Coefficient alpha and the internal structure of tests. *Psychometrics, 16*, 297–334.

Daniere, A.G., & Takahashi, L.M. (1999). Environmental behaviors in Bangkok, Thailand: A portrait of attitudes, values and behaviors. *Economic Development and Cultural Change, 47*, 525–557.

Davies, J., Foxall, G.R., & Pallister, J. (2002). Beyond the intention-behavior mythology: An integrated model of recycling. *Marketing Theory, 2*(1), 29–113.

Diamantopoulos, A., Schlegelmilch, B.B., Sinkovics, R.R., & Bohlen, G.B. (2003). Can socio-demographics still play a role in profiling green consumers? A review of the evidence and an empirical investigation. *Journal of Business Research, 56*, 465–480.

Dyer, G., Harvey, F., Kazmin, A., & Wheatley, J. (2009). Climate change alliance crumbles as accord is labelled a 'great failure'. *Financial Times*, December 23, p. 1.

Ellen, P.S., Wiener, J.L., & Cobb-Walgren, C. (1991). The role of perceived consumer effectiveness in motivating environmentally-conscious behaviours. *Journal of Public Policy & Marketing*, 19(2), 102–117.

Ferrell, O.C., & Gresham, L. (1985). A contingency framework for understanding ethical decision-making in marketing. *Journal of Marketing*, 49, 87–96.

Flamm, B. (2009). The impacts of environmental knowledge and attitudes on vehicle ownership and use. *Transportation Research, Part D: Transport and Environment*, 14(4), 272–279.

Fraj-Andres, E., & Martínez-Salinas, E. (2007). Impact of environmental knowledge on ecological consumer behaviour: An empirical analysis. *Journal of International Consumer Marketing*, 19, 73–102.

Fransson, N., & Gärling, T. (1999). Environmental concern: Conceptual definitions, measurement methods and research findings. *Journal of Environmental Psychology*, 19(4), 369–382.

Fornell, C., & Larcker, D. (1981). Evaluating structural equation models with unobservable variables and measurement error. *Journal of Marketing Research*, 18, 39–50.

Fryxell, G.E., & Lo, C.W.H. (2003). The influence of environmental knowledge and values on managerial behaviours on behalf of the environment: an empirical examination of managers in China. *Journal of Business Ethics*, 46(1), 45–69.

GfK Roper Consulting. (2007). *Green gauge*. Retrieved 10 November 2009 from: http://www.gfkamerica.com

Goldenhar, L.M., & Connell, C.M. (1993). Understanding and predicting recycling behavior: An application of the theory of reasoned action. *Journal of Environmental Systems*, 22, 91–103.

Gram-Hanssen, K. (2010). Standby consumption in households analyzed with a practice theory approach. *Journal of Industrial Ecology*, 14(1), 150–165.

Green-Demers, I., Pelletier, L.G., & Ménard, S. (1997). The impact of behavioural difficulty on the saliency of the association between self-determined motivation and environmental behaviours. *Canadian Journal of Behavioural Science*, 29(3), 157–166.

Harris Interactive. (2010). *Fewer Americans 'going green'*. Retrieved 10 March 2011 from http://www.harrisinteractive.com/NewsRoom/HarrisPolls/tabid/447/mid/1508/articleId/667/ctl/ReadCustom%20Default/Default.aspx

Heinzerling, A. (2010). *Global carbon dioxide emissions fall in 2009 – Past decade still sees rapid emissions growth*. Retrieved 10 March 2011 from http://www.earth-policy.org/indicators/C52

Hines, J.M., Hungerford, H.R., & Tomera, A.N. (1986). Analysis of research on responsible environmental behaviour: A meta-analysis. *Journal of Environmental Education*, 18, 1–8.

Howell, R.A. (2011). Lights, camera . . . action? Altered attitudes and behaviour in response to the climate change film, *The Age of Stupid*. *Global Environmental Change*, 21(1), 177–187.

Ivy, T., Geok-Chin, L., Kim-Eng, C., & Chuan, G.K. (1998). A survey of environmental knowledge, attitudes and behavior in students in Singapore. *International Research in Geographical and Environmental Education*, 7, 181–202.

Jones, R.E. (1990). Understanding paper recycling in an institutionally supportive setting: An application of the theory of reasoned action. *Journal of Environmental Systems*, 19, 307–321.

Kahn, M.E. (2007). Do greens drive hummers or hybrids? Environmental ideology as a determinant of consumer choice. *Journal of Environmental Economics and Management*, 54, 129–145.

Kaiser, F.G., Wolfing, S., & Fuhrer, U. (1999). Environmental attitude and ecological behavior. *Journal of Environmental Psychology*, 19, 1–19.

Kilbourne, W., & Pickett, G. (2008). How materialism affects environmental beliefs, concern, and environmentally responsible behavior. *Journal of Business Research*, 61, 885–893.

Kollmuss, A., Zink, H., & Polycaro, C. (2008). *Making sense of the voluntary carbon marketing: A comparison of carbon offset standards*. Retrieved from http://tricorona.de/files/93ea78fc52f9fdaf0048dcf866d73004wwf_standcomp_080305_web.pdf

Kotchen, M., & Reiling, S. (2000). Environmental attitudes, motivations, and contingent valuation of nonuse values: A case study involving endangered species. *Ecological Economics*, 32, 93–107.

Kotler, P. (2011). Reinventing marketing to manage the environmental imperative. *Journal of Marketing*, 75(4), 132–135.

Leonidou, C.N., & Leonidou, L.C. (2011). Research into environmental marketing/management: A bibliographic analysis. *European Journal of Marketing*, 45, 68–103.

Leonidou, L.C., Leonidou, C.N., & Kvasova, O. (2010). Antecedents and outcomes of consumer environmentally-friendly attitudes and behaviour. *Journal of Marketing Management*, 26, 1319–1344.

Lynne, G.D., & Rola, L.R. (1988). Improving attitude–behavior prediction models with economic variables: Farmer actions towards soil conservation. *Journal of Social Psychology*, 128, 19–28.

Maloney, M.P., & Ward, M.P. (1973). Ecology: Let's hear from the people: An objective scale for the measurement of ecological attitudes and knowledge. *American Psychologist*, 28, 583–586.

Maloney, M.P., Ward, M.P., & Braucht, G.N. (1975). A revised scale for the measurement of ecological attitudes and knowledge. *American Psychologist*, 30, 787–790.

McKercher, B., Prideaux, B., Cheung, C., & Law, R. (2010). Achieving voluntary reductions in the carbon footprint of tourism and climate change. *Journal of Sustainable Tourism*, 18, 297–317.

MacKerron, G.J., Egerton, C., Gaskill, C., Parpia, A., & Mourato, S. (2009). Willingness to pay for carbon offsets certification and co-benefits among (high-)flying young adults in the UK. *Energy Policy*, 37, 1372–1381.

Majoras, D.P. (2008). *Carbon offset workshop opening remarks*. FTC, Washington DC. Retrieved 10 December 2008 from: http://www.ftc.gov/speeches/majoras/080108carbonow.pdf

Mohr, L.A., Eroglu, D., & Ellen, P.S. (1998). The development and testing of a measure of skepticism toward environmental claims in marketers' communications. *Journal of Consumer Affairs*, 32(1), 30–55.

Moisander, J. (2007). Motivational complexity of green consumerism. *International Journal of Consumer Studies*, 32, 516–525.

Mostafa, M.M. (2007). A hierarchical analysis of the green consciousness of the Egyptian consumer. *Psychology and Marketing*, 24, 445–473.

Offset Offerings: A Breakdown. (2007, June). *The Washington Post*. Retrieved 10 December 2008 from http://www.washingtonpost.com/wp-dyn/content/article/2007/06/08/AR2007060801131.html

Onishi, A. (2007). The impact of CO2 emissions on the world economy: Policy simulations of FUGI global model. *Journal of Policy Modeling*, 29, 797–819.

Oreg, S., & Katz-Gerro, T. (2006). Predicting pro-environmental behavior cross-nationally: Values, the theory of planned behavior, and value-belief-norm theory. *Environment and Behavior*, 38, 462–483.

Pickett-Baker, J., & Ozaki, R. (2008). Pro-environmental products: Marketing influence on consumer purchase decision. *Journal of Consumer Marketing*, 25, 281–293.

Podsakoff, P.M., & Organ, D.W. (1986). Self-reports in organizational research: Problems and prospects. *Journal of Management*, 12, 531–543.

Polonsky, M.J., Carlson, L., Prothero, A., & Kapelianis, D. (2002). A cross-cultural examination of the environmental information on packaging: Implications for advertisers. *Advances in International Marketing*, 12, 153–174.

Polonsky, M.J., & Rosenberger, P.J. (2001). Re-evaluating green marketing – An integrated approach. *Business Horizons*, *44*(5), 21–30.

Ramseur, J.L. (2007). Voluntary carbon offsets: Overview and assessment. *Congressional Research Service*. Retrieved 15 April 2008 from http://assets.opencrs.com/rpts/RL34241_20071107.pdf

Ristino, L.A. (2008). It's not easy being green: Reflections on the American carbon offset market. *Policy*, *34*, 34–37.

Rokka, J., & Uusitalo, L. (2008). Preference for green packaging in consumer product choices – Do consumers care? *International Journal of Consumer Studies*, *32*, 516–525.

Satorra, A. (2000). Scaled and adjusted restricted tests in multisample analysis of moment structures. In D.D.H. Heijmails, D.S.G. Pollock, & A. Satorra (Eds.), *Innovations in multivariate statistical analysis: A Festschrift for Heinz Neudecker* (pp. 233–247). Dordrecht, The Netherlands: Kluwer.

Schahn, J., & Holzer, E. (1990). Studies of individual environmental concern: The role of knowledge, gender, and background variables. *Environment and Behavior*, *22*, 767–786.

Schlegelmilch, B.B., Bohlen, G., & Diamantopoulos, A. (1996). The link between green purchasing decisions and measures of environmental consciousness. *European Journal of Marketing*, *30*, 33–55.

Schwartz, S.H. (1973). Normative explanations of helping behaviour: A critique, proposal, and empirical test. *Journal of Experimental Social Psychology*, *9*, 349–364.

Seth, J.N., Sethia, N.K., & Srinvas, S. (2011). Mindful consumption: A customer-centric approach to sustainability. *Journal of the Academy of Marketing Science*, *39*, 21–39.

Shi, W., Wang, S., & Yang, Q. (2010). Climate change and global warming. *Reviews in Environmental Science and Biotechnology*, *9*, 99–102.

Steg, L., & Vleka, C. (2009). Encouraging pro-environmental behaviour: An integrative review and research agenda. *Journal of Environmental Psychology*, *29*, 309–317.

Stone, G., Barnes, J.H., & Montgomery, C. (1995). ECOSCALE: A scale for the measurement of environmentally-responsible consumers. *Psychology and Marketing*, *12*, 595–612.

Stutzman, T.M., & Green, S.B. (1982). Factors affecting energy consumption: Two field tests of the Fishbein–Ajzen model. *Journal of Social Psychology*, *117*, 183–201.

Tanner, C., & Kast, S.W. (2003). Promoting sustainable consumption: Determinants of green purchases by Swiss consumers. *Psychology and Marketing*, *20*, 883–902.

Taylor, S., & Todd, P. (1995). Understanding household garbage reduction behavior: A test of an integrated model. *Journal of Public Policy and Marketing*, *14*, 192–205.

Thøgersen, J. (1999). The ethical consumer: Moral norms and packaging choice. *Journal of Consumer Psychology*, *22*, 439–460.

Thøgersen, J. (2004). A cognitive dissonance interpretation of consistencies and inconsistencies in environmentally-responsible behavior. *Journal of Environmental Psychology*, *24*, 93–103.

Thøgersen, J. (2006). Media attention and the market for 'green' consumer products. *Business Strategy and the Environment*, *15*, 145–156.

Thøgersen, J., & Ölander, F. (2003). Spillover of environmentally-friendly consumer behavior. *Journal of Environmental Psychology*, *23*, 225–236.

Thøgersen, J., & Ölander, F. (2006). To what degree are environmentally-beneficial choices reflective of a general conservation stance? *Environment and Behavior*, *38*, 550–569.

uStamp (2010). *Consumers' voice is transforming market research via online panels, social media and technology*. Business Wire. Retrieved 15 March 2010 from: http://www.businesswire.com

Uusitalo, L. (1989). Economic man or social man – Exploring free-riding in the production of collective goods. In K. Grunert & F. Ölander (Eds.), *Understanding economic behavior* (pp. 267–283). Dordrecht, The Netherlands: Kluwer.

Uusitalo, L. (1990a). Are environmental attitudes and behavior inconsistent? Findings from a Finish study. *Scandinavian Political Studies*, *13*, 211–226.

Uusitalo, L. (1990b). Consumer preferences of environmental quality and other social goals. *Journal of Consumer Policy*, *13*, 231–251.

Vanclay, J.K., Shortiss, J., Aulsebrook, S., Gillespie, A.M., Howell, B.C., Johanni, R., et al. (2011). Customer response to carbon labelling of groceries. *Journal Consumer Policy*, *34*, 153–160.

Van Liere, K.D., & Dunlap, R.E. (1981). Environmental concern: Does it make a difference how it is measured? *Environment and Behavior*, *13*, 651–676.

Zellner, A., & Theil, H. (1962). Three-stage least squares: Simultaneous estimation of simultaneous equations. *Econometrica*, *30*(1), 54–78.

## Appendix 1. Environmental knowledge scales

| General environmental knowledge | Carbon offset knowledge |
| --- | --- |
| Most smog in our big cities comes from industrial plants (e.g. factories) (**FALSE**) | Carbon offsets involve firms reducing their pollution (**FALSE**) |
| Mercury has been found at unacceptable levels in seafood (**TRUE**) | Firms that offer carbon offsets can receive a tax incentive for doing so (**TRUE**) |
| Diesel fuel pollutes less than unleaded fuel (**TRUE**) | Firms that offer carbon offsets are environmentally responsible (**FALSE**) |
| Ecology assumes that man is an integral part of nature (**TRUE**) | All carbon offset programs are government regulated/approved (**FALSE**) |
| Aluminium takes longer to decompose than iron or steel (**TRUE**) | Independent organisations audit the outcomes of a firm's offset program (**FALSE**) |
| Traditional plastic bags do not decompose in landfills (**TRUE**) | Carbon offsets offered by US firms always reduce the carbon produced in the United States (**FALSE**) |
| Products on sleep-mode do not use any electricity (**FALSE**) | Carbon offsets are priced as a percentage of the overall price of the good/service (**FALSE**) |
| Most water in the United States is used in agriculture (**TRUE**) | Carbon offset programs may invest in activities that only reduce carbon in the future (**TRUE**) |

# Understanding local food shopping: Unpacking the ethical dimension

Phil Megicks, *University of Plymouth, UK*
Juliet Memery, *University of Plymouth, UK*
Robert J. Angell, *University of Plymouth, UK*

**Abstract** Analysing shopping in the local food sector is an area of contemporary consumer research that has received considerable interest in recent times. The significance of the topic relates not only to underlying consumer behaviour theory, but also to the perceived role of local food in environmentally responsible purchasing practices, and consequently sustainable food policies. However, previous empirical investigation of local food buying behaviour is limited, and this research extends current work through adopting a mixed methods approach that comprised qualitative focus groups with an online survey of consumers. Multivariate analysis techniques were utilised to identify a set of drivers of and inhibitors to local food buying. Following this, two types of local food buyers were distinguished based upon the reasons for buying/not buying, and these were further categorised using demographic and location variables. An integrated modelling process was then used to establish the effects of the different influences on behavioural intentions and actual buying behaviour. Results identified a complex range of outcomes which indicate that the ethical sustainability dimension of local food shopping does not positively affect consumer buying in this market. The implications for related areas of theory and the future marketing practices of local food suppliers and retailers are then considered.

## Introduction

The study of the purchase and consumption of local food has become an increasingly popular research theme in recent times, not only from a consumer behaviour perspective (Zepeda & Deal, 2009) but also in terms of its significance as a generally recognised facet of environmentally responsible buying (McEachern, Warnaby, Carrigan, & Szmigin, 2010), and the consequential implications for sustainable food policy (Defra, 2002). Additionally research has considered local food's role inter alia in the future of rural economies, developing rural–urban linkage, and promoting local food tourism (Khan & Prior, 2010). Opportunities for competitive advantage across the spectrum of retail providers from farm shops, food cooperatives, and farmers' markets to national supermarket chains in exploiting the trend in favour of local food consumption have also been identified (Seyfang, 2007; Weatherell, Tregear, & Allinson, 2003). Such investigation has been undertaken against the backdrop of key economic, political, and social events in the food arena (Morris & Buller, 2003). Specifically, on the supply side, agricultural crises including BSE and Foot and Mouth Disease (Tregear & Ness, 2005) have heightened consumers' awareness of food supply chains and their fears of food safety. Simultaneously, from a demand-side viewpoint, there has been an increase in the expectations of food consumers relating to product quality, customer service, and the shopping experience generally, including the ethical and social responsibility dimension (Megicks, Memery, & Williams, 2008). In sum, therefore, a strong platform for the growth of the local food sector has been presented, and this paper sets out to analyse the complex combination of contributory factors in its development, giving particular emphasis to explaining the underlying behaviour of buyers. It therefore builds upon previous research, which has provided useful insights into the various influences on consumer buying (specifically focusing on the end-user rather than retail buyers), and makes a significant contribution to the deeper understanding of the factors affecting intended and actual behaviour through extensive empirical research in the market for local food products in England.

## Definition and development of the local food sector

Any investigation of contextual consumer behaviour requires an appreciation of the nature of the product that is the focus of the buyer's attention. In the case of local food sector, the 'locality' aspect is interpreted in a number of ways (see, e.g., Morris & Buller, 2003; Ricketts Hein, Ilbery, & Kneafsey, 2006) but predominantly relates to two specific characteristics of the produce: its origination from a stated area, and recognition by consumers that that the food is derived from a 'local' source (Pearson et al., 2011). Although clear definitions in terms of geographical distance from the point of purchase or within a defined socio-administrative area are often referred to (e.g. '30–50 miles of the sellers' location'; 'within the county boundaries'; SERIO, 2008), for the purposes of this study, the second perspective is adopted, which places the emphasis on the interpretation of the consumer of what is local to them both in terms of distance and how this translates into specific buying and consumption outcomes (COI/FSA, 2003).

Despite the debate around definitional issues, there is wide-ranging agreement on the rise in the local food sector's significance over the past decade. This is evidenced through a number of studies that have identified the growth of the sector in financial terms, and the growing awareness of consumers, retailers, and policymakers of the potential that it holds with respect to meeting specific needs of the market together with the associated benefits in the downstream agri-food supply chain (Weatherell et al., 2003). Recent research by Mintel (2011) estimates the local food market to be worth more than £5 billion in 2010, having grown by 27% over the past five years. It is forecasted that this will approach nearly £6 billion by 2015, with much of the growth being based upon large supermarkets' strategies to support the sale of locally sourced food within their corporate social responsibility agendas. As part of the heightening of attention to local food consumption, further understanding of the nature of consumer buying has emerged. An IGD (2008) report identified that 65% of consumers buy local produce, and that more frequent purchasing had led to a growth in market size (Khan & Prior, 2010). Additionally, an investigation undertaken by SERIO (2008) identified that almost 75% of consumers had bought local produce in the last month, with the main categories of food being fruit and vegetables, dairy produce, and meat, which were bought from a range of different retail outlets. Of particular interest, however, is the pattern of local food consumption across demographic types that is revealed in a number of recent studies, with significant variation being evident around the choices of rural and urban consumers, buyers of different ages, and across socio-economic groupings. In general terms, local food buying tends to be more evident amongst rural consumers that are older and in higher social bandings (IGD, 2005; Mintel, 2011). Such characteristics are important contributors to understanding the nature of buying behaviour in this market, but these must be taken into account only in conjunction with a more wide-ranging assessment of the essential factors that affect consumer decisions, including the perceived environmental and sustainability advantages that buying local food may offer (Pearson et al., 2011).

## Local food and ethical and socially responsible buying

Buying local has become inextricably associated with ethical and socially responsible consumption for a number of reasons that reflect its intrinsic beneficial nature in this regard, especially in the case of food produce. Hence, as greater attention has been afforded to ethical buying (de Pelsmacker, Driesen, & Rayp, 2005; Harrison, Newholm, & Shaw, 2005), so the focus on how purchasing locally derived food can provide positive fulfilment of consumers' ethical needs has intensified. This has been especially relevant in the realm of realising sustainable consumption motives (see Jackson, 2005) where the ethical environmental benefits of buying local such as reduced food miles, support for local suppliers and retailers, and improved animal welfare (Tregear & Ness, 2005) can offer consumers extensive possibilities to achieve this. Recent research has also identified a lower incidence of supplier exploitation, chemical-free food, and reduced packaging as further possible ethical and socially responsible benefits of local food consumption (McEachern et al., 2010). In essence, therefore, purchasing local food is often considered as sustainable consumption where consumers' decision making takes wider issues into account, as well as individual needs.

Consumer acceptance of ethical and socially responsible products into their regular purchasing patterns, especially in the food sector, is heavily driven by such factors as social and institutional norms, convenience, price, availability, and habit. With this in mind, openness to sustainable food buying and positive action in this direction is often subject to a mismatch between behavioural intentions to buy and actual buying behaviour. As Vermeir and Verbeke, (2004) point out, this is based upon the extent to which 'interested consumers turn their expressed interest into actual purchasing habits, in that even where consumers have concerns about conventionally produced food, their support for alternatives is usually conditional and often determined by price or availability issues' (p. 4). This theme, which is rooted in attitudinal and behavioural differences, has been widely considered in ethical consumer research (see, e.g., Carrigan & Attalla, 2001), and is often regarded as key to understanding the limited adoption of ethical products even amongst ethically minded consumers (Carrington, Neville, & Whitwell, 2010). Given the association of local food buying with ethical and socially responsible consumption, a similar pattern of behaviour could be expected in this market, which could be further exacerbated in the current environment of economic uncertainty, as unemployment rises and pressure on consumer expenditure increases (Carrigan & de Plesmacker, 2009).

## Buying local food as a shopping experience

Food buying is generally considered to be a shopping activity and therefore subject to greater scrutiny from the perspective of the motivations of consumers in this respect. For many years, shopping was predominantly regarded as a utilitarian, functional activity, fulfilling the need to be 'task-related and rational' (Batra & Ahtola, 1991) in the acquisition of products. More recently, however, researchers have widened the understanding of shopping as an 'experience' that includes a hedonic aspect that has been particularly stimulated by recognition of the importance of its entertainment and emotional worth. Acceptance of this can take food shopping into a different domain for some consumers, away from Miller's (1998) provisioning activity, towards a more complex set of motives that relate to the experiential, sensory, emotive, and 'fantasy' aspects of consumption (Hirschman & Holbrook, 1982). Against this backdrop, shopping for local food lends itself well to wider interpretation, as some studies of hedonic shopping indicate that the contextual setting may stimulate shoppers to engage in the shopping experience to achieve non-functional outcomes (e.g. Babin, Darden, & Griffin, 1994). Although evidence suggests that the supermarket shopping experience predominates the purchasing of local food (SERIO, 2008), the relationship of local food with particular retail formats such as farmers' markets and farm shops can be interpreted in the context of hedonic shopping motives. For example, these could relate to a sense of escapism and adventure, the enjoyment of bargaining and haggling, and the mood-altering possibilities of shopping (Arnold & Reynolds, 2003), which are experiences that may often be far more significant than the mere acquisition of products (Sherry, 1990). Additionally, the scope for considering local food buying as a means of achieving greater understanding of the personal and social identity of shoppers fits well with the activities under investigation in this research (Woodruffe-Burton & Wakenshaw, 2011). Conceptualising shopping in this wider sense broadens its relevance to local food consumption, and offers meaningful opportunities for greater insights into the motivations and characteristics of consumers in this market. This is further supported by the understanding that factors which influence shopping behaviour are generally considered to be a combination of both personal and social motives that relate to a range of psychological and other needs with utilitarian and hedonic elements (see Tauber, 1972). Moreover, they are often used as a basis for identifying shopper types in taxonomies of retail consumers (Jarratt, 1996; Westbrook & Black, 1985). There is therefore scope to understand more about local food consumption from these approaches that identify wide-ranging shopper motives, and additionally make it possible to develop shopper segments that in some cases might align with core expectations in this area (e.g. those 'ethical shoppers' who are moralistic in their support for local merchants as identified by Darden & Reynolds, 1971).

## Previous studies of influences on local food buying

According to COI/FSA (2007), the main reasons for buying local food are: supporting local businesses and the local community; food quality issues, including where the food comes from and its freshness; and environmental factors such as reducing food miles and pollution. An IGD report (2005) generally concurs with this and summarises the reasons for buying local food into three groups: product quality, sustainability, and the shopping experience. In the same study, the main barriers to customers buying are identified as lack of awareness of local and regional produce, a lack of practical access to outlets and being out of their price range, and uncertainty about availability to plan into their food shopping.

Two recent academic studies specifically investigating consumer behaviour towards local food are worthy of consideration. Weatherell et al. (2003) suggest that the practical benefits of food (e.g. freshness, taste, healthiness, appearance, and availability) dominate decisions when choosing food over what they term 'civic' factors, even amongst the 'issue aware' respondents. They also identify numerous significant differences between respondents' views according to their urban/rural residency, particularly from the standpoint of 'civic' issues of food choice, which tend to be a much higher priority of those located in rural areas, as does concern over food provisioning issues and interest in local foods. These researchers also find evidence to support an identified group of 'concerned consumers' who give priority to all food-related issues except price and who are particularly interested in buying local foods. Nonetheless, even this group put practical buying criteria and moral and health concerns before the origin of food when making choices, thus signifying that trade-offs can take place between broader concerns and pragmatic factors when shopping for local food. Further to this, Tregear and Ness (2005) attempt to identify features that distinguish interest amongst consumers in food, and extrapolate this into the local food focus of their research. Their findings indicate that in addition to extrinsic food features (e.g. environment, welfare, and origin), pragmatic features of food (i.e. price and intrinsic characteristics such as quality, taste, and freshness) are important determinants of interest. They also identify that rurally resident consumers have a higher interest in local food issues compared with those in urban areas, and concur with other research that older respondents are more interested in local food compared with younger ones. The findings of both these studies were supported in a similarly configured investigation undertaken by Khan and Prior (2010) which identifies a range of reasons for, and barriers to, buying local food consistent with previous work.

A further investigation worthy of note relates explicitly to the buying of a particular customer type (conscious consumers) in farmers' markets (McEachern et al., 2010). This study presents very helpful insights into a specific facet of local food buying and establishes strong evidence for the significance of a set of identified motivations when buying in this context. This is especially so in regard to the ethical and socially responsible purpose of consumers when shopping for local food, and the perception that shopping for local food at these outlets is often regarded as a leisure pursuit. It therefore emphasises the trade-offs that consumers make between principles, cost, and convenience, and highlights the tension between intended and actual behaviour. Although this work goes some way towards recognising associations between local food buying and a range of explanatory influences, along with the other empirical studies considered here, it does not establish a measurable relationship that assesses the effects of each factor on consumers' local food purchasing behaviour. Consequently, the aim of the research presented here is to fill the gap by developing an understanding of which factors stimulate and detract from buying local food, and the relative importance of each, which includes consideration of any differences between intended and actual behaviour. It further sets out to establish variations in these influences on local food buying in identified consumer segments in the market. In order to achieve this, the research employs a sequential, two-phase integrative qualitative and quantitative framework.

## Qualitative investigation

Exploratory qualitative research was conducted through 20 focus groups, comprising an average of 10 members each, with the purpose of identifying the factors that influence consumers purchasing local food. Discussions were held throughout England, with the composition of each group being determined by an interlocking quota sampling approach to gain coverage and develop understanding across the range of different consumers. As displayed in Table 1, two focus groups were held in each of the nine English regions (ONS, 2003), one urban and one rural, with an

**Table 1** Focus group sample.

| Region | Urban | Rural | Gender | SE group | Life stage* |
|---|---|---|---|---|---|
| London | North London | | Male | ABC1 | Pre/no family |
| | South London | | Female | C2DE | Older Children |
| South East | Brighton | | Female | C2DE | Pre/no family |
| | Reading | | Female | ABC1 | Older children |
| | | Crowthorne | Male | C2DE | 3rd age/retired |
| | | East Grinstead | Female | ABC1 | Young children |
| East of England | Norwich | | Female | ABC1 | 3rd age/retired |
| | | Diss | Female | C2DE | Young children |
| South West | Bristol | | Female | C2DE | Young children |
| | | St Austell | Female | ABC1 | 3rd age/retired |
| West Midlands | Birmingham | | Female | ABC1 | Older children |
| | | Stourbridge | Female | C2DE | Young children |
| East Midlands | Nottingham | | Female | C2DE | Older children |
| | | Long Eaton | Female | ABC1 | Pre/no children |
| North West | Manchester | | Female | C2DE | Young children |
| | | Colne | Male | ABC1 | Older children |
| North East | Newcastle | | Female | ABC1 | Pre/no family |
| | | Morpeth | Female | C2DE | 3rd age/retired |
| Yorkshire & Humber | Leeds | | Male | ABC1 | Young children |
| | | Ripon | Female | C2DE | 3rd age/retired |

*Life stage: pre/no children = single or all adult household (HH); young children = HH with all or most children at pre- or primary school age (≤11yrs); older children = HH with all or most children at secondary school age (12yrs+); 3rd age/retired = 'empty-nesters' and/or no longer working.

additional two groups in the South-East to take account of population distribution. Respondents in the sample were asked six questions relating to their attitudes to foods and purchasing behaviour when recruited, and the responses to these questions were used to ensure the focus groups consisted of a mix of those currently predisposed to buying and using local food products, and those who are not. Additionally, respondents in the sample were selected as being representative of grocery shoppers generally, hence age, gender, socio-economics, geodemographics, family size, and composition were used to establish group membership.

A discussion outline was employed, following the guidelines of Kruger and Casey (2000), with several structured questions initiating conversation and establishing respondent shopping behaviours such as frequency, location, and so on. Subsequent discussion was more spontaneous, and directed at identifying insights into attitudes and behaviours, motivations for use and non-use, and intended consumption patterns. All focus groups were digitally recorded and transcribed. Content analysis was used to categorise key local food buying influences and shopping behaviours. Transcripts were read through a number of times by the authors, and each individually, then collectively, identified reoccurring themes which were then coded and sorted into categories based on similar characteristics in line with the work of Lincoln and Guba (1985). Conceptual definitions and labels for the resulting categorisations were constructed, and these were viewed by a Faculty Panel familiar with the subject area for content validity. Two categories of influences emerged from the qualitative stage: drivers and inhibitors. Drivers are those influences that motivate consumers to buy local food and are associated with positive feelings or outcomes (e.g. it makes the shopping experience satisfying; it supports local producers). On the other hand, inhibitors consist of influences that prevent or constrain consumers from buying such products and are often associated with time-poor lifestyles (e.g. it is inconvenient; it is time-consuming).

### Item generation

Items for use in the quantitative phase are based on the findings from the qualitative stage as well as the extant literature. The initial item-generation process revealed 43 items: 30 drivers and 13 inhibitors. A panel of experts were given the conceptual definitions and illustrative quotes, and asked to retain items that represented the domain and were clearly worded, hence evaluating the items for content and face validity. Any items they viewed as not representative or that could be misinterpreted (Babin et al., 1994) were deleted from the pool after discussion. The final item pool consisted of 29 items: 18 drivers and 11 inhibitors, which were taken forward to the quantitative phase. Illustrative quotes to support the inclusion of these items are shown in Appendix 1.

## Quantitative investigation

The second phase of the study involved an online survey of 1223 grocery shoppers located in England who were the main/joint decision maker in shopping decisions in the household. Based upon an understanding of market behaviour gleaned from the qualitative phase, a less complex and pragmatic interlocking quota sampling procedure was utilised for this phase, based upon gender, age, and regional location. The survey instrument comprised a set of closed questions to capture essential demographic, psychographic, attitudinal, and behavioural characteristics, and batteries of seven-point 'strongly agree'–'strongly disagree' Likert-type questions to assess the importance of particular factors in decision making, and how this translates into actual and intended purchasing behaviour.

## Descriptive statistics

The main characteristics of respondents in the sample are shown in Table 2. Additionally, most people indicated that they shop for groceries two or three times per week (42.6%) with a further 35.6% taking a weekly trip. Interestingly, only 6.7% shop less frequently than once every week. A fairly even spread of respondents can be seen with regard to the distance they travelled to shop from a store. As such, 29.0% live within one mile, 33.3% within one to two miles, 28.3% between two and five miles, and just 9.5% of respondents live farther than five miles away from where they do their main shopping. In terms of getting to the store to purchase groceries, the majority of respondents travel by car 78.0%. The second most used mode of

**Table 2** Respondent characteristics of quantitative sample.

| Demographic characteristics | | | |
|---|---|---|---|
| **Variable** | **Category** | **Count** | **%** |
| Gender | Female | 775 | 63.4 |
| | Male | 448 | 36.6 |
| Age | 18–24 years | 125 | 10.2 |
| | 25–34 years | 233 | 19.1 |
| | 35–44 years | 244 | 20.0 |
| | 45–54 years | 210 | 17.2 |
| | 55+ years | 411 | 33.6 |
| Location | Urban | 801 | 65.5 |
| | Rural | 422 | 34.5 |
| Region | East Anglia | 137 | 11.2 |
| | East Midlands | 111 | 9.1 |
| | London | 172 | 14.1 |
| | North East | 84 | 6.9 |
| | North West | 158 | 12.9 |
| | South East | 201 | 16.4 |
| | South West | 124 | 10.1 |
| | West Midlands | 97 | 7.9 |
| | Yorkshire & Humber | 139 | 11.4 |
| Socio-economic | A | 143 | 11.7 |
| | B | 103 | 8.4 |
| | C1 | 288 | 23.5 |
| | C2 | 299 | 24.4 |
| | D | 283 | 23.1 |
| | E | 107 | 8.7 |

## CONTEMPORARY ISSUES IN GREEN AND ETHICAL MARKETING

transport that people indicate using regularly is by foot (38.8%), followed by public bus (16.0%).

### *Identifying local food purchasing factors*

For the initial stage of scale development, item analysis was performed on the influences affecting the purchase of local food. Corrected item-to-total correlations between items were examined, which led to all of the original items being retained and taken forward to the next stage of analysis (>.5; Tian, Bearden, & Hunter, 2001). Exploratory factor analysis (EFA) was conducted using principal components extraction with varimax rotation as the estimation procedure (Kline, 2000). In the first instance, the scale for drivers of local food purchasing was integrated into the model. With parameters organised to assess solutions with eigenvalues in excess of 1.0, the analysis indicated a four-factor solution with the sampling adequacy at an acceptable level (KMO = .955; df = 136; $p$ = .01). The total variance explained in the observed items by the four-factor solution is 67.05%, indicating a well-explained factorial structure. The rotated components matrix reveals a clear and substantively explainable set of factors (Nunnally & Bernstein, 1994). Results of the EFA for drivers of buying local food are shown in Table 3.

The first factor accounts for 22.63% of the variance in the model and consists of seven items. Because these items relate to the physical properties evident in local produce, this factor is labelled *intrinsic quality*. The second factor contains three items, explaining 18.74% of variance in the model. These variables relate most strongly to the importance ascribed to the product's origin and supporting producers and retailers from the local community. Hence, this factor is labelled *local support and provenance*. The third factor consists of three items and explains 12.87% of variance in the overall solution. Substantively, these variables related most strongly to wider ethical and environmental issues. As such, this factor is named *ethical sustainability*. The final factor to emerge from the drivers scale consists of five items accounting for 12.81% of variance in the model. These variables relate most strongly to the feelings and emotions experienced as a result of shopping for local produce. As a result, this factor is labelled *shopping benefits*. To assess the internal consistency of each of the factors within the scale, Cronbach's coefficient alpha was employed, with all yielding adequate solutions above the .70 threshold advocated by authorities such as Peter (1981) and DeVellis (2003), as shown in Table 3.

A second factor analysis was implemented, this time using the scale items for inhibitors of purchasing local produce. From the qualitative research, 11 items were carried forward for quantitative testing. The rotated solution produced a two-factor structure with acceptable sampling adequacy (KMO = .95; df = 55; $p$ < .01). In total, 67.0% of the variance in the observed items was explained by this solution. Substantively, factor one refers to items concerning product-related explanations for the non-purchase of local foods and is therefore labelled *product distracters*. Overall, this factor consists of seven items and explains 36.12% of total variance in the model. The second factor incorporates the remaining four items, all relating to the non-fiscal costs involved in sourcing and purchasing local produce. As such, the factor is named *buying inconvenience* and accounts for 31.15% of total variance in the rotated model. As before, the internal consistency of both factors was found to be above commonly acceptable thresholds with alpha coefficients of .90 and .89 respectively as indicated in Table 4.

**Table 3** Exploratory factor analysis for drivers of buying local produce.

| Drivers of purchasing local produce | Intrinsic quality | Local support and provenance | Ethical sustainability | Shopping benefits |
|---|---|---|---|---|
| I buy local produce because it is free from preservatives | .751 | | | |
| I buy local produce because it is free from chemicals | .732 | | | |
| I buy local produce because it is natural | .710 | | | |
| I buy local produce because it is wholesome | .676 | | | |
| I buy local produce because it has a good appearance | .658 | | | |
| I buy local produce because I can buy the amount I want | .616 | | | |
| I buy local produce because it lasts longer | .596 | | | |
| I buy local produce because it supports local producers | | .771 | | |
| I buy local produce because it supports local retailers | | .748 | | |
| I buy local produce because I know where it comes from | | .656 | | |
| I buy local produce because it reduces food miles | | | .725 | |
| I buy local produce because it is environmentally friendly | | | .721 | |
| I buy local produce because it is ethical | | | .634 | |
| I buy local produce because shopping because it brings back memories of the past | | | | .747 |
| I buy local produce because shopping for it is fun | | | | .678 |
| I buy local produce because it is nostalgic | | | | .677 |
| I buy local produce because I feel guilty if I do not | | | | .596 |
| I buy local produce because the shopping experience is satisfying | | | | .594 |
| Variance explained (%) | 22.63 | 18.74 | 12.87 | 12.81 |
| Cronbach's coefficient alpha | .93 | .89 | .88 | .78 |

## Distinguishing shopper segments of local produce

To identify different types of shopper for local food purchasing, a two-stage clustering process was adopted, combining both hierarchical and non-hierarchical methods (Hair, Black, Babin, & Anderson, 2009). The driver and inhibitor factors were used as

**Table 4** Exploratory factor analysis for inhibitors of buying local produce.

| Inhibitors of purchasing local produce | Product distracters | Buying inconvenience |
|---|---|---|
| I don't buy local produce because the range of products is limited | .750 | |
| I don't buy local produce because food produced elsewhere is sometimes better | .748 | |
| I don't buy local produce because it is not well promoted | .736 | |
| I don't buy local produce because it is not well labelled | .696 | |
| I don't buy local produce because the price is not always clear | .662 | |
| I don't buy local produce because it is not readily available | .657 | |
| I don't buy local produce because it is expensive | .634 | |
| I don't buy local produce because to do so is time consuming | | .798 |
| I don't buy local produce because it requires extra effort | | .789 |
| I don't buy local produce because it is inconvenient | | .783 |
| I don't buy local produce because I have to travel farther to do so | | .761 |
| Variance explained (%) | 36.12 | 31.15 |
| Cronbach's coefficient alpha | .90 | .89 |

the basis for distinguishing the shopper types initially using Ward's (squared Euclidian distances) method to establish the number of groups within the data and the initial cluster centres. A range of solutions (2–4) were identified (Punj & Stewart, 1983), and, following inspection of the dendogram, the resulting two-cluster solution was found to be both theoretically and practically representative of the data. The next step employed a k-means method using the cluster centres from the hierarchical analysis as the initial seeds; this assigned the cases to the two clusters, consisting of 646 and 577 respondents respectively. The robustness of the solution was tested in line with Klastorin (1983). A discriminant function analysis indicated that approaching 100% of the cases were correctly classified, and a two-dimensional scatter-plot of the clusters revealed distinct positions between the groupings. In addition, a one-way analysis of variance (ANOVA) of the differences in the means of the clusters for all the factors included was found to be significantly different at the $p < 0.001$ level.

The results of the cluster analysis are presented in Table 5. This provides the mean scores on each of the clusters for the drivers and inhibitors. The data also include additional items for actual shopping behaviour for local produce based on purchases in the last three months, and a second, focused on future intentions, by asking how likely the respondent was to buy local food in the next fortnight. Independent samples $t$-tests were used to establish whether the differences in mean score between clusters were statistically significant; in all cases this was verified. This also applied

# CONTEMPORARY ISSUES IN GREEN AND ETHICAL MARKETING

**Table 5** Differences in factor mean scores and buying behaviour by cluster membership.

| Statement (1 = 'low'–7 = 'high' Likert-type scales) | Aggregate sample mean (n = 1223) | Cluster 1 mean (n = 646) | Cluster 2 mean (n = 577) | t-test (sig) |
|---|---|---|---|---|
| Intrinsic quality | 4.41 | 5.21 | 3.51 | $t = 30.43$ $(p < .01)$ |
| Local support and provenance | 5.27 | 6.25 | 4.18 | $t = 35.24$ $(p < .01)$ |
| Ethical sustainability | 4.85 | 5.79 | 3.80 | $t = 30.00$ $(p < .01)$ |
| Shopping benefits | 3.38 | 3.84 | 2.86 | $t = 15.87$ $(p < .01)$ |
| Product distracters | 3.28 | 2.67 | 3.97 | $t = -19.91$ $(p < .01)$ |
| Buying inconvenience | 2.93 | 2.30 | 3.62 | $t = -19.00$ $(p < .01)$ |
| How often have you bought local food for use at home in the past three months? | 4.45 | 5.20 | 3.44 | $t = 19.40$ $(p < .01)$ |
| Do you intend to buy local food for use at home in the next fortnight? | 4.96 | 5.72 | 3.87 | $t = 21.75$ $(p < .01)$ |

for the measures for actual buying and intention to buy between the two different groups.

For further interpretation of the two clusters, a series of post-hoc tests was performed incorporating a range of demographic and geographic variables. Chi-square tests were used to establish whether statistical differences exist between the proportions of responses in each of the categories. This type of profiling provided deeper insight into the characteristics of the cluster members. Overall, the results in Table 6 reveal that cluster 1 and 2 differ with regard to gender, age, and location. Income and education are not found to differ significantly between the two clusters.

The profiles and behaviours of the two clusters reveal some key differences, and it is possible to classify them broadly as follows.

## Cluster 1

This group of consumers representing 53% of the sample is positively disposed towards local food with particularly strong scores for *local support and provenance* and *ethical sustainability* drivers, and also a high score for the *intrinsic quality* of local food. The *shopping benefits* driver score, although not as high, is greater than the mean score for the sample as a whole. In contrast, the scores for both the *product distracters* and *buying inconvenience* factors are low. In general, this cluster has a high propensity to recognise the value of consuming local food and does not regard the distracters as a real impediment to buying. This is exhibited in the very high intention

# CONTEMPORARY ISSUES IN GREEN AND ETHICAL MARKETING

**Table 6** Post-hoc tests for establishing cluster profiles.

| Variable | Cluster 1 | Cluster 2 | $\chi^2$ test |
|---|---|---|---|
| *Gender* | | | |
| Male | 31.9% | 41.9% | $\chi^2 = 13.27$ |
| Female | 68.1% | 58.1% | $p < .01$ |
| *Age (yrs)* | | | |
| 18–24 | 7.0% | 13.9% | $\chi^2 = 34.32$ |
| 25–34 | 15.9% | 22.5% | $p < .01$ |
| 35–44 | 19.7% | 20.3% | |
| 45–54 | 18.4% | 15.8% | |
| 55+ | 39.0% | 27.6% | |
| *Location* | | | |
| Urban | 60.7% | 70.9% | $\chi^2 = 14.04$ |
| Rural | 39.3% | 29.1% | $p < .01$ |
| *Income* | | | |
| £0–24,999 | 59.4% | 59.6% | $\chi^2 = 5.84$ |
| £25,000–49,999 | 33.2% | 32.1% | $p = .56$ |
| £50,000–74,999 | 6.5% | 6.1% | |
| £75,000–99,999 | 1.5% | .5% | |
| £100,000+ | .9% | 1.3% | |
| *Education* | | | |
| School level | 41.5% | 39.0% | $\chi^2 = 16.67$ |
| College level | 31.0% | 33.1% | $p = .06$ |
| University level | 21.2% | 21.0% | |
| Graduate level | 6.4% | 6.9% | |

to buy score and a high level of actual purchasing behaviour. The group's make-up in terms of socio-economic characteristics indicates that there are significantly more female and older members, and there is a greater proportion of rurally located consumers. There is no significant variation in income and education.

## Cluster 2

This segment represents 47% of consumers and comprises those that have generally low scores for the *intrinsic quality*, *ethical sustainability*, and *shopping benefits* driver factors. Although a little higher, the *local support and provenance* score is still well below the mean for the sample. For both the *product distracters* and *buying inconvenience* factors, the group scores significantly higher that the sample mean. The low frequency of purchase and intention to buy scores reflect the group members having a stronger affinity with the negative effects of local food distracters, rather than the positive motives for buying. The socio-economics of the group display a greater proportion of men and younger consumers, and more being located in urban areas. As with the other segment, income and education differences are not significant.

## Influences on local food purchasing intentions and Behaviours

The main aim of this research was to identify the degree to which various influences affect local food buying behaviour. To achieve this aim, data were interrogated using a multiple regression procedure. Two outcomes – intentions and behaviour – were employed as dependent variables in separate regression models whereby the former was represented by the item: *Do you intend to buy local food/drink for use at home in the next fortnight?* The latter was represented by the item: *How often have you bought local food/drink for use at home in the past three months?* In assessment of the two dependent variables, separate regression models incorporating linear composites for each of the four drivers and two inhibitor factors, as independent variables, were developed. In addition, a further variable included in the model assessed the role that geographical location has on the purchasing of local food. To explore this, a dummy variable was used to understand better whether living in either a rural or urban area has an influence on buying intentions or behaviour. The analysis was undertaken at an aggregate level for the whole sample, and separately for both of the two identified cluster segments.

From inspection of the aggregate regression results in Table 7, it is apparent that the factors influencing purchasing intentions and behaviour for local produce are not identical, which is also reflected in the difference in $R^2$ values for each of the models (cf. .46 for intentions with .39 for behaviour). In the structural element of the model, the regression parameters explaining purchase intentions indicate that four variables have a significant influence on the dependent variable: *intrinsic quality*, *local support and provenance*, *product distracters*, and *buying inconvenience*. Of these, the two drivers have a significant positive effect on intentions (*intrinsic quality* = .152; *local support and provenance* = .387) and the two inhibitors have a negative significant influence (*product distracters* = −.087; *buying inconvenience* = −.182). This suggests that the most important driver of future intentions to buy local food is *local support and provenance*, and the most influential inhibitor is *buying inconvenience*. *Ethical sustainability*, *shopping benefits*, and *location* are not revealed as significant factors of influence in the intentions process. For the second regression model, behaviour, the standardised regression coefficients indicate that *intrinsic quality* (.160), *local support and provenance* (0282), *shopping benefits* (.123), *product distracters* (−.129), and *buying inconvenience* (−.16) all had a significant influence on purchasing behaviour for local produce. In addition, location was found to have a significant effect on the dependent variable in this model. Using a two-category item as a dummy variable for urban consumers, the estimates show that people living in those locations have a lower level of actual buying than in the reference category (i.e. rural). As in the intentions model, the main positive buying driver for actual purchases is *local support and provenance*, and the main inhibitor is *buying inconvenience*. For the model that analyses actual buying behaviour, two further influences, *shopping benefits* and *rural/urban location*, are significant compared with the intentions to buy model.

Analysis of regression coefficients for the cluster groups reveals variation in the effects that the different factors have on intentions and behaviour both within and between the groups. For cluster 1, there is again variation in the $R^2$ values, with .23 of variation being explained in the intentions model compared with .18 for behaviour. When inspecting the results for intentions in this cluster, *local support and provenance* (.312), *product distracters* (−.150), and *buying inconvenience* (−.123) all significantly influence this outcome, plus there is a significant (−.076) effect for the

**Table 7** Multiple regression analysis for local food purchasing intentions and behaviour.

| | Standardized coefficients $\beta$ (standard error) | | | | | |
| | Aggregate model | | Cluster 1 | | Cluster 2 | |
| | Intentions | Behaviour | Intentions | Behaviour | Intentions | Behaviour |
|---|---|---|---|---|---|---|
| Intrinsic quality | .152 (.050)** | .160 (.055)** | .040 (.066) | .112 (.077)** | .230 (.079)** | .153 (.081)** |
| Local support and provenance | .387 (.043)** | .282 (.048)** | .312 (.078)** | .430 (.077)** | .315 (.060)** | .226 (.061)** |
| Ethical sustainability | .001 (.041) | −.036 (.045) | .058 (.057) | −.13 (.091) | −.69 (.060) | −.070 (.062) |
| Shopping benefits | .031 (.042) | .123 (.046)** | −.019 (.052) | .034 (.061) | .075 (.068) | .233 (.070)** |
| Product distracters | −.087 (.048)* | −.129 (.052)** | −.150 (.064)** | −.210 (.075)** | −.42 (.074) | −.059 (.076) |
| Buying inconvenience | −.182 (.045)** | −.156 (.050)** | −.123 (.068)* | −.040 (.080) | −.234 (.063)** | −.238 (.065)** |
| Location: Urban/rural | −.044 (.108) | −.060 (.118)* | −.076 (.144)* | −.108 (.168)** | −.039 (.162) | −.032 (.167) |
| Model $R^2$ | .46 | .39 | .23 | .18 | .28 | .26 |

**Significant at the $p < .01$ level; *significant at the $p < .05$ level. *Note*: Before assessing the two regression models, the variables were tested to ensure that they did not violate the necessary assumptions as outlined in Tabachnick and Fidell (2007).

dummy variable, indicating that urban consumers have a lower intention to buy compared with their rural counterparts. Similarly, when considering actual behaviour in this group, *local support and provenance* (.430), *product distracters* (−.210), and the location effect against urban consumers (−.108) are again significant. However, in this model, the effect of *buying inconvenience* is no longer significant, whereas there is now a positive significant effect for *intrinsic quality* (.11). In the cluster 2 models, there is a difference in $R^2$ values between intentions and behaviour of .28 compared with .26 respectively. In the model for intentions, *intrinsic quality* (.230), *local support and provenance* (.315), and *buying inconvenience* (−.234) are the only significant factors. The significant effects on behaviour come from the same three variables: *intrinsic quality* (.153), *local support and provenance* (.226), and *buying inconvenience* (−.238). However, for actual buying in this segment, the positive effect of *shopping benefits* (.226) is also significant. Key differences between the clusters reveal that, in cluster 2, three factors are significant, whilst they are not in cluster 1. One of these relates to the model for intentions (*intrinsic quality*) and two to the model for behaviour (*shopping benefits* and *buying inconvenience*). By way of contrast, in cluster 1, *product distracters* and the urban location factor are significant for both the models, whereas they are not significant in cluster 2.

## Discussion and conclusions

### Research implications

The range of factors identified from our analysis have been categorised as four drivers and two inhibitors of buying: *intrinsic quality*, *local support and provenance*, *ethical sustainability*, *shopping benefits*, *product distracters*, and *buying inconvenience*. Establishing these factors from empirical research provides a strong foundation for further understanding of how consumers make decisions in this important market, which can be viewed from several perspectives. When buying local foods, consumers are often choosing to do so for reasons that not only relate to the product itself but also their priorities and perceptions of food-related issues, such as support for local businesses and communities and a positive association with the environment and sustainable consumption. Further to this, the process of buying is fundamentally linked to the act of shopping, which can be regarded as a strong motive for buying local food because of the satisfaction that it may bring from that experience. Yet this aspect can also be regarded negatively, particularly from a convenience viewpoint and in relation to some of the specific issues that consumers have to encounter in the way that local produce is presented for sale and marketed. Recognising that consumers have a multifaceted appreciation of what local food buying can offer in terms of its extensive benefits, and the difficulties that they may encounter when acquiring it, makes a significant contribution to understanding local food shopping, and enriches the previous studies in the area. In particular, this work adds to the research of Tregear and Ness (2005) and Weatherell et al. (2003) who identify some similar influences on food buying behaviour in a local context. This study, however, provides more substantive outcomes, as it is a national study, and also looks specifically at the reasons for local food buying, which encompasses a number of different buying dimensions. These include not just food choice priorities but, in line with general shopping motivations theory, some additional facets of buying such as shopping-related benefits (Dawson, Bloch, & Ridgway, 1990) and drawbacks (Khan & Prior, 2010) and associated ethical and social responsibility issues (Megicks et al., 2008). Moreover, the complex nature of local food shopping, which involves trade-offs by consumers between the perceived advantages and shortcomings of purchasing, helps to provide insights into the differences between intentions to purchase and actual buying in this market. The gap between consumers' intentions to buy and what they actually purchase is clearly distinguishable in the local food market, which is a key feature of 'ethically motivated buying' (Carrigan & Attalla, 2001; Carrington et al., 2010) and related to negative buying factors such as price and availability outweighing the perceived positive outcomes (Vermeir & Verbeke, 2004). Here, as Peattie (1999) indicates, consumers are deciding when considering transactions around local food choices whether or not to engage in this form of behaviour.

Such variation in buying can be more fully understood if further analysis is undertaken to identify differences in the types of customer that may exist in the local food sector. Our research leads to two segments of local food buyers being identified based upon differences in their purchasing behaviour, the degree of emphasis given to different factors in buying decision making, and their demographic and locational characteristics. Direct comparison of the two groups, which were broadly similar in size across the total sample, indicates that they are clearly distinguishable in terms of the differences in emphasis given to the positive drivers of local food buying and the negative inhibitors, and the behaviour of consumers in each. The composition of cluster 1 in terms of it comprising older consumers concurs with research that has indicated that these consumers have a greater sense of social obligation (Carrigan, Szmigin, & Wright, 2004). Additionally, females are regarded as being strongly associated with ethical and environmentally concerned (Minton & Rose, 1997), and rural consumers identify with, and are interested in, environmental issues (Prothero, 1990). On the other hand, cluster 2 is depicted as having negative associations with local food buying through high scores on both the inhibitor factors. Its make-up with higher proportions of younger, male, and urban consumers is consistent with previous research in local food and ethical consumption (see Khan & Prior, 2010; Roberts, 1996).

The contribution that this study makes to understanding the factors of influence on consumer shopping behaviour in the local food sector is noteworthy, as it analyses the effects of a number of important drivers and inhibitors on both behavioural intentions and actual buying. The findings indicate that the most important factor in explaining both buying intentions and actual behaviour in this market is support for local business and the provenance of the food, which is consistent with the more general results of previous work (McEachern et al., 2010; Tregear & Ness, 2005). In addition, the results reveal that the intrinsic qualities of the food produce are important in influencing buying intentions and behaviour, especially in cluster 2. This may be partly due to the greater product range exposure of urban consumers in this segment having more choice, and having to make more discernible decisions relating to the benefits provided by the local produce. Another outcome of note is that the benefits of shopping for local food do not significantly influence behavioural intentions at any level, but affect actual behaviour in both the aggregate model and cluster 2. It is possible that these consumers make a retrospective judgement after they have engaged in a specific local food buying experience, and therefore do not see it as an important determinant of shopping for food before the event, but recognise it as being so in actual behaviour. In addition, it is interesting to note that the shopping benefits are not important in cluster 1 at all, which could suggest that they put greater emphasis on other factors, or are simply used to shopping in this way so do not see it as an 'out-of-the-ordinary' event in an experiential sense. Further to this, and of notable importance, are the effects of the ethical factor in all the models; although identified as a driver factor, the actual relationship between the consumer behaviour outcomes of local food buying and this variable are sometimes negative but insignificant. Even though previous research on this relationship is inconclusive (see Tregear & Ness, 2005), it is clear from the findings here that consumers buying local food is not associated with wider ethical and sustainability issues but rather focuses on the key immediate concern of support for the locality in which they reside. Consideration of the negative effects of the inhibiters shows that the product distracter factor and the inconvenience of buying local are both influential in explaining decreases in intentions and behaviour. The fact that these distracters are only significant in cluster 1 is of particular interest, as it suggests that the buying of members of this group will be negatively affected by an increase in this variable, whereas in cluster 2 there is not a significant effect on buying intentions and behaviour. In this latter segment, increasing the product distracters will not make a significant change to consumers purchasing, but buying inconvenience has a major influence and will deter people from buying, as these shoppers are more likely to be sensitive to increased inconvenience. This also translates into overall buying across both segments, but in cluster 1, increasing buying inconvenience does not significantly affect the actual purchasing behaviour of these customers, suggesting that they are prepared to accept some inconvenience in seeking out local food, or that they do not regard it as such. In sum, it is possible to conclude that some factors are clearly important in explaining behaviour across the local food sector as a whole, but analysis of the two distinguishable customer segments reveals variability in the extent to which different factors influence behavioural intentions and actual buying behaviour.

### *Practitioner implications*

The outcomes of this research have major implications for the producers and retailers of local food, particularly with regard to their future marketing effort. Identification of the key drivers and inhibitors of buying provide a focus for concentrating the marketing effort on promoting the main perceived benefits, whilst at the same time challenging the perceived drawbacks that discourage shoppers from buying. There are lessons to learn, therefore, for local food suppliers and retailers (large and small) when it comes to conveying relevant messages and enhancing this through appropriate service support. With local support and provenance being the most influential driver for buying behaviour and intentions, it must be incorporated into all external, in-store, and on-pack messages. Retail staff need to be made aware of this as the main selling point, and they should be able to communicate this effectively in their interaction with customers. Similarly, product features that make explicit the intrinsic qualities such as 'natural' and 'wholesome' should also be used as important positioning elements of marketing local food generally and specific product lines. Additionally, it is critical that suppliers ensure that the produce does actually meet the specific needs of customers in this respect: chemical and preservative free, a good appearance, freshness, and being available in required amounts. Effective marketing of local food relates equally to supermarket shopping and buying from independently owned outlets. However, promoting the shopping experience dimension of certain types of local food buying situations can provide a significant advantage for niche retailers who operate farm shops or pick-your-own outlets, and often further enhance the support for the local community and provenance benefits. A key message to convey to those responsible for marketing in this sector is that customers' buying is not affected by ethical and sustainability issues linked to the environment, and that although this may have been something that was considered a valid approach in the past, it is more likely to have a negative impact on behaviour in current market conditions. There are also important insights for producers and retailers in overcoming the distractive characteristics of local food buying, which has implications across a wide range of marketing activities, including clearer promotion and labelling, in particular, making customers aware of availability and ensuring that variety is provided. Similarly, suppliers and shopkeepers need to be cognisant of the way that price is communicated and addressing the perception that local produce is expensive. Furthermore, buying inconvenience can be a major barrier to local food shopping which can be tackled in a number of ways, including making more local food available through supermarket chains, and increasing the opportunities for access to local foods by increasing the numbers of available outlets (e.g. specialist traders, and traditional and farmers' markets). In addition, the perception that such inconvenience cannot be surmounted or is not worthwhile in terms of trading it off against the positive benefits could form the focus of a promotional effort that emphasises the main drivers of buying. The identification of the different buying types gives local food marketers a strong platform from which to target their activities, particularly in terms of product placement, promotional messages, in-store communications, packaging, and pricing. Notwithstanding the complexities of the varying influences on buying in the two segments, producers and retailers alike should be able to configure appropriate 'offers' to take account of the specific needs of different shoppers. What is important is the degree of emphasis given to each, which should be in line with customers' expectations relating to the drivers and inhibitors identified. Moreover, it is critical to be aware of any differences in the effects that each factor has on buying intentions and behaviour in the different shopper groups, and where such differences exist, appropriate emphasis is given to those factors that relate directly to actual buying by consumers.

### Limitations and further research

The research presented here is based upon extensive qualitative and quantitative investigation of a representative sample of local food shoppers in England. Its findings therefore may not hold up to generalisation in the UK as a whole, and in international contexts, particularly in economies that do not have complex agri-food chain systems and highly developed retail sectors. The opportunity to undertake a comparable study in other countries at a similar stage of development, or with more basic food chain infrastructures therefore exists. This research considers local food as a 'homogeneous' product class, whereas further research could be undertaken to investigate buying behaviour in different food categories, which may reveal varying results and have more specific implications for marketing at an individual category level. Although extensive multivariate analysis is undertaken, the cross-sectional data used only permit associations between buying behaviour and factors of influence to be identified. Further research using longitudinal data would allow more substantive findings in terms of cause and effect with regard to both buying intentions and actual purchasing. This could also be achieved by undertaking a more detailed analysis of the wealth of qualitative data collected in the focus groups that were used in this research to underpin and inform the quantitative survey work presented here. The opportunity exists to interrogate these data using interpretive techniques that may identify key relationships between the factors that affect buying in this context from the perspective of the different dimensions of shopping, and the complex trade-offs that are involved in buying local food.

# References

Arnold, M.J., & Reynolds, K.E. (2003). Hedonic shopping motivations. *Journal of Retailing*, 79, 77–95.

Babin, B.J., Darden, W.R., & Griffin, M. (1994). Work and/or fun: Measuring hedonic and utilitarian shopping value. *Journal of Consumer Research*, 20, 411–423.

Batra, R., & Ahtola O. (1991). Measuring the hedonic and utilitarian sources of consumer attitudes. *Marketing Letters*, 2, 159–170.

Carrigan, M., & Attalla, A. (2001). The myth of the ethical consumer: Do ethics matter in purchase behaviour? *Journal of Consumer Marketing*, 18(7), 560–578.

Carrigan, M., & de Pelsmacker, P. (2009). Will ethical consumers sustain their values in the global credit crunch? *International Marketing Review*, 26(6), 674–687.

Carrigan, M., Szmigin, I., & Wright, J. (2004). Shopping for a better world? An interpretive study of the potential for ethical consumption within the older market. *Journal of Consumer Marketing*, 21(6), 401–417.

Carrington, M.J., Neville, B.A., & Whitwell, G.J. (2010). Why ethical consumers don't walk their talk: Towards a framework for understanding the gap between the ethical purchase intentions and actual buying behaviour of ethically minded consumers. *Journal of Business Ethics*, 97(1), 139–158.

COI Communications/Food Standards Agency. (2003). *Local food: Report on qualitative research*. Food Standards Agency.

COI Communications/Food Standards Agency. (2007). Omnibus research report prepared for the Food Standards Agency. In W.R. Darden & F.D. Reynolds (1971). Shopping orientations and product usage roles. *Journal of Marketing Research*, 8, 505–508.

Darden, W.R., & Reynolds, F.D. (1971). Shopping Orientations and Product Usage Roles. *Journal of Marketing Research*, 8, 505–508.

Dawson, S., Bloch, P.H., & Ridgway, N.M. (1990). Shopping motives, emotional states, and retail outcomes. *Journal of Retailing*, 66(4), 408–427.

Department for Environment, Food and Rural Affairs. (2002). *The strategy for sustainable farming and food: Facing the future*. London: Defra.

de Pelsmacker, P., Driesen, L., & Rayp, G. (2005). Do consumers care about ethics? Willingness to pay for Fairtrade coffee. *The Journal of Consumer Affairs*, 39(2), 363–385.

DeVellis, R.F. (2003). *Scale development: Theory and applications* (2nd ed.). Thousand Oaks, CA: Sage.

Hair, J.F., Jr., Black, W.C., Babin, B.J., & Anderson, R.E. (2009). *Multivariate data analysis* (7th ed.). Upper Saddle River, NJ: Prentice Hall.

Harrison, R., Newholm, T., & Shaw, D. (Eds.). (2005). *The ethical consumer*. London: Sage.

Hirschman, E.C., & Holbrook, M.B. (1982). Hedonic consumption: Emerging concepts, methods and propositions. *Journal of Marketing*, 46, 92–101.

Institute of Grocery Distribution. (2005). *The local and regional food opportunity*. Watford, England: IGD.

Institute of Grocery Distribution. (2008). *Home or away – The role of provenance*. Watford, UK: IGD.

Jackson, T. (2005). Motivating sustainable consumption: A review of evidence on consumer behaviour and behavioural change, a report to the Sustainable Development Research Network. London: Policy Studies Institute.

Jarratt, D. (1996). A shopper taxonomy for retail strategy development. *The International Review of Retail, Distribution and Consumer Research*, 6(2), 196–215.

Khan, F., & Prior, C. (2010). Evaluating the urban consumer with regard to sourcing local food: A heart of England study. *International Journal of Consumer Studies*, 34, 161–168.

Klastonn, T. (1983). Assessing Cluster Analysis Results. *Journal of Marketing Research*, 20(1), 92–98.

Kline, P. (2000). *An easy guide to factor analysis*. London: Routledge.

Kruger, R.A., & Casey, M.A. (2000). *Focus groups: A practical guide for applied research* (3rd ed.). Thousand Oaks, CA: Sage.

Lincoln, Y., & Guba, E. (1985). *Naturalistic inquiry*. Beverly Hills, CA: Sage.

McEachern, M.G., Warnaby, G., Carrigan, M., & Szmigin, I. (2010). Thinking locally, acting locally? Conscious consumers and farmers' markets. *Journal of Marketing Management*, 26(5/6), 395–412.

Megicks, P., Memery, J., & Williams, J. (2008). Influences on ethical and socially responsible shopping: Evidence from the UK grocery sector. *Journal of Marketing Management*, 24(5–6), 637–659.

Miller, D. (1998). *A theory of shopping*. Cambridge, England: Polity.

Mintel. (2011). *Food provenance – UK*. London: Mintel.

Minton, A.P., & Rose, R.L. (1997). The Effects of Environmental Concern on Environmentally Friendly Consumer Behaviour: An Exploratory Study. *Journal of Business Research*, 40, 37–48.

Morris, C., & Buller, H. (2003). The local food sector: A preliminary assessment of its form and impact in Gloucestershire. *British Food Journal*, 105(8), 559–566.

ONS. (2003). Retrieved from: http://www.statistics.gov.uk/geography/downloads/uk_gor_cty.pdf

Nunnally, J., & Bernstein, I. (1994). *Psychometric theory* (3rd ed.). New York: McGraw Hill.

Pearson, D., Henryks, J., Trott, A., Jones, P., Parker, G., Dumaresq, D., et al. (2011). Local food: Understanding consumer motivations in innovative retail formats. *British Food Journal*, 113(7), 886–899.

Peattie, K. (1999). Trappings versus substance in the greening of marketing planning. *Journal of Strategic Marketing*, 7, 131–148.

Peter, J.P. (1981). Construct validity: A review of psychometric basic issues and recent marketing practices. *Journal of Marketing Research*, 18(2), 133–145.

Prothero, A. (1990), Green consumerism and the societal marketing concept: Marketing strategies for the 1990s. *Journal of Marketing Management*, 6(2), 87–103.

Punj, G., & Stewart, D.W. (1983). Cluster analysis in marketing research: Review and suggestions for application. *Journal of Marketing Research*, XX, 134–148.

Ricketts Hein, J., Ilbery, B., & Kneafsey, M. (2006). Distribution of local food activity in England and Wales: An index of food relocalization. *Regional Studies*, 40, 289–301.

Roberts, J.A. (1996). Green consumers in the 1990s: Profile and implications for advertising. *Journal of Business Research*, 36(3), 217–231.

SERIO (Socio-Economic Research and Intelligence Observatory). (2008). *Understanding of consumer attitudes and actual purchasing behaviour with reference to local and regional foods*. London: Defra.

Seyfang, G. (2007). Growing sustainable consumption communities: The case of local organic food networks. *International Journal of Sociology and Social Policy*, 27(3/4), 120–134.

Sherry, J.F., Jr. (1990). A sociocultural analysis of a Midwestern American flea market. *Journal of Consumer Research*, 17, 13–30.

Tabachnick, B.G., & Fidell, L.S. (2007). *Using multivariate statistics* (5th ed.). Boston: Allyn & Bacon/Pearson Education.

Tauber, E.M. (1972). Why do people shop? *Journal of Marketing*, 36, 46–49.

Tian, K., Bearden, W., & Hunter, G. (2001). Consumers' need for uniqueness: Scale development and validation. *Journal of Consumer Research*, 28, 50–66.

Tregear, A., & Ness, M. (2005). Discriminant analysis of consumer interest in buying locally produced foods. *Journal of Marketing Management*, 21, 19–35.

Vermeir, I., & Verbeke, W. (2004). *Sustainable food consumption: Exploring the consumers attitude–behaviour gap*. Unpublished master's thesis, Ghent University, Belgium.

Weatherell, C., Tregear, A., & Allinson, J. (2003). In search of the concerned consumer: UK public perceptions of food, farming and buying local. *Journal of Rural Studies*, 19, 233–244.

Westbrook, R.A., & Black, W.C. (1985). A Motivation-based shopper typology. *Journal of Retailing*, 61(1), 78–103.

Woodruffe-Burton, H., & Wakenshaw, S. (2011). Revisiting experiential values of shopping: Consumers' self and identity. *Marketing Intelligence and Planning*, 29(1), 69–85.

Zepeda, L., & Deal, D. (2009). Organic and local food consumer behaviour: Alphabet theory. *International Journal of Consumer Studies*, 33, 697–705.

# CONTEMPORARY ISSUES IN GREEN AND ETHICAL MARKETING

**Appendix**. Local food items remaining after content and face validity and supporting quotes.

| Local food item | Supporting quote |
| --- | --- |
| ***Drivers:*** | |
| I buy local produce because it is free from preservatives | 'They've got no preservatives in them and that's a good sign' (Brighton)<br>'. . . if you buy fresh from the baker, it's not going to be loaded with preservatives' (Esher) |
| I buy local produce because it is free from chemicals | 'But they're [local veg] not sprayed are they; you know how they're grown and I think that's really important' (Esher)<br>'No chemicals on it' (Ripon) |
| I buy local produce because it is natural | 'It's healthier . . . more natural' (Reading)<br>'A lot of local produce, because you can buy it from sources, it's more of a natural state' (East Grinstead) |
| I buy local produce because it is wholesome | 'Much better for you' (Norwich)<br>'The less additives the better – organic, sugar-free' (Bristol) |
| I buy local produce because it has a good appearance | 'I expect something that looks perfect' (Brighton)<br>'[Local food] . . . it looks good and fresh' (Crowthorne) |
| I buy local produce because I can buy the amount I want | 'You can choose which bit you want and how much you want, even the broccoli' (Diss)<br>'You don't have to buy a bag of potatoes. If you want one potato and one carrot you can go and do that' (Birmingham) |
| I buy local produce because it lasts longer | 'If it's fresher, it's likely to last longer with fruit' (Edgware)<br>'A lot of market fruit and veg lasts a long time' (Stourbridge) |
| I buy local produce because it supports local producers | '. . . support your local farmers . . . I'm happy to do that' (Newcastle)<br>'You're supporting the local growers and farms, supporting your own community, you feel like you're part of it, you're sustaining each other' (Reading) |
| I buy local produce because it supports local retailers | 'I really like supporting local businesses' (Brighton)<br>'You're supporting the local shops; you're getting a good rapport going with them'(Colne) |
| I buy local produce because I know where it comes from | 'You know where it's come from' (Nottingham)<br>'I know if I buy meat from the farm then it comes from that farm' (Bristol) |
| I buy local produce because it reduces food miles | 'I'd rather have stuff that's local because it hasn't travelled so far' (Norwich)<br>'If it was local, I would favour it more because it hasn't had the transportation time' (East Grinstead) |

*(Continued)*

**Appendix**. (Continued).

| Local food item | Supporting quote |
|---|---|
| I buy local produce because it is environmentally friendly | 'It's helping the environment as well really' (Norwich)<br>'Environmentally friendly is definitely high on the list. I'd go for organic and free-range as well' (Colne) |
| I buy local produce because it is ethical | 'A moral and a health choice' (Colne)<br>'Morally . . . [I] don't want any green beans flown in from Kenya' (Crowthorne) |
| I buy local produce because shopping for it brings back memories of the past | 'My mother bought me a leg of Welsh lamb . . . They've just come back from Wales and that's where she comes from and she goes to the local butcher who she knew as a child and got four legs of lamb' (Brighton)<br>'My parents always buy local produce; it's how I've been brought up. My mum always bought her vegetables from a stall, and I really remember that and . . . local fruit and veg' (Brighton) |
| I buy local produce because shopping for it is fun | 'it's more for fun' (East Grinstead)<br>'I buy local fruit and vegetables and PYO whenever fruit comes in season . . . it's always a fun thing to do' (Reading) |
| I buy local produce because it is nostalgic | 'I miss the days when you could market shop with your mum' (Leeds)<br>'I can remember on a Saturday, my Nan used to have a greengrocer van come round and you used to stand on the back of it and buy your vegetables' (Esher) |
| I buy local produce because I feel guilty if I do not | '[Fresh local Christmas turkey] . . . was £30 or something, and it was boned and it was massive, it was for 18 people and it was delicious and it really made me feel good' (East Grinstead)<br>'Conscience, just . . . the need to support our local farmers' (Edgware) |
| I buy local produce because the shopping experience is satisfying | 'I go [to a local farm] once a week in the season, and it's a therapeutic thing, picking strawberries and raspberries and there's a lark singing. You don't get that in Tesco!' (Crowthorne)<br>'As soon as I knew it was good for me, that was part of the shopping experience for me' (Leeds) |
| **Inhibitors:** | |
| I don't buy local produce because the range of products is limited | '[A disadvantage of buying local foods is] choice' (Edgware)<br>'the lack of variety' (Newcastle) |
| I don't buy local produce because food produced elsewhere is sometimes better | 'You just don't associate wine with England' (Birmingham)<br>'It's not good quality [compared with France]' (Bristol) |

*(Continued)*

# CONTEMPORARY ISSUES IN GREEN AND ETHICAL MARKETING

**Appendix**. (Continued).

| Local food item | Supporting quote |
|---|---|
| I don't buy local produce because it is not well promoted | 'It would be good if [supplier] did a week where they did a promotion, to promote something that was locally grown and really push it, but they don't really' (Manchester)<br>'They've got to advertise it, because we're not even aware' (Stourbridge) |
| I don't buy local produce because it is not well labelled | 'In France, where I come from, you tend to buy what is right at the right time. In England, unless you know what's in season, no-one tells you' (Bristol)<br>'They say it's a local farmers' market, you expect it to be local, but you don't really know . . . They don't label it to say "we are from Evesham"' (Stourbridge) |
| I don't buy local produce because the price is not always clear | 'If I do find a butcher . . . you think "that much?" . . . because when it's pre-packed you know what you're going to pay. I feel too embarrassed to ask how much one chop is . . . embarrassed by the cost' (South London)<br>'There's a local shop I like to go to . . . they've got everything in little packets' (St Austell) |
| I don't buy local produce because it is not readily available | 'If you live in the country or nearer a farm, you have access to the local products, but if you live in a city you have to buy from a supermarket; that's just the way society works' (Leeds)<br>'Supply – it's not always available' (Edgware) |
| I don't buy local produce because it is expensive | 'I wouldn't pay the price that you have to pay for those. The fruit to me is gorgeous but I just can't afford some of the prices. It's down to money most of time' (Long Eaton)<br>'They're more expensive definitely . . . Yes, that puts me off' (Morpeth) |
| I don't buy local produce because to do so is time-consuming | 'The fact that if you've got to buy different things from different places then it's very, very time consuming' (Manchester)<br>'To a lot of people, the biggest barrier is time' (Colne) |
| I don't buy local produce because it requires extra effort | 'I think with things like the organic and local produce, it's not as accessible. You've got to go out of your way to order it or go to a specialist shop' (East Grinstead)<br>'If I had the time and the choice, I would choose local, but it's easier sometimes to grab what's there' (Newcastle) |
| I don't buy local produce because it is inconvenient | 'Fast food is easy' (Newcastle)<br>'It's the real convenience stuff [I buy] – frozen foods and packed meals' (East Grinstead) |

*(Continued)*

# CONTEMPORARY ISSUES IN GREEN AND ETHICAL MARKETING

**Appendix**. (Continued).

| Local food item | Supporting quote |
| --- | --- |
| I don't buy local produce because I have to travel farther to do so | 'Your butcher just down here, and you have to go all down North Street for fresh fruit and veg – it's the distance' (Ripon)<br>'The time to make a special journey. You still have to go to the supermarket to get all the other stuff; it's an extra' (Crowthorne) |

# A cross-cultural analysis of pro-environmental consumer behaviour among seniors

Lynn Sudbury Riley, *Liverpool John Moores University, UK*
Florian Kohlbacher, *German Institute for Japanese Studies (DIJ), Japan*
Agnes Hofmeister, *Corvinus University of Budapest, Hungary*

---

**Abstract** This paper presents the results of a cross-national study into the ecologically conscious consumer behaviour of senior consumers (aged 50+, mean age 64 years) in the UK, Germany, Japan, and Hungary. Using a survey, the study ($n = 1275$) utilises a modified version of the Ecologically Conscious Consumer Behaviour Scale, in addition to a battery of variables to measure wider ethical purchasing behaviour and sociodemographic characteristics. Findings suggest that there are segments of older consumers in all countries under study who demonstrate ecologically conscious consumer behaviour, and at the same time there are segments that do not. These segments cannot be identified by sociodemographic variables, but do differ in their wider ethical purchasing behaviour. The study is the first of its kind to measure actual ecologically conscious consumer behaviour in the senior market across different nations.

---

## Introduction

Over the last decade, there have been significant and important additions to the body of knowledge pertaining to contemporary issues in ethical and environmental marketing. However, four notable gaps remain. First, research into ethical issues is still dominated by corporate, as opposed to consumer, ethics (Schlegelmilch & Oberseder, 2010). Second, cross-cultural consumer ethics is still very much under researched (Newholm & Shaw, 2007; Ramsey, Marshall, Johnston, & Deeter-Schmelz, 2007). Third, there is a noted attitude–behaviour gap, in that 'there appears to be a gap between what consumers say about the importance of ethical issues and what they do at the checkout counter' (Auger & Devinney, 2007, p. 361). Finally, Vitell, Lumpkin, and Rawwas (1991) noted more than a decade ago that virtually no studies have examined the ethical beliefs of elderly consumers, despite the fact that this 'represents an important and rapidly growing segment of the population' (p. 366), and with only a few exceptions (Carrigan, Szmigin, & Wright, 2004) this situation remains as true today as it was then. The research presented here was designed based on these gaps, and presents the results of a cross-national survey into the ecologically conscious consumer behaviour of senior consumers. In so doing, it also concentrates on four nations (UK, Japan, Germany, and Hungary) which are important from a senior consumer perspective, and yet previous research conducted in these nations lags far behind what is known about the older consumer in the United States.

The paper begins with a review of current knowledge pertaining to overall ethical consumer behaviour and beliefs, before presenting an overview of the importance of older consumers in the nations under study. The review section finishes with a summary of the small amounts of literature which focuses on older consumers and ethical consumption. Details of the measurement instruments and methods used to collect the data in the four nations are then presented, before moving onto the results, which, due to issues of measurement invariance, are presented on a country-by-county basis. Nevertheless, tentative cross-national comparisons are made in the subsequent discussion section. The paper concludes with implications for managers and sets out a research agenda.

## Ethical consumer behaviour and beliefs

The ethical consumer movement is now well recognised (Carrigan & Attalla, 2001; Harrison, Newholm, & Shaw, 2006), with the term 'ethical consumer behaviour' incorporating a variety of consumption activities, including the purchasing of Fairtrade and environmentally friendly products and the conscious boycotting of products that have been produced by companies with a poor ethical reputation. Ethical consumer behaviour is without doubt increasing, and the UK is now the biggest market in Europe for Fairtrade goods (Varul & Wilson-Kovacs, 2008), with consumption of ethical products and services in the UK rising by 15% between 2006 and 2007 to an estimated value of £35.5 billion (Co-operative Bank, 2008). While the Japanese Fairtrade market is still comparatively small, it has been showing tremendous growth rates in recent years, pointing to a new consumption trend in Japan (Kohlbacher & Langbecker, 2010). The phenomenal growth in ethical products, spurred partly by the Fairtrade movement which provided an alternative model of trade, gave many companies a radical edge (Low & Davenport, 2005). Indeed, it has been argued that this radical edge became a source of competitive advantage which attracted the attention of major companies, and today Fairtrade, Rainforest Alliance, and other ethical products are found in mainstream as opposed to niche markets (Doherty & Tranchell, 2007).

This shift from niche to mainstream is producing a parallel shift in the way researchers view ethical consumption. Ethical purchasing, and indeed the boycotting of unethical brands, has long been recognised as a way of expressing one's political and moral concerns (Irving, Harrison, & Rayner, 2002; Sassatelli, 2006; Shaw, 2007). However, as Low and Davenport (2007) suggest, the move of ethical products from niche to mainstream high street has resulted in the dilution of highly politicised programmes into the belief among many people that product choices can create social and political change. Given that today's seniors comprise 'the Woodstock generation', it is reasonable to assume that they would not be afraid to utilise their significant purchasing power for political reasons. At the same time, perceived consumer effectiveness has been shown to moderate pro-environmental behaviour

(Kim & Choi, 2005; Laskova, 2007). Thus it may be that some seniors, who are all too used to being ignored by marketers and advertisers (Carrigan & Szmigin, 1999; Simcock & Sudbury, 2006), may perceive their behaviour to be of little effect.

One major problem identified in the literature is the so-called 'attitude–behaviour gap'. As Cowe and Williams (2000) point out, far more consumers profess to care about ethical issues than actually purchase ethical products, while Schröder and McEachern (2004) note that while claiming to be ethical, some consumers delegate responsibility for ethical standards to the corporation. Moreover, Carrigan and Attalla (2001) note that consumer sophistication does not necessarily equate to ethical consumption. Thus awareness of ethical products, and indeed approval of them, does not guarantee purchase, and other factors need to be considered (Szmigin, Carrigan, & McEachern, 2008). One constant factor in the literature is price. It would appear that consumers are unwilling to pay a large premium in order to put their beliefs into practice (Sudbury & Böltner, 2010). Iwanow, McEachern, and Jeffrey (2005) found price and quality to have greater influence on purchase decisions for clothing items, while, importantly, their study found price to be the primary influence affecting purchase decision among older consumers in Gap. McEachern, Warnaby, Carrigan and Szmigin (2010) also found that for some consumers the price-hike to buy ethical products was just too great, leading them to conclude, 'conscious consumers perceive limits to their ethical behaviours arising from . . . cost, even though they have an "ethical" orientation toward consumption' (p. 406). One important study (Loureiro, McCluskey, & Mittelhammer, 2002), which assessed consumer's willingness to pay for eco-labelled apples, found that females with strong environmental and food safety concerns were willing to pay more, but that this was only a small amount, leading these authors to conclude that it is difficult to get the balance right between environmentally friendly products and positioning and price. Of particular note is that this study was conducted in a grocery store. Thus the usual problems of recall with survey data were avoided, and of equal importance was the sample, which was upscale in comparison to the general population of the United States. Thus it seems as though ability to pay does not equate to willingness to pay a premium for environmentally friendly or ethically produced goods. Indeed, Pepper, Jackson, and Uzzell (2009) send out the reminder that energy use is related primarily to income and household size – not consumer's ethical and pro-environmental beliefs. Overall, then, it appears that price is a far more important issue to many consumers than are ethical issues. Indeed, Carrigan and Attalla (2001) discuss the 'depressing reality is that many ethical abuses can still continue to be carried out by companies without any negative impact on consumer buyer behaviour' (p. 571). This attitude–behaviour gap is well recognised across a number of studies conducted with different demographics and in a variety of countries (Auger, Burke, Devinney, & Louviere, 2003; Chatzidakis, Hibbert, & Smith, 2007; Eckhardt, Belk, & Devinney, 2010; Schröder & McEachern, 2005; Szmigin et al., 2008).

In contrast to studies that concentrate on older consumers, there is a body of literature that investigates cross-national and cross-cultural ethical issues. However, the gap comes from the lack of studies pertaining to ethical consumer behaviour across borders, as opposed to ethical beliefs and attitudes. Previous multinational investigations include a study into the perceived role of ethics and corporate social responsibility (Vitell & Paolillo, 2004), business ethics (Whipple & Swords, 1992), and Machiavellianism (Al-Khatib, D'Suria Stanton, & Rawwas, 2005).

Research into ethical consumption and ethical beliefs has identified a number of underlying antecedents, which include the pro-environmental behaviour of others (Pieters, Bijmolt, van Raaij, & de Kruijk, 1998), overall environmental consciousness (Schlegelmilch, Bohlen, & Diamantopoulous, 1996), perceived consumer effectiveness (Straughan & Roberts, 1999), values (Pepper et al., 2009), environmental consciousness and willingness to pay (Vlosky, Ozanne, & Fontenot, 1999), the modified Theory of Planned Behaviour (Shaw, Shiu, & Clarke, 2000), religiosity (Vitell & Paolillo, 2003), and attitudes towards business (Vitell, Singh, & Paolillo, 2007). However, previous research has shown socio-demographics to be poor determinants of ethical purchasing behaviour, with Schlegelmilch, Diamantopoulos, and Bohlen (1994) concluding, 'there is very little value in the use of socio-demographic characteristics for profiling environmentally-conscious consumers in the UK' (p. 343). Roberts (1996) found sex, income, education, and age to be significant predictors of ecologically conscious consumer behaviour, but these variables explained only 6% of the variance. This increased to 45% when he added attitudinal variables to his regression model.

While some studies have found no gender differences (Carrigan & Attalla, 2001), several have found females to be significantly more likely to demonstrate ethical attitudes than their male counterparts (Laroche, Bergeron, & Barbaro-Forleo, 2001; Loureiro et al., 2002), and Roberts (1996) found this pattern to be true for ecologically conscious consumer behaviour. More importantly, one of the few socio-demographic characteristics that does differentiate ethical beliefs is age. Age has been found to be a significant determinant in most of the ethical beliefs measured by Vitell et al. (2007); older adults have been shown to reject questionable activities (Swaidan, Vitell, & Rawwas, 2003; Vitell et al., 1991) and show a higher level of agreement with a code of ethics (Kim & Choi, 2003) than younger people, as well as be more positive towards Fairtrade (De Pelsmacker, Janssens, Sterckx, & Mielants, 2006), more environmentally concerned (Sandahl & Robertson, 1989), differ in their perceptions of unethical sales tactics, (Ramsey et al. 2007), and display higher levels of ecologically conscious consumer behaviour (Roberts, 1996).

## The senior consumer

The current ageing of the world's population is probably the most profound demographic change in the history of humankind. It is a pervasive and truly global phenomenon, without precedent or parallel, largely irreversible, and, with the young populations of the past, unlikely to occur again. Indeed, at the world level, the number of older persons will exceed the number of children by 2047, which has already occurred in many developed regions. The profundity of this demographic change will impact on economic growth, labour markets, pensions, health care, housing, migration, politics, and of course consumption (UN, 2007). Although retirement ages, and indeed median age, differ across countries, tentatively it can be suggested that senior consumers are those aged 50 and above. Consensus among gerontologists (e.g. English Longitudinal Study of Ageing), charities (e.g. Age UK), academics (Carrigan, 1998; Simcock, Sudbury, & Wright, 2006), and practitioners (e.g. SilverSurfers.net, SAGA) has resulted in age 50 becoming the inclusion point for studies, policies, and target markets. Globally, therefore, according to the US Census

**Table 1** Age classifications by country.

|  | Japan | Germany | UK | Hungary |
|---|---|---|---|---|
| UN ageing league table position | 1 | 3 | 17 | 19 |
| Per cent of population aged 65+ | 23 | 20 | 17 | 17 |
| Size of senior consumer market (millions) | 57 | 30 | 20 | 3.7 |

Bureau (2011), the over-50s market comprises 1.4 billion consumers, or 20.8% of the world's population.

Despite the importance of this market in terms of its size and indeed purchasing power, it remains an under-researched segment. This situation is particularly true of research conducted on seniors outside the United States (Kohlbacher & Chéron, 2010; Kohlbacher, Sudbury, & Hofmeister, 2011). The present study therefore makes a contribution to knowledge by focusing on four disparate nations (Japan, UK, Germany, Hungary) outside the United States, all of which are important from an older consumer perspective. Table 1 presents the United Nation's ageing population league table position, percentage of population over 65 years, and the number of adults who are classified as senior consumers (aged 50+) in each of these countries.

Japan is the country most severely affected by the demographic shift (Coulmas, 2007; Coulmas, Conrad, Schad-Seifert, & Vogt, 2008). Its population started to shrink in 2005, and as of October 2010, people aged 65 and older account for more than 23% of the population, the highest ratio in the world. Japanese private households with heads 50 years of age and older spend considerably more money per head than the age group between 30 and 49, and this high purchasing power of seniors also stems from their financial wealth. As a matter of fact, according to the latest estimates from 2009, older people hold a disproportionately large amount of personal financial assets, with those in their 50s and their 60s owning 21% and 31% respectively of the total, and those aged 70 years and older holding 28%, which means that people aged 50 years and older hold about 80% of total personal financial assets in Japan (Nikkei Weekly, 2010a). Older consumers in Japan thus obviously form an attractive market segment, and they have already overtaken younger age groups in terms of average household purchasing power and consumption, a trend that is forecast to increase even further over the next three years (Nikkei Weekly, 2010b). This is also one of the reasons why experts have pointed to the fact that managers and marketers around the globe can learn from experimenting in the Japanese lead market and why some foreign companies have already invested to take advantage of attractive opportunities represented by the demographic trend in Japan (Kohlbacher, Gudorf, & Herstatt, 2011).

Currently, the business world in Japan is highly attentive to the baby boomer generation, which represents the most important group of older customers (Dentsu Shinia Purojekuto, 2007; Hakuhodo Institute, 2003). The Japanese baby boomers – those born between 1947 and 1951 – have always been highly active, energetic, and consumption-oriented, and formed a wealthy subgroup, being curious about technological innovations and having a shopping-related mentality (McCreery, 2000). Along with retirement comes newly gained free time. This is the reason why the baby boomer generation, which has high purchasing power and propensity to consume, is a very attractive potential target group for companies in the silver market (Kohlbacher, 2011; Sekizawa, 2008).

Germany is ranked third in the ageing league tables produced by the UN, with a median age of 43 years (CIA, 2011). Population projections indicate that the old-age dependency ratio will almost double over the next 50 years in Germany (Hoffman & Menning, 2004). Indeed, according to Eitner, Enste, Naegele, and Leve (2011), while approximately every fifth inhabitant of Germany was older than 65 in 2008, it is expected that by 2060 this will apply to every third inhabitant. At the same time, following the projections, the share of younger inhabitants below the age of 20 will fall from 19% in 2008 to 15% in 2060. According to the data, the number of adults 65 years and older will increase from around 16.5 million at present to approximately 22 million in 2060, and approximately 14% (9 million) will be 80 years and older (Statistisches Bundesamt, 2009). During recent years, the expenditures on private consumption in households with persons aged 65 and older rose far above average. In 2007, the 55–65 age group showed slightly above average consumption, spending €2137 per month (compared to the national average of €2067 per month). At the same time, this rise in consumption is markedly higher than the rise in income. In other words, the growth in consumption is effected at the expense of saving (Deutsches Institut fuer Wirtschaftsforschung, 2007; Statistisches Bundesamt, 2009).

The German 50-plus group consists of approximately 30 million people who have spent a large part of their lives in a divided nation, giving them a specific set of experiences. Apart from this influence, these consumers are also influenced by when they were born; some of them experienced two World Wars, as well as economic crises, and the so-called baby boomers 'have largely been influenced by the hippie movement, Woodstock and the idea of sexual liberation' (Leyhausen & Vossen, 2011, p. 177).

The UK is ranked 17th from a total of 192 countries in the United Nation's league table on population ageing, and the median age in the UK is 40.5 years. According to the Office for National Statistics (ONS, 2009), life expectancy is now 81.5 for females and 77 for males (which is in stark contrast to life expectancy in 1901 which was 49 and 45 years respectively (ONS, 2004)). The addition of the baby boomers (the UK baby boom comprises those born 1947–1964) to this group has resulted in the emergence of a market comprising more than 20 million people, a 45% increase over five decades. This number is projected to increase by a further 36% by 2031, when there will be 27.2 million people aged 50 and over (ONS, 2004). Moreover, better nutrition and advances in health care have led to suggestions that a *healthy* life expectancy is increasing (Academy of Medical Sciences, 2009). Although there are pockets of very real deprivation in this segment (Arber, 2004), there is also a large degree of relative affluence and financial wellness (Baek & DeVaney, 2004). There are groups within this cohort, particularly those who came to maturity during the 1960s, who experienced a distinct zeitgeist characterised by abundance, education, opportunity, diversity, and freedom, leading to high levels of self-reliance and optimism (McKean Skaff, 2006). Moreover, in many respects, it was the baby boomers who *shaped* modern marketing in the UK (Thompson & Thompson, 2007), and consumers aged 50–64 years are amongst the highest spenders on a range of products and services in the UK (ONS, 2009).

Hungary is ranked 19th in the UN (2007) population ageing league tables, with a median age of 39.7 years (CIA, 2011). It is an important country on which to focus because it already has the oldest population in Eastern Europe, and projections indicated that by 2010 its proportion of over 55s was higher than that for the United States (Velkoff, 1992). Recognition of the implications of Hungary's ageing population came in the recent altering of the official retirement age, which is also the age that a person is recognised as 'elderly', when it was increased from 60 to 65 years (Monostori, 2009). While some older Hungarians still live in poverty, comparative studies indicate that pensioner households have improved their relative income position during the economic transition, and indeed the incidence of poverty among the Hungarian old is lower than among all other age groups (UN, 2009). Moreover, compared to salaries, pensions in Hungary are higher than the European average (Monostori, 2009).

## Senior consumers and ethical behaviour

An unexpected finding to emerge from a recent qualitative diary study into seniors and packaging (Sudbury & Simcock, 2010) was the level of concern shown by many older adults regarding packaging's environmental impact. Whilst the study revealed them to be consumers of high quality and expensive products, perhaps somewhat paradoxically these diaries also showed them to be socially and environmentally concerned and assiduous recyclers. Senior consumers are 'increasingly likely to be among the ranks of the ethically motivated and adventurous' (Szmigin, Maddock, & Carrigan, 2003, p. 548). Moreover, a study conducted in Belgium (De Pelsmacker et al., 2006) found 'the older the respondents, the more positive they tended to be towards Fairtrade issues. Inclination to action, concern and buying behaviour increased with age ... and older people appeared to be more positive about the price level of Fairtrade products' (p. 134). Indeed, an interpretive study conducted by Carrigan et al. (2004) led these authors to suggest that 'older consumers are a significant force within the consumer resistance movement ... they are inherently diverse in nature, yet present some consistency in their attitudes towards certain aspects of ethical purchasing' (pp. 412–413). Yet, an extensive literature review has failed to uncover a single large-scale study that focuses on the actual ethical purchasing behaviour of older consumers.

## Method

The study comprised part of a major piece of international research into older consumers across several culturally disparate nations, and utilised questionnaires. The lower age parameter of 50 was selected on the basis that this is (a) the most commonly used definition in the relevant literature (Moschis & Ong, 2011), and (b) the starting point for many age-related services offered to older consumers (e.g. SAGA, Silverserfer.net). The questionnaire was translated and back translated by teams in Japan, Germany, and Hungary before being piloted across all four countries. Several adjustments to the original questionnaire were made based on piloting (see below for details of scale adjustment). Three lists were purchased – one German ($n = 6000$), one British ($n = 5000$), and one Japanese ($n = 1044$) – that contained randomly selected names and addresses of people aged 50+, and a questionnaire and pre-paid envelope was posted to them all. Piloting in Hungary demonstrated the difficulties of self-completion among many older Hungarian adults. Thus the distribution strategy was adapted in that country, and consequently a team of trained

**Table 2** Sample characteristics by nationality and age.

| Country | n | Mean age | Std. deviation |
|---|---|---|---|
| UK | 450 | 66.27 | 8.277 |
| Germany | 213 | 63.15 | 8.396 |
| Japan | 412 | 63.87 | 8.484 |
| Hungary | 200 | 58.66 | 5.635 |
| *Total* | *1275* | *63.78* | *8.392* |

researchers administered the questionnaire face-to-face to 200 adults aged 50+. This resulted in a usable sample of 1275 seniors, details of which are provided in Table 2.

Respondents completed an adapted version of the Ecologically Conscious Consumer Behaviour (ECCB) Scale (Roberts, 1996; Roberts & Bacon, 1997). The scale was chosen because it measures actual ecologically conscious purchase behaviour (e.g. 'I have switched products for environmental reasons' and 'When there is a choice, I always choose the product that contributes to the least amount of environmental damage'), as opposed to intentions or attitudes. Indeed, given the major attitude–behaviour gap outlined in the literature, it was felt that the ECCB was superior to alternatives precisely because it appears to measure actual as opposed to intended behaviour. Piloting revealed that respondents perceived there to be too much similarity between some of the items (e.g. 'I buy toilet paper made from recycled paper', 'I buy Kleenex made from recycled paper', 'I buy paper towels made from recycled paper', and 'I make every effort to buy paper products from recycled paper' comprised four individual items). Thus these were merged into a single item ('I make every effort to buy paper products (toilet paper, tissues, etc.) made from recycled paper'). Some terminology was also amended, for example the term 'pollution' was replaced with 'environmental damage'. This process resulted in an adapted ECCB scale consisting of 11 items, measured using the standard five-point Likert-type scale comprising 'never true', 'rarely true', 'sometimes true', 'mostly true', and 'always true'. A higher score is indicative of a greater level of ECCB.

In recognition that the concept of environmentalism is broadly defined yet the ECCB scale is rather limited, a battery of questions pertaining to Fairtrade, ethical financial products, freedom foods, and animal testing were included in the questionnaire. These latter variables were included because they have been often ignored in previous studies (McEachern, Schröder, Willock, Whitelock, & Mason, 2007). These comprised 'When there is a choice, I choose the Fairtrade option for all food products', 'When there is a choice, I choose the Fairtrade option for all clothing products', 'When there is a choice, I choose ethical financial products and investments', 'When there is a choice, I choose the free-range/freedom food option', and 'I do not buy cosmetics and toiletries that have been tested on animals'. The original four response categories of 'always', 'most of the time', 'occasionally', and 'never' were extended to five ('I am unaware of these choices') after piloting revealed some seniors were unaware of some of these choices.

Additionally, respondents were asked about their actual behaviour relating to whether or not they had ever taken action (e.g. taken part in a demonstration, written to an organisation, used an Internet forum, or attended an event, etc.) about any ethical, environmental, or conservation issue which they felt strongly about, and whether or not they (a) were members of any environmental group or cause, or (b) regularly donated to any environmental charities.

Finally, respondents completed a battery of sociodemographic questions. These questions included the usual sociodemographic variables of gender, income (in bands), socio-economic status (ascertained by asking people what their job is or was if they were already retired), and work status (working, retired, unemployed, housewife). Three types of age (chronological, cognitive, and age identity) were also included because chronological age has been shown to have many limitations when using an older sample (Sudbury, 2004; Szmigin & Carrigan, 2000). Cognitive age (Barak & Schiffman, 1981) is a multidimensional method of measuring self-perceived age that is now used extensively in marketing research, and has been used successfully across cultures (Barak, Mathur, Zhang, Lee, & Erondu, 2003; Guiot, 2001; Kohlbacher & Chéron, 2010; Ong, Yap-Ying, & Abessi, 2009; Sudbury, 2004). Age identity is a gerontology scale which asks people to categorise themselves as young, middle-aged, or old, and is the most popular technique amongst gerontologists for measuring self-perceived age (Barak, 1987). Additionally, respondents were asked if they had children and grandchildren. The rationale for these latter questions was the assumption that those with progeny may view the issue of sustainability differently to those who are childless.

Research undertaken in a small number of countries can provide rich insights into national-level factors that are not well understood, but it precludes generalisations, and theory testing may not be appropriate (Cadogan, 2010). Indeed, had the purpose of the study been to test theory, confirmatory factor analysis would have been the next step. However, given the pioneering nature of the current study, the dearth of previous large-scale multinational research into older adults and their ethical purchasing behaviour, and the lack of appropriate and validated scales to measure actual ethical purchasing behaviour, the decision to use exploratory factor analysis was made.

The 11 items of the adapted ECCB Scale were therefore subjected to principal components analysis (PCA) with Oblimin rotation in all four countries individually. One item 'I recycle my household rubbish' showed low loadings, and a reliability analysis suggested it should be removed from the scale as well, which was duly done. The Kaiser-Meyer-Olkin measure verified the adequacy of the sample for the analysis, exceeding the recommended value of .6 (Kaiser, 1970) in all countries (UK: KMO = .898; Germany: .877; Japan: .836; Hungary: .895), while Bartlett's test of sphericity (UK: $\chi^2$ (45) = 7759.92, $p < .001$; Germany: 1179.32, $p < .001$; Japan: 1704.17, $p < .001$; Hungary: 1387.49, $p < .001$) indicated that the correlations between items were sufficiently large for PCA. The PCA on the 10 ECCB items resulted in a single-factor solution in the UK, Germany, and Hungary. Only in Japan did a second component with an eigenvalue exceeding 1 emerge, but an inspection of the scree plot lent support to a one-factor solution. A further PCA with a forced one-factor solution demonstrated all items to load strongly onto a single factor across all countries, explaining 60.65% of the variance in the UK, 54.21% in Germany, 44.66% in Japan, and 60.69% in Hungary.

Overall ECCB was therefore measured by summing the 10 remaining items, with higher scores indicative of a greater propensity to demonstrate ecologically conscious consumer behaviour. The reliability of the resulting 10-item scale was checked using Cronbach's alpha and item–total correlations. Alphas were .925 in the UK, .904 in Germany, .859 in Japan, and .927 in Hungary, revealing high internal consistency in all four countries. Corrected item–total correlations were all above .4 and in most cases even above .6.

Given the exploratory approach of this study, the focus of the analysis that follows is on a country-by-country basis, as cross-national comparisons of the raw data require measurement invariance. Nevertheless, based on the PCA and the factorial similarity it revealed, structural equivalence (Byrne & Watkins, 2003; Fischer & Fontaine, 2011) is assumed with confidence.

## Results

Within all countries, scores on the ECCB scale ranged from a minimum of 10 to a maximum of 50. However, as can be seen from Table 3, higher scores (indicative of a greater degree of ecologically conscious consumer behaviour) were found in Japan (mean score 35.3) and Germany (means score 36.8), while the UK and Hungary produced mean scores of 32.7 and 32.3 respectively.

Turning to socio-economic variables, ECCB did not correlate with either income band or socio-economic status in any of the nations under study. Likewise, ANOVAs confirmed that ECCB is unrelated to work status. A very weak positive correlation was found with age and ECCB ($r = .105$, $n = 412$, $p < .05$) in the Japanese sample, but this relationship failed to emerge in any of the other countries. Likewise, no relationship was found with cognitive age in the UK, Germany, or Japan, while only a weak negative correlation ($r = -.162$, $n = 200$, $p < .05$) was found in the Hungarian sample. Age identity, too, failed to show any relationship to ECCB. Contrary to expectations, $t$-tests found no significant differences in the ECCB between parents and those who have no children, or between grandparents and those who have no grandchildren, and this was true across all the countries.

As can be seen from Figure 1, gender was the only socio-economic variable to emerge as potentially important in differentiating ECCB, with significant differences emerging in both Germany ($t = -2.920$, df $= 206.261$, $p < .01$) and the UK ($t = -5.498$, df $= 415.488$, $p < .001$). In both cases, females demonstrated significantly greater ecologically conscious consumer behaviour than did their male counterparts.

In contrast to the socio-economic variables, those variables pertaining to behaviour relating to environmentalism did indeed demonstrate significant differences across all countries. As can be seen from Figure 2, those who have taken action (e.g. taken part in a demonstration, written to an organisation, used an Internet forum, or attended an event etc.) about any ethical, environmental, or conservation issue which they

**Table 3** Mean ECCB score by country.

| Country | Mean | *n* | Std. deviation |
| --- | --- | --- | --- |
| UK | 32 7156 | 450 | 8.39 |
| Germany | 36 8028 | 213 | 7.56 |
| Japan | 35 2743 | 412 | 6.07 |
| Hungary | 32 2700 | 200 | 8.91 |
| *Total* | *34 1553* | *1275* | *7.84* |

**Figure 1** ECCB by country and gender.

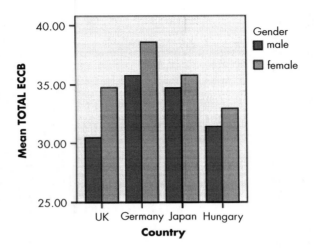

**Figure 2** ECCB by country and action taken.

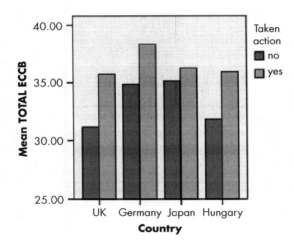

felt strongly about demonstrate higher ECCB than do those who have never taken any action. This finding is true across all the countries, and $t$-tests revealed these differences to be significant in the UK ($t = 6.170$, df $= 401.085$, $p < .001$), Germany ($t = 3.383$, df $= 208$, $p < .001$), and Hungary ($t = 2.048$, df $= 198$, $p < .05$).

Significant differences in ecologically conscious consumer behaviour is also found between those who are members of ethical or environmental/conservation groups or causes (Figure 3 UK: $t = 3.824$, df $= 92.702$, $p < .001$; Germany: $t = 3.246$, df $= 210$, $p < .001$; Japan: $t = 3.057$, df $= 409$, $p < .01$; Hungary: $t = 4.011$, df $= 30.490$, $p < .001$) and those who regularly donate to environmental or conservation charities (Figure 4 UK: $t = 6.812$, df $= 323.106$, $p < .001$; Germany: $t = 4.269$, df $= 208$, $p < .001$; Japan: $t = 3.593$, df $= 410$, $p < .001$; Hungary: $t = 2.724$, df $= 198$, $p < .01$).

**Figure 3** ECCB by country and environmental group membership.

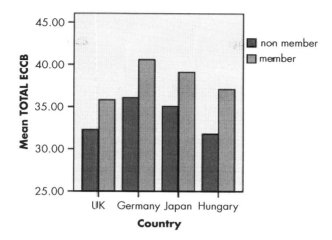

**Figure 4** ECCB by country and environmental charity donation.

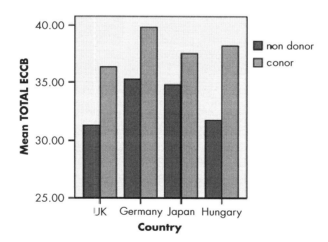

As noted earlier, piloting revealed concepts such as Fairtrade and freedom foods to be unfamiliar to some senior consumers, thus the final questionnaire included a response category 'I am unaware of these choices' for these questions. Table 4 details the percentage of respondents from each country who are unaware of the various Fairtrade and ethical choices.

As can be seen from Table 4, the UK leads the way with the majority of British respondents being aware of most of these choices. Fewer than 5% of UK seniors are unaware of Fairtrade food. In contrast, more than 20% of Germans and more than 33% of Japanese and Hungarians have never heard of Fairtrade food. Likewise, while almost 90% of UK respondents are aware of Fairtrade clothing, more than 25% of Germans and 33% of Japanese and Hungarians are not. Ethical finance is the least

## CONTEMPORARY ISSUES IN GREEN AND ETHICAL MARKETING

**Table 4** Percentage of respondents unaware of various ethical product choices by country.

| Choice | UK | Germany | Japan | Hungary |
|---|---|---|---|---|
| Fairtrade food | 4.7 | 20.5 | 34.1 | 38.0 |
| Fairtrade clothing | 11.1 | 26.2 | 36.0 | 39.0 |
| Ethical finance | 16.5 | 34.8 | 36.4 | 18.0 |
| Free-range food | 2.8 | 10.5 | 22.2 | 14.0 |
| Not tested on animals | 13.5 | 23.8 | 50.6 | 22.0 |

**Table 5** ECCB and ethical product choices correlations by country.

| | UK ECCB | Germany ECCB | JAPAN ECCB | Hungary ECCB |
|---|---|---|---|---|
| Fairtrade food | .578** | .443** | .293** | .427** |
| Fairtrade clothing | .461** | .389** | .312** | .414** |
| Ethical finance | .454** | .491** | .192** | .200* |
| Free-range food | .473** | .584** | .355** | .260** |
| Not tested on animals | .283** | .381** | .260** | .308** |

*Correlation is significant at the .05 level (two-tailed); **correlation is significant at the .01 level (two-tailed).

well known of all these concepts in the UK, with 16.5% of respondents unaware of this choice and similar percentages of older Hungarians (18%), while relatively large numbers of German and Japanese seniors (35% and 36% respectively) have not heard of this concept at all. Those unaware of products that are not tested on animals fall between 13.5% in the UK to more than 50% of Japan's seniors in this study.

The analysis that follows is therefore limited to those respondents who were aware of these ethical product choices. As Table 5 shows, significant and positive correlations were found with each of these choices and ECCB across all nations.

## Discussion

Despite the fact that direct statistical analyses between the nations cannot be made, it is still possible to compare the results. Interestingly, although the UK sample demonstrated higher levels of awareness of a variety of ethical product choices than any of the other nations studied here, these British seniors scored lower on the ECCB scale than did older Germans and Japanese, and only marginally higher than older Hungarians. Previous research (Al-Khatib et al., 2005; Vitell & Paolillo, 2004; Whipple & Swords, 1992) has shown the importance of nationality and culture as significant predictors of ethical beliefs and behaviours, and the present study contributes to that body of knowledge. The underlying reason for these apparent differences needs further investigation.

As Ramsey et al. (2007) note, demographic differences among consumer groups are important to the development of marketing strategies. However, the present study found few sociodemographic differences in the ecologically conscious consumer behaviour of seniors. Ethical product choices sometimes carry a price premium, but no differences were found between income groups, socio-economic groups, or indeed between those who are still working and those who are retired. Nevertheless, as the literature review pointed out, previous studies have found that ability to pay is not correlated with actual purchase of ethical products, and thus there is still a need to investigate the underlying price–quality–ethical dimension to consumer behaviour. Neutralisation theory has been used to explain why consumers do not take their ethical beliefs to the checkout (Chatzidakis et al., 2007). This theory suggests that consumers are able to eliminate any dissonance that may arise when they make a product choice that is not ethical, and of course it is possible that a price premium gives consumers a reason to neutralise that dissonance. Certainly, previous research (Sudbury & Böltner, 2010) has shown that once consumers are probed as to why they do not act on their beliefs they cite a wide variety of reasons, many of which project blame from the individual to the company.

The proposition that people with children and grandchildren would demonstrate their concern with sustainability to a greater extent than those without progeny found no support. The weak correlations found in the Japanese sample with chronological age and in the Hungarian sample with cognitive age are so small they are almost meaningless. Thus while some previous research has found older consumers to be more ethical than their younger counterparts (Kim & Choi, 2003; Swaidan et al., 2003; Vitell et al., 2007), it would seem that there are few age differences *within* the senior market, a finding that supports the work of Diamantopoulos, Schlegelmilch, Sinkovics, and Bohlen (2003). It would appear that meaningful age differences emerge only when a full range of ages is used in the study.

The only sociodemographic variable that did emerge as potentially important was gender. However, although older females scored higher on the ECCB scale than did their male counterparts in all four nationalities, these differences failed to reach statistical significance in the Japanese and Hungarian samples. This is an interesting finding because, on the one hand, a body of research suggests that women are more likely than men to behave ethically (Laroche et al., 2000; Loureiro et al., 2002). On the other hand, a body of gerontology literature suggest that as people age, they become more androgynous. Indeed, it is well documented that in mid-life there begins a change that is marked by males showing feminine traits, whilst women demonstrate male traits (Gutman, 1979). The finding that older British and German females demonstrate higher ECCB than their male counterparts is therefore consistent with previous ethics literature, while the finding that there are no significant gender differences between older Japanese and Hungarian seniors could be explained by gerontological theories. Clearly, more research into gender differences with regard to ethical consumer behaviour is warranted.

The finding that people who score highly on the ECCB scale actually demonstrate different behaviour to those whose scores are low is an important one. This behaviour manifests itself in deeds such as taking action (such as taking part in a demonstration, writing to an organisation, using an Internet forum, or attending an event etc.) about any ethical, environmental, or conservation issue they feel strongly about, making regular donations to environmental charities, and being members of environmental groups or causes. Importantly, the consumer behaviour that is demonstrated includes making wider ethical product choices, including Fairtrade foods and clothing, ethical financial products, free-range foods, and products that are not tested on animals.

This finding holds true in all the countries under study, and has two important implications. First, the finding adds validity to the ECCB scale, which is important because there are few scales that actually appear to measure behaviour as opposed to intentions. Second, the findings suggest that ecologically conscious consumer behaviour is related to wider ethical purchasing, and while this seems intuitively obvious, no previous empirical evidence has demonstrated this relationship. Thus future researchers that utilise the ECCB scale can have greater confidence that the scale can act as a proxy for a wide variety of ethical behaviours.

In addition to confirming that there are substantial numbers of seniors who are consumers of ethical and environmentally friendly products, this research has shown that there are also substantial numbers of older persons who are not yet aware of these choices. This untapped market potential needs to be addressed, given that previous research has demonstrated that older adults are more ethical than younger consumers who are all too often the focus of marketing effort (Carrigan & Szmigin, 1999).

## Conclusions and implications for research and practice

This study, the first of its kind, investigated the pro-environmental consumer behaviour of seniors in Japan, Germany, the UK, and Hungary. Using a modified version of the ECCB scale, the study found differences between the nations, with older Japanese and German consumers demonstrating more ecologically conscious consumer behaviour than their British and Hungarian counterparts. In line with previous research, the study found sociodemographic factors to be poor indicators of ecologically conscious consumer behaviour, although females were found to score higher on the ECCB scale than were males. An important finding was that people with higher ECCB scores actually behave differently to those with lower scores, and this behaviour includes taking part in demonstrations, blogging and using Internet forums, and/or giving to environmental charities. Finally, results revealed large numbers of senior consumers are still unaware of many ethical product choices.

The study therefore makes some significant contributions, and addresses some important gaps. First, the study makes a contribution to the literature pertaining to consumer, as opposed to corporate, ethics, which is comparatively under-researched. Second, the fact that it investigates consumer ethics in a cross-cultural setting is not to be underestimated. Too often studies are conducted in one culture or with small samples, and while these are useful, they are limited in their applicability to the wider population or to other nations. Random samples were used in this study, which adds to its usefulness. Third, the study is important because it measures actual, as opposed to intended, consumer behaviour, and given the well-documented attitude–behaviour gap, this is a significant issue. Indeed, the finding that consumers who score high on the ECCB scale do actually behave differently to those with low scores is a vital one. Moreover, the modifications to the ECCB scale, which were made as a result of extensive piloting across four different nations, adds to the validity and usefulness of the scale. Future researchers can now utilise the scale with more faith in its validity and reliability, and can have confidence in cross-national settings. A further significant contribution, made because of the recognised limitations of the ECCB scale, was the inclusion of questions pertaining to Fairtrade, ethical financial products, free-range and freedom goods, and animal testing. The study therefore includes wider behaviours than have previously been measured using solely ECCB scale items.

Finally, the fact that the study concentrates on senior consumers makes a valuable contribution to the older consumer literature, and this is especially important given that the study was conducted outside the United States, where the vast majority of knowledge pertaining to older consumers originates. Additionally, the inclusion of questions pertaining to progeny and various types of self-perceived age are unique in an ethics study, and while these variables were not found to be significant in terms of ethical consumer behaviour, their inclusion in studies is important from a senior consumer perspective.

Clearly, investigation is needed into the underlying reasons why, despite higher levels of awareness of ethical product choices, older UK consumers do not score as high on the ECCB scale as those in Germany and Japan. Possible reasons for this paradox include those ethical or environmentally friendly products are perceived as too expensive, and where price and ethical concerns conflict, Shaw and Clarke (1999) found a restricted number of ethical purchases were made. Thus, while many seniors are affluent, there are others who are less well-off who may not be able to afford a full range of ethical products. Other possibilities include the perception of inferior quality, or it may be a packaging issue: a previous study (D'Souza, Taghian, Lamb, & Peretiatko, 2007) found older Australian consumers to be more dissatisfied with environmental labelling than their younger counterparts.

Communication to those who are unaware is of course crucial, and clearly there are major untapped marketing opportunities here. Those marketing and advertising managers whose brands are positioned ethically need to begin to tap into these potential new senior markets, while keeping in mind that information provision has been shown to be crucial as an influencer to ethical purchasing (Valor, 2007). Furthermore, there is a move to challenge manufacturers to prove the ethical claims they make (Strong, 1996), particularly as ethical consumers have been found to be sceptical of advertising (Shrum, McCarty, & Lowrey, 1995). Moreover, it has been noted that there is a gap in the literature with respect to the design of advertising which aims to promote sustainable consumption (Golding, 2008). Given the proven fact that seniors are underrepresented in advertising (Carrigan & Szmigin, 2000; Prieler, Kohlbacher, Hagiwara, & Arima, 2011; Simcock & Sudbury, 2006), it may be quite a steep learning curve for marketers to learn to target a segment effectively that are proving to comprise astute and sophisticated consumers (Sudbury & Simcock, 2010).

Citizenship and consumption are often portrayed as oppositional, but, as Soper (2007) argues, the two do not have to be mutually exclusive. Rather, there is the possibility that some affluent consumers simply choose to consume in a different way, and the identification of such seniors in the current study lends support for such a theory. Indeed, previous research suggests that customer service and product quality are important motivators even when purchasing ethical products (Megicks, Memery, & Williams, 2008). Thus it is unlikely that many of today's affluent seniors are willing to compromise on quality or service for the sake of an ethically sourced or produced product.

One of the limitations of the study is, due to its exploratory nature, direct cross-cultural comparisons are not made, as more confirmatory methods would be necessary to establish measurement equivalence. The next step in this research is to establish measurement equivalence, and examine the antecedents of ecologically conscious consumer behaviour among seniors in these different nations. The study has therefore set a research agenda, and the potential antecedents to be investigated in the near future include the different value bases of these seniors, their ethical ideologies, anomie, and their attitudes and beliefs from a new environmental paradigm perspective. Perhaps the most pressing implication from this research from a practitioner perspective is the need for an investigation into the major untapped marketing opportunities that this study reveals. There are large groups of relatively wealthy, relatively ethical consumers to be found across the nations under study that are unaware of some ethical product choices. Research needs to be conducted to ascertain why many ethical positioning strategies appear to be missed by so many senior consumers. By taking the time to understand the needs and motivations of an increasingly important demographic, marketers of ethical products may be able to restore the radical edge they lost when ethical products moved from niche to mainstream.

## References

Academy of Medical Sciences. (2009). *Rejuvenating ageing research*. Retrieved 3 January 2010 from: http://www.acmedsci.ac.uk/p99puid161.html

Al-Khatib, J.A., D'Auria Stanton, A., & Rawwas, M.Y.A. (2005). Ethical segmentation of consumers in developing countries: A comparative analysis. *International Marketing Review*, 22(2), 225–246.

Arber, S. (2004). Gender, marital status and ageing: Linking material, health and social resources. *Journal of Aging Studies*, 18, 91–108.

Auger, P., Burke, P., Devinney, T.M., & Louviere, J.J. (2003). What will consumers pay for social product features? *Journal of Business Ethics*, 42, 281–304.

Auger, P., & Devinney, T.M. (2007). Do what consumer say matter? The misalignment of preferences with unconstrained ethical intentions. *Journal of Business Ethics*, 76, 361–383.

Baek, E., & DeVaney, S.A. (2004). Assessing the baby boomers' financial wellness using financial ratios and a subjective measure. *Family and Consumer Sciences Research Journal*, 32, 321–348.

Barak, B. (1987). Cognitive age: A new multidimensional approach to measuring age identity. *International Journal of Aging and Human Development*, 25(2), 109–128.

Barak, B., Mathur, A., Zhang, Y., Lee, K., & Erondu, E. (2003). Inner-age satisfaction in Africa and Asia: A cross-cultural exploration. *Asia Pacific Journal of Marketing and Logistics*, 15(1/2), 3–26.

Barak, B., & Schiffman, L.G. (1981). Cognitive age: A nonchronological age variable. *Advances in Consumer Research*, 8, 602–606.

Byrne, B.M., & Watkins, D. (2003). The issue of measurement invariance revisited. *Journal of Cross-Cultural Psychology*, 34(2), 155–175.

Cadogan, J. (2010). Comparative, cross-cultural, and cross-national research: A comment on good and bad practice. *International Marketing Review*, 27(6), 601–605.

Carrigan, M. (1998). Segmenting the grey market: The case for fifty-plus 'lifegroups'. *Journal of Marketing Practice: Applied Marketing Science*, 4(2), 43–56.

Carrigan, M., & Attalla, A. (2001). The myth of the ethical consumer – Do ethics matter in purchase behaviour? *Journal of Consumer Marketing*, 18(7), 560–577.

Carrigan, M., & Szmigin, I. (1999). In pursuit of youth: What's wrong with the older market? *Marketing Intelligence and Planning*, 17(5), 222–230.

Carrigan, M., & Szmigin, I. (2000). Advertising in an ageing society. *Ageing and Society*, 20, 217–233.

Carrigan, M., Szmigin, I., & Wright, J. (2004). Shopping for a better world? An interpretive study of the potential for ethical consumption within the older market. *Journal of Consumer Marketing*, 21(6), 401–417.

Chatzidakis, A., Hibbert, S., & Smith, A.P. (2007). Why people don't take their concerns about Fairtrade to the supermarket: The role of neutralisation. *Journal of Business Ethics*, 74, 89–100.

CIA. (2011). The world factbook. Retrieved 4 February 2011 from https://www.cia.gov/library/publications/the-world-factbook/fields/2177.html

Co-operative Bank. (2008). Ten years of Ethical Consumerism 1999–2008. Retrieved from http://www.cooperativebank.co.uk/servlet/Satellite?

Coulmas, F. (2007). *Population decline and ageing in Japan – The social consequences*. London: Routledge.

Coulmas, F., Conrad, H., Schad-Seifert, A., & Vogt, G. (Eds.). (2008). *The demographic challenge: A handbook about Japan*. Leiden, The Netherlands: Brill.

Cowe, R., & Williams, S. (2000). *Who are the ethical consumers?* London: The Co-Operative Bank.

D'Souza, C., Taghian, M., Lamb, P., & Peretiatko, R. (2007). Green decisions: Demographics and consumer understanding of environmental labels. *International Journal of Consumer Studies*, 31, 371–376.

De Pelsmacker, P., Janssens, W., Sterckx, E., & Mielants, C. (2006). Fairtrade beliefs, attitudes and buying behaviour of Belgian consumers. *International Journal of Non-profit and Voluntary Sector Marketing*, 11, 125–138.

Dentsu Shinia Purojekuto. (2007). *Dankai maketingu (baby boomer marketing)*. Tokyo: Dentsu.

Deutsches Institut fuer Wirtschaftsforschung. (2007). *Auswirkungen des demographischen Wandels auf die private Nachfrage nach Guetern und Dienstleistungen in Deutschland bis 2050*. Berlin: DIW.

Diamantopoulos, A., Schlegelmilch, B.B., Sinkovics, R.R., & Bohlen, G.M. (2003). Can socio-demographics still play a role in profiling green consumers? A review of the evidence and an empirical investigation. *Journal of Business Research*, 56, 465–480.

Doherty, B., & Tranchell, S. (2007). Radical mainstreaming of Fairtrade: The case of the Day chocolate company. *Equal Opportunities International*, 26(7), 693–711.

Eckhardt, G.M., Belk, R., & Devinney, T.M. (2010). Why don't consumers consumer ethically? *Journal of Consumer Behaviour*, 9(6), 426–436.

Eitner, C., Enste, P., Naegele, G., & Leve, V. (2011). The discovery and development of the silver market in Germany. In F. Kohlbacher & C. Herstatt (Eds.), *The silver market phenomenon: Marketing and innovation in the aging society* (2nd ed., pp. 309–324). Heidelberg, Germany: Springer.

Fischer, R., & Fontaine, J.R.J. (2011). Methods for investigating structural equivalence. In D. Matsumoto & F.J.R. Van de Vijver (Eds.), *Cross-cultural research methods in psychology* (pp. 179–215). New York: Cambridge University Press.

Golding, K.M. (2008). Fairtrade's dual aspect – The communications challenge of Fairtrade marketing. *Journal of Macromarketing*, 00, 1–12.

Guiot, D. (2001). Antecedents of subjective age biases among senior women. *Psychology and Marketing*, 18(10), 1049–1071.

Gutman, D. (1979). Individual adaptation in the middle years. In J. Hendricks & D. Hendricks (Eds.), *Dimensions of aging* (pp. 150–159). Cambridge, MA: Winthrop.

Hakuhodo Institute of Life and Living, & Hakuhodo Inc. Elder Business Development Division. (2003). *Kyodai shijō 'erudā' no tanjō [The birth of the colossal 'elder market']*. Tokyo: Purejidentosha.

Harrison, R., Newholm, T., & Shaw, D. (2006). *The ethical consumer*. London: Sage.

Hoffman, E., & Menning, S. (2004). A century of population aging in Germany. *Science of Aging Knowledge Environment*, 37, 35.

Irving, S., Harrison, R., & Rayner, M. (2002). Ethical consumerism – Democracy through the wallet. *Journal of Research for Consumers*, 3, 1–20.

Iwanow, H., McEachern, M.G., & Jeffrey, A. (2005). The influence of ethical trading policies on consumer apparel purchase decisions. *International Journal of Retail and Distribution Management*, 33(5), 371–387.

Kaiser, H. (1970). A second generation little jiffy. *Psychometricka*, 35, 401–415.

Kim, Y., & Choi, S.M. (2003). Ethical standards appear to change with age and ideology: A survey of practitioners. *Public Relations Review*, 29, 78–89.

Kim, Y., & Choi, S.M. (2005). Antecedents of green purchase behaviour: An examination of collectivism, environmental concern, and PCE. *Advances in Consumer Research*, 32, 592–599.

Kohlbacher, F. (2011). Business implications of demographic change in Japan: Chances and challenges for human resource and marketing management. In F. Coulmas & R. Lützeler (Eds.), *Imploding populations in Japan and Germany: A comparison*. Leiden, The Netherlands: Brill.

Kohlbacher, F., & Chéron, E. (2010, June). *Segmenting the silver market using cognitive age and the list of values: Empirical evidence from Japan*. European Advances in Consumer Research (EACR) Conference, London.

Kohlbacher, F., Gudorf, P., & Herstatt, C. (2011). Japan's growing silver market – An attractive business opportunity for foreign companies? In M. Boppel, S. Boehm, & S. Kunisch (Eds.), *From grey to silver: Managing the demographic change successfully* (pp. 189–205). Heidelberg, Germany: Springer.

Kohlbacher, F., & Langbecker, N. (2010). Cash and conscience: Examining the state of Fairtrade in Japan. *The American Chamber of Commerce Japan (ACCJ) Journal*, November, 30–33.

Kohlbacher, F., Sudbury, L., & Hofmeister, A. (2011). *Self-perceived age among older consumers: A cross-national investigation*. American Marketing Association Winter Marketing Educators' Conference, Austin, Texas.

Laroche, M., Bergeron, J., & Barbaro-Forleo, G. (2001). Targeting consumers who are willing to pay more for environmentally friendly products. *Journal of Consumer Marketing*, 18(6), 503–520.

Laskova, A. (2007). *Perceived consumer effectiveness and environmental concerns*. Paper presented at the 13th Asia-Pacific Management Conference, Melbourne, Australia.

Leyhausen, F., & Vossen, A. (2011). We could have known better – Consumer-oriented marketing in Germany's ageing market. In M. Boppel, S. Boehm, & S. Kunisch (Eds.), *From grey to silver: Managing the demographic change successfully* (pp. 175–184). Heidelberg, Germany: Springer.

Loureiro, M.L., McCluskey, J.J., & Mittelhammer, R.C. (2002). Will consumers pay a premium for eco-labelled apples? *The Journal of Consumer Affairs*, 36(2), 203–219.

Low, W., & Davenport, E. (2007). To boldly go . . . exploring ethical spaces to re-politicise ethical consumption and Fairtrade. *Journal of Consumer Behaviour*, 6, 336–348.

McCreery, J. (2000). *Japanese consumer behavior: From worker bees to wary shoppers*. Honolulu: University of Hawai'i Press.

McEachern, M.G., Schröder, M.J.A., Willock, J., Whitelock, J., & Mason, R. (2007). Exploring ethical brand extensions and consumer buying behaviour: The RSPCA and the 'freedom food' brand. *Journal of Product and Brand Management*, 16(3), 168–177.

McEachern, M.G., Warnably, G., Carrigan, M., & Szmigin, I. (2010). Thinking locally, acting locally? Conscious consumers and farmers' markets. *Journal of Marketing Management*, 26(5/6), 395–412.

McKean Skaff, M. (2006). The view from the driver's seat: Sense of control in the baby boomers at midlife. In S.K. Whitbourne & S.L. Willis (Eds.), *The baby boomers grow up: Contemporary perspectives on midlife* (pp. 185–204). Mahwah, NJ: Lawrence Erlbaum.

Megicks, P., Memery, J., & Williams, J. (2008). Influences on ethical and socially responsible shopping: Evidence from the UK grocery sector. *Journal of Marketing Management, 24*(5–6), 637–659.

Monostori, J. (2009). Ageing. *Demográfia portré*, 81. Retrieved from http://www.demografia.hu/letoltes/kiadvanyok/DemPort_angol/Demoangol.pdf

Moschis, G.P., & Ong, F.S. (2011). Religiosity and consumer behaviour of older adults: A study of sub cultural influences in Malaysia. *Journal of Consumer Behaviour, 10*(1), 8–17.

Newholm, T., & Shaw, D. (2007). Studying the Ethical Consumer: A Review of Research. *Journal of Consumer Behaviour, 6*, 253–70.

Office for National Statistics. (2004). *Focus on older people*. London: Government Publications. Retrieved 16 January 2005 from http://www.statistics.gov.uk/focuson/olderpeople/

Office for National Statistics. (2008). *Family spending – A report on the expenditure and food survey*. London: Government Publications. Retrieved 15 October 2009 from http://www.statistics.gov.uk/StatBase/Product.asp?vlnk=361&More=Y

Office for National Statistics. (2009). *Social trends*. London: Government Publications. Retrieved 16 April 2009 from http://www.statistics.gov.uk/socialtrends39/

Ong, F.S., Yap-Ying L., & Abessi, M. (2009). The correlates of cognitive ageing and adoption of defensive-ageing strategies among older adults. *Asia Pacific Journal of Marketing and Logistics, 21*(2), 294–305.

Pepper, M., Jackson, T., & Uzzell, D. (2009). An examination of the values that motivate socially conscious and frugal consumer behaviours. *International Journal of Consumer Studies, 33*, 126–136.

Pieters, R., Bijmolt, T., van Raaij, F., & de Kruijk, M. (1998). Consumers' attributions of pro-environmental behaviour, motivations, and ability to self and others. *Journal of Public Policy and Marketing, 17*(2), 215–225.

Prieler, M., Kohlbacher, F., Hagiwara, S., & Arima, A. (2011). Gender representation of older people in Japanese television advertisements. *Sex Roles: A Journal of Research, 1*(5–6), 405–415.

Ramsey, R.P., Marshall, G.W., Johnston, M.W., & Deeter-Schmelz, D.R. (2007). Ethical ideologies and older consumer perceptions of unethical sales tactics. *Journal of Business Ethics, 70*(2), 191–207.

Roberts, J.A. (1996). Green consumers in the 1990: Profile and implications for advertising. *Journal of Business Research, 36*, 217–231.

Roberts, J.A., & Bacon, D.R. (1997). Exploring the subtle relationship between environmental concern and ecologically conscious consumer behaviour. *Journal of Business Research, 40*, 79–89.

Sandahl, D.M., & Robertson, R. (1989). Social determinants of environmental concern: Specification and test of the model. *Environment and Behaviour, 21*(1), 57–81.

Sassatelli, R. (2006). Virtue, responsibility and consumer choice: Framing critical consumerism. In J. Brewer & R. Trentman (Eds.), *Consuming cultures* (pp. 219–258). Oxford: Berg.

Schlegelmilch, B.B., Bohlen, G.M., & Diamantopoulos, A. (1996). The link between green purchasing decisions and measures of environmental consciousness. *European Journal of Marketing, 30* (5), 35–55.

Schlegelmilch, B.B., Diamantopoulos, A., & Bohlen, G.M. (1994). *The value of socio-demographic characteristics for predicting environmental consciousness*. Paper presented at the American Marketing Association Winter Conference, Chicago, IL.

Schlegelmilch, B.B., & Obersecer, M. (2010). Half a century of marketing ethics: Shifting perspectives and emerging trends. *Journal of Business Ethics, 93*, 1–19.

Schröder, M.J.A., & McEachern, M.G. (2004). Consumer value conflicts surrounding ethical food purchase decisions: A focus on animal welfare. *International Journal of Consumer Studies, 28*(2), 168–177.

Schröder, M.J.A., & McEachern, M.G. (2005). Fast foods and ethical consumer value: A focus on McDonald's and KFC. *British Food Journal, 107*(4), 212–224.

Sekizawa, H. (2008). The impact of the ageing of society on consumer behaviour and consumer markets. In F. Coulmas, H. Conrad, A. Schad-Seifert, & G. Vogt (Eds.), *The demographic challenge: A handbook about Japan* (pp. 999–1016). Leiden, The Netherlands: Brill.

Shaw, D. (2007). Consumer voters in imagined communities. *International Journal of Sociology and Social Policy, 27*(3/4), 135–150.

Shaw, D., & Clarke, I. (1999). Belief formation in ethical consumer groups: An exploratory study. *Marketing Intelligence and Planning, 17*(2), 109–119.

Shaw, D., Shiu, E., & Clarke, I. (2000). The contribution of ethical obligation and self-identity to the theory of planned behaviour: An exploration of ethical consumers. *Journal of Marketing Management, 16*, 879–894.

Shrum, L.J., McCarty, J.A. & Lowrey, T.M. (1995). Buyer characteristics of the green consumer and their implications for advertising strategy. *Journal of Advertising, 24*(2), 71–82.

Simcock, P., & Sudbury, L. (2006). The invisible majority? Older models in UK television advertising. *International Journal of Advertising, 25*(1), 87–106.

Simcock, P., Sudbury, L., & Wright, G. (2006). Age, perceived risk and satisfaction in consumer decision making: A review and extension. *Journal of Marketing Management, 22*, 355–378.

Soper, K. (2007). Re-thinking the good life: The citizenship dimension of consumer disaffection with consumerism. *Journal of Consumer Culture, 7*, 205–229.

Statistisches Bundesamt. (2009). Wirtschaftsrechnungen. Laufende Wirtschaftsrechnungen. Einnahmen und Ausgaben privater Haushalte 2007, Fachserie 15 Reihe 1, Wiesbaden.

Straughan, R.D., & Roberts, J.A. (1999). Environmental segmentation alternatives: A look at green consumer behaviour in the new millennium. *Journal of Consumer Marketing, 16*(6), 558–575.

Strong, C. (1996). Features contributing to the growth of ethical consumerism – A preliminary investigation. *Marketing Intelligence and Planning, 14*(5), 5–13.

Sudbury, L. (2004). Subjective age perceptions in the UK: An empirical study. *Quality in Ageing and Older Adults, 5*, 4–13.

Sudbury, L., & Böltner, S. (2010). Fashion marketing and the ethical movement versus individualist consumption: Analysing the attitude behaviour gap. *European Advances in Consumer Research, 9*.

Sudbury, L., & Simcock, P. (2010). *Using qualitative diary research to analyse older consumers' packaging experiences*. Paper presented at the American Marketing Association Summer Marketing Educators' Conference, Boston, MA.

Swaidan, Z., Vitell, S.J., & Rawwas, M.Y.A. (2003). Consumer ethics: Determinants of ethical beliefs of African Americans. *Journal of Business Ethics, 46*, 175–186.

Szmigin, I., & Carrigan, M. (2000). The older consumer as innovator: does cognitive age hold the key? *Journal of Marketing Management, 16*, 505–527.

Szmigin, I., Carrigan, M., & McEachern, M.G. (2008). Flexibility, dissonance and the conscious consumer. *European Advances in Consumer Research, 8*, 379–380.

Szmigin, I., Maddock, S., & Carrigan, M. (2003). Conceptualizing community consumption. *British Food Journal, 105*(8), 542–550.

The Nikkei Weekly. (2010a, January 11). *Boomers wield financial clout*, p. 3.

The Nikkei Weekly. (2010b, April 12). *Older generations carry consumption*, p. 5.

Thompson, K.E., & Thompson, N.S. (2007, July). *Advertising to older consumers: Theory into practice*. Paper presented at the Academy of Marketing Conference, Kingston University, UK.

United Nations (UN). (2009). Older persons as consumers. Retrieved 3 January 2010 from http://www.unece.org/fileadmin/DAM/pau/_docs/age/2009/Policy_briefs/3-PolicyBrief_Older_Persons_Eng.pdf

US Census Bureau (2011). The International Database. Retrieved from http://www.census.gov/population/international/data/idb/informationGateway.php

Valor, C. (2007). The influence of information about labour abuses on consumer choice of clothes: A grounded theory approach. *Journal of Marketing Management*, 23(7–8), 675–695.

Varul, M.Z., & Wilson-Kovacs, D. (2008). Fairtrade consumerism as an everyday ethical perspective – A comparative perspective. *ESRC Results and Policy Implications*. Retrieved from http://people.exeter.ac.uk/mzv201/FT%20Results.pdf

Velkoff, V.A. (1992). Ageing trends. *Journal of Cross-Cultural Gerontology*, 7(4), 429–437.

Vitell, S.J., Lumpkin, J.R., & Rawwas, M.Y.A. (1991). Consumer ethics: An investigation of the ethical beliefs of elderly consumers. *Journal of Business Ethics*, 10, 365–375.

Vitell, S.J. & Paolillo, J.G.P. (2003). Consumer ethics: The role of religiosity. *Journal of Business Ethics*, 46, 151–162

Vitell, S.J. & Paolillo, J.G.P. (2004). A cross-cultural study of the antecedents of the perceived role of ethics and social responsibility. *Business Ethics: A European Review*, 13(2/3), 185–199.

Vitell, S.J., Singh, J.J., & Paolillo, J.G.P. (2007). Consumers' ethical beliefs: The roles of money, religiosity and attitude toward business. *Journal of Business Ethics*, 73, 369–379.

Vlosky, R.P., Ozanne, L.K., & Fontenot, R.J. (1999). A conceptual model of US consumer willingness to pay for environmentally certified wood products. *Journal of Consumer Marketing*, 16(2), 122–136.

Whipple, T.W., & Swords, D.F. (1992). Business ethics judgments: A cross-cultural comparison. *Journal of Business Ethics*, 11, 671–678.

# Chinese consumers' adoption of a 'green' innovation – The case of organic food

John Thøgersen, *Aarhus University, Denmark*
Yanfeng Zhou, *Sun Yat-Sen University, Guangzhou, People's Republic of China*

---

**Abstract** Little research has been published on Chinese consumer-citizens' adoption of or willingness to adopt sustainable lifestyle elements. A case in point is organic food – a more sustainable alternative to conventional food. Organic food is a Western invention. However, organic food products are now available in upscale supermarkets in East and South-East China metropolises such as Shanghai, Beijing, and Guangzhou. This paper reports the results of a study investigating what motivates early adopters of organic food in China. The data were collected in Guangzhou by means of a mall-intercept survey. As in Western Europe, the early adoption of organic food in China is positively related to what Schwartz termed 'universalism values'. Also as in the West, the personal attitude towards buying organic food in China is strongly linked to beliefs about its healthiness, taste, and environmental friendliness. Social norms play a minor role for the intention to buy organic food, probably because the early adopters have few role models and face few expectations in this respect.

---

## Introduction

Private consumption is expanding rapidly in China, and it is an official goal to transform China to a consumer society during the next five-year plan. From a global perspective, it is imperative that Chinese consumers do not adopt the unsustainable consumption patterns of consumers in developed countries but that instead they adopt a consumption pattern that is both fulfilling and sustainable. This is unlikely to happen automatically, but will demand a concerted effort from all stakeholders, including the central and local government(s), businesses, and individual consumers and citizens. Mobilising Chinese consumer-citizens for a sustainable transition to a consumer society should be based on thorough knowledge of their motivation, as well as their experienced impediments. However, so far little research has been published on Chinese consumer-citizens' adoption of or willingness to adopt sustainable lifestyle elements (but see Chan, 2001; Yin, Wu, Du, & Chen, 2010). Insight into

Chinese consumer motives in this respect is important for both Chinese and foreign businesses catering to Chinese consumers (Madden, 2009). It is no less important for public regulators looking for effective ways to deal with environmental and other detrimental consequences of the expansion of private consumption in China (Liu, Wang, & Yang, 2009).

Organic food, which is a more sustainable alternative to conventional food (Thøgersen, 2010a), is a Western invention (Lockeretz, 2007). However, organic food products are now available in upscale supermarkets in East and South-East China metropolises such as Shanghai, Beijing, and Guangzhou (Yin et al., 2010). Hence, there seems to be an emerging market in China for this type of food. This makes organic food a useful case to study in order to obtain much-needed insights into consumer responses to 'green' innovations in China.

It is often argued that consumer motives for adopting any new idea, sustainable or not, are a product of the media and of the cultural, legal, and other relevant contexts (Shaw & Clarke, 1998; Solomon, 2008; Usunier & Lee, 2009). The Chinese cultural, legal, and economic context is as different from Western European or North American ones as they come (e.g. Kim, Pan, & Park, 1998). Hence, based on this line of reasoning, we might expect Chinese consumer motives to buy organic food to differ widely from consumer motives in Europe or North America. On the other hand, the physical products are the same, and it is basically the same (process) characteristics that differentiate organic from conventional food products in the West, in China, and in the rest of the world. To the extent that consumer motives are derived from these differentiating characteristics, they should only differ a little between countries and cultures.

The aim of this paper is to obtain a deeper understanding of the early adoption of and consumer purchase motives regarding an environmentally and ethically 'extended' (or 'green') type of consumer products in China, focusing on organic food. The reasons why consumers in Europe – the continent where the concept was invented – buy or refrain from buying organic food are well described in the literature. An important sub-question is whether the early adoption of this kind of product in China is based on the same functional (including ethical and environmentalist) reasons and value priorities as in Europe, or whether they are based on completely different reasons and priorities.

## An innovation adoption model

Prior to the full-fledged adoption of an innovation, the typical adopter has gone through a number of stages from exposure to the innovation and/or information about it, over forming an understanding of and a positive attitude towards the innovation, to trying it out (Rogers, 2003). Consumers may stall or reject the innovation at any stage of this process. Hence, having taken the first step(s) in the adoption process is no guarantee that an individual consumer will eventually adopt the innovation.

Research on consumer decision making often distinguishes between a 'high-effort' and a 'low-effort' path to a decision, including the decision to adopt an innovation (Hoyer & MacInnis, 2006). It is usually assumed that the adoption of an innovation follows a high-effort path, which begins with understanding and inference, continues through to liking, and ends with trial and continued adoption (Kotler & Roberto,

1989). A high-effort path is usually followed when adopters are highly involved in the decision making, and the alternatives are at the same time highly differentiated (Hoyer & MacInnis, 2006; McGuire, Lindzey, & Aronson, 1985), which is usually assumed to be the case for an innovation (at least) because of its novelty (Kotler & Roberto, 1989). However, low-risk incremental innovations may be adopted through a 'low-effort' process where trial directly follows after awareness of the innovation, without prior information acquisition or attitude formation (Hoyer & MacInnis, 2006).

When it comes to the adoption of organic food in China, there are reasons to expect that a high-effort path is most common. Most importantly, consumers often fear being cheated by unscrupulous sellers when products are promoted with 'green' claims (D'Souza, 2004; Ellison, 2008) and Chinese consumers no less so than Western consumers (Yin et al., 2010). The perceived risk of being cheated when buying organic food is the most important reason to expect a high-effort adoption process in this case (Fazio, 1990; Hoyer & MacInnis, 2006).

In addition, it is usually assumed that consumers who buy organic food products are highly involved in these products (e.g. Zanoli & Naspetti, 2002). In China, the evidence regarding this matter is limited to studies identifying segments of consumers that are highly involved in protecting the environment or in more specific environmental and/or ethical issues related to consumption (e.g. Chan & Lau, 2000; Madden, 2007; Shen & Saijo, 2008). Although in a somewhat indirect way, this evidence further suggests the existence of a segment of Chinese consumers that are positively involved in organic food products.

Figure 1 presents a simplified model of the individual-level adoption process for organic food in China (cf. Thøgersen, Haugaard, & Olesen, 2010). As indicated,

**Figure 1** An innovation adoption model for organic food.

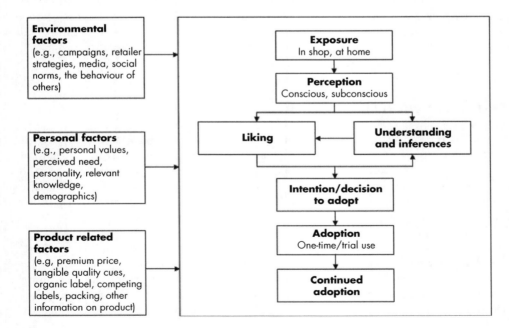

perception, understanding, and a positive attitude (liking) are contingent on exposure to organic food products, either in the store or in promotion material. In the studied case and context, this is not a trivial requirement. The Chinese organic market is still in its early infancy. China only recently, in 2005, got a state-authorised definition and control of organic food and organic food production and a certified organic label (USDA, 2005), 15 to 20 years after most European countries (Lockeretz, 2007). Also, the chances of being accidentally exposed to organic food products in Chinese retail outlets are rather slim when organic food accounts for only .08% of total food consumption even in large Chinese cities such as Beijing, Shanghai, and Guangzhou, according to recent estimates (Yin et al., 2010).

Starting the adoption process and proceeding through the stages is also contingent on or influenced by a number of personal, environmental, and product-related factors. Important product-related factors, when it comes to adopting organic food products, include their price and quality relative to their conventional counterparts (e.g. Hughner, McDonagh, Prothero, Shultz, & Stanton, 2007; Yin et al., 2010).

Important environmental factors include supportive or conflicting social norms and how many people have already adopted the new products, as well as campaigns promoting and educating consumers about organic food (Fisher & Price, 1992; McDonagh, 2002). Important personal factors include consumers' particular knowledge about organic farming and the organic label, their individual value priorities, and, related to this, their perceived need for organic food (Grankvist, Lekedal, & Marmendal, 2007).

We apply this decision-making/adoption of innovation theory frame of reference to the study of Chinese consumers' adoption of organic food products. Since our study is limited to a single innovation and context, we focus especially on personal factors, but references are also made to important product characteristics and characteristics of the adoption environment.

## Research on motives for buying organic food

A number of reviews of the international research on consumers' reasons for buying or rejecting organic food products have been published recently (Hughner et al., 2007; Thøgersen, 2010a; Torjusen, Sangstad, Jensen, & Kjærnes, 2004). These reviews reveal a high degree of consensus in research on this question. It is unanimously found that a positive attitude towards buying organic food is related to believing that organic food is healthier, tastes better, and is better for the environment, and the most important reasons for not buying organic food are high prices and limited availability. A recent, exploratory study in Guangzhou, Zhenzen, and Zhuhai found basically the same reasons for buying or not buying organic food among Chinese consumers (Yin et al., 2010).

A large-scale study of consumer purchase of organic food products in eight Western European countries found large differences between countries in the extent to which buying intentions regarding organic food is transformed into behaviour (Thøgersen, 2009). In the countries with the most developed organic market, a strong relationship between consumer intentions and behaviour was found. This was not so in countries with a less developed organic market, however. Here, the intention–behaviour relationship was weak, and how easy or difficult buying organic food was perceived to be (i.e. perceived control) was a relatively stronger predictor of behaviour.

A few studies in Europe have investigated how the purchase of organic food is related to consumers' basic value priorities (e.g. Dreezens, Martijn, Tenbult, Kok, & de Vries, 2005; Honkanen, Verplanken, & Olsen, 2006; Thøgersen, 2011; Thøgersen & Ölander, 2006). Studies employing a comprehensive instrument for measuring human values find that buying organic food is most strongly related to what Schwartz (1992, 1994) terms 'universalism values', and when universalism is controlled, no other value is both positively and significantly related to the purchase of organic food (e.g. Dreezens et al., 2005; Thøgersen, 2011). Similar findings have been reported in the United States (Zepeda & Deal, 2009) and also with regard to ethical (Shaw, Grehan, Shiu, Hassan, & Thomson, 2005) and Fairtrade products (Doran, 2009). According to Schwartz (1992, 1994), the motivational goal of universalism is understanding, appreciation, tolerance, and protection of the welfare for all people and for nature. Hence, the relationship between universalism and buying organic food is consistent with organic food being perceived as a more sustainable alternative to conventional food (Thøgersen, 2011).

Viewed in a global perspective, Western European countries share fairly similar cultural value priorities (e.g. Schwartz, 1999). In addition, the harmonisation of the legal system within the EU has implications for the organic market in terms of subsidies, common guidelines, and also labelling initiatives (Lockeretz, 2007). Because of their geographical closeness and the cooperation within the EU, there is also some synchronisation of media agendas (Thøgersen, 2010b). The fact that the media and the cultural, legal, and other relevant environments are fairly homogeneous across Western European countries may account for the practically identical consumer motives and motivations for buying organic food in this region of the world.

Similarities in consumer motives and motivations for buying organic food on a global scale call for other explanations, however. An obvious contributing factor to international harmonisation is product standardisation, that is, that the core differentiating characteristics of organic food products are the same, irrespective of national contexts. Among other things, cooperation in the international organic growers' association, IFOAM, secures this (Lockeretz, 2007; Willer, Yussefi-Menzler, & Sorensen, 2008). Organic food products appeal to a – larger or smaller – segment of consumers in each country who values these attributes.

This product-centred explanation implies that contextual factors such as cultural value priorities, legal framework, and so on mainly influence the size of the organic market, not so much the meaning attributed to organic products or the reasons and motives for buying them.

## Hypotheses

People selectively pay attention to aspects of their environment that are relevant to them and that they are able to comprehend (Hoyer & MacInnis, 2006). Therefore, noticing a new product when exposed to it depends on the consumer's relevant knowledge and experience, as well as on the new product's perceived relevance. We assume that general knowledge regarding organic food is correlated with education, and that level of education therefore can serve as a proxy for general knowledge in this area.

Relevance depends on the one hand on the perceived usefulness of the new product (i.e. organic food) to reach the consumer's personal goals and values, on the other hand on whether or not he or she can afford it, that is, on the person's (or family's) income. As regards the latter, household disposable incomes in China lag far behind Europe and North America, even in the most economically advanced metropolitan areas in East and South-East China (McEwen, Fang, Zhang, & Burkholder, 2006; Polsa, So, & Speece, 2005). At the same time, the typical price premium for organic food products in China is considerably higher than the 10–40% that Europeans and North Americans are used to (Winter & Davis, 2006). According to our own observations in Guangzhou at the time of data collection, organic vegetables, for example, were typically priced about a factor five times their conventional counterparts. This price premium alone is likely to make organic food products irrelevant to most Chinese consumers.

As previously mentioned, buying organic food is usually found to be guided by universalism values, and in Western Europe no other value is both positively and significantly related to the purchase of organic food when universalism is controlled for (e.g. Dreezens et al., 2005; Thøgersen, 2011). However, it is possible that the adoption of organic food is linked to other value priorities in China, where cultural value priorities differ radically from the West (Chan & Lau, 2000). For example, in studies of cultural value priorities, China and Western Europe are found on opposite poles of key dimensions, including Hofstede's (1980) 'individualism–collectivism' dimension[1] and Schwartz's (1999) 'harmony–mastery' and 'hierarchy–egalitarianism' dimensions.

Based on these reflections, we hypothesise:

*H1: The likelihood that a Chinese consumer notices an organic food product in the early phase after its introduction in the local market and thereby starts the adoption process is positively related to education level, income, and the priority given to what Schwartz termed 'universalism' values.*

Different attitude theories make different predictions about the sources of Chinese consumers' attitudes towards buying organic food (i.e. 'liking'). Some theories assume that consumers form attitudes based on their understanding of and inferences regarding the attitude object; others that the attitude is formed automatically based on a quick, holistic first impression. In the first category are expectancy-value attitude theories, which assume that people form attitudes towards, for example, buying a product by integrating their evaluation of salient aspects and outcomes of doing so (Fishbein & Ajzen, 2009). A number of studies have successfully applied this theory to the study of attitudes towards buying organic food (e.g. Dean, Raats, & Shepherd, 2008; Magnusson, Arvola, Hursti, Åberg, & Sjöden, 2001; Thøgersen, 1997). These studies have especially linked positive attitudes towards buying organic food to beliefs about its healthiness, taste, and environmental friendliness (Hughner et al., 2007; Yin

---

[1]According to Hofstede (1980), collectivism versus individualism is the degree to which individuals are integrated into groups. In individualist societies, ties between individuals are loose: everyone is expected to look after him/herself and his/her immediate family. In collectivist societies, people are integrated into strong, cohesive in-groups, often extended families, which continuously protect them in exchange for unquestioning loyalty.

et al., 2010). However, looming evidence suggests that this is at least not the whole story and that people are not always as rational or systematic when forming attitudes as assumed by the expectancy–value attitude theory (Eagly & Chaiken, 1993). This has led to alternative hypotheses, including that people sometimes infer their attitudes towards specific objects from their previous behaviour with regard to the attitude object (Bem, 1972). We view these theories and hypotheses as complementary rather than necessarily competing accounts of the formation of an attitude towards buying organic food. Hence, we hypothesise:

*H2a: As in Western Europe, positive attitudes towards buying organic food products in China are related to consumers' perceptions and inferences about their healthiness, taste, and environmental friendliness.*

*H2b: Chinese consumers' buying experience with regard to organic food account for additional variance in the attitude towards buying an organic food product after controlling for salient beliefs about doing so.*

A positive attitude ('liking' in Figure 1) is usually a necessary, but often not a sufficient, condition for a consumer to proceed to the next stage of the adoption process: making a decision or forming an intention to actually adopt the new product.

The decision to adopt a new product, service, or idea at an early stage is different from the decision to adopt at a later stage, both because of different opportunities for social learning (Bandura, 2001) and because social and other motives behind the adoption depend on the number of people that have already adopted the innovation (Fisher & Price, 1992). Only a small minority is usually willing to adopt a new product, service, or idea without knowing (or believing) that others have (successfully) done so before. Most people need some kind of 'social proof' (Cialdini, 2001) before adopting. Compared to later adopters, early adopters have a relatively low need for social proof, which may be due to their personality (e.g. a high need for novelty, a positive attitude towards change), the possession of expert knowledge, or because of a strong involvement with the new product, service, or idea (Rogers, 2003).

In addition to a positive attitude and 'social proof' (an environmental factor), social-cognitive theories of action have identified a number of factors that may be involved in making a decision or formation of an intention to adopt a new product, service, or idea, including expectations regarding others' approval or disapproval (i.e. perceptions about injunctive social norms, cf. Cialdini et al., 2006) and perceptions regarding how easy or difficult it would be to do so (e.g. Bandura, 2001; Fishbein & Ajzen, 2009).

Many studies report that social motives are more important and individual motives less important in a collectivist culture as compared to an individualist culture (e.g. Bagozzi, Wong, Abe, & Bergami, 2000; Chan & Lau, 2001; C. Lee & Green, 1991; J.A. Lee, 2000). Yamagishi, Hashimoto, and Schug (2008) added the important qualification that what is often perceived as an East Asian 'preference' for conformity is actually a strategy to avoid negative responses and reputation. Their carefully crafted experiments demonstrate that when a situation is defined in such a way that there is no possibility for negative evaluations, East Asians act according to their personal preferences.

In the present case, we analyse Chinese consumer responses to a new and uncommon phenomenon – organic food. If there are still no clear and well-defined norms about this behaviour among Chinese consumers, perhaps nobody expects negative evaluations for not buying organic food? In that case, one can derive the hypothesis from Yamagishi's institutional approach to cultural differences in behaviour that in this early phase of introducing organic food in China, consumers act on their personal preferences, rather than on their concern for others' view upon them, when they decide whether or not to adopt.

*H3: Despite the Chinese culture being characterised by collectivism and due to the lack of social models and of social expectations in the introduction phase, social factors play a minor role for early adopters' decision to adopt organic food. The decision to adopt is based mostly on personal preferences.*

Implementing a decision to adopt a new product, service, or idea can be more or less difficult, depending on how facilitating the environment is and on how demanding it is to carry out the decision in terms of money, time, and effort. This is reflected in research finding that the purchase of organic food is more strongly related to consumer buying intentions and less to perceptions about how easy or difficult it is to perform this behaviour (i.e. self-efficacy, Bandura, 1982, or perceived behavioural control, Ajzen, 1991) in European countries with a more developed organic market compared to those countries with less developed ones (Thøgersen, 2009). Extending this pattern to China, we hypothesise that:

*H4: The final adoption of an organic food product in China, given the current early stage of the development of the organic market here, is more strongly related to control factors than to buying intentions.*

## Method

A mall-intercept questionnaire survey was collected in April 2009 outside five upscale supermarkets that sell organic food products in one of the largest Chinese metropolises, Guangzhou. The questionnaire was developed in English, for a European study,[2] but adapted and translated to Chinese. Back-translation was used to control the quality of the translation. The questionnaire was pretested with 47 Chinese MBA students at Sun Yat-Sen University in Guangzhou and after discussions in the research group some formulations were slightly adjusted to capture the intended meaning more precisely.

Potential participants were intercepted as they left the supermarket after food shopping. This secures that participants have at least shared responsibility for their household's food shopping. The first questions in the questionnaire screened participants with regard to knowledge of organic food. If they did not have a reasonably accurate knowledge about organic food, participants were not asked further questions about organic food. Hence, after answering questions about descriptive background characteristics and general values, these participants were

[2]The CONDOR project (http://www.condor-organic.org) has been reported in a number of publications (e.g. Krystallis, Vassallo, Chryssohoidis, & Perrea, 2008; Thøgersen, 2009, 2011).

excused. No log was made of the number of people approached that refused to participate. Of the 771 persons who agreed to participate, 213 did not know about organic food and 29 changed their minds after starting to fill out the questionnaire. The gender composition was 83 female/17% male. The age composition of the participants was 31% aged 18–25 years, 34% aged 26–34 years, 13% aged 35–44 years, and 21% aged 45–60 years. The sample was relatively highly educated (49% had a college/university degree) and had a relatively high family income (47% more than 5000 RMB/month, 11% more than 10,000 RMB/month).

### Variables

All responses were made on a seven-point scale unless stated otherwise. Whereas the knowledge questions focused on organic food in general, the rest of the questions about organic food were specified to organic vegetables. This narrower product category was chosen in order to make the questions less ambiguous and because vegetables are usually among the first types of organic products that a consumer will adopt.

The final adoption of organic vegetables (i.e. behaviour) was recorded by the item: 'How often, in the past 10 times where you bought vegetables, were these organic?' using a eleven point scale from '0 times' to '10 times'.

Buying intentions were measured with two items: 'I intend to buy organic vegetables instead of conventional ones in the near future' (response categories ranging from definitely 'do not' to 'definitely do'), and 'I will buy organic vegetables instead of conventional ones in the near future' (response categories ranging from 'extremely unlikely' to 'extremely likely'). The two-item scale has an acceptable construct reliability (Cronbach's $\alpha = .65$).

Attitudes towards buying organic vegetables were measured by means of four items, reflecting cognitive as well as affective evaluations. The two cognitive attitude items were of the following semantic differentials: 'Buying organic vegetables instead of conventional ones is . . . ' (harmful–beneficial, foolish–wise). The two affective attitude items were of the following semantic differentials: 'Buying organic vegetables instead of conventional ones would make me feel...' (bad–good, displeased–pleased). The four-item scale had an acceptable construct reliability (Cronbach's $\alpha = .74$).

Two aspects of social influence regarding buying organic vegetables, often referred to as injunctive and descriptive norms (Cialdini et al., 2006; Rivis & Sheeran, 2003), were measured with one item each. Expectations regarding others' approval or disapproval (or injunctive norms) were measured with the item: 'Most people who are important to me think that . . . "I should not buy" to "I should buy" . . . organic vegetables instead of conventional ones'. Perceptions regarding relevant others' behaviour (or descriptive norms) were measured with the item: 'Most people who I value would buy organic vegetables instead of conventional ones' (response categories ranging from 'strongly disagree' to 'strongly agree'). The two items are too weakly correlated to be considered reflective of the same latent disposition ($r = .17$). Hence, they are used as two separate constructs in the following.

Perceptions regarding how easy or difficult it would be to buy organic vegetables (i.e. perceived behavioural control) were measured by two items: 'In general, for me to buy organic vegetables instead of conventional ones would be . . . ' (response categories ranging from 'difficult' to 'easy'), and 'If I want to, I could easily buy organic vegetables instead of conventional ones' (response categories ranging from 'strongly disagree' to 'strongly agree'). In the following analyses, both items are coded so that a higher number indicates higher perceived control. The construct reliability of the two-item scale is below the normally acceptable threshold (Cronbach's $\alpha = .51$). The interpretation and implications of this will be discussed in the following section.

The nine perceptions and inferences about organic food included in the survey (see Appendix 1) are so-called 'modal salient beliefs' (Ajzen & Fishbein, 1980) based on interviews with a separate convenience sample of 14 individuals from the studied population using an open-ended questionnaire format. All items had the same format as this example: 'Organic vegetables are healthier', with response categories ranging from $1 =$ 'strongly disagree' to $7 =$ 'strongly agree' (7). The list included tangible 'search attributes', such as the price and the appearance of the products, 'experience attributes', such as taste, and intangible 'credence attributes', such as environmentally friendliness and health (cf. Darby & Karni, 1973). The full list of belief items is shown in Appendix 1.

Personal experience with buying organic food was measured by the item: 'If you buy organic foods, please estimate for how many months or years you have been buying them' (a six-point scale with response categories ranging from 'less than 3 months' to 'more than 5 years'). This question was only asked to participants who reported buying organic food. Participants who did not buy organic food were coded as 0 on this item.

Schwartz's 40-item Portrait Value Questionnaire (PVQ) was used to measure individual value priorities (Schwartz et al., 2001). The PVQ includes short verbal portraits of 40 imaginary persons. Each portrait describes a person's goals, aspirations, or wishes that point implicitly to the importance of a value. For each portrait, respondents are asked: 'How much like you is this person?' Responses were given on a five-point graded scale from 'very much like me' (coded as 6) to 'not like me at all' (coded as 1). The 40 items are assumed to reflect 10 basic motivational value domains, each represented by three to six items. The construct reliabilities of the 10 value domains vary from the acceptable to the not acceptable (Cronbach's $\alpha$: Stimulation $= .70$, Universalism $= .69$, Security $= .65$, Achievement $= .64$, Benevolence $= .63$, Hedonism $= .60$, Conformity $= .52$, Self-direction $= .49$, Tradition $= .49$, Power $= .41$).

### Statistical method

AMOS 16 (Arbuckle, 2006) is used for the confirmatory factor analysis (CFA) and structural equation modelling (SEM). The main advantage of SEM is that it is possible to account explicitly for measurement error when a latent variable of interest is represented by multiple manifest variables. Measures of 'fit', that is, of the extent to which the implied variance–covariance matrix, based on the parameter estimates, reflects the observed sample variance–covariance matrix can be used to determine whether the hypothesised model gives an acceptable representation of the analysed data.

The usual assumptions about uncorrelated unique ('error') terms and a simple structure factor pattern in the measurement model were applied, but the first of these assumptions had to be relaxed in one case (an error correlation in the measurement model for the attitude) in order to secure an acceptable model fit. When there is only one item representing a latent construct, as for example with injunctive and descriptive norms in the present study, the measurement error cannot be estimated but has to be set to a fixed value. For single-item constructs used as dependent variables (i.e. behaviour), we fixed the error variance to zero. For constructs used as predictor variables (i.e. injunctive and descriptive norms, beliefs), we fixed it to 20% of the item's total variance (which is 'typical' for survey measures, cf. Andrews, 1984).

# Results

### Characterising participants who have started the process of adopting organic food

Since we intercepted participants as they left a supermarket that sold organic food, we could be sure they had been exposed to organic food. As mentioned earlier, we initially screened the participants according to whether or not they had a reasonably precise idea about what organic food is. We infer that participants who passed the screening have noticed organic food and understood what it is and in this respect have started the adoption process. In Table 1, we compare those who passed the screening and those who failed on key demographic characteristics.

As predicted by Hypothesis 1, participants who know organic food (i.e. passed the screening) are more educated and have a higher income than those who do not, on average (Table 1). The two groups do not differ significantly in terms of gender composition (both groups are mostly female), age, or family size.

In order to investigate whether the two groups also differ in terms of value priorities, as predicted, $t$-tests were calculated for each of the 10 value types using as input averages of the items belonging to each value type centred around the person's mean score on all 10 value types. The centring was done to control for individual variation in scale use (cf. Schwartz, 1992). A significant difference in value priorities was found, but only for one motivational value type. Those who know organic food gave higher priority to what Schwartz (1992, 1994) termed 'universalism' values ($M = .49$) than those who did not know organic food ($M = .38$), on average ($t = 2.467, p = .01$).

In sum, these analyses strongly suggest that it is not accidental which Chinese shoppers know or do not know organic food. Especially, Chinese shoppers are more

**Table 1** Descriptive background characteristics for participants who have ('know')/do not have ('don't know') a reasonably precise idea of what organic food is.

|  | Know organic food | Don't know organic food |
| --- | --- | --- |
| Education[1] | 4.56 | 4.35 |
| Income[2] | 2.58 | 2.27 |
| Gender ($M = 1, F = 2$) | 1.83 | 1.81 |
| Age[3] | 2.24 | 2.27 |
| Household size | 3.61 | 3.85 |

*Note*: $N = 742$. [1]No formal schooling = 1, <primary school = 2, primary school = 3, secondary school = 4, tertiary education = 5, post-graduate degree = 6. Difference significant, independent samples Mann–Whitney $U$ test, $p < .001$. [2]Monthly household income: <3000Y = 1, 3–5000Y = 2, 5–8000Y = 3, 8–10,000Y = 4, >10,000Y = 5. Difference significant, independent samples Mann–Whitney $U$ test, $p < .001$. [3]18–25 years = 1, 26–34 years = 2, 35–44 years = 3, 45–60 years = 4.

likely to have noticed organic food and to have a reasonably accurate understanding of what it is – a first step in the process of adopting organic food – if they are more educated, but also if they have a higher income (and, hence, the ability to buy it) and if the products match their value priorities (and they are, therefore, motivated to buy it). For consumers with a low income or whose value priorities do not 'fit' organic products, these new products are not very relevant, and therefore these consumers are less likely to pay attention to them or to information about them.

### *From knowing to liking*

As previously mentioned, we draw on two attitude theories to investigate why some Chinese consumers are more likely than others to proceed from knowing to liking organic food (expectancy–value attitude theory and Bem's self-perception theory). In the analysis reported in Figure 2, we view these theories as complementary accounts of attitude formation. Hence, we control for possible antecedents of Chinese consumers' attitude towards buying organic vegetables suggested by both views, specifically salient beliefs about consequences of buying organic vegetables and the length of personal experiences with doing so. In order to simplify the model and reduce the risk of multicollinearity, we used a stepwise procedure to identify relevant beliefs. First, we included the 'modal belief' item that was most strongly correlated with the attitude as predictor. Next, we added belief items to the model, one by one, in the order of their bivariate correlations, checking the significance of the items at each step, and deleting non-significant predictors again. Based on this stepwise procedure, the final model includes four beliefs contributing significantly to attitudinal variance (Figure 2).

**Figure 2** Antecedents of attitudes towards buying organic food in Guangzhou, China. Standardized solution, $N = 529$. Model fit: chi-square = 31.264, 17 df, CFI = .99, RMSEA = .040 (90% confidence interval: .016–.062). In order to save space, only the structural model is shown in this figure and in the following SEM analyses. The rest of the AMOS output can be acquired from the first author.

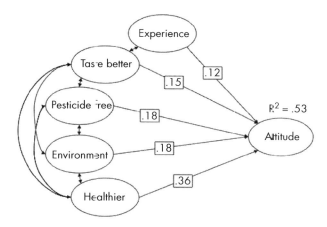

According to the fit indices, the model reported in Figure 2 gives an acceptable representation of the data.[3] The included antecedents account for 53% of the variance in these Chinese consumers' attitudes towards buying organic vegetables. This amount of explained variance is usually considered respectable in multivariate statistical analyses, but it is much lower than in the following analysis, suggesting either that there are still important antecedents that are unaccounted for in our model or, even more likely in a case such as this, that there is a rather large random element in the responses due to many respondents feeling uncertain about what to answer.

When looking at the relationships in the model, it is striking that the same four beliefs are significant predictors of the attitude towards buying organic vegetables in China as have been found to be most important in Western Europe (beliefs about its healthiness, pesticide residues, environmental friendliness, and taste), and the same goes for experience (Thøgersen, 2009). This finding is consistent with Hypothesis 2a and with an exploratory study carried out in the same area of China at about the same time as this one but using a different questionnaire format (Yin et al., 2010). Consistent with Hypothesis 2b, this analysis also found that Chinese consumers' buying experience with regard to organic food account for additional variance in the attitude towards buying organic vegetables, after controlling for salient beliefs about doing so (Figure 2).

### From liking to deciding to buy organic food

As mentioned earlier, it is possible for social motives to both speed up and hamper the innovation adoption process. However, in the introduction phase where few have adopted the innovation, there is a lack of social models or social expectations to back up a decision to adopt. For an innovation such as organic food, there is hardly any resistance against adoption in the social system either. Under these circumstances, social motives are probably less important than personal motives for deciding to adopt an innovation such as this, even in a collectivistic culture. Our analysis of the relative weight of personal and social motives for intentions to buy organic vegetables in China, while also controlling for perceived behavioural control, is presented in Figure 3.

According to the fit indices, the model gives an acceptable representation of the data. Also, the included antecedents predict buying intentions regarding organic vegetables to a very high extent. Intentions to buy seem to depend primarily on the person's attitude to buying these products, whereas social norms, injunctive as well as descriptive, play no role when personal attitudes are controlled for. This is consistent with Hypothesis 3. Since the two norm constructs were measured with only a single item each, the estimates of their impact may be attenuated, but it is unlikely that attenuation can fully explain the big difference between the impacts of attitudes and norms.

---

[3] As previously mentioned, we had four attitude items measuring two aspects of the attitude: a cognitive and an affective evaluation of buying organic food. Because they measured the same aspect, the unique (i.e. error) variances of the two cognitive items proved to be correlated. Hence, in order to improve the model fit, we dropped the assumption about uncorrelated error terms for the correlation between these two error terms.

**Figure 3** Antecedents of intentions to buy organic vegetables. Standardized solution, N = 529. Model fit: chi-square = 128.235, 26 df, CFI = .92, RMSEA = .086 (90% confidence interval: .072–.101).

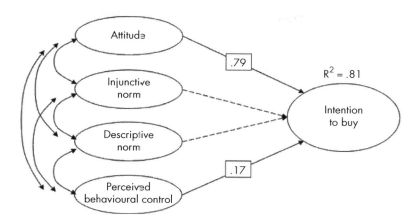

Perceived behavioural control contributes significantly to explaining the variance in intentions in the expected direction. Given the high prices and very selective distribution (i.e. low availability) of organic food, one might have expected a bigger contribution from this variable. Perhaps the effect of perceptions about how easy or difficult it is to buy organic food was attenuated because the interviews were carried out outside supermarkets selling organic food. Further, the low reliability of this construct, as reported earlier, suggests that Chinese consumers hold these perceptions with a high degree of uncertainty. A low reliability also tends to attenuate relationships between constructs. Be that as it may, the participating consumers seem to base their reported intentions to buy organic vegetables squarely on their personal attitudes while apparently only making small adjustments for restrictive objective conditions or perceived social expectations.

### From intentions to behaviour

Finally, we report our analysis of the relationship between buying intentions and organic buying behaviour among the participating Chinese consumers while also controlling for perceived control and income; a variable reflecting actual control (Fishbein & Ajzen, 2009) regarding the purchase of expensive products such as these. We hypothesised that in China, where the organic market is still in its infancy, the relative importance of buying intentions and control factors for organic buying behaviour should resemble that of European countries with a less developed organic market. Hence, control factors should mean more than intentions when it comes to the final adoption of organic vegetables. This is exactly what our analysis show (Figure 4).

Again, the fit indices show that the model gives an acceptable (actually, very good) representation of the data. Next, Figure 4 shows that, as expected, the buying behaviour regarding organic vegetables is positively related to behavioural intentions. However, the relationship is rather weak. We also find that perceived behavioural control is a stronger predictor than behavioural intentions. This is consistent with

**Figure 4** From intention to action. $N = 529$. Model fit: chi-square $= 8.450$, 5 df, CFI $= .99$, RMSEA $= .036$ (90% confidence interval: .000–.077).

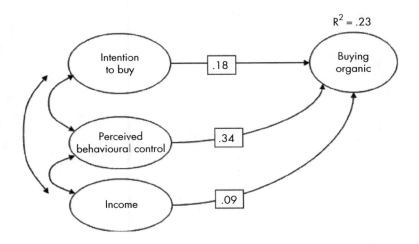

Hypothesis 4 and with what has previously been reported from less developed organic markets in Europe (Thøgersen, 2009). Finally, family income accounts for additional explained variance. Considering the rather restrictive conditions for buying organic food in China, one might have expected an even bigger contribution from control factors. Again, the estimated paths may be attenuated due to low construct reliabilities, not least due to the fact that both behaviour and income were measured with only one item each. The fact that the interviews were carried out outside supermarkets selling organic food may also have attenuated the impact of perceived control.

The included antecedents only account for 23% of the variance in these Chinese consumers' self-reported buying behaviour. The low explained variance is partly due to measurement issues (notably that the dependent variable is measured by a single item only), and partly due to behavioural antecedents not being accounted for. It is likely that the impeding socio-structural conditions for buying organic food in China, even in big metropolises, increase the random element in respondents' reports about this issue. Also, if properly measured and included in the analysis, further actual control factors (i.e. objective structural conditions) might have accounted for additional variance.

## Discussion

### Summary of findings

As expected, the early adopters of organic food in China are characterised by relatively high education and income and by giving relatively high priority to what Schwartz termed 'universalism' values. Like in the West, no other value types are significantly related to the adoption of organic food when universalism is controlled for. Also like in the West, a positive attitude towards buying organic food in China is linked to believing that it is healthier, tastes better, and is better for the environment.

Past experience has an additional, positive effect on attitude towards buying organic food, which suggests that there are self-reinforcing mechanisms promoting this behaviour. In this early phase of the introduction of organic food in China, personal preferences (attitudes or liking) are decisive for the formation of an intention to buy organic food. Social norms play no role in this connection, probably because the early adopters have few role models to look at and face few expectations either way. Perhaps partly because the interviews were carried out outside supermarkets selling organic food, perceptions about how easy or difficult they are to get played a minor role for intention formation as well. However, taking the final step from intention to adoption is obviously not as easy in the current Chinese society, as reflected in perceived control being more strongly related to behaviour than intentions. Not surprisingly, taking the last step from intention to actually buying organic food is also more likely the higher the family income is, given the same level of intentions and perceived control.

### Limitations

This study was carried out in a context where organic food is a new and not very well-known concept. Among other things, this has had negative implications for the reliability of a number of the measured constructs, and the presented results should be interpreted with that reservation in mind. We attempted to reduce the uncertainty of participants' reports by screening for knowledge of organic food, but even consumers that in principle know what organic food is may be uncertain about what that means in practice. Consumer uncertainty can be reduced by means of consumer education and campaigns (Thøgersen, 2005). Increased public debate about the concept as it diffuses through the market may also contribute to reducing uncertainty.

Another important limitation is that this research is based on a non-random sample of consumers from a single city. Hence, it cannot be assumed that the findings are representative for China as a whole. In order to obtain a more representative picture of Chinese consumers' motives and motivation to adopt organic food, studies based on representative samples or replications of this study in other parts of China are needed. Still, in the current situation, our results may provide a more useful picture of the actual market situation for organic food in big-city China than a representative sample of the whole population would have done.

We base this argument on the finding that who has and who lacks knowledge about organic food in China is not accidental. Knowing organic food is related to how relevant this new concept is to the consumer as reflected both in its relation to motivation (i.e. universalism values) and to the ability to buy (i.e. education and income). Hence, when studying the emerging market for a sustainable consumption alternative, such as organic food in China, limiting the sampling to geographical locations with a relatively high concentration of potential early adopters and screening for knowledge of the concept are cost-effective means to focus on the segment of consumers that are currently in the market for that type of product.

### Implications

The similarities between what this study reports for China and what previous studies have reported for Europe regarding the motives and motivation to buy organic food products are striking. Early adopters of organic food in China are seemingly guided by the same value priorities and motivated by the same beliefs about consequences of doing so as have been previously found in Europe (e.g. Thøgersen, 2009). Hence, it seems that the basic drivers behind buying organic food are identical across these very different cultural contexts. Further, the motives for buying organic food seem to be derived from their specific, defining characteristics, and the basic motivation has to do with organic food been perceived as beneficial for 'the common good' in both cultures (Thøgersen, 2011). This is a finding of great practical relevance for cross-cultural research and for marketing, and future research should investigate whether it can be replicated in yet other cultural contexts.

In the current situation, personal motives mean relatively more and social motives less for the intention to buy organic food in China than in Europe (cf. Thøgersen, 2009), despite China's culture being characterised as more collectivistic and Europe's as more individualistic. As previously argued, Yamagishi's institutional approach to cultural differences in behaviour can explain this apparent paradox. According to Yamagishi et al. (2008), even in a collectivistic culture people follow their personal preferences in contexts where there is no risk of social disapproval. We argue that the early introduction phase of an innovation is such a context. This also means that this situation is likely to change in the future. Hence, we predict that social norms will become more important for Chinese consumers' buying intentions and behaviour as the market for organic food in China matures. Future research should test this prediction.

Under all circumstances, the first individuals who are willing to adopt an innovation are vital for getting the diffusion process started (Kotler & Roberto, 1989). In later phases of the diffusion process, the fact that others have already adopted the innovation is an important asset for its promotion to more reluctant adopter groups, as is positive word of mouth from earlier adopters acting as referents or opinion leaders (Hoyer & MacInnis, 2006). In this connection, it is an advantage that the early adopters of organic food have relatively high incomes and are better educated than average. This bodes well for their ability to function as role models and opinion leaders. Hence, it is likely that marketers promoting organic food products in China can benefit from building their communication strategies on the early adopters, acting as spokes people, role models, and opinion leaders.

Due to the average consumer's need for 'social proof' and the human propensity to imitate others, innovations that are not observable, for instance because they are used in private, tend to diffuse more slowly than innovations that are observable (Hoyer & MacInnis, 2006; Rogers, 2003). Since food products bought in a supermarket are usually consumed in private and organic food products are not visually different from conventional, except for the organic label, this aspect is bound to hamper the diffusion of organic food. Hence, marketing communication is needed for organic food to activate the mentioned social dynamics and speed up the diffusion process.

Chinese consumer intentions are currently less important than control factors for their final adoption of organic food. Thus in hindsight, it might have been better to spend more efforts to capture important control factors (and beliefs) to see which control factors relate most to determine actual behaviour. Be that as it may, this finding is consistent with what has previously been found in European countries with less developed organic markets, but different from what has been found in the countries with the most developed organic markets. Hence, it is likely that this finding is related to the maturity of the market rather than to culture-specific conditions. The impediments for buying organic food are bigger in China than in most European countries, especially in terms of availability – organic food only being available in a handful of upscale supermarkets in a metropolis like Guangzhou – and its much higher premium price. That low availability and high prices are the main barriers reducing consumer purchase of organic food has also been found in another study in China (Yin et al., 2010), as well as in most other international contexts (Hughner et al., 2007; Thøgersen, 2010a). Hence, in order to facilitate future growth of the organic market in China, these two impediments need to be targeted. More intensive but also more low-cost distribution strategies are called for, as well as a lowering of the premium prices (Thøgersen, 2010a).

# References

Ajzen, I. (1991). The Theory of Planned Behavior. *Organizational Behavior and Decision Processes*, 50, 179–211.

Ajzen, I., & Fishbein, M. (1980). *Understanding attitudes and predicting social behavior.* Englewood Cliffs, NJ: Prentice-Hall.

Andrews, F.M. (1984). Construct validity and error components of survey measures: A structural modeling approach. *Public Opinion Quarterly*, 48, 409–442.

Arbuckle, J.L. (2006). *Amos 7.0 user's guide.* Chicago: SPSS.

Bagozzi, R.P., Wong, N., Abe, S., & Bergami, M. (2000). Cultural and situational contingencies and the theory of reasoned action: Application to fast-food and restaurant consumption. *Journal of Consumer Psychology*, 9, 97–106.

Bandura, A. (1982). Self-efficacy mechanism in human agency. *American Psychologist*, 37, 122–147.

Bandura, A. (2001). Social cognitive theory: An agentic perspective. *Annual Review of Psychology*, 52, 1–26.

Bem, D.J. (1972). Self-perception theory. In L. Berkowitz (Ed.), *Advances in experimental social psychology* (pp. 1–62). New York: Academic Press.

Chan, R.Y.K. (2001). Determinants of Chinese consumers' green purchase behavior. *Psychology and Marketing*, 18, 389–413.

Chan, R.Y.K., & Lau, L.B.Y. (2000). Antecedents of green purchases: A survey in China. *Journal of Consumer Marketing*, 17, 338–357.

Chan, R.Y.K., & Lau, L.B.Y. (2001). Explaining green purchasing behavior: A cross-cultural study on American and Chinese consumers. *Journal of International Consumer Marketing*, 14(2/3), 9–40.

Cialdini, R.B. (2001). *Influence: Science and practice* (4th ed.). Boston: Allyn and Bacon.

Cialdini, R.B., Demaine, L.J., Sagarin, B.J., Barrett, D.W., Rhoads, K., & Winter, P.L. (2006). Managing social norms for persuasive impact. *Social Influence*, 1, 3–15.

D'Souza, C. (2004). Ecolabel programmes: A stakeholder (consumer) perspective. *Corporate Communications*, 9, 179–188.

Darby, M.R., & Karni, E. (1973). Free competition and the optimal amount of fraud. *Journal of Law and Economics*, 16, 67–88.

Dean, M., Raats, M.M., & Shepherd, R. (2008). Moral concerns and consumer choice of fresh and processed organic foods. *Journal of Applied Social Psychology*, 38, 2088–2107.

Doran, C. (2009). The role of personal values in fair trade consumption. *Journal of Business Ethics*, 84, 549–563.

Dreezens, E., Martijn, C., Tenbult, P., Kok, G., & de Vries, N.K. (2005). Food and values: An examination of values underlying attitudes toward genetically modified and organically grown food products. *Appetite*, 44, 115–122.

Eagly, A.H., & Chaiken, S. (1993). *The psychology of attitudes.* Fort Worth, TX: Harcourt Brace Jovanovich College.

Ellison, J. (2008, June 28). Save the planet, lose the guilt. *Newsweek*.

Fazio, R.H. (1990). Multiple processes by which attitudes guide behavior: The MODE model as an integrative framework. In M.P. Zanna (Ed.), *Advances in experimental social psychology* (Vol. 23; pp. 75–109). New York: Academic Press.

Fishbein, M., & Ajzen, I. (2009). *Predicting and changing behavior: The reasoned action approach*. New York: Psychology Press.

Fisher, R.J., & Price, L.L. (1992). An investigation into the social context of early adoption behavior. *Journal of Consumer Research*, 19, 477–486.

Grankvist, G., Lekedal, H., & Marmendal, M. (2007). Values and eco- and fair-trade labelled products. *British Food Journal*, 109, 169–181.

Hofstede, G. (1980). *Culture's consequences: International differences in work-related values*. Beverly Hills, CA: Sage.

Honkanen, P., Verplanken, B., & Olsen, S.O. (2006). Ethical values and motives driving organic food choice. *Journal of Consumer Behaviour*, 5, 420–430.

Hoyer, W.D., & MacInnis, D.J. (2006). *Consumer behavior* (4th ed.). Boston: Houghton Mifflin.

Hughner, R.S., McDonagh, P., Prothero, A., Shultz, C., & Stanton, J. (2007). Who are organic food consumers? A compilation and review of why people purchase organic food. *Journal of Consumer Behaviour*, 6, 94–110.

Kim, D., Pan, Y., & Park, H.S. (1998). High-versus low-context culture: A comparison of Chinese, Korean, and American cultures. *Psychology and Marketing*, 15, 507–521.

Kotler, P., & Roberto, E.L. (1989). *Social marketing. Strategies for changing public behavior*. New York: Free Press.

Krystallis, A., Vassallo, M., Chryssohoidis, G., & Perrea, T. (2008). Societal and individualistic drivers as predictors of organic purchasing revealed through a portrait value questionnaire (PVQ)-based inventory. *Journal of Consumer Behaviour*, 7, 164–187.

Lee, C., & Green, R.T. (1991). Cross-cultural examination of the Fishbein behavioural intention model. *Journal of International Business Studies*, 22, 289–305.

Lee, J.A. (2000). Adapting Triandis's model of subjective culture and social behaviour relations to consumer behaviour. *Journal of Consumer Psychology*, 9, 117–126.

Liu, J., Wang, R., & Yang, J.-X. (2009). Environment consumption patterns of Chinese urban households and their policy implications. *International Journal of Sustainable Development and World Ecology*, 16(1), 9–14.

Lockeretz, W. (Ed.). (2007). *Organic farming: An international history*. Wallingford, UK: CABI.

Madden, N. (2007). Are Chinese going green? *AdAge China*.

Madden, N. (2009). 20 trends changing China you should know about. *AdAge China*.

Magnusson, M.K., Arvola, A., Hursti, U.-K. K., Åberg, L., & Sjöden, P.-O. (2001). Attitudes towards organic foods among Swedish consumers. *British Food Journal*, 103, 209–226.

McDonagh, P. (2002). Communicative campaigns to effect anti-slavery and fair trade. The case of Rugmark and Cafédirect. *European Journal of Marketing*, 36, 642–666.

McEwen, W., Fang, X., Zhang, C., & Burkholder, R. (2006). Inside the mind of the Chinese consumer. *Harvard Business Review*, 84(3), 68–76.

McGuire, W.J., Lindzey, I.G., & Aronson, E. (1985). Attitudes and attitude change. *Handbook in social psychology* (pp. 233–345). New York: Random House.

Polsa, P., So, S.L.M., & Speece, M.W. (2005). The People's Republic of China. In A. Pecotich & C.J. Shultz II (Eds.), *Handbook of markets and economies: East Asia, Southeast Asia, Australia, New Zealand*. Armonk, NY: M.E. Sharpe.

Rivis, A., & Sheeran, P. (2003). Descriptive norms as an additional predictor in the theory of planned behaviour: A meta-analysis. *Current Psychology*, 22, 218–233.

Rogers, E.M. (2003). *Diffusion of innovations* (5th ed.). New York: Free Press.

Schwartz, S.H. (1992). Universals in the content and structure of values: Theoretical advances and empirical tests in 20 countries. In M.P. Zanna (Ed.), *Advances in experimental social psychology* (pp. 1–65). San Diego, CA: Academic Press.

Schwartz, S.H. (1994). Are there universal aspects in the structure and content of human values? *Journal of Social Issues*, 50(4), 19–45.

Schwartz, S.H. (1999). A theory of cultural values and some implications for work. *Applied Psychology: An International Review*, 48, 23–48.

Schwartz, S.H., Melech, G., Lehmann, A., Burgess, S., Harris, M., & Owens, V. (2001). Extending the cross-cultural validity of the theory of basic human values with a different method of measurement. *Journal of Cross-Cultural Psychology*, 32, 519–542.

Shaw, D., & Clarke, I. (1998). Culture, consumption and choice: Towards a conceptual relationship. *Journal of Consumer Studies and Home Economics*, 22, 163–168.

Shaw, D., Grehan, E., Shiu, E., Hassan, L., & Thomson, J. (2005). An exploration of values in ethical consumer decision making. *Journal of Consumer Behaviour*, 4, 185–200.

Shen, J., & Saijo, T. (2008). Reexamining the relations between socio-demographic characteristics and individual environmental concern: Evidence from Shanghai data. *Journal of Environmental Psychology*, 28, 42–50.

Solomon, M.R. (2008). *Consumer behavior* (8th ed.). Upper Saddle River, NJ: Prentice Hall.

Thøgersen, J. (1997). *Understanding behaviours with mixed motives. An application of a modified Theory of Reasoned Action on consumer purchase of organic food products*. Paper presented at the The Association for Consumer Research 1997 European Conference, Stockholm.

Thøgersen, J. (2005). Consumer behaviour and the environment: Which role for information? In S. Krarup & C.S. Russell (Eds.), *Environment, information and consumer behaviour* (pp. 51–63). Cheltenham, UK: Edward Elgar.

Thøgersen, J. (2009). Consumer decision-making with regard to organic food products. In M.T.d.N. Vaz, P. Nijkamp, & J.L. Rastoin (Eds.), *Traditional food production facing sustainability: A European challenge* (pp. 173–194). Farnham, England: Ashgate.

Thøgersen, J. (2010a). Country differences in sustainable consumption: The case of organic food. *Journal of Macromarketing*, 30, 171–185.

Thøgersen, J. (2010b). Pro-environmental consumption. In K.M. Ekström (Ed.), *Consumer behaviour – A Nordic perspective* (pp. 95–115). Lund, Sweden: Studentlitteratur.

Thøgersen, J. (2011). Green shopping: For selfish reasons or the common good? *American Behavioral Scientist*, 55, 1052–1076.

Thøgersen, J., Haugaard, P., & Olesen, A. (2010). Understanding consumer responses to ecolabels. *European Journal of Marketing*, 44, 1787–1810.

Thøgersen, J., & Ölander, F. (2006). To what degree are environmentally beneficial choices reflective of a general conservation stance? *Environment and Behavior*, 38, 550–569.

Torjusen, H., Sangstad, L., Jensen, K.O.D., & Kjærnes, U. (2004). *European consumers' conceptions of organic food. A review of available research*. Oslo, Norway: National Institute for Consumer Research.

USDA (2005). *Administrative measures for certification of organic products in People's Republic of China*. Washington, DC: USDA.

Usunier, J.C., & Lee, J.A. (2009). *Marketing across cultures* (5th ed.). Harlow, UK: Pearson.

Willer, H., Yussefi-Menzler, M., & Sorensen, N. (Eds.). (2008). *The world of organic agriculture – Statistics and emerging trends 2008*. London: Earthscan.

Winter, C.K., & Davis, S.F. (2006). Organic foods. *Journal of Food Science*, 71(9), R117–R124.

Yamagishi, T., Hashimoto, H., & Schug, J. (2008). Preferences versus strategies as explanations for culture-specific behavior. *Psychological Science*, 19, 579–584.

Yin, S., Wu, L., Du, L., & Chen, M. (2010). Consumers' purchase intention of organic food in China. *Journal of the Science of Food and Agriculture*, 90, 1361–1367.

Zanoli, R., & Naspetti, S. (2002). Consumer motivations in the purchase of organic food. A means-end approach. *British Food Journal*, 104, 643–653.

Zepeda, L., & Deal, D. (2009). Organic and local food consumer behaviour: Alphabet Theory. *International Journal of Consumer Studies*, 33, 697–705.

## Appendix 1. A full list of the items used in capturing the behavioural beliefs[4]

1. Organic food is free from chemicals such as residues from fertilisers, pesticides.
2. Organic vegetables are more expensive.
3. Organic vegetables taste better.
4. Organic vegetables are produced in a way that is better for the environment.
5. Organic vegetables keep fresh for less time.
6. Organic vegetables are better for the health.
7. The appearance of organic vegetables is less attractive.
8. Organic vegetables are more natural.
9. Vegetables sold as 'organic' are not really organic.

[4] In all cases, seven-point scales were used. Scale endpoints were 'strongly disagree' to 'strongly agree'.

# Consumer attitudes towards sustainability aspects of food production: Insights from three continents

Athanasios Krystallis, *Aarhus University, Denmark*
Klaus G. Grunert, *Aarhus University, Denmark*
Marcia D. de Barcellos, *Federal University of Rio Grande do Sul, Brazil*
Toula Perrea, *Aarhus University, Denmark*
Wim Verbeke, *Ghent University, Belgium*

**Abstract** This study aims to analyse citizens' sustainability attitudes towards food production in the EU, Brazil, and China ($n = 2885$), using pork as an exemplary production system. The objective is to map citizens' attitudes towards sustainable characteristics of pig production systems, and investigate whether these attitudes coincide with people's general attitudes towards sustainability, on one hand, and their consumption of specific pork products, on the other. A conjoint experiment was designed to evaluate citizens' preferences towards pig production systems with varying sustainability levels. Conjoint analysis results were then used for a subsequent cluster analysis in order to identify international citizen clusters across the three continents. Respondents' sociodemographic profile, attitudes towards sustainability issues, and consumption frequency of various pork products are used to profile resulting segments. Results for the three continents point out that general sustainability attitudes relate to citizens' attitudes towards pig farming only for specific small-sized social groups. However, what the large majority of respondents think in their role as citizens related to pig production did not appear to influence their pork consumption choices significantly. The main implication of this finding is that while critical attitudes only weakly influence purchasing behaviour, they may, however, still be expressed in the public debate and influence policy formation at national and global levels. This study therefore provides valuable insights to policymakers and practitioners for improvements in an integrated management of food chains to meet consumer sustainability-related expectations better.

## Introduction

A significant part of society nowadays lives and works under extreme pressure caused by the necessity to act upon many expectations and obligations in a limited period of time. In terms of everyday consumption patterns, a growing tendency of over-consumption can be observed, which is becoming more alarming and is being highly prioritised in the political and social agenda. Research also underlines the concerns about the consequences of unmonitored consumption practices within a 'throw-away' society, which can lead to environmental, social, and economic degeneration (Hume, 2009). Recently, attempts have been increasingly made by various stakeholders to engage citizens in more sustainable behavioural practices and to make them embody those practices in their everyday consumption behaviour. Social scientists have contributed significantly to this effort by examining consumers' motivations behind diverse consumption behaviours and their outcomes, pointing to the economic activities with the highest environmental impact: transportation, energy use, construction, and food (mainly meat and dairy) production (Tukker, Emmert, Charter, Vezzoli, & Sto, 2008). However, many consumers seem to give little thought to the links between their consumption behaviours and the process of food production (de Boer, Boersema, & Aiking, 2009).

The present study analyses citizens' attitudes towards food production in three continents, using pork farming as an example of a contemporary debated food production system. The overall objective of the study is to map the attitudes of people in three continents in relation to characteristics of pig production systems, and investigate whether these attitudes are related to their general attitudes towards (environmental and social) sustainability, on one hand, and demand for specific pork products, on the other. The study uses empirical evidence from individuals in four European countries with higher-than-average per capita pork consumption (national representative samples from Belgium, Denmark, Poland, and Germany), as well as from individuals from eight cities in South America (Brazil) and individuals from six cities in Asia (mainland China). Based on the above-described overall objective of the study, our main research questions are as follows:

*RQ1: How are citizens' attitudes to pig production affected by aspects of sustainability of those systems?*

*RQ2: Do citizens who have positive attitudes to more sustainable pig farming practices also have stronger environmental or social concerns in general?*

*RQ3: Do citizens who have positive attitudes to more sustainable pig farming practices consume certain types of pork products less frequently?*

More specifically, in this study we investigate if citizen preferences for pig production depend on key sustainable characteristics of those systems. Through a series of conjoint experiments conducted in the six target countries, the study investigates whether selected sustainable pig farming characteristics have an effect on citizens' preferences for pig production systems. Based on the conjoint results, cluster analyses are run at the continent level (EU, Brazil, China) in order to distinguish citizen groups who differ in how sustainable characteristics of pig production systems affect their preferences, and whether these groups also differ in terms of their general environmental, social, and economic sustainability attitudes. Moreover, if and how those attitudes are reflected in consumers' consumption frequency of a broad range of specific pork products is analysed. Answers to the above questions can provide valuable insights to policymakers and practitioners for improvements in an integrated management of food chains to meet consumer sustainability-related expectations better.

## Sustainable pig production characteristics and citizen attitudes

The role of food production and consumption is central in the debate on sustainability. Recent research has provided empirical insights into the influence of processes involved in the entire life cycle of food, from production to consumption, and its enormous negative impact on the environment in terms of farmland erosion, waste, emission of greenhouse gases, and so on. (Tanner, Kaiser, & Wolfing Kast, 2004). Furthermore, the social component involved in the production of food, in terms of faraway growers and producers of some of the most frequently consumed products like coffee, tea, fruits, sugar, and so on, though often neglected, has an equally significant role in sustaining overall welfare.

The development of agriculture and food production in the second half of the twentieth century focused on providing enough and safe food to the population of Western countries, and production system intensification was one of the driving forces behind this task (Brom, Visak, & Mejiboom, 2007). However, the increase in agricultural efficiency had a drawback: the economic rationale behind it created unwanted environmental consequences and compromised animal welfare. For many years, this trade-off did not constrain intensive food production systems, but citizens' awareness and concern related to its consequences is now growing accordingly (see, e.g., European Commission, 2006). In addition, a distance between producers and consumers is mentally and physically created, mainly as a result of urbanisation (Brom et al., 2007). Stimulated by mass media news coverage and advertisements, modern consumers often have a 'romantic' view of agriculture and food production and, when confronted with the intensive, mainstream agricultural production systems, negative attitudes towards agriculture and food production and technology might emerge (e.g. Frewer, Kole, Van de Kroon, & De Lauwere, 2005; Grunert, 2005; Kanis, Groen, & De Greef, 2003; Søndergaard, Grunert, & Scholderer, 2005; Verbeke, Van Oekel, Warnants, Viane, & Boucque, 1999).

Pig production systems' sustainability, including strategies to achieve economic, social, and environmental goals, has been an extensively researched topic worldwide (e.g. Cavalett, De Queiroz, & Ortega, 2006; Olsson & Pickova, 2005; Siegford, Powers, & Grimes-Casey, 2008; Yang, 2007). The study by Stern et al. (2005) in particular evaluated the cost of different sustainable pig production scenarios that each focused on animal welfare, low impacts on the environment, or the delivery of specific product quality and safety. The evaluation results indicated that the animal welfare scenario had the highest cost per pork kilo, whereas the environmental scenario and the product-quality scenario had the lowest and the highest environmental impact respectively (Stern et al., 2005).

*Economic* goals in relation to sustainability relate to the system's ability to provide a fair income for pig meat producers, as well as affordable pork prices to consumers. In this respect, there is an important duality between intensive pig production systems that provide standard quality bulk products at low cost versus extensive pig production systems that borrow their economic viability from quality differentiation and price premiums. Farm size in general (Darby, Batte, Ernst, & Roe, 2008) or size of the herd (Vanhonacker, Verbeke, Van Poucke, & Tuyttens, 2008) is a relevant indicator when people form attitudes related to intensity in pig production. Farm size is typically expressed as the number of animals on the farm, or to be more specific, as the number of breeding sows in farrowing or mixed farrowing/finishing farms (Wognum et al., 2009). Recent research suggests that 'larger gains in terms of animal welfare image among the public can be realised from providing farm animals with more space relative to reducing animal group size' (Vanhonacker, Verbeke, Van Poucke, Buijs, & Tuyttens, 2009, p. 16).

The *social* component of sustainability concerns an integration of pig production into the priorities and needs of society, which form the basis for an appreciation and support for the sector from society and government. A crucial issue in this respect pertains to animal welfare. Housing in general and floor type in particular have been mentioned as key attributes for individuals, especially lay persons, for evaluating a pork production system's animal friendliness and its societal acceptability (Millet, Moons, Van Oeckel, & Janssens, 2005; Vanhonacker et al., 2008). Furthermore, the provision of safe-to-consume, healthy, and fit-for-use quality pork can be assumed to be related to the system's societal acceptability (Meuwissen, Van der Lans, & Huirne, 2007)[1].

The *environmental* component refers to the system's impact on the natural and living environment and quality of life for humans. The association of pig production with environmental pollution pertains to its negative externalities in terms of degradation of water, air, and soil quality (Petit & Van der Werf, 2003; Pomar, Dubeau, Letourneau-Montnimy, Boucher, & Julien, 2007). Initiatives to implement practices beyond simple compliance with environmental regulations (Siegford et al., 2008) are likely to guide citizens' evaluations of pig production systems.

## Materials and methods

In this study, we extract major attributes of pig production systems relating to all three aspects of sustainability (economic, social, and environmental), as described above. By combining these attributes, we investigate how sustainable characteristics of production systems affect citizens' attitudes to pig production (RQ1). Based on this, the research aims at identifying clusters in the four EU countries, Brazil, and China based on differences in how the above sustainable characteristics of pig production systems affect attitudes to pig farming through a series of conjoint experiments and subsequent cluster analyses. Countries were selected taking into account not only their cultural diversity but also their important role in the global pork sector: China is the world's largest pig producer, followed by the EU (second largest), and Brazil (fourth largest). In terms of foreign trade, China is third in terms of pork imports, whilst the EU, Brazil, and China are second, fourth, and fifth respectively in terms of pork exports. Finally, per capita consumption in the EU, China, and Brazil is 41.8 kg, 37.1 kg, and 14 kg, ranking first, second, and fourth in the world respectively (USDA, 2010).

Then, following research questions 2 and 3, each cluster in each of the three continents is profiled based on: (a) their general attitudes towards wider environmental and economic sustainability themes, such as attitudes towards environment and nature, industrial food production, technological progress, animal

---

[1]Note that food safety is not considered a social component of sustainability, since at least in the Western part of the world, safety is considered a non-tradable good and a non-negotiable attribute from citizen/consumer perspective. People want and expect all food to be safe; otherwise, it should not enter the market (Van Wezemael, Verbeke, Kügler, de Barcellos, & Grunert, 2010). However, this is not always the case with many populations in emerging countries, such as in China, and this will be further depicted in the present research design.

welfare, food and environment, local employment, and local economy (RQ2); and (b) their consumption frequency of various common pork product types (RQ3), and citizens' sociodemographic characteristics.

### Samples and questionnaires

Data were collected through questionnaire-based consumer surveys in the three continents ($N = 2885$).

In Europe (Belgium, Denmark, Poland, and Germany), participants were randomly selected by a professional market research agency from nationally representative online panels. All contact and questionnaire administration procedures were carried out electronically. Questionnaire completion was self-administered without involvement from interviewers. The target population in the four countries was intentionally specified as individuals between 20 and 70 years old, with specific quotas according to age (half the sample in the 20–44 age group and the other half in the 45–70 age group) and residence in relation to pig meat production intensity (urban residence, rural with low pig meat production density, and rural with high pig meat production density).

In Brazil, the survey was conducted in two areas of the country, South and Central-West, which represent different models of pig production. The South, with most of its population descending from immigrants mainly from Germany, Italy, and the Netherlands, can be characterised as a very traditional and conventional pork production region. On the other hand, the Central-West region represents a rather new pork production centre, less populated but rapidly expanding. Data were collected through consumer surveys in eight cities: Porto Alegre, Santa Rosa, Curitiba, and Ponta Grossa in the South), and Cuiabá, Campo Verde, Goiânia, and Rio Verde in the Central-West. The participants were randomly recruited by a professional research agency according to predetermined selection criteria. The target population was intentionally specified as individuals belonging equally to both genders, with specific age quotas (one third of the sample in the 18–30 age group, one third in the 31–50 age group, and one third older than 50) and type of residence in relation to pig meat production (urban vs. rural area with high pig production density).

In China, data collection was concentrated on major cities, as this is where major changes in eating habits are predominantly taking place. Regional allocation was done focusing on the top provinces in terms of pork production and consumption. Six cities across the country were selected: Nanjing (South-East coast); Chengdu (South-West), Wuhan (Centre), Changchun (North-East), Beijing (North), and Guangzhou (South). Data were collected by personal interviews in the six chosen cities. The target population was intentionally specified as individuals belonging equally to both genders, with specific age quotas (one third in the 18–30 age group, one third in the 31–50 age group, and one third older than 50).

The questionnaire used for data collection in all six countries included four sections, although certain modifications were deemed necessary to grasp strong cultural differences that exist among the three continents: (a) attitudes towards environment and nature (in all countries), industrial food production (in the EU and Brazil), technological progress (in the EU and China), animal welfare (in the EU), food and environment (in all countries), local employment (in all countries), and local economy (in all countries); (b) consumption frequencies of various common pork products grouped in five categories, as follows: first fresh cut, fresh minimally processed, further processed, pork-based dishes, and pork meat products; (c) 15 verbal descriptions of various pig farms based on a conjoint design, which were presented to respondents and their opinions collected; and (d) sociodemographic characteristics of the respondents.

All the attitudinal scales used were drawn from the literature. Attitude towards environment and nature was measured using a reduced five-item version of the New Environmental Paradigm (NEP) scale (Dunlap, Van Liere, Mertig, & Jones, 2000). Attitude towards industrial food production was measured with five items developed by Beckmann Brokmose, and Lind (2001). Attitude towards technological progress was measured with five items used by Hamstra (1991). Attitude towards animal welfare was measured with six items from Kendall, Lobao, and Sharp (2006), plus two items from Lindeman and Väänänen (2000). Attitudes towards food and environment were measured with three items from Lindeman and Väänänen (2000). Finally, part of the Consumer Ethnocentric Scale (CETSCALE; Shimp & Sharma, 1987) was used, including five items on local economy and three items on local employment. The scales described above have been tested in many countries and found to exhibit stability and cross-cultural validity. All attitudinal items were measured on seven-point Likert-type agreement scales with end points 1 = 'strongly disagree' to 7 = 'strongly agree'.

The master questionnaires were developed in English and translated into the national languages using the procedure of back-translation. Researchers carefully tested the questionnaire through personal interviews with 15–20 respondents in each of the countries in order to identify and eliminate potential problems and to ensure linguistic equivalence.

### Measurement of attitude towards pig meat production systems/the conjoint experiment

The investigation of attitudes towards pig meat production systems was done by means of a conjoint experiment. In the frame of the present survey, the factors in the conjoint experiment had to tap essential aspects of pig meat farming that could be used by citizens, who are mostly lay persons as far as pig farming practices are concerned, as criteria for their overall evaluation. Moreover, those factors had to reflect all three components of sustainability in food production as described above, and at the same time take into consideration existing differences in the sociocultural and economic background of the populations under study. Thus, based on extensive consultation with experts on pig production systems and the relevant literature described before, the factors described in Table 1 were identified per country.

Especially in China, due to certain unique features of the pork supply and demand (i.e. 75–80% of pork meat is produced in very small family farms or rural backyards; Wang, 2005), Chinese consumers are particularly concerned about food safety. Since the majority of producers in the food processing and catering industry are still small workshops and enterprises that tend to ignore food hygiene and food safety requirements (Xinhuanet, 2007), it was decided to put more emphasis on the social and economic angles of sustainability, approaching food safety as a social sustainability attribute.

The total number of combinations (conjoint 'profiles') of the above factor levels is $3^5 = 243$ (five factors with three levels each) for EU and Brazil and $3^2 \times 2^3 = 72$ for China. The number of combinations to be shown to respondents out of

**Table 1** Conjoint factors and factor levels per country.

| EU and Brazil | China |
|---|---|
| *1. Stocking density* | *1. Farm size* |
| Fewer than 100 sows | Small (family farm with 1–5 sows) |
| About 400 sows | Medium (large-scale family farm with up to 400 sows) |
| 800 or more sows | Large (industrial pig farm with several thousands of sows) |
| *2. Housing and floor type* | *2. Animals' breed* |
| Slatted floor | Traditional Chinese |
| Litter bedding | European |
| Outdoors access | |
| *3. Effort to protect soil, air, water* | *3. Food safety efforts at the farm level* |
| Minimal | Not a special consideration |
| Some | Special attention (regular veterinary control and hygiene regulations) |
| Maximum | Maximum attention (strict veterinary control and hygiene regulations) |
| *4. Fat content according to feed* | *4. Meat type* |
| Standard | Tasty |
| Lower fat | Lean |
| Healthier fat | |
| *5. Quality type of the product* | *5. Quality type of the product* |
| Consistent | Consistent |
| Variable | Variable |
| Demanded by key customers | |

the total number of combinations (the model's 'fractional factorial design') was generated through an orthogonal design procedure (SPSS v15.0). Orthogonality was perfect, assuming no correlation between the conjoint factors (simple linear model with no interaction effects). All factor level combinations that correspond to different versions of pig meat production systems were realistic and thus any multicollinearity problems due to correlation among factors were eliminated. The orthoplan procedure generated 15 fully orthogonal factor level combinations, corresponding to 15 different types of pig farming. An example of the verbal description of the 15 pig farms can be seen in Table 2.

### Data collection procedure

Fieldwork started after editing, correcting, electronic programming (in the EU), and additional pretesting of the questionnaire. The fieldwork in the EU countries took place during January 2008. A total of 1931 respondents completed the questionnaire. In Brazil, the fieldwork took place during March 2008. Questionnaire completion was achieved through face-to-face interviews. A total of 475 respondents completed the questionnaire. In China, fieldwork was mainly done by local researchers. The fieldwork took place between January and March 2008. Each interviewee filled in

# CONTEMPORARY ISSUES IN GREEN AND ETHICAL MARKETING

**Table 2** Examples of verbal description of survey's fractional factorial design (full orthogonality), EU countries.

| Profile no. | Profile description |
|---|---|
| 1 | Consider a farm with about 400 sows. The animals are housed on litter. There is some effort to reduce the production system's ecological impact on soil, water, and air. Pigs' feeding aims for lower fat content. The farm produces pigs with similar meat quality every time. |
| 2 | Consider a farm with about 400 sows. The animals are housed on slatted floors. The effort to reduce the production system's ecological impact on soil, water, and air is maximum. Pigs' feeding aims for standard fat content. The farm produces pigs with the qualities demanded only by their main customers. |
| 3 | Consider a small farm with fewer than 100 sows and other livestock. The animals are housed on litter. The effort to reduce the production system's ecological impact on soil, water, and air is maximum. Pigs' feeding aims for standard fat content. The farm produces pigs with different quality because of biological variations and changing local conditions. |
| 4 | Consider a farm with up to or more than 800 sows with hired labour. The animals have outdoors access. The effort to reduce the production system's ecological impact on soil, water, and air is maximum. Pigs' feeding aims for healthy fat. The farm produces pigs with similar meat quality every time. |
| 5 | Consider a small farm with fewer than 100 sows and other livestock. The animals are housed on slatted floors. The effort to reduce the production system's ecological impact on soil, water, and air is minimal. Pigs' feeding aims for standard fat content. The farm produces pigs with similar meat quality every time. |
| 6 | Consider a small farm with fewer than 100 sows and other livestock. The animals are housed on slatted floors. There is some effort to reduce the production system's ecological impact on soil, water, and air. Pigs' feeding aims for healthy fat. The farm produces pigs with similar meat quality every time. |
| 7 | Consider a farm with up to or more than 800 sows with hired labour. The animals are housed on slatted floors. There is some effort to reduce the production system's ecological impact on soil, water, and air. Pigs' feeding aims for standard fat content. The farm produces pigs with the qualities demanded only by their main customers. |
| 8 | Consider a small farm with fewer than 100 sows and other livestock. The animals have outdoors access. The effort to reduce the production system's ecological impact on soil, water, and air is minimal. Pigs' feeding aims for lower fat content. The farm produces pigs with the qualities demanded only by their main customers. |
| 9 | Consider a small farm with fewer than 100 sows and other livestock. The animals have outdoors access. There is some effort to reduce the production system's ecological impact on soil, water, and air. Pigs' feeding aims for standard fat content. The farm produces pigs with different quality because of biological variations and changing local conditions. |
| 10 | Consider a farm with about 400 sows. The animals have outdoors access. The effort to reduce the production system's ecological impact on soil, water, and air is minimal. Pigs' feeding aims for standard fat content. The farm produces pigs with similar meat quality every time. |

(*Continued*)

# CONTEMPORARY ISSUES IN GREEN AND ETHICAL MARKETING

**Table 2** (Continued).

| Profile no. | Profile description |
|---|---|
| 11 | Consider a farm with up to or more than 800 sows with hired labour. The animals are housed on slatted floors. The effort to reduce the production system's ecological impact on soil, water, and air is minimal. Pigs' feeding aims for lower fat content. The farm produces pigs with different quality because of biological variations and changing local conditions. |
| 12 | Consider a farm with about 400 sows. The animals are housed on slatted floors. The effort to reduce the production system's ecological impact on soil, water, and air is minimal. Pigs' feeding aims for healthy fat. The farm produces pigs with different quality because of biological variations and changing local conditions. |
| 13 | Consider a small farm with fewer than 100 sows and other livestock. The animals are housed on slatted floors. The effort to reduce the production system's ecological impact on soil, water, and air is maximum. Pigs' feeding aims for lower fat content. The farm produces pigs with similar meat quality every time. |
| 14 | Consider a farm with up to or more than 800 sows with hired labour. The animals are housed on litter. The effort to reduce the production system's ecological impact on soil, water, and air is minimal. Pigs' feeding aims for standard fat content. The farm produces pigs with similar meat quality every time. |
| 15 | Consider a small farm with fewer than 100 sows and other livestock. The animals are housed on litter. The effort to reduce the production system's ecological impact on soil, water, and air is minimal. Pigs' feeding aims for healthy fat. The farm produces pigs with similar meat quality every time. |

the questionnaire under the guidance and supervision of the interviewer. A total of 479 respondents completed the questionnaire.

The following procedure for the conjoint experiment was applied in every country: all respondents had to look at each of the 15 verbal descriptions (conjoint profiles) of pig meat production systems, which were presented to them in a randomised order. As explained above, the combination of the attribute alternatives made each production system unique. Each respondent had to indicate how much s/he liked the described system by assigning a score to each on an 11-point liking rating scale, with end points $-5$ = 'dislike very much' to $+5$ = 'like very much'. Before the conjoint rating task was executed, respondents filled in the attitudinal parts of the questionnaire and the pork consumption frequency per type part. After the conjoint task, respondents filled in the sociodemographic part. Completed questionnaires were edited to ensure precision of the response prior to data coding and transcription using SPSS v15.0.

## Results

The mean age of the respondents in the EU countries was 44 years ($SD = 13$), in Brazil 42 years ($SD = 15$), and in China 39 years ($SD = 12$). The detailed sociodemographic profile of the samples can be seen in Table 3. The samples in the EU and China are

CONTEMPORARY ISSUES IN GREEN AND ETHICAL MARKETING

**Table 3** Samples' sociodemographic characteristics ($n = 2885$), %.

| | EU<br>$N_{EU} = 1931$ | Brazil<br>$N_{BRA} = 475$ | China<br>$N_{CHI} = 479$ |
|---|---|---|---|
| *Country/city* | BELGIUM 25.4 | *SOUTH*<br>Porto Alegre: 12.6 | *SOUTH-EAST*<br>Nanjing: 16.7 |
| | DENMARK 24.9 | Santa Rosa: 13.1<br>Curitiba: 12.6 | *SOUTH-WEST*<br>Chengdu: 16.7 |
| | POLAND: 24.9 | Ponta Grossa: 12.0<br>*CENTRAL-WEST* | *CENTRE*<br>Wuhan:16.7 |
| | GERMANY 24.8 | Cuiabá: 12.8<br>Campo Verde: 12.4 | *NORTH-EAST*<br>Changchun: 16.7 |
| | | Goiânia: 12.4<br>Rio Verde: 12.0 | *NORTH*<br>Beijing: 16.7<br>*SOUTH*<br>Guangzhou: 16.7 |
| *Area of residence* | Urban: 33.4 | Urban: 75.6 | Urban: 100 |
| | Non-urban, but low pork farm density: 33.1 | Rural: 24.2 | – |
| | Non-urban, and high pork farm density: 33.5 | – | – |
| *Gender*<br>Male | 49.7 | 49.7 | 50.1 |
| *Age (years)*<br>Mean (*SD*) | 44 (13) | 42 (15) | 39 (12) |
| *Marital status*<br>Married | 53.6 | 50.1 | 72.2 |
| *Education*<br>University or beyond | 43.8 | 11.2 | 41.5 |
| *Financial situation*<br>Reasonable | 47.3 | 31.6 | 19.6 |
| Well-off | 8.2 | 9.7 | 2.1 |
| *Occupation*<br>Salaried employment | 30.7 | 23.6 | 47.4 |
| Managerial employment | 6.7 | 0.8 | 2.7 |

somewhat biased towards higher education, which may be attributed to the use of an electronic survey method (EU) and the participation of urban consumers (China).

All seven attitudinal scales that were used in the present research have first been tested for reliability. Cronbach's alpha values ranged from modest to very high (Table 4), usually exceeding the threshold of .7 (Nunnally, 1978). Based upon average scores, concerns about the environment and nature and the quest for environmental friendly food production were quite strong across all three continents and especially in Brazil. In all, attitudes most strongly held across all three continents were related to environmental sustainability, whereas different expressions of social sustainability were maintained in Brazil (e.g. need to support national employment and economy),

**Table 4** Attitudinal scales' description, mean scores and reliabilities ($n = 2285$).

| Attitudes | EU | BRA | CHI |
|---|---|---|---|
| *Attitude towards environment and nature Cronbach's alpha:* | *.681* | *.573* | *.698* |
| 1. Humans are severely abusing the environment | 5.82 | 6.63 | 5.21 |
| 2. The balance of nature is strong enough to cope with the impacts of modern industrial nations (R)* | 5.26 | 4.84 | – |
| 3. The so-called 'ecological crisis' facing humankind has been greatly exaggerated (R) | 4.66 | 4.60 | – |
| 4. The earth is like a spaceship with very limited room and resources | 5.43 | 5.78 | 5.66 |
| 5. If things continue on their present course, we will soon experience a major ecological catastrophe | 5.12 | – | 5.20 |
| Mean | 5.26 | 5.46 | 5.35 |
| *Attitude towards industrial food production Cronbach's alpha:* | *.701* | *.742* | – |
| 6. Most food manufacturers are more interested in money than in the nutritional quality of their products | 5.58 | 2.63 | – |
| 7. Modern food production removes vitamins and minerals from food products | 4.47 | 2.71 | – |
| 8. The food industry is very concerned about the nutritional value of their products (R) | 4.28 | – | – |
| 9. Most foods are so processed that they have lost their nutritional value | 4.62 | 2.51 | – |
| 10. The majority of food products can be eaten without risk (R) | 3.74 | 3.88 | – |
| Mean | 4.53 | 2.93 | – |
| *Attitude towards technological progress Cronbach's alpha:* | *.736* | – | *.663* |
| 11. The degree of civilisation can be measured from the degree of technological development | 4.40 | – | 4.86 |
| 12. New technological inventions and applications make up the driving force of progress of society | 5.22 | – | 5.48 |
| 13. In [country], we are probably better off than ever thanks to the tremendous progress in technology | 4.87 | – | 4.67 |
| 14. Throughout the ages, technological know-how has been the most important weapon in the struggle for life | 4.86 | – | 5.37 |
| 15. Because of the development of technology, we will be able to face up to the problems of tomorrow's society | 4.14 | – | 4.88 |
| Mean | 4.69 | – | 5.05 |

(*Continued*)

**Table 4** (Continued).

| Attitudes | EU | BRA | CHI |
|---|---|---|---|
| *Attitude towards animal welfare Cronbach's alpha:* | 0.790 | | |
| 16. It is important that the food I eat on a typical day has been produced in a way that animals have not experienced pain | 5.84 | – | – |
| 17. It is important that the food I eat on a typical day has been produced in a way that animals' rights have been respected | 5.80 | – | – |
| 18. In general, humans have too little respect for the quality of life of animals | 5.59 | – | – |
| 19. Increased regulation of the treatment of animals in farming is needed | 5.59 | – | – |
| 20. Animal agriculture raises serious ethical questions about the treatment of animal | 5.10 | – | – |
| 21. As long as animals do not suffer pain, humans should be able to use them for any purpose (R) | 4.53 | – | – |
| 22. It is acceptable to use animals to test consumer products such as soaps, cosmetics, and cleaners (R) | 5.36 | – | – |
| 23. Hunting animals for sport is an acceptable form of recreation (R) | 5.35 | – | – |
| Mean | 5.39 | – | – |
| *Attitude towards food and environment Cronbach's alpha:* | .912 | .810 | .720 |
| 24. It is important that the food I eat on a typical day has been prepared in an environmentally friendly way | 5.54 | 6.55 | 5.35 |
| 25. It is important that the food I eat on a typical day has been produced in a way which has not shaken the balance of nature | 5.52 | 6.57 | 5.26 |
| 26. It is important that the food I eat on a typical day is packaged in an environmentally friendly way | 5.61 | 6.73 | 5.48 |
| **Mean** | **5.55** | **6.61** | **5.36** |
| *Attitude towards local employment Cronbach's alpha:* | .742 | .538 | .661 |
| 27. Buying [country]-made products keeps [country] working | 4.96 | 6.34 | 5.26 |
| 28. [Country] consumers who purchase products made in other countries are responsible for putting their fellow [country] out of work | 3.42 | 5.88 | 3.83 |
| 29. Buying [country] produced products supports the local community's livelihood | 5.28 | 5.71 | 5.43 |
| **Mean** | **4.55** | **5.97** | **4.84** |
| *Attitude towards local economy Cronbach's alpha:* | .903 | .828 | .804 |
| 30. [Country] products first, last, and foremost | 4.27 | 5.50 | 4.93 |
| 31. A real [country] should always buy [country]-made products | 3.56 | 5.37 | 4.79 |
| 32. We should purchase products manufactured in [country] instead of letting other countries get rich off us | 4.42 | 5.75 | 4.37 |
| 33. It's always best to purchase [country] products | 4.28 | 5.74 | 3.62 |
| 34. It may cost me in the long-run, but I prefer to support [country] products | 4.55 | 5.61 | – |
| **Mean** | **4.21** | **5.59** | **4.42** |

*(R): item was reverse-coded.

China (e.g. technology as leverage of social progress), and the EU (e.g. animal welfare).

## Conjoint analysis results

Conjoint analysis implemented through SPSS v15.0 per continent led to the results graphically depicted in Figure 1, where part-worth utilities per factor level are presented for EU/Brazil and China.

In Europe, it was clear that the factors 'housing and floor type' and 'efforts to protect soil, air, and water at the farm' had the strongest influence on the respondents' evaluation of pig production systems. Accordingly, in terms of factor levels, the most positive evaluations resulted from 'outdoor access' and 'maximum effort' to protect

**Figure 1** Conjoint analysis of part-worth utilities per factor level ($N = 1931$).

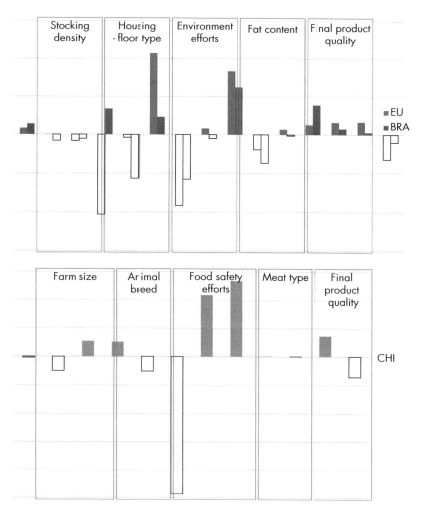

soil, air, and water. In Brazil, the factor 'efforts to protect soil, air, and water at the farm' also had the strongest influence on the respondents' evaluation of pig production systems, followed by 'housing and floor type' and 'fat content'. In terms of factor levels, the most positive evaluations resulted from 'maximum effort' to protect soil, air, and water, followed by 'healthier' fat, 'slatted floor' type, and 'outdoor access'. In China, the factor 'food safety efforts' had by far the strongest influence on respondents' evaluation of pig production systems. In terms of factor levels, the most positive evaluations resulted from 'maximum' and 'extra' food safety efforts.

### Cluster analysis results

The second phase of the analysis was the implementation of a segmentation task through a two-stage cluster analysis. Respondents' grouping criteria were the 15 part-worth variables emerging from the conjoint analysis. After initial implementation of hierarchical cluster analysis (stage I), the k-means procedure on the hierarchical clusters' centroids followed, with the option of identifying three to seven clusters (stage II). In Europe, a four-cluster solution was selected as the one with the highest correlation between the hierarchical and the k-means cluster membership variables (Pearson correlation .723, $p < .01$). In Brazil and in China, a three-cluster solution was the best (Pearson correlations .987, $p < .01$ and .794, $p < .01$ respectively). The profile of each cluster per sample was developed by cross-tabulating the cluster membership variable with three sets of variables: (a) the sociodemographic variables, (b) the attitudinal variables, and (c) the pork consumption frequency variables. Chi-square tests for the sociodemographics and the pork consumption frequencies and Duncan–Scheffe post-hoc ANOVA tests for the attitudinal questions tested the hypothesised statistically significant differences among the clusters in the three continents in respect to those three sets of variables (see Appendix 1, Tables 1–4).

### EU

Cluster 1 (17.1% of the sample) puts (almost exclusively) the strongest emphasis on the maximum effort to protect the environment at the farm level. It was thus defined as the 'environmental conscious' citizens. It is an international cluster with citizens from all four EU countries that were part of this survey (Appendix 1, Table 2). In terms of its sociodemographic profile, cluster 1 constitutes a type of European 'elite' (better educated, well-off, etc.). Cluster 1 holds the second most pessimistic attitude towards the environment and nature, and the strongest attitude towards the need for an environmentally friendly food production (Appendix 1, Table 3). Finally, it includes the second highest percentage of regular pork eaters for most of the products examined (Appendix 1, Table 3).

Cluster 2 (59.1% of the sample) presents the weakest evaluations of the pig farming characteristics under evaluation. It is thus defined as the 'indifferent, ambivalent' citizens. In general, cluster 2 closely resembles the profile of the overall sample, and respondents also hold the least strong sustainability attitudes – but the strongest attitudes towards local economy. It has the highest percentage of regular pork eaters for almost all product categories under examination.

Cluster 3 (12.3% of the sample) puts almost exclusively emphasis on the type of housing and floor, favouring outdoor access. It was thus interpreted as the 'animal welfare conscious' citizens. It consists of respondents mainly from Germany and

Denmark, less urban, with a larger percentage of people residing closer to centres of dense pig farming, more women, and with the smallest percentage of highly educated people. Cluster 3 members held the second strongest attitude towards animal welfare, and show the lowest or second-lowest regular consumption for most of the pork products under examination.

Finally, cluster 4 (11.5% of the sample) prefers all the attributes that characterise the extensive type of pig farming (e.g. small stock density, outdoor access, maximum environmental effort, different quality of the final product). Cluster 4 is thus defined as the 'sustainability-oriented' citizens. They originate mainly in Denmark and Germany, are more urban than the 'animal welfare conscious' citizens of cluster 3, and have among them the highest percentage of reasonable income earners. Furthermore, cluster 4 members hold the strongest (most pessimistic) attitude towards the environment and nature, the strongest attitude towards animal welfare, and the second-strongest attitude towards the need for an environmentally friendly food production. Cluster 4 has the lowest or second-lowest regular consumption for most of the pork products under consideration, similarly to cluster 3.

## Brazil

No statistically significant differences were found among the clusters in regard to farm size and fat content. Respondents in all clusters preferred small size farms (fewer than 100 sows) and 'healthier' fat, but without emphasising those pig farming characteristics too much. Apart from the above-described similarities, the description of the three clusters is as follows (Appendix 1, Tables 1–4). Cluster 1 (71.6% of the sample) shows indifference for almost all factors under examination. It is thus termed the 'indifferent, ambivalent' citizens. Their sociodemographic characteristics, attitudinal profiles, and regular pork consumption frequencies across all product types under examination are very close to the relevant figures of the overall sample. Respondents in cluster 2 (16.0% of the sample) put the strongest emphasis on the maximum effort to reduce the impact on the environment at the farm level. They are thus characterised as the 'environmental conscious' citizens. They express the strongest concerns towards the environment and nature, and the second-strongest request for environmental friendly food production. They show the lowest or second-lowest regular consumption for most of the other products under examination. Finally, respondents in cluster 3 (12.4% of the sample) mostly prefer slatted floor or outdoors housing, while they also favour the maximum effort to reduce the impact on the environment at the farm level, and pork products of 'health' fat content. Based on these preferences, cluster 3 members are termed the 'sustainability-oriented' citizens. They hold the most negative attitudes towards industrial food production and food and environment, strongly favouring local employment and local economy. Cluster 3 members exhibit the highest regular pork consumption across almost all pork types under examination.

## China

Respondents in cluster 1 (31.5% of the sample) put almost exclusively the strongest emphasis on the special or maximum food safety efforts. They are thus characterised as the 'food safety conscious' citizens. They express the strongest concerns towards the environment, the most positive attitude towards technological progress, and the strongest request for environmental friendly food production. Cluster 1 members usually exhibit the lowest regular pork consumption across all pork types under examination. In cluster 2 (44.1% of the sample), respondents show indifference towards almost all factors under examination. At the same time, they favour special or maximum food safety efforts to a lesser extent compared to the other two clusters. Based on that, cluster 2 members are termed the 'indifferent' citizens. They hold the weakest attitudes towards all sustainability attitudes under consideration, and exhibit the highest regular pork consumption across all pork types. Finally, cluster 3 (23.0% of the sample) mostly prefer industrial/extensive pig farming characteristics, such as large size and similar quality of the final product. So they are termed the 'industrial production oriented' citizens. Their attitudinal profile and regular pork product consumption are close to that of the overall sample.

## Discussion and conclusion

The results presented above for the three continents at both the sample level and the specific cluster level provide substantial insights for food production chains, marketing, and public policy. Across the three continents, people's attitudes towards environment and nature, animal welfare, and industrial food production turned out to be on average rather moderately strong. On the other hand, numerous past surveys proclaimed that sustainability issues are high in the social agenda when it comes to agriculture, and food and meat production (e.g. Frewer et al., 2005; Grunert, 2006; Kanis et al., 2003; Søndergaard et al., 2005; Stern et al., 2005; Verbeke et al., 1999; Vermeir & Verbeke, 2006; Yang, 2007). Their on average weak attitudes may influence the way citizens see pig farming and may be related to the finding that the biggest clusters across continents, with more than half of the respondents overall, had only weak opinions about differences between pig farming systems. At the same time, pork appears to play a substantial role in the diet of most respondents in the six countries of this study, as indicated by the percentages of the regular pork eaters across the product categories under investigation.

The results of the conjoint experiment show that, among the pig farming characteristics studied, people in the EU and Brazil assign most importance to animal and environmental well-being as criteria to discriminate between 'good' and 'bad' pig farming practices, despite the fact that their attitudes towards environmental protection, animal welfare, and industrial food production are only moderately strong. In the absence of strong opinions, it is quite possible that citizens adopt 'politically correct' stances that minimise exposure to criticism and the possibility of misjudgement. This is further supported by the finding that end-product-related attributes (i.e. quality of the final product or fat content according to feed type) were assigned less importance as evaluation criteria in the conjoint experiment (especially in the EU) compared to livestock production-related attributes. This may be because although consumers might consider pork quality and healthiness already quite good (as indicated by their overall good level of satisfaction with pork and pork products; Resano et al., 2011), what consumers want with respect to pork quality and healthiness (e.g. fat content) is widely a personal and subjective choice; on the other hand, people often have clearer opinions – possibly aided by the media – about how production practices (rather than end-product characteristics) ought to be in general.

The results of the cluster analysis also allow a more differentiated view (see Table 5 for a comparative approach of the three continents). Small-sized, clear-cut segments of citizens were identified in both the EU and Brazil, which paid attention to specific pig farming attributes: environmentally conscious respondents, animal welfare conscious citizens (in the EU), and respondents who support small-scale, extensive pig farming, in addition to the main clusters that cover the bulk of indifferent average citizens. The sociodemographic profile of each cluster is also meaningful. For instance, European urban elites would favour more technocratic, economically efficient pig farming systems, without neglecting issues of top priority in the public discourse (i.e. environmental protection). On the other hand, certain small but conscious social groups would favour more socially responsible types of pig farming (i.e. small-sized, local, animal conscious, beneficial for consumers in terms of healthiness and quality). Furthermore, the profile of the clusters in terms of the potentially relevant attitudes is also quite consistent, with small but conscious social groups always holding stronger sustainability attitudes.

In China, pig production is under rapid change. Both demand and supply have been rising. The small family farm raising a few pigs mainly for its own consumption, while still the dominant segment in the sector, is giving way to large industrial pig farms. At the same time, there is a widespread concern about food safety, which reflects Chinese policymakers' characterisation of food safety as a social sustainability component. In this respect, the results of the cluster analysis in China also allow for a differentiated picture to be drawn, as in the case of the EU and Brazil. Smaller-sized, clear-cut segments of citizens were identified, which paid attention to specific pig farming attributes (e.g. food safety). One may speculate that the three clusters that emerged in China form stages in a diffusion process: there is a social group that is not concerned about social sustainability (i.e. food safety) issues (stage 1); there is another social group that has become concerned about the way pork is produced because there is a safety issue (stage 2); and there is a third social group that also believes that they see the solution to this issue, namely by transforming the value chain to large-scale industrial production (stage 3). This interpretation coincides with the process of long-term change and differentiation of consumer preferences for food in a growing economy. Government favours industrialisation and industrial actors push it even further, so it is communicated as a socially beneficial development.

From the above, it becomes clear that sustainability attitudes, no matter how they are expressed in varying cultural contexts, indeed relate to citizens' attitudes towards pig farming, but only for some specific social groups. People with stronger attitudes towards eco- and social-friendly food production also tend to belong to clusters with stronger opinions towards pig production systems, and vice versa. The emergence of small clusters that emphasise the sustainability aspects of pig production is in line with most of the relevant past literature (e.g. Kanis et al., 2003; Meuwissen et al., 2007; Olsson & Piskova, 2005; Petit & Van der Werf, 2003; Stern et al., 2005).

Finally, another outcome of the survey pertains to the comparison of people's role as citizens, as expressed in their evaluation of pig production systems, and their role as consumers, as verified by their pork consumption behaviour. It becomes

**Table 5** Comparison among types of citizens in terms of sustainability-related characteristics in the three continents ($n = 2885$).

| | EU | | | | BRAZIL | | | CHINA | | |
|---|---|---|---|---|---|---|---|---|---|---|
| | Indifferent, ambivalent | Environmentally conscious | Animal well-being conscious | Small farming supporters | Indifferent, ambivalent | Environmentally conscious | Small farming supporters | Indifferent | Food safety conscious | Industrial production-oriented |
| 1. Cluster no. | **2** | **1** | **3** | **4** | **1** | **2** | **3** | **2** | **1** | **3** |
| 2. Cluster size, % | 59.1 | 17.1 | 12.3 | 11.5 | 71.6 | 16.0 | 12.4 | 44.1 | 31.5 | 23.0 |
| 3. Pig meat production system preference | Weakest evaluation of characteristics under examination | Strongest emphasis on maximum effort to protect the environment at the farm level | Strongest emphasis on the type of housing and floor | Strong emphasis on all attributes that characterise extensive type of farming | Weakest evaluation of characteristics under examination | Strongest emphasis on maximum effort to protect the environment at the farm level | Strong emphasis on all attributes that characterise extensive type of farming | Weakest evaluation of characteristics under examination | Strongest emphasis on special or maximum food safety efforts | Strong emphasis on all attributes that characterise industrial type of farming |
| 4. Sustainability-related attitudes | Least-strong attitudes across most constructs (close to sample's average); strongest 'local economy' | Strongest 'food and environment'; second-strongest 'environment and nature' | Second-strongest 'animal welfare' | Strongest 'environment and nature' and 'animal welfare'; second strongest 'food and environment' and 'local economy' | Least-strong or second least-strong attitudes across all types (close to sample's average) | Strongest 'environment and nature'; second-strongest 'food and environment'; second-strongest 'local economy' | Strongest 'industrial food production', 'food and environment',. 'local employment', 'local economy' | Least-strong attitudes across all constructs | Strongest 'environment and nature', 'technological progress', 'food and environment' | Close to sample's average across all other attitudes |

(*Continued*)

**Table 5** (Continued).

| | EU | | | | BRAZIL | | | CHINA | | |
|---|---|---|---|---|---|---|---|---|---|---|
| | Indifferent, ambivalent | Environmentally conscious | Animal well-being conscious | Small farming supporters | Indifferent, ambivalent | Environmentally conscious | Small farming supporters | Indifferent | Food safety conscious | Industrial production-oriented |
| 5. Sociodemographics | Mostly from BE and PL; close to overall sample's profile | International cluster, mainly PL and GE; urban 'elite' (more educated, well-off) | Mostly from GE and DK; less urban, more familiar with pig farming, less educated | Mostly from DK and OE, less urban, more familiar with pig farming, more educated | Close to overall sample's profile | Central-West; urban, female, more educated | South; more familiar with pig farming, males, least educated | Not substantial sociodemographic differences among the clusters beyond city of residence | | |
| 6. Pork consumption | Highest frequency across most pork product types | Second-highest frequency across most pork product types | Second-lowest frequency across most pork product types | Usually lowest frequency across most pork product types | Close to overall sample's frequency across most pork product types | Lowest or second-lowest frequency across most pork product types | Highest frequency across most pork product types | Highest frequency across all pork producttypes | Usually lowest or second-lowest frequency across most pork product types | Close to overall sample's frequency across all pork product types |

BE = Belgium, DK = Denmark, GE = Germany, PL = Poland.

apparent that only weak relationships can be identified between citizen attitudes and consumers' behaviour at the cluster level. Statistically significant differences among the clusters in terms of pork consumption emerge for the majority of pork products under examination, but these differences are small and apply to all pork products irrespective of their degree of processing. One might expect that small farm-supporting citizens usually consume less processed pork products (e.g. quality-differentiated fresh first cut), while the large farm supporting citizens might usually consume pork meat products highly processed from standard bulk pork. However, it turns out that in the EU and China, the indifferent consumers are by far the most regular pork consumers, while even the European environmental conscious citizens and the Brazilian small farming supporters constitute the second most regular types of consumer across almost all pork products under examination. As for the remaining smaller clusters, animal welfare conscious and small farm supporters in the EU, environmental conscious citizens in Brazil, and food safety concerned citizens in China consume pork meat less regularly of almost all types included in the present survey, indicating that consistency between sustainability attitudes and behaviour appears for selected social groups only.

The here-presented work is not free of certain limitations, each of which may constitute a new direction for future research to accommodate. These limitations steam to a large extent from the cross-cultural nature of the research and the adaptations necessary in its design. For instance, the reliability of some attitudinal scales (e.g. attitude towards environment and towards local employment in Brazil, or attitudes towards technological progress in China) is acceptable but poor (Nunnally, 1978). When applying scales in a cross-cultural study, however, by necessity average reliability will be lower due to the unavoidable differences in culture-specific meaning of items, which makes scale optimisation for internal consistency more difficult than when using of the same scales in single-country studies (Hui & Triandis, 1985). Another limitation of same nature is the necessary adjustment of the conjoint research design in China to accommodate cultural differences, which makes the results across geographical samples not directly comparable. However, what we aimed to reveal is the existence of sustainability-favourable trend across continents independent of how sustainability-relevant concern of citizens in these continents is expressed in terms of concrete production method parameters or the absolute preference of citizens thereafter.

Relevant to research design but not related to the cross-cultural nature of the study are some other possible limitations. For instance, some factor levels in the EU and Brazil conjoint designs might be too technical for consumers to comprehend (e.g. 'litter' and 'slatted floor'), creating certain biased preference for other more straightforward options (e.g. 'outdoor access'), especially since respondents read and evaluated the conjoint profiles without help from interviewers and their scoring was thus based on their individual subjective interpretation. This weakness is, however, consistent across all samples, the scoring of which simply was a reflection of beliefs and perceptions that are of course coloured as compared to facts or reality. Despite pretesting in all countries not revealing any comprehension problems, possible lack of knowledge was not exclusively remedied in the research design so to avoid the introduction of bias as opposed to genuine beliefs and perceptions of the respondents. Since this survey is not an information experiment, measurement of the impact of the provision of factual information or knowledge was not included in our aims.

A similar point here is related to the requirement that participants make 15 evaluations of alternative systems that each one is quite complex, the possibly resulting fatigue, and its impact on the evaluation task's validity. Yet 15 profiles are not rare in conjoint applications, and neither is it the use of verbal conjoint profile descriptions (e.g. Grunert, Bech-Larsen, Lahteenmaki, Ueland, & Astrom, 2004). Moreover, the questionnaire was pretested in all countries, and no problems were reported. The translation of the profiles was done in consultation with (European) pig production specialists. And since the results have face validity, it seems plausible to assume that the conjoint factors and profiles have been more or less understood. Nevertheless, future conjoint applications with special or technical factors should take under consideration the balance between respondents' comprehension abilities and the introduction of informational bias in consumers' evaluation.

Several of the above limitations can probably be taken as point of departure for some academic implications. For instance, measurement scales that were proven to be valid and reliable in a European (or Western) context do not perform equally well in culturally varied (e.g. Brazilian or Chinese) context. The academic implication of this is that similar scales need to be developed or existing ones refined, adapted, and validated in those contexts or settings. Moreover, lack of direct comparisons of outcomes across cultures as a result of adjustments in research design across cultures is a non-unusual reality in consumer research. Although such adaptations in research designs are necessary simply because some concepts may have a different meaning in different settings, the development of methods that can allow for a direct cross-cultural comparison remains one of the strongest academic challenges.

Overall, the major managerial implication from the above-described findings is that people's attitudes to pig production may be more important for pig producers' long-term licence to produce than for the sales of their products. While critical attitudes (to the extent they exist) only weakly influence purchase behaviour, they may still be expressed in the public debate and influence policy formation at regional, national, and global levels. On the other hand, we cannot completely rule out that a stronger relationship between attitudes to pig production and consumer demand would develop if more products clearly positioned with regard to small farming, animal welfare, environmental impact, and/or food safety (at least in world markets where food safety is still demanded and remains a social sustainability element), while retaining good eating quality and an attractive price, were on the market.

## Acknowledgements

The authors gratefully acknowledge the European Community financial participation under the Sixth Framework Programme for Research, Technological Development and Demonstration Activities, for the Integrated Project Q-PORKCHAINS FOOD-CT-2007-036245. The views expressed in this publication are the sole responsibility of the author(s) and do not necessarily reflect their view of the European Commission. Neither the European Commission nor any person acting on behalf of the Commission is responsible for the use that might be made of the information. The information in this document is provided as is and no guarantee or warranty is given that the information is fit for any particular purpose. The user thereof uses the information at its sole risk and liability.

# References

Beckmann, S.C., Brokmose, S., & Lind, R.L. (2001). *Danish consumers and organic foods.* Copenhagen: (Working Paper). Copenhagen Business School [in Danish].

Brom, F.W., Visak, T., & Mejiboom, F. (2007). Food, citizens and the market: The quest for responsible consuming. In L. Frewer, H. & Van Trijp, H. (Eds.), *Understanding consumers of food products* (pp. 610–623). Cambridge, MA: Woodhead.

Cavalett, O., De Queiroz, J.F., & Ortega, E. (2006). Energy assessment of integrated production systems of grains, pig and fish in small farms in South Brazil. *Ecological Modelling*, 296, 205–224.

Darby, K., Batte, M.T., Ernst, S., & Roe, B. (2008). Decomposing local: A conjoint analysis of locally produced foods. *American Journal of Agricultural Economics*, 90, 476–486.

De Boer, J., Boersema, J.J., & Aiking, H. (2009). Consumers' motivational associations favouring free-range meat or less meat. *Ecology and Economy*, 68, 850–860.

Dunlap, R.E., Van Liere, K.D., Mertig, A.C., & Jones, R.E. (2000). Measuring endorsement of the new ecological paradigm: A revised NEP scale. *Journal of Social Issues*, 56, 425–442.

European Commission. (2006). Special Eurobarometer 238. Risk Issues. February. Retrieved 10 March 2007 from http://www.bfr.bund.de/cm/221/risk_issues_executive_summary_on_food_safety.pdf.

Frewer, L.J., Kole, A., Van de Kroon, S.M.A., & De Lauwere, C. (2005). Consumer attitudes towards the development of animal-friendly husbandry systems. *Journal of Agriculture and Environmental Ethics*, 18, 345–367.

Grunert, K.G. (2006). Future trends and consumer lifestyles with regard to meat consumption. *Meat Science*, 74, 149–160.

Grunert, K.G., Bech-Larsen, T., Lahteenmaki, L., Ueland, O., & Astrom, A. (2004). Attitudes towards the use of GMOs in food production and their impact on buying intention: The role of positive sensory experience. *Agribusiness*, 20, 95–107.

Hamstra, A.M. (1991). *Biotechnology in foodstuffs: Towards a model of consumer acceptance.* The Hague: The SWOKA Institute.

Hui, C.H., & Triandis, H.C. (1985). Measurement in cross-cultural psychology, a review and comparison of strategies. *Journal of Cross-Cultural Psychology*, 16, 131–152.

Hume, M. (2009). Compassion without action: Examining the young consumers consumption and attitude to sustainable consumption. *Journal of World Business*, 45, 385–394.

Kanis, E., Groen, A.F., & De Greef, K.H. (2003). Societal concerns about pork and pork production and their relationships to the production system. *Journal of Agriculture and Environmental Ethics*, 16, 137–162.

Kendall, H.A., Lobao, L.M., & Sharp, J.S. (2006). Public concern with animal well-being: Place, social structural location, and individual experience. *Rural Sociology*, 71, 399–428.

Lindeman, M., & Väänänen, M. (2000). Measurement of ethical food choices motives. *Appetite*, 34, 55–59.

Meuwissen, M.P.M., Van der Lans, I.A., & Huirne, R.B.M. (2007). Consumer preferences for pork supply chain attributes. *NJAS-Wageningen Journal of Life Sciences*, 54, 293–312.

Millet, S., Moons, C.P.H., Van Oeckel, M.J., & Janssens, G.P.J. (2005). Welfare, performance and meat quality of fattening pigs in alternative housing and management systems: A review. *Journal of the Science of Food and Agriculture*, 85, 709–719.

Nunnally, J.C. (1978). *Psychometric theory* (2nd ed.). New York: McGraw-Hill.

Olsson, V., & Pickova, J. (2005). The influence of production systems on meat quality, with emphasis on pork. *AMBIO*, 34, 338–343.

Petit, J., & Van der Werf, H.M.G. (2003). Perception of the environmental impacts of current and alternative modes of pig production by stakeholder groups. *Journal of Environmental Management*, 68, 377–386.

Pomar, C., Dubeau, F., Letourneau-Montnimy, M.P., Boucher, C., & Julien, P.O. (2007). Reducing phosphorous concentration in pig diets by adding an environmental objective to the traditional feed formulation algorithm. *Livestock Science, 111*, 16–27.

Resano, H., Perez-Cueto, F.J.A., Verbeke, W., Olsen, N., de Barcellos, M.D., & Grunert, K.G. (2011). Consumer satisfaction with pork meat and derived products in five EU countries. *Appetite, 56*, 167–170.

Siegford, J.M., Powers, W., & Grimes-Casey, H.G. (2008). Environmental aspects of ethical animal production. *Poultry Science, 87*, 380–386.

Søndergaard, H.A., Grunert, K.G., & Scholderer, J. (2005). Consumer attitudes to enzymes in food production. *Trends in Food Science and Technology, 16*, 466–474.

Stern, S., Sonesson, U., Gunnarsson, O., Oborn, I., Kumm, K.I., & Nybrant, T. (2005). Sustainable development of food production: A case study on scenarios for pig production. *AMBIO, 34*, 402–407.

Van Wezemael, L., Verbeke, W., Kügler, J.O., de Barcellos, M.D., & Grunert, K.G. (2010). European consumers and beef safety: Perceptions, expectations and uncertainty reduction strategies. *Food Control, 21*, 835–844.

Vanhonacker, F., Verbeke, W., Van Poucke, E., Buijs, S., & Tuyttens, F. (2009). Societal concern related to stocking density, pen size and group size in farm animal production. *Livestock Science, 123*, 16–22.

Vanhonacker, F., Verbeke, W., Van Poucke, E., & Tuyttens, F. (2008). Do citizens and farmers interpret the concept of farm animal welfare differently? *Livestock Science, 116*, 126–136.

Verbeke, W., Van Oekel, M.J., Warnants, N., Viane, J., & Boucque, Ch.V. (1999). Consumer perception, facts and possibilities to improve the acceptability of health and sensory characteristics of pork. *Meat Science, 53*, 77–99.

Vermeir, I., & Verbeke, W. (2006). Sustainable food consumption: Exploring the consumer 'attitude–behavioral intention' gap. *Journal of Agriculture and Environmental Ethics, 19*, 169–194.

Shimp, T.A., & Sharma, S. (1987). Consumer ethnocentrism: Construction and validation of the CETSCALE. *Journal of Marketing Research, 24*, 280–289.

Tanner, C., Kaiser, F.G., & Wolfing Kast, S. (2004). Contextual conditions of ecological consumerism – A food-purchasing survey. *Environment and Behaviour, 36*, 94–111.

Tukker, A., Emmert, S., Charter, M., Vezzoli, C., & Sto, E. (2008). Fostering change to sustainable consumption and production: An evidence based view. *Journal of Cleaner Production, 16*, 1218–1225.

USDA (2010). Livestock and poultry: World markets and trade. *Foreign Agricultural Service*. Retrieved 29 May 2011, from http://www.fas.usda.gov/dlp/circular/2010/livestock_poultryfull101510.pdf

Wang, Y.Z. (2005). A study on horizontal and vertical configuration of food safety administration. *China Industrial Economy, 12*, 64–70.

Wognum, N., Trienekens, J., Wever, M., Vlajic, J., Van der Vorst, J., Omta, O., Hermansen, J., & Nguyen, T.L.T. (2009). Organisation, logistics and environmental issues in the European pork chain. In J. Trienekens, B. Petersen, N. Wognum, & D. Brinkmann (Eds.), *European pork chains: Diversity and quality challenges in consumer-oriented production and distribution* (pp. 41–72), Wageningen: Wageningen Academic.

Xinhuanet. (2007). Retrieved 4 January 2007, from http://news.xinhuanet.com/life/2007-01/04/content_5563242.htm

Yang, T.S. (2007). Environmental sustainability and social desirability issues in pig feeding. *Asian-Australian Journal of Animal Science, 20*, 605–614.

**Appendix 1**

**Table A1** Cluster profiles in terms of part-worth utilities ($n = 2885$).

| | | EU | | | | | BRAZIL | | | | | CHINA | | |
|---|---|---|---|---|---|---|---|---|---|---|---|---|---|---|
| | | Cluster 1 | Cluster 2 | Cluster 3 | Cluster 4 | | Cluster 1 | Cluster 2 | Cluster 3 | | | Cluster 1 | Cluster 2 | Cluster 3 |
| Conjoint factors and factor levels | Sig | $N_1 =$ 298, 17.1% | $N_2 =$ 1036, 59.1% | $N_3 =$ 216, 12.3% | $N_4 =$ 201, 11.5% | Sig | $N_1 =$ 340, 71.6% | $N_2 =$ 76, 16.0% | $N_3 =$ 59, 12.4% | Conjoint factors and factor levels | Sig | $N_2 =$ 151, 31.5% | $N_1 =$ 211, 44.1% | $N_2 =$ 110, 23.0% |
| 1. Stocking density | * | | | | | n.s. | | | | 1. Farm size | * | | | |
| Fewer than 100 sows | | −.199 | .232[a] | .013 | .299[a] | | .134 | .082 | .213 | Small | | .010[a] | −.066[a] | .010[a] |
| About 400 sows | | .496 | −.011 | .127 | −.132 | | −.077 | −.034 | −.159 | Medium | | −.102[a] | .046[a] | −1.009[a] |
| 800 or more sows | | −.296[a] | −.220[a,b] | −.140 | −.167[b] | | −.056 | −.047 | −.054 | Large | | .092[a] | .019[a] | .999 |
| 2. Housing and floor type | * | | | | | * | | | | 2. Animals' breed | * | | | |
| Slatted floor | | −1.551 | −.567 | −4.357 | −2.908 | | .111[a] | .018[a] | 2.057 | Chinese | | .352 | .181[a] | .296[a] |
| Litter bedding | | .962 | .204[a] | 1.899 | .212[a] | | .351 | −.164 | −4.074 | European | | −.352[a] | −.181 | −.296[a] |
| Outdoors access | | .589 | .362 | 2.457 | 2.696 | | .053 | −.369 | 2.017 | | | | | |

(Continued)

**Table A1** (Continued).

| Conjoint factors and factor levels | Sig | EU Cluster 1 $N_1 =$ 298, 17.1% | EU Cluster 2 $N_2 =$ 1036, 59.1% | EU Cluster 3 $N_3 =$ 216, 12.3% | EU Cluster 4 $N_4 =$ 201, 11.5% | Sig | BRAZIL Cluster 1 $N_1 =$ 340, 71.6% | BRAZIL Cluster 2 $N_2 =$ 76, 16.0% | BRAZIL Cluster 3 $N_3 =$ 59, 12.4% | Conjoint factors and factor levels | Sig | CHINA Cluster 1 $N_2 =$ 151, 31.5% | CHINA Cluster 2 $N_1 =$ 211, 44.1% | CHINA Cluster 3 $N_2 =$ 110, 23.0% |
|---|---|---|---|---|---|---|---|---|---|---|---|---|---|---|
| 3. Effort protect soil air water | * | | | | | * | | | | 3. Food safety efforts | * | | | |
| Minimal | | −2.599 | −.618[a] | −.441 | −.660[a] | | −.033 | −2.259 | −1.531 | Not special attention | | −4.314 | −1.107 | −2.398 |
| Some | | .360 | .108[a] | .032[a] | .006[a] | | .023[a] | −.538 | .153[a] | Special attention | | 1.974 | 0.439 | 1.147 |
| Maximum | | 2.234 | .509[a] | .408[a] | .653 | | .010 | 2.797 | 1.378 | Maximum attention | | 2.339 | 0.667 | 1.251 |
| 4. Fat according to feed | * | | | | | n.s. | | | | 4. Meat type | * | | | |
| Standard | | −.390 | −.153[a] | .036 | −.128[a] | | −.341 | −.512 | −.377 | Tasty | | −.047 | .146 | −.234 |
| Lower | | .379 | .004[a,b] | −.069[a] | .055[b] | | −.032 | .069 | −.023 | Lean | | .047 | −.146 | .234 |
| Healthier | | 010[a] | .149[b] | .033[a] | .073[a,b] | | .374 | .442 | .401 | | | | | |
| 5. Quality of the final product | * | | | | | * | | | | 5. Quality of the final product | * | | | |
| Consistent | | .036 | .243 | −.078 | −.362 | | .029[a] | .027[a] | .404 | Consistent | | .050[a] | .176[a] | 1.159 |
| Variable | | .250 | .075 | −.064 | .907 | | .179 | −.176 | −.578 | Variable | | −.050[a] | −.176[a] | −1.159 |
| Demanded by key customers | | −.286 | −.318 | .142 | −.544 | | −.208 | .149[a] | .174[a] | | | | | |

*Paired Duncan–Scheffe post-hoc ANOVA tests; $p < .05$; n.s: not statistically significant differences.
[a, b]Not statistically significant differences in paired comparisons.

**Table A2** Cluster profiles in terms of sociodemographic characteristics ($n = 2885$), %.

| | Sig | EU Cluster 1 $N_1 = 298,$ 17.0% | Cluster 2 $N_2 = 1036,$ 59.1% | Cluster 3 $N_3 = 216,$ 12.3% | Cluster 4 $N_4 = 201,$ 11.5% | | Sig | BRAZIL Cluster 1 $N_1 = 340,$ 71.6% | Cluster 2 $N_2 = 76,$ 16.0% | Cluster 3 $N_3 = 59,$ 12.4% | | Sig | CHINA Cluster 1 $N_2 = 151,$ 31.5% | Cluster 2 $N_1 = 211,$ 44.1% | Cluster 3 $N_2 = 110,$ 23.0% |
|---|---|---|---|---|---|---|---|---|---|---|---|---|---|---|---|
| *Country* | ** | | | | | *City/area* | ** | | | | *City* | *** | | | |
| Belgium | | 23.2 | 31.6 | 7.9 | 8.0 | Porto Alegre | | 13.8 | 17.1 | 0.0 | Nanjing | | 15.9 | 19.0 | 10.9 |
| Denmark | | 18.5 | 19.7 | 37.5 | 53.7 | Santa Rosa | | 1.5 | 1.3 | 94.9 | Chengdu | | 11.9 | 12.8 | 29.1 |
| Poland | | 30.9 | 30.2 | 2.3 | 5.5 | Curitiba | | 17.4 | 1.3 | 0.0 | Wuhan | | 15.2 | 20.4 | 11.8 |
| Germany | | 27.5 | 18.5 | 52.3 | 32.8 | Ponta Grossa | | 16.8 | 0.0 | 0.0 | Changchun | | 29.8 | 9.0 | 14.5 |
| | | | | | | Cuiabá | | 12.1 | 26.3 | 0.0 | Beijing | | 17.9 | 16.1 | 17.3 |
| | | | | | | Campo Verde | | 8.8 | 38.2 | 0.0 | Guangzhou | | 9.3 | 22.7 | 16.4 |
| | | | | | | Goiânia | | 13.8 | 15.8 | 0.0 | | | | | |
| | | | | | | Rio Verde | | 15.9 | 0.0 | 5.1 | | | | | |
| *Area of residence* | * | | | | | *Area of residence* | ** | | | | *Area of residence* | n.s. | | | |
| Urban | | 39.9 | 31.8 | 29.6 | 33.3 | Urban | | 74.4 | 61.8 | 0.0 | Urban | | 100.0 | 100.0 | 100.0 |
| Non-urban, low pork farm density | | 28.5 | 35.0 | 30.1 | 31.3 | Rural | | 25.6 | 38.2 | 100 | | | | | |
| Non-urban, high pork farm density | | 31.5 | 33.2 | 40.3 | 35.3 | | | | | | | | | | |

(Continued)

**Table A2** (Continued).

| | Sig | EU Cluster 1 $N_1 = $ 298, 17.0% | EU Cluster 2 $N_2 = $ 1036, 59.1% | EU Cluster 3 $N_3 = $ 216, 12.3% | EU Cluster 4 $N_4 = $ 201, 11.5% | | Sig | BRAZIL Cluster 1 $N_1 = $ 340, 71.6% | BRAZIL Cluster 2 $N_2 = $ 76, 16.0% | BRAZIL Cluster 3 $N_3 = $ 59, 12.4% | | Sig | CHINA Cluster 1 $N_2 = $ 151, 31.5% | CHINA Cluster 2 $N_1 = $ 211, 44.1% | CHINA Cluster 3 $N_2 = $ 110, 23.0% |
|---|---|---|---|---|---|---|---|---|---|---|---|---|---|---|---|
| *Gender* | ** | | | | | *Gender* | n.s. | | | | *Gender* | n.s. | | | |
| Male | | 57.0 | 53.5 | 42.1 | 38.3 | Male | | 50.9 | 43.4 | 50.8 | Male | | 47.7 | 53.6 | 47.3 |
| *Age (years)* | n.s. | | | | | *Age (years)* | n.s. | | | | *Age (years)* | n.s. | | | |
| Mean | | 43.9 | 44.1 | 44.6 | 43.4 | Mean | | 40 | 46 | 41 | Mean | | 39 | 39 | 38.5 |
| (SD) | | (13.4) | (13.1) | (13.1) | (11.8) | (SD) | | (14.8) | (16.1) | (13.9) | (SD) | | (12.0) | (11.16) | (12.0) |
| *Marital status* | n.s. | 54.0 | 56.0 | 51.4 | 49.8 | *Marital status* | ** | 49.7 | 55.3 | 45.8 | *Marital status* | n.s. | 79.5 | 68.7 | 67.0 |
| Married | | | | | | Married | | | | | Married | | | | |
| *Education* | ** | | | | | *Education* | n.s. | | | | *Education* | n.s. | | | |
| University or beyond | | 49.0 | 45.0 | 30.6 | 43.3 | University or beyond | | 11.8 | 13.2 | 5.1 | University or beyond | | 41.4 | 45.0 | 37.3 |
| *Financial situation* | ** | | | | | – | | | | | *Financial situation* | n.s. | | | |
| Reasonable | | 45.6 | 51.3 | 32.9 | 46.8 | | | | | | Reasonable | | 17.9 | 21.3 | 20.4 |
| Well-off | | 12.4 | 7.3 | 9.3 | 7.5 | | | | | | Well-off | | 2.0 | 1.9 | 2.8 |
| *Occupation* | ** | | | | | *Occupation* | n.s. | | | | *Occupation* | n.s. | | | |
| Salaried employment | | 32.2 | 29.5 | 28.7 | 36.8 | Salaried employment | | 24.4 | 18.4 | 25.4 | Salaried employment | | 46.2 | 45.0 | 51.7 |
| Managerial employment | | 9.1 | 6.5 | 6.0 | 5.5 | Managerial employment | | 0.3 | 1.3 | 3.4 | Managerial employment | | 5.8 | 1.4 | 1.2 |

***Chi-square tests, $p < .001$; **chi-square tests, $p < .01$; *chi-square tests, $p < .05$; n.s.: not statistically significant differences.

**Table A3** Cluster profiles in terms of attitudes ($n = 2885$), mean scores[a].

| | Sig | EU | | | | Sig | BRAZIL | | | Sig | CHINA | | |
|---|---|---|---|---|---|---|---|---|---|---|---|---|---|
| | | Cluster 1 $N_1 =$ 298, 17.0% | Cluster 2 $N_2 =$ 1036, 59.1% | Cluster 3 $N_3 =$ 216, 12.3% | Cluster 4 $N_4 =$ 201, 11.5% | | Cluster 1 $N_1 =$ 340, 71.6% | Cluster 2 $N_2 =$ 76, 16.0% | Cluster 3 $N_3 =$ 59, 12.4% | | Cluster 1 $N_2 =$ 151, 31.5% | Cluster 2 $N_1 =$ 211, 44.1% | Cluster 3 $N_2 =$ 110, 23.0% |
| *Environment and nature* | | | | | | | | | | | | | |
| 1. Humans are severely abusing the environment | ** | 6.07 | 5.96 | 6.18 | **6.20** | * | 6.58 | **6.92** | 6.53 | n.s. | 5.08 | 5.19 | 5.44 |
| 2. The balance of nature is strong enough to cope with the impacts of modern industrial nations (R) | ** | 5.65 | 5.12 | 5.59 | **5.81** | ** | 4.65 | **6.28** | 4.12 | – | | | |
| 3. The so-called 'ecological crisis' facing humankind has been greatly exaggerated (R) | ** | 5.12 | 4.55 | 4.57 | **5.19** | ** | 4.19 | **6.22** | 4.86 | – | | | |
| 4. The earth is like a spaceship with very limited room and resources | ** | **5.80** | 5.33 | 5.67 | 5.68 | ** | 5.64 | **6.47** | 5.68 | ** | 5.79 | 5.47 | **5.91** |

(*Continued*)

**Table A3** (Continued).

| | | EU | | | | | BRAZIL | | | | CHINA | | |
|---|---|---|---|---|---|---|---|---|---|---|---|---|---|
| | | Cluster 1 | Cluster 2 | Cluster 3 | Cluster 4 | | Cluster 1 | Cluster 2 | Cluster 3 | | Cluster 1 | Cluster 2 | Cluster 3 |
| | Sig | $N_1 =$ 298, 17.0% | $N_2 =$ 1036, 59.1% | $N_3 =$ 216, 12.3% | $N_4 =$ 201, 11.5% | Sig | $N_1 =$ 340, 71.6% | $N_2 =$ 76, 16.0% | $N_3 =$ 59, 12.4% | Sig | $N_2 =$ 151, 31.5% | $N_1 =$ 211, 44.1% | $N_2 =$ 110, 23.0% |
| 5. If things continue on their present course, we will soon experience a major ecological catastrophe | ** | 5.27 | 5.07 | 5.39 | **5.39** | – | – | – | – | * | **5.47** | 5.03 | 5.15 |
| *Industrial food production* | | | | | | | | | | | | | |
| 6. Most food manufacturers are more interested in money than in the nutritional quality of their products | n.s. | 5.72 | 5.57 | 5.63 | 5.64 | ** | 2.37 | 2.05 | **4.85** | – | | | |
| 7. Modern food production removes vitamins and minerals from food products | n.s. | 4.43 | 4.49 | 4.50 | 4.43 | ** | 2.59 | 2.03 | **4.29** | – | | | |
| 8. The food industry is very concerned about the nutritional value of their products (R) | ** | 4.43 | 4.14 | 4.37 | **4.64** | – | – | – | **–** | – | | | |

| Item | | | | | | | | | | | | | |
|---|---|---|---|---|---|---|---|---|---|---|---|---|---|
| 9. Most foods are so processed that they have lost their nutritional value | n.s. | 4.53 | 4.67 | 4.45 | 4.71 | ** | 2.35 | 1.79 | **4.51** | – | | | |
| 10. The majority of food products can be eaten without risk (R) | n.s. | 4.26 | 3.72 | 3.77 | 3.98 | ** | 3.96 | 1.68 | **6.27** | – | | | |
| *Technological progress* | | | | | | | | | | | | | |
| 11. The degree of civilisation can be measured from the degree of technological development | ** | 4.33 | **4.55** | 4.17 | 4.01 | – | | | | n.s. | 4.92 | 4.82 | 4.88 |
| 12. New technological inventions and applications make up the driving force of progress of society | n.s. | 5.35 | 5.28 | 5.25 | 5.02 | – | | | | *** | 5.72 | 5.27 | **5.65** |
| 13. In [country], we are probably better off than ever, thanks to the tremendous progress in technology | n.s. | 4.95 | 4.93 | 4.84 | 4.79 | – | | | | n.s. | 4.80 | 4.57 | 4.71 |
| 14. Throughout the ages, technological know-how has been the most important weapon in the struggle for life | n.s. | 4.93 | 4.90 | 4.88 | 4.60 | – | | | | ** | 5.57 | 5.16 | **5.51** |

*(Continued)*

**Table A3** (Continued).

| | Sig | EU | | | | Sig | BRAZIL | | | Sig | CHINA | | |
|---|---|---|---|---|---|---|---|---|---|---|---|---|---|
| | | Cluster 1 $N_1 =$ 298, 17.0% | Cluster 2 $N_2 =$ 1036, 59.1% | Cluster 3 $N_3 =$ 216, 12.3% | Cluster 4 $N_4 =$ 201, 11.5% | | Cluster 1 $N_1 =$ 340, 71.6% | Cluster 2 $N_2 =$ 76, 16.0% | Cluster 3 $N_3 =$ 59, 12.4% | | Cluster 1 $N_2 =$ 151, 31.5% | Cluster 2 $N_1 =$ 211, 44.1% | Cluster 3 $N_2 =$ 110, 23.0% |
| 15. Because of the development of tcchnology, wo will be able to face up to the problems of tomorrow's society | ** | 4.19 | 4.29 | 3.93 | 3.67 | – | | | | n.s. | 4.88 | 4.78 | 5.10 |
| *Animal welfare* | | | | | | | | | | | | | |
| 16. It is important that the food I eat on a typical day has been produced in a way that animals have not experienced pain | ** | 5.95 | 5.69 | 6.38 | **6.40** | – | | | | – | | | |
| 17. It is important that the food I eat on a typical day has been produced in a way that animals' rights have been respected | ** | 6.00 | 5.69 | 6.26 | **6.37** | – | | | | – | | | |

| | | | | | | | |
|---|---|---|---|---|---|---|---|
| 18. In general, humans have too little respect for the quality of the life of animals | ** | 5.64 | 5.51 | 5.87 | **6.18** | – | – |
| 19. Increased regulation of the treatment of animals in farming is needed | ** | 5.66 | 5.50 | 5.98 | **6.16** | – | – |
| 20. Animal agriculture raises serious ethical questions about the treatment of animal | n.s. | 5.17 | 5.06 | 5.25 | 5.42 | – | – |
| 21. As long as animals do not suffer pain, humans should be able to use them for any purpose (R) | ** | 4.45 | 4.38 | 4.96 | **5.25** | – | – |
| 22. It is acceptable to use animals to test consumer products such as soaps, cosmetics, and cleaners (R) | ** | 5.36 | 5.18 | 5.88 | **6.04** | – | – |
| 23. Hunting animals for sport is an acceptable form of recreation (R) | ** | 5.45 | 5.10 | **6.00** | 5.93 | – | – |

(*Continued*)

**Table A3** (Continued).

| | | EU | | | | | BRAZIL | | | | CHINA | | |
|---|---|---|---|---|---|---|---|---|---|---|---|---|---|
| | Sig | Cluster 1 $N_1 =$ 298, 17.0% | Cluster 2 $N_2 =$ 1036, 59.1% | Cluster 3 $N_3 =$ 216, 12.3% | Cluster 4 $N_4 =$ 201, 11.5% | Sig | Cluster 1 $N_1 =$ 340, 71.6% | Cluster 2 $N_2 =$ 76, 16.0% | Cluster 3 $N_3 =$ 59, 12.4% | Sig | Cluster 1 $N_2 =$ 151, 31.5% | Cluster 2 $N_1 =$ 211, 44.1% | Cluster 3 $N_2 =$ 110, 23.0% |
| *Food and environment* | | | | | | | | | | | | | |
| 24. It is important that the food I eat on a typical day has been prepared in an environmentally friendly way | ** | **5.84** | 5.49 | 5.74 | 5.76 | ** | 6.46 | 6.62 | **6.98** | ** | **5.55** | 5.15 | 5.49 |
| 25. It is important that the food I eat on a typical day has been produced in a way which has not shaken the balance of nature | ** | 5.80 | 5.46 | 5.79 | **5.81** | ** | 6.53 | 6.45 | **6.98** | ** | **5.49** | 5.05 | 5.37 |
| 26. It is important that the food I eat on a typical day is packaged in an environmentally friendly way | ** | **5.97** | 5.56 | 5.83 | 5.83 | * | 6.66 | 6.86 | **6.98** | n.s. | 5.60 | 5.35 | 5.61 |
| *Local employment* | | | | | | | | | | | | | |
| 27. Buying [country]-made products keeps Brazil working | n.s. | 4.93 | 4.98 | 4.81 | 5.03 | * | 6.27 | 6.34 | **6.75** | n.s. | 5.41 | 5.13 | 5.25 |

| | | | | | | | | | | | | |
|---|---|---|---|---|---|---|---|---|---|---|---|---|
| 28. [Country] consumers who purchase products made in other countries are responsible for putting their fellow [country] out of work | * | 3.21 | **3.53** | 3.20 | 3.42 | ** | 5.84 | 5.49 | **6.61** | n.s. | 3.84 | 3.91 | 3.64 |
| 29. Buying [country] produced products supports the local community's livelihood | n.s. | 5.33 | 5.27 | 5.16 | 5.43 | ** | 5.68 | 5.01 | **6.80** | ** | 5.60 | 5.21 | **5.56** |
| *Local economy* | | | | | | | | | | | | | |
| 30. [Country] products first, last, and foremost | * | 4.00 | **4.35** | 4.18 | **4.35** | ** | 5.35 | 5.14 | **6.85** | n.s. | 4.88 | 4.92 | 4.95 |
| 31. A real [country] should always buy [country]-made products | *** | 3.18 | **3.76** | 3.20 | 3.52 | ** | 5.28 | 4.67 | **6.81** | n.s. | 4.92 | 4.73 | 4.64 |

*(Continued)*

**Table A3** (Continued).

| | Sig | EU | | | | Sig | BRAZIL | | | Sig | CHINA | | |
|---|---|---|---|---|---|---|---|---|---|---|---|---|---|
| | | Cluster 1 $N_1 =$ 298, 17.0% | Cluster 2 $N_2 =$ 1036, 59.1% | Cluster 3 $N_3 =$ 216, 12.3% | Cluster 4 $N_4 =$ 201, 11.5% | | Cluster 1 $N_1 =$ 340, 71.6% | Cluster 2 $N_2 =$ 76, 16.0% | Cluster 3 $N_3 =$ 59, 12.4% | | Cluster 1 $N_2 =$ 151, 31.5% | Cluster 2 $N_1 =$ 211, 44.1% | Cluster 3 $N_2 =$ 110, 23.0% |
| 32. We should purchase products manufactured in [country] instead of letting other countries get rich | n.s. | 4.19 | 4.48 | 4.47 | 4.36 | * | 5.61 | 5.57 | **6.75** | n.s. | 4.49 | 4.29 | 4.34 |
| 33. It's always best to purchase [country] products | * | 4.04 | **4.37** | 4.20 | 4.22 | ** | 5.90 | 4.17 | **6.81** | n.s. | 3.60 | 3.61 | 3.54 |
| 34. It may cost me in the long-run, but I prefer to support [country] products | n.s. | 4.53 | 4.53 | 4.47 | 4.84 | ** | 5.40 | 5.59 | **6.85** | – | | | |

[a]Seven-point scale with end points 1 = 'strongly disagree' to 7 = 'strongly agree'; *ANOVA tests, $p < .05$; **ANOVA tests, $p < .01$; ***ANOVA tests, $p < .001$; n.s: not statistically significant differences.

**Table A4** Cluster profiles in terms of regular[a] pork consumption frequency ($n = 2885$).

| | | EU | | | | | | BRAZIL | | | | | CHINA | | |
|---|---|---|---|---|---|---|---|---|---|---|---|---|---|---|---|
| | | Cluster 1 | Cluster 2 | Cluster 3 | Cluster 4 | | | Cluster 1 | Cluster 2 | Cluster 3 | | | Cluster 1 | Cluster 2 | Cluster 3 |
| | | $N_1 =$ 298, | $N_2 =$ 1036, | $N_3 =$ 216, | $N_4 =$ 201, | | | $N_1 =$ 340, | $N_2 =$ 76, | $N_3 =$ 59, | | | $N_2 =$ 151, | $N_1 =$ 211, | $N_2 =$ 110, |
| | Sig | 17.0% | 59.1% | 12.3% | 11.5% | | Sig | 71.6% | 16.0% | 12.4% | | Sig | 31.5% | 44.1% | 23.0% |
| *A. Fresh first cut* | | | | | | | | | | | | | | | |
| 1. Tenderloin | *** | 33.6 | **34.6** | 24.1 | 20.4 | 1. Pork ribs | * | 19.8 | 21.1 | **37.3** | 1. Lean meat | n.s. | 88.7 | 84.8 | 91.0 |
| 2. Mignonette | * | 58.7 | **61.5** | 52.8 | 49.8 | 2. Loins | * | 22.4 | 15.7 | **27.2** | 2. Side pork | n.s. | 68.2 | 60.2 | 57.3 |
| 3. Pork ribs | n.s | 39.6 | 44.1 | 43.5 | 41.8 | 3. Pork leg | n.s. | 15.7 | 13.2 | 20.4 | 3. Pork ribs | n.s. | 57.3 | 59.5 | 55.5 |
| 4. Pork offal/entrails | * | 6.7 | **10.5** | 4.2 | 2.5 | 4. Others (entrails, fat, tail, ear) | ** | **14.4** | 13.1 | 5.7 | 4. Offal | *** | 15.1 | **29.5** | 19.3 |
| | | | | | | | | | | | 5. Trotters | | 19.4 | **33.1** | 20.4 |
| *B. Fresh minimally processed* | | | | | | | | | | | | | | | |
| 5. Minced pork meat | n.s. | 54.7 | 58.9 | 52.3 | 54.2 | 5. Sausages (fresh), packaged meat | * | 22.1 | 18.4 | **28.8** | 6. Ground meat | n.s. | 42.7 | 41.9 | 39.0 |
| 6. Sausages (fresh) | * | 34.2 | **42.4** | 36.1 | 31.3 | | | | | | 7. Meat stuffing | *** | 31.2 | **41.9** | 33.6 |
| 7. Pork based brochette | *** | 19.8 | 16.6 | **27.3** | 22.9 | – | | | | | 8. Meatball | *** | 23.9 | **35.3** | 30.3 |
| 8. Small cuts (barbeque etc.) | n.s. | 13.4 | 14.1 | 12.0 | 15.9 | – | | | | | 9. Seasoned pork | * | 15.6 | **25.1** | 21.7 |
| *C. Further processed* | | | | | | | | | | | | | | | |

(Continued)

**Table A4** (Continued).

| | | EU | | | | | | BRAZIL | | | | | CHINA | | |
|---|---|---|---|---|---|---|---|---|---|---|---|---|---|---|---|
| | | Cluster 1 | Cluster 2 | Cluster 3 | Cluster 4 | | | Cluster 1 | Cluster 2 | Cluster 3 | | | Cluster 1 | Cluster 2 | Cluster 3 |
| | Sig | $N_1 =$ 298, 17.0% | $N_2 =$ 1036, 59.1% | $N_3 =$ 216, 12.3% | $N_4 =$ 201, 11.5% | | Sig | $N_1 =$ 340, 71.6% | $N_2 =$ 76, 16.0% | $N_3 =$ 59, 12.4% | | Sig | $N_2 =$ 151, 31.5% | $N_1 =$ 211, 44.1% | $N_2 =$ 110, 23.0% |
| 9. Pork escalope/schnitzel | *** | 23.5 | **27.7** | 9.7 | 12.4 | 7. Stuffed meat, | | | | | 10. Barbecued pork | * | 15.4 | **26.5** | 19.2 |
| 10. Pork cordon bleu | *** | 4.0 | **8.4** | 4.2 | 6.0 | pork escalope, | | | | | 11. Roast pork | ** | 15.2 | **19.6** | 17.6 |
| 11. Stuffed meat | *** | 11.4 | **16.4** | 3.7 | 6.5 | roasted meat, | * | 15.0 | 11.8 | **30.6** | 12. Braised pork | n.s. | 12.6 | 22.7 | 20.0 |
| 12. Mixed gyros-pita meat | *** | 14.8 | 10.3 | **22.2** | 14.9 | marinated meat, | | | | | 13. Ham sausage | n.s. | 26.5 | 32.7 | 30.9 |
| 13. Remaining mixed meat | *** | 3.4 | **5.5** | 3.7 | **5.5** | seasoned meat | | | | | | | | | |
| 14. Other pork roasted, cooked, baked | n.s. | 24.2 | 27.5 | 22.7 | 20.4 | – | | | | | | | | | |
| 15. Marinated | * | 6.4 | **9.4** | 5.6 | 6.5 | – | | | | | | | | | |
| *D. Pork-based dishes* | | | | | | | | | | | | | | | |
| 16. Lasagne | n.s. | 17.1 | 15.7 | 16.7 | 17.9 | 12. Lasagne, | | | | | 14. Gravy pork noodles | n.s. | 39.1 | 39.4 | 45.5 |
| 17. Spaghetti Bolognese | n.s. | 40.6 | 45.6 | 43.1 | 42.3 | pizza, Brazilian | n.s. | 33.0 | 40.7 | 30.5 | 15. Meat bun | n.s. | 46.5 | 55.7 | 58.1 |

| | | | | | | | | | | | | | | |
|---|---|---|---|---|---|---|---|---|---|---|---|---|---|---|
| 18. Pizza | n.s. | 27.5 | 26.9 | 30.6 | 27.4 | 'feijoada'/black | | | | 16. Pork stuffing dumpling | n.s. | 40.7 | 43.1 | 39.9 |
| | | | | | | beans | | | | 17. Pork pie | * | 20.9 | **34.1** | 22.3 |
| *E. Pork meat products* | | | | | | 15. Cold meat | | | | 18. Preserved meat | *** | 12.1 | **22.3** | 14.5 |
| 19. Salami | *** | 34.6 | **41.2** | 34.7 | 34.3 | | | | | | | | | |
| 20. Cooked ham | *** | 51.0 | **54.5** | 38.9 | 37.3 | (salami, ham, | ** | 58.2 | 73.8 | **86.5** | 19. Chinese sausage | *** | 13.2 | **33.5** | 14.6 |
| 21. Dry cured ham | *** | 30.5 | **36.5** | 21.8 | 18.9 | mortadella) | | | | 20. Ham | ** | 18.5 | **23.3** | 20.9 |
| 22. Dry cured products (bacon) | * | 30.2 | **35.0** | 22.2 | 15.4 | 18. Bacon | ** | 32.3 | **46.0** | 10.2 | 21. Canned meat | * | 4.0 | **13.6** | 6.4 |
| 23. Sausage Vienna, Frankfurter | *** | 27.2 | **34.8** | 21.8 | 24.9 | 19. Sausages | ** | 46.2 | **73.7** | 59.2 | 22. Dried meat floss | * | 8.0 | **19.0** | 9.9 |
| 24. Sausages cooked | *** | 22.5 | **33.1** | 21.3 | 21.4 | 20. Paté | * | 16.2 | 11.8 | **20.4** | 23. Pork jerk | ** | 5.3 | **15.1** | 7.2 |
| 25. Liver pate | n.s. | 26.8 | 34.3 | 25.9 | 39.8 | – | | | | | | | | |
| 26. Toppings | n.s. | 23.8 | 26.1 | 22.7 | 28.4 | – | | | | | | | | |
| 27. Canned meat | *** | 7.0 | **10.6** | 6.9 | **10.4** | – | | | | | | | | |

***Chi-square tests, $p < .001$; **chi-square tests, $p < .01$; *chi-square tests, $p < .05$.

[a]EU and Brazilian respondents who consume any pork product from 'several times a month' to 'daily'; in China, relevant numbers represent consumption from 'once a week' to 'daily'.

# Individual values and motivational complexities in ethical clothing consumption: A means-end approach

Thomas Jägel, *University of Manchester, UK*
Kathy Keeling, *University of Manchester, UK*
Alexander Reppel, *University of London, UK*
Thorsten Gruber, *University of Manchester, UK*

**Abstract** With the expansion of ethical consumption, there is an increased need to understand the variety of consumer motives for consumer engagement in such behaviour. For the rapidly growing area of ethical clothing, this study explores consumers' desired consumption outcomes and personal values that drive ethical product preferences. Analysis of data obtained through a semi-qualitative laddering approach ($n = 93$ ethical clothing consumers) reveals five dominant perceptual patterns relating not only to environmental and altruist ethical concerns, but also more individual motives of value for money, personal image, and well-being. Further analysis shows that consumers have to compromise and balance between their conflicting end-goals. The study augments previous findings in ethical clothing research, as researchers can better understand how specific attributes of products relate to the emotional and symbolic aspects and link back to consumer values. Though limited in scope by its exploratory character, the study contributes towards a deeper understanding of ethical consumer behaviour. Implications for theory practice and further research are discussed.

## Introduction

The market size for ethical consumption in the UK has almost tripled within the last decade (Co-operative Bank, 2009). Even in times of economic crisis, many consumers still exhibit ethical consumption behaviour (Carrigan & de Pelsmacker, 2009) such as downshifting, recycling, boycotting, or purchasing ethical goods. The small but exponentially growing market of ethical clothing (Mintel, 2009) represents an especially promising research area within this field. The notion of ethical clothing is multifaceted, as reflected by the use of various terms such as eco, Fairtrade, organic, sustainable, or recycled clothing (Mintel, 2009; Thomas, 2008), and customers' changing approach towards clothing recycling and disposal and boycotting of unethical clothing companies adds further to its relevance.

Until recently, the role of ethical concern on clothing choice seemed marginal (Carrigan & Attala, 2001; Iwanow, McEachern, & Jeffrey, 2005; Joergens, 2006), but currently, results suggest that ethical clothing consumption is relevant for a growing number of consumers (e.g. Niinimäki, 2010). Issues around understanding ethical clothing consumption have been attributed to the complex pursuit of multiple personal values that underlie consumers' choice criteria in clothing consumption (Butler & Francis, 1997; Kim & Damhorst, 1998), but these values themselves are not well understood (Niinimäki, 2010). This is important, as values are often linked to strong positive and negative affective responses as they 'represent important consequences that are personally relevant' (Peter, Olson, & Grunert, 1999, p. 71). Schlegelmilch (1996) argues that the level of involvement in environmentally concerned purchases leads to central rather than peripheral, heuristic information processing, and so concerned consumers consider concrete facts rather than emotional appeals. Hartmann, Ibáñez, and Sainz (2005) suggest that a combination of factual and emotional benefits works best to position environmentally friendly products. Certainly, some debates around the nature of consumption argue for the 'privileged place' (Cova, 1999) of emotions and symbolic aspects of products (Cova, 1999; Elliot, 1994). Hence, an understanding of how product attributes link back to personal values seems a worthy focus of attention.

This study therefore explores consumers' product preferences in ethical clothing and how these are linked back to personal values, thus contributing towards an understanding of the values that consumers seek from ethical apparel. After a review of the literature on ethical clothing and the role of personal values in ethical consumption, we describe a study using the semi-structured laddering technique to develop consumer motivational chains among a sample of ethical clothing consumers. The study reveals the dominant motivational patterns behind ethical clothing choice, and discusses the implications and research directions in the context of ethical fashion.

Further, in highlighting the importance of personal values as determinants of ethical consumption, this paper contributes to the broader literature on green and ethical consumption, as the study reflects recent shifts in consumer practice and research focus. Our study sheds light on the motivational complexities faced by ethical consumers (Szmigin, Carrigan, & McEachern, 2009) and supports the broadening of consumer involvement from a purely 'green' environmentally concerned consumer towards an 'ethical' consumer who is also socially aware (Harrison, Newholm, & Shaw, 2005). Our study finally aims to make a methodological contribution by applying the semi-structured interviewing technique of laddering to ethical clothing.

## Ethical clothing consumption

The purchase of clothing that uses environmentally friendly production, as well as fairly traded clothing (with the focus on achieving better prices and working conditions) is closely related to clothing boycotts and buying second-hand for recycling reasons, which, all taken together, accounted for a market size worth about £1 billion in the UK in 2009 (Co-operative Bank, 2010). Hence, an inclusive definition of ethical clothing covers all clothing produced and traded with regard to its impact on the environment and the people involved (Mintel, 2009). Mintel (2009) estimates that spending on ethical clothing has quadrupled within four years, and predicts further growth, driven by a stronger consumer demand for fairly produced and sustainable clothing. Although research interest in ethical clothing consumption has increased in recent years, studies tend to focus on single issues: on eco clothing (e.g. Niinimäki, 2010), organic clothing (e.g. Lin, 2009), Fairtrade (Shaw, Hogg, Wilson, Shiu, & Hassan, 2006), buying from socially responsible businesses (Dickson, 2000), clothing disposal and donating (Ha-Brookshire & Hodges, 2009), and clothing recycling (Shim, 1995). This can make drawing generalisations about the importance of product versus ethical attributes difficult. Further, some differences in the outcomes of studies may be attributed to the type of sample. For example, Joergens (2006) and Iwanow et al. (2005), in studies of all clothing consumers, conclude that price, style, and quality are the primary influence on clothes purchase; ethical considerations are of secondary importance. In contrast, Dickson and Littrell (1996) and Sneddon, Lee, and Soutar (2009) specifically research ethical consumers, finding ethical concerns do have relevance for clothing purchase decisions. Thus, at least for a subset of consumers, ethical product attributes present important choice criteria.

However, it can be concluded that there is a complex mix of 'multiple end-goals such as self-expression, aesthetic satisfaction and group conformity' (Kim & Damhorst, 1998, p. 132) behind ethical clothing consumption. Consumers may not simply try to reduce and avoid feelings of guilt by recycling or re-using their old clothing, they may simultaneously seek utilitarian value (Ha-Brookshire & Hodges, 2009; Lin, 2009), or feel themselves driven by an 'ethical obligation' (Shaw et al., 2006). Ethical clothing consumers may also search to express their ideology and self-identity through their clothing, that is, egoistic motives (Niinimäki, 2010).

In sum, the review of literature reveals a wide range of motives behind consumers' ethical clothing consumption. Dickson (2000) and Dickson and Littrell (1996) using path analysis, specifically theorise and demonstrate a hierarchical system of effects with global values as the most abstract level affecting more specific attitudes. Importantly, the attitude towards the behaviour of purchasing apparel in an ethical context was a better predictor of purchase behaviour than was attitude towards the apparel itself (Dickson & Littrell, 1996). Thus the use of a laddering exercise, with its power to show the full account of how personal values in relation to ethical clothing are satisfied through the interrelation and interaction of product attributes and consequences, appears valid. Our study therefore aims to capture as much of the complexity of relevant product preferences and benefits sought by buyers of ethical clothing as possible, and to show how these are linked to underlying personal values.

## Values as drivers in ethical consumption

Values, defined as 'desirable, trans-situational goals' serve 'as a guiding principle in peoples' lives' (Schwartz, 1994, p. 21) and thereby have an important role in determining and limiting ethical consumption (Kilbourne & Beckmann, 1998).

For Schwartz (1992), human values are characterised by two orthogonal dimensions – self-enhancement versus. self-transcendence, and openness to change versus conservation – resulting in four distinct value orientations. First, self-enhancement as a value orientation includes power and achievement values, thereby highlighting self-interest, while, second, self-transcendence, in contrast, emphasises concern for others. Third, openness to change highlights independent action and thought, whereas, fourth, conservation is characterised by self-restriction and resistance to change (Schwartz, 1992). Personal values can therefore be conflicting in nature.

Schwartz's value framework and the use of the Schwartz (1992) value survey have provided useful insight into environmentally friendly (Gilg & Ford, 2005), socially conscious, and frugal consumer behaviour (Pepper, Jackson, & Uzzell 2009) and consumption of Fairtrade products (Doran, 2009). Stern, Dietz, and Kalof (1993) adapt Schwartz's framework in stating that three values – biospheric values, altruistic values, and egoistic values – determine consumers' environmental concerns. Biospheric (or ecocentric) values reflect a concern for the non-human species, plant, or animal, and the conservation of the planet in general; egoistic values manifest in trying to maximise individual outcomes, and altruistic values reflect concern for social justice and the welfare of other human beings (Stern et al., 1993). Shaw, Grehan, Shiu, Hassan, and Thompson (2005) also find a set of relevant values related to the Schwartz (1992) framework for ethical consumer purchasing, including traditionalist values (such as security) or values related to openness to change (such as independence).

However, whilst undoubtedly providing insight and structure on the nature of values in ethical consumer purchasing, criticisms of these studies are that the predefined value sets risk missing other relevant constructs, and it is not always clear how values translate into consumers' concrete choice criteria for ethical products. Consequently, the flexibility of means-end theory (Gutman, 1982; see below) initially used in the context of product and brand positioning (Gutman, 1982; Reynolds & Gutman, 1988) represents a potentially valuable framework to understand pro-environmental and pro-social behaviour in terms of the underlying personal values (Jackson, 2005).

## Means-end approaches and laddering technique

While Hines and O'Neill's (1995) study on determinants of clothing quality provides a rare example of an application of the laddering approach related to clothing, laddering techniques and their foundation in means-end theory have sporadically been used when researching ethical consumer behaviour (Jackson, 2005), recycling behaviour (Bagozzi & Dabholkar, 1994), preferences, categories, and differences between countries relating to organic food (Baker, Thompson, Egelken, & Huntley, 2004; Padel & Foster, 2005; Zanoli & Naspetti, 2002). These studies reveal the divergence and complexity of perceptual and motivational patterns of consumers when buying ethical products. In particular, how ethical and non-ethical considerations interact, for instance, ecological product features such as the absence of chemicals, are also linked to the self-related motivations of health and personal well-being (e.g. Zanoli & Naspetti, 2002).

Means-end chain theory (Gutman, 1982) posits that consumers use means (products, activities) to attain ends (valued states of being). More specifically, the theory assumes that consumers' preferences towards certain offerings (*attributes*) are determined by functional and psychological *consequences* for the consumers, which help them to strive for underlying terminal *values* (Reynolds & Gutman, 1988). The means-end theory thereby frames consumer decision making as the basic problem and assumes that consumers strive for maximising positive outcomes (benefits) and avoiding negative outcomes (risks) that these consumption decisions entail (Olsen & Reynolds, 2001). The evaluation of what are positive and negative outcomes is in turn determined by personal values that people want to attain (Gutman, 1982).

Values are the consumers' universal life goals and represent the most personal and general consequences individuals are striving for (Rokeach, 1973). Importantly, attributes and consequences can differ in nature. Attributes can be very concrete or rather abstract (Grunert, Beckmann, & Sørensen, 2001), whilst consequences can be either functional and tangible (often experienced directly after a purchase) or take more personal or emotional forms, thus representing psychological and social consequences (Olsen & Reynolds, 2001). Overall, attributes, consequences, and values form interrelated and hierarchical structures in consumers' minds (Reynolds & Gutman, 1988). For the present research, means-end theory represents a suitable framework, as it clearly specifies how product purchase decisions are linked to values and accounts for the fact that different attributes, consequences, and values can be present in a given context. It puts special emphasis on the linkages between components, as these carry the majority of the meaning (Reynolds, Dethloff, & Westberg, 2001).

Within research using means-end approaches, there is no agreement whether the obtained structures should be interpreted as cognitive maps or context-dependent motivational structures (Grunert et al., 2001). We agree with Claeys and Vanden Abeele (2001) that a main contribution of means-end chain theory can be seen in reconciling the motivational and cognitive schools in consumer research, as product knowledge (on preference) level is linked to more personal concepts such as values. Thus means-end chains can be interpreted as cognitive and motivational structures alike.

Means-end chain theory is closely linked to the qualitative interviewing technique of laddering (Reynolds & Gutman, 1988), which elicits, rather than imposes, the consumer attitude and value structures. This represents a methodological advantage to closed-question survey-based approaches that do not necessarily allow for sufficient respondent reflection on the relevant values for their decision making (Dietz, Fitzgerald, & Shwom, 2005). Laddering usually involves semi-standardised personal in-depth interviews, with the interviewer probing to reveal attribute–consequence–value chains (i.e. 'ladders'). The interviewer repeatedly questions why an attribute, a consequence, or a value is important to the respondent. The answer then acts as the starting point for further questioning, until saturation is reached. Cognitive concepts obtained during the laddering interview and analysis are summarised in a graphical representation of a set of means-end chains termed a Hierarchical Value Map (HVM) (Reynolds & Gutman, 1988).

## Study design

Velodu-de-Oliveira, Ikeda, and Campomar (2006) identify barriers to the use of laddering in marketing research: interviews can be time-consuming and expensive; sets of answers can be artificial, as questions focus on reaching a higher level of abstraction; and respondents might feel uncomfortable talking about questions at value level. The researcher might bias the interview and analysis process through pre-established expectations, and might therefore analyse the results overly simplistically.

We addressed most of these issues relating to the interview process by choosing a non-interviewer-based 'hard' laddering approach via questionnaires with open-ended questions. Hard laddering can be distinguished from the 'soft' laddering approach, which uses in-depth interviews (Botschen, Thelen, & Pieters, 1999). Whilst producing similar results to soft laddering (Botschen et al., 1999), hard laddering is more efficient for collecting data than soft laddering, as it is easier and less costly to administer, so enabling larger and more representative samples (Russell et al., 2004). Furthermore, hard laddering can reduce social response bias, as social pressure is lower than in soft laddering (Russell et al., 2004) and eliminates a considerable part of researcher bias (Grunert et al., 2001). Nevertheless, Philipps and Reynolds (2009) criticise hard laddering approaches, as respondents might not reach high levels of abstraction due to a lack of probing opportunity by an interviewer. We addressed this serious criticism by taking advantage of the technical advantages of conducting our questionnaire online, and programmed in extra help and prompts.

There are important benefits for hard laddering in an online environment, for example lower transcription errors; it is cheaper, faster, and more convenient than a pen-and-paper approach (Russell et al., 2004). Further, the online questionnaire software allowed a more flexible, interactive, and appealing design than a pen-and-paper based equivalent.[1]

Based on an earlier instrument, we developed a detailed laddering questionnaire and explanation based on multi-step exploration and piloting. This research phase included face-to-face laddering interviews and a pen-and-paper version of the questionnaire, which was then revised upon feedback, adapted to an online version, and pretested again. The final questionnaire started with simple definitions of the terms ethical and eco clothing, adopted from Mintel (2009), in order to ensure a shared understanding among all participants. As recommended for laddering interviews, the questionnaire continued with sociodemographics and warm-up questions to activate participant cognitions about the topic. Consumers were asked to indicate which of a list ethical and eco-clothing acquisition behaviours they had done during the last six months.

A tutorial followed to explain the constructs of attributes, values, and consequences, and the laddering process, using an example from outside green/ethical marketing, so later results were not influenced by the tutorial. In addition to the explanations given in the tutorial, to help consumers to understand attributes further, participants were encouraged to consider the wide range of attributes relating to ethical and eco clothing and that they should not feel limited in their choice. Participants were further asked to think of decisive attributes for past ethical purchases, similar to a difference by occasion elicitation (Reynolds & Gutman, 1988) and also those attributes that would make it (more) likely for them

---

[1] The exact content of the online version is available on request.

to buy in the future. This question had proven to work well at the piloting stage and is similar to the Reynolds (2006) and Philipps et al. (2010) concept of 'on the margin' elicitation, asking a question that identifies main barriers to a purchasing decision. As the aim of the research was to obtain the whole range of attributes, these barriers should be taken into account. With this in mind, respondents were asked:

> First, please try to think about the three most important features or attributes that an item of ethical and eco clothing should ideally possess. Choose those attributes that have convinced you to buy ethical and eco clothing in the past or which could convince you to buy it in the future.

This procedure helped elicit a wide range of consumer preferences in relation to ethical and eco clothing.

At the next step, respondents used a large open text box to answer why the first attribute they had just identified was important to them. In subsequent steps, respondents explained why what they indicated in the previous boxes was *in turn* important to them. Participants could maximally fill in five text boxes per ladder. After completion of the first ladder, the process was repeated for the second and third attribute. If participants wanted help to answer the laddering question, they could tick a dedicated help button, which provided an additional question based on probing techniques for soft laddering interviews (Reynolds & Gutman, 1988) with the aim of helping structure respondent thoughts, for example postulation of absence of the attribute 'what would happen if the product did not possess the attribute?'; evoking the situational context 'Can you think of a specific situation in relation to your previous statement?'; third-person probing 'It might help to picture others in your situation and why it might matter to them'.

The sampling was handled by a UK research agency by sending out invitations to randomly chosen members of their large and demographically diverse existing panel of potential respondents, rewarded by small, non-monetary incentives. Panel maintenance involves routine membership, and fraud and data quality screening to ensure valid and unique responses. Grunert and Grunert (1995) argue that for the success of a hard laddering approach, the mean respondent involvement with the product category should not be too low (as cognitive structures would be too weak) or too high (as cognitive structures would be too complex for a hard laddering approach). Therefore, screening questions ensured only consumers reporting at least one relevant ethical clothing acquisition behaviour could take the survey (i.e. bought eco clothing or fairly traded clothing, engaged in recycled clothing acquisition, or boycotted unethical clothing retailers and brands). Equally, the screening requirements were low enough to ensure the sample covered a range of respondent involvement with ethical clothing acquisition and fashion. The Zaichkowsky (1994) measure of product involvement provided a check on respondent involvement.

Respondents were predominantly female, and 90% were aged between 25 and 65 years (see Table 1). Further, 48% of the sample reported incomes at or below £20,000. As the average UK wage is circa £25,900 (ONS, 2010), this is not completely consistent to Mintel (2009) findings that potential buyers of ethical clothing come from upper socio-economic groups. One possible explanation is that participants in this study actually *bought*, whereas Mintel focuses on *potential* buyers. Furthermore, the proportions of female, retired, and part-time workers in this study come from sectors with lower than average wages (ONS, 2010), and Mintel's

# CONTEMPORARY ISSUES IN GREEN AND ETHICAL MARKETING

**Table 1** Sociodemographic characteristics of the sample.

| Total = 98 respondents | | | | | |
|---|---|---|---|---|---|
| *Gender* | Male | 27% | *Ethical* | Bought eco clothing | 70% |
| | Female | 71% | *Clothing* | | |
| *Age* | 20–24 | 3% | *Acquisition Behaviour* | Bought fairly traded clothing | 50% |
| | 25–34 | 20% | | | |
| | 35–44 | 29% | | Bought from ethical company or boycotted unethical companies | 42% |
| | 45–54 | 16% | | | |
| | 55–64 | 23% | | Engaged in recycled clothing acquisition | 57% |
| | 65+ | 7% | | | |
| *Employment status* | Full-time | 52% | *Income* | Up to £10,000 | 20% |
| | Part-time | 14% | | £10,001–£20,000 | 28% |
| | Retired | 19% | | £20,001–£30,000 | 22% |
| | Unemployed | 10% | | £30,000–£40,000 | 13% |
| | Other (caring, etc.) | 5% | | £40,000+ | 16% |
| *Education* | Secondary school | 20% | | College | 47% |
| | Further education | 16% | | Postgraduate | 15% |

(2009) research focus does not include boycotting or recycled clothing acquisition. Age-wise, Mintel (2009) describe a similar skew to this study.

As an indicator of the sample suitability for the hard laddering approach (Grunert & Grunert, 1995), involvement with the product category (Zaichkowsky, 1994) provided a satisfactory level (mean = 4.9, scale 1–7). Therefore, it can be assumed that for the majority of respondents, the effectiveness of a hard laddering approach was not negatively influenced by the lack or complexity of cognitive structures (Grunert & Grunert, 1995).The sample size derived from the intention to reach full theoretical saturation. Theoretical saturation in this context means that no new relevant category emerges from further analysis, that categories are well-developed, and links between categories well-established. Most hard laddering techniques operate with sample sizes of about 50. In the present study, the larger sample size ensured that categories were well developed, even at value level, and allowed us to gain insights into the relative importance of different constructs and the links between concepts in order to detect dominant perceptual patterns.

## Analysis

The analysis of the laddering data comprised three main steps, following the guidelines as set out by Gengler and Reynolds (1995), Grunert et al. (2001), and Reynolds and Gutman (1988). First, for each respondent, responses were grouped into 'chunks' of meaning (Gengler & Reynolds, 1995) to specify the elements of means-end chain for each respondent. This way, individual ladders, consisting of attributes, consequences, and values, were constructed separately for each respondent (Reynolds & Gutman, 1988).

We then developed meaningful categories based on phrases and key words based on comprehensive lists of clothing attributes and personal values (Schwartz, 1992). Where applicable, we defined categories in line with existing concepts from the literature. The coding procedure was iterative and labour-intensive, including splitting, combining, and redefining categories in line with content analysis techniques. We reduced the number of concepts until we reached a manageable number of 50 (Gengler & Reynolds, 1995; see Tables 2–4).

Initially carried out by a single researcher, a second researcher with expertise in ethical consumer research and a third researcher with laddering expertise carried out a cross-check of whether the categories were clear, distinguishable, and theoretically consistent (Grunert & Grunert, 1995). Some categories were reshaped after these reviews. The resulting data were then entered into the software LADDERMAP (Gengler & Reynolds, 1993). LADDERMAP assists construction of an implications matrix displaying how often an element leads to each other element in the laddering data directly and indirectly (Gutman & Reynolds 1988). The implications matrix bridges the qualitative and quantitative elements of the laddering technique, and allows examination of the different types of relationships and determination of the dominant paths likely to appear in an aggregate map (Reynolds & Gutman, 1988). This aggregate map, the hierarchical value map, displays dominant perceptual patterns (Reynolds & Gutman, 1988), with the size of nodes and thickness of lines representing the number within the laddering data. Since the HVM must be interpretable to allow managerial implications (Gengler & Reynolds, 1995), only linkages mentioned by a certain amount of respondents are graphically represented. Three different cut-off points were tried and compared to identify the most meaningful and interpretable map (Christensen & Olson, 2002) given the Gengler and Reynolds' (1995) recommendations that no less than 70% of the direct linkages are represented. We chose a cut-off level of four, as the resulting map keeps the balance between data reduction and retention (Gengler, Klenosky, & Mulvey, 1995; see Figure 1).

## Results and discussion

Using the 98 interviews, we identified 11 attributes, 12 consequences, and 8 values to appear on the HVM (see Figure 1). The attributes level at the base of the HVM (unshaded circles) forms the product preferences of buyers of ethical clothing. These include both generic product attributes (such as price, quality, style, and comfort) and attributes that relate to the ethical character of the product, such as recycled and natural materials, environmentally friendly production techniques, and fair working conditions and wages for the workers.

The breadth of attributes may be attributable to the sample composition; respondents reported a wide spread of involvement with ethical clothing issues. However, the range also supports other research showing that consumers who buy ethical clothing often base their choice not solely on product or ethical attributes but on a combination of both (e.g. Dickson & Littrell, 1996; Iwanow et al., 2005; Joergens, 2006; Niinimäki, 2010), and the pronounced role of product performance

# CONTEMPORARY ISSUES IN GREEN AND ETHICAL MARKETING

**Table 2** Table of all attributes.

| Name of attribute | Number of times mentioned | Characteristics |
|---|---|---|
| Natural materials | 37 | Ethical clothing should be made from natural materials such as organic cotton and bamboo and not be synthetic |
| Product performance | 34 | Consumers want their clothing to be fit for purpose, hard-wearing, and durable |
| Fair wages | 33 | Consumers want to ensure fair payment of factory workers and raw material suppliers when buying ethical clothing |
| Environmentally friendly production techniques | 32 | Ethical clothing should be produced with a minimum effect on the environment (no gases, low carbon footprint) and animals |
| Comfort and fit | 31 | Ethical clothing should be soft, comfortable and provide a good fit |
| Style | 30 | Consumers look for design and style in ethical clothing |
| Quality | 29 | Ethical clothing should provide high quality in materials and stitching |
| Fair working conditions | 27 | Ethical clothing should be made under safe and healthy working conditions, without child labour or sweatshops |
| Price | 26 | Ethical clothing should be fairly priced and be affordable for consumers |
| Recycled | 15 | Consumers seek clothing which is recycled or reused, and which is recyclable |
| Local sourcing | 14 | Consumers avoid certain countries of origin and prefer local production of ethical clothing |
| Brand | 10 | Consumers look for trusted brands as to ensure they buy ethical |
| Information | 9 | Consumers want to information on labels to ensure that clothing is really ethical |
| Sustainable | 9 | Ethical clothing should be made ensuring a long-term benefit for environment and local workers, as by using renewable resources |
| Choice and availability | 4 | Consumers look for a wide range of ethical clothing to choose from |
| Clean | 4 | Ethical clothing should be in a good and clean condition, even if it is recycled |

is in line with Niinimäki's (2010) observation that ethical consumers want clothing to be durable.

On the next step of the ladder, the consequence level (light shading), the 14 categories reveal a wide range of perceived consumption benefits and risk. This sample of consumers wants to 'support the environment' and 'promote better living

**Table 3** Table of all consequences.

| Name of consequence | Number of times mentioned | Characteristics |
|---|---|---|
| Support the environment | 52 | Consumer want to help the environment and reduce their own and their products' negative impact |
| Avoid exploitation | 38 | Consumers don't want to be involved in exploiting others and avoid unethical companies |
| Feel of wearing | 37 | Consumers want a comfortable feel when wearing ethical clothing and want to avoid sweating |
| Look good | 32 | Consumers want to look good, smart, fashionable, and feel dressed properly. |
| Stay in budget | 31 | Consumers can afford ethical clothing, stay within their budget, and save money for other things |
| Assume responsibility | 28 | Consumers feel they have a responsibility and ethical obligation to contribute and 'do their bit' |
| Value for money | 24 | Consumers feel they get good use of the money they invest in ethical clothing |
| Produce less waste | 22 | Consumers can reduce and avoid waste |
| Promote better living conditions | 21 | Consumers want to have a positive impact on other peoples' lives by buying ethical clothing |
| Reduce buying | 20 | Consumers want their clothing to last so they need to replace them less often |
| Promote health | 9 | Consumers want to sustain their health, and avoid skin irritations or allergies |
| Act as an ambassador | 9 | Consumers act as an ambassador of ecological and social issues in their social environment |
| Avoid feelings of guilt | 8 | Consumers would feel guilty if they did not buy ethical clothing, and want to avoid the feeling of guilt |
| Ensure paying for a right cause | 6 | Consumers want to feel sure that they are truly paying for a right cause |
| Recycle and re-use | 5 | Consumers want to recycle and reuse clothing themselves, and want to resell and donate it |
| Fight unethical companies | 5 | Consumers take action against companies that engage in unethical clothing production and trade |
| Promote local economy | 5 | Consumers aim to assist workers, shops, and companies in their communities and in the UK |
| Animal welfare | 4 | Consumers want to help animals and wildlife |
| Convenience | 3 | Consumers can save time and avoid stress related to the maintenance of ethical clothing |

**Table 4** Table of all values.

| Name of value | Number of times mentioned | Characteristics |
|---|---|---|
| Feel good | 26 | Consumers seek personal and emotional well-being |
| Equality | 23 | Consumers believe that everyone deserves equal treatment and opportunity |
| Social justice | 19 | Consumers care for the weak and wish more caring and sharing of wealth in society |
| Save resources and prevent pollution | 15 | Consumers strive for saving the world's scarce resources and prevent it from being polluted |
| Provide for future generations | 13 | Consumers want to sustain the environment for generations to come |
| Protect the environment | 12 | Consumers feel strongly about preserving nature |
| Self-respect | 11 | Consumers want to believe in their own worth, be self-confident, and act self-congruent |
| Social recognition | 9 | Consumers want respect from others and are concerned about the image they project to them |
| Security | 8 | Consumers seek safety and security for themselves and their families |
| Influence | 6 | Consumers want to have an impact on their immediate environment |
| Benevolence | 4 | Consumers strongly feel about helping people in their closer environment |
| Health | 4 | Consumers ultimately seek to live a healthy live |
| Uniqueness | 4 | Consumers want to feel individual and one of a kind |
| Unity with nature | 2 | Consumers want to live in harmony with nature and animals |

conditions' for workers by buying ethical products. This also has psychological consequences for consumers, as they enact their responsibility by helping the environment, and try to avoid the risk of responsibility for others suffering due to their choice in clothing ('avoid exploitation'). This supports Shaw et al.'s (2006) notion of an ethical obligation that drives these consumers. At the same time, the presence of constructs such as 'look good', 'stay within budget', and 'feel of wearing' on the HVM shows that consumers still search for individual benefit and take into account personal and financial needs in ethical clothing consumption.

On the value level of the means-end chains (darker shading), consumers engaging in ethical and eco clothing identify eight different values, demonstrating the pivotal importance and complexity of personal values as drivers of ethical clothing consumption. Three different values directly centre on saving the environment, and can therefore be classified as biospheric.

**Figure 1** Hierarchical value map for ethical clothing consumption.

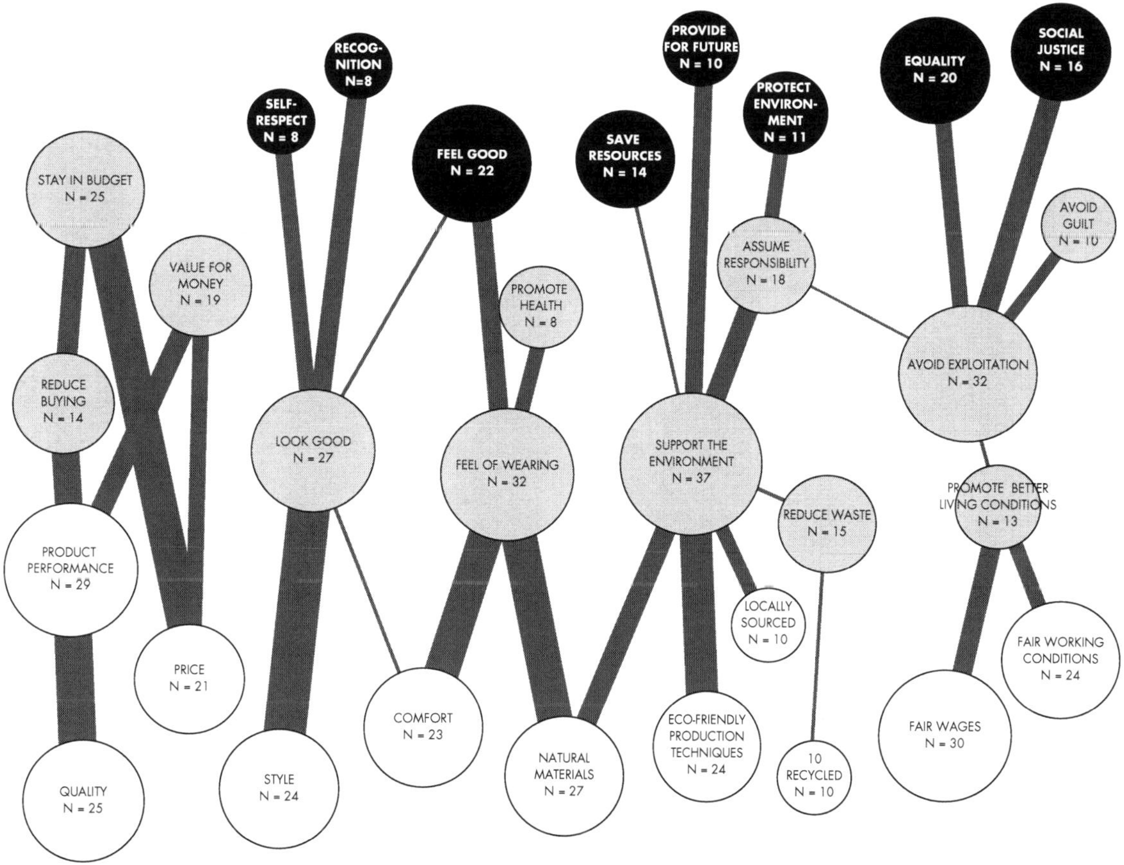

Altruism also drives ethical clothing consumption, as the concepts of 'social justice' and 'equality' demonstrate, although egoistic motives are also apparent ('social recognition' and 'self-respect'). This supports Kim and Damhorst's (1998) claim that self-expression and group conformity must not be neglected in explaining ethical clothing consumption. The importance of accounting for individual desires and needs in ethical and eco clothing is also reflected by consumers' drive for emotional well-being ('feel good').

The relationships between constructs and their strengths allow for a discussion of how the revealed values impact on product preferences in ethical clothing. By focusing on the strong links between attributes, consequences, and values, five dominant perceptual patterns can be revealed (see Figure 2).

## *Dominant patterns*

1. In the first perceptual pattern, 'quality' emerges as intrinsically linked to aspects of product performance. Respondents infer durability and maintaining shape from their general requirement of quality for two main reasons. First, durable and well-performing clothing reduce the need to replace clothing quickly. Respondents link these attributes to saving money and staying within a limited clothing budget. Second, consumers want to get value for money. Consistently, 'price' links equally strongly to budgetary considerations and to 'value for money'. This perceptual pattern is clearly driven by individual, and more specifically, financial benefits and utilitarian value.

2. For the attribute 'style', buyers of ethical and eco fashion follow a relatively straightforward perceptual pattern. They have a preference for style and design because they want to 'look good', which ultimately helps to convey a desired image to others ('social recognition'). Similarly, the benefit of looking good helps ethical consumers to create a better self-image and feel more confident ('self-respect'). Ultimately, consumers following this pattern use ethical clothing to convey a certain image to others and to express their self-identity, concurring with similar comments from Niinimäki (2010).

3. The concepts of 'comfort and fit' and of 'natural materials' are both strongly linked to the consequence of 'feel of wearing'. Consumers seek to feel comfortable in their clothes. For some respondents, the feel of wearing of eco materials is also related to health issues ('promote health'). This pattern supports Lin's (2009) suggestion that a segment of consumers buying in this clothing sector is driven by need rather than want, as clothing choice is motivated by their personal health. Yet for the majority of respondents following this perceptual pattern, emphasis on comfort, fit, and natural materials are driven by a desire for well-being and 'feeling good'.

4. The fourth dominant pattern centres on consumers' environmental concern. It is characterised by the richness of concepts on the attribute and value levels. Here, 'recycled' and its consequence to reduce waste appear, highlighting the interrelatedness of clothing acquisition and disposal. Besides eco-friendly materials and modes of production, consumers following this pattern also care for the geographic origin of their clothing. This supports the findings of Niinimäki (2010). The biospheric values associated with this pattern also vary in nature. Buyers of eco clothing wishing to 'protect the environment' have a very

**Figure 2** Dominant patterns in the hierarchical value map.

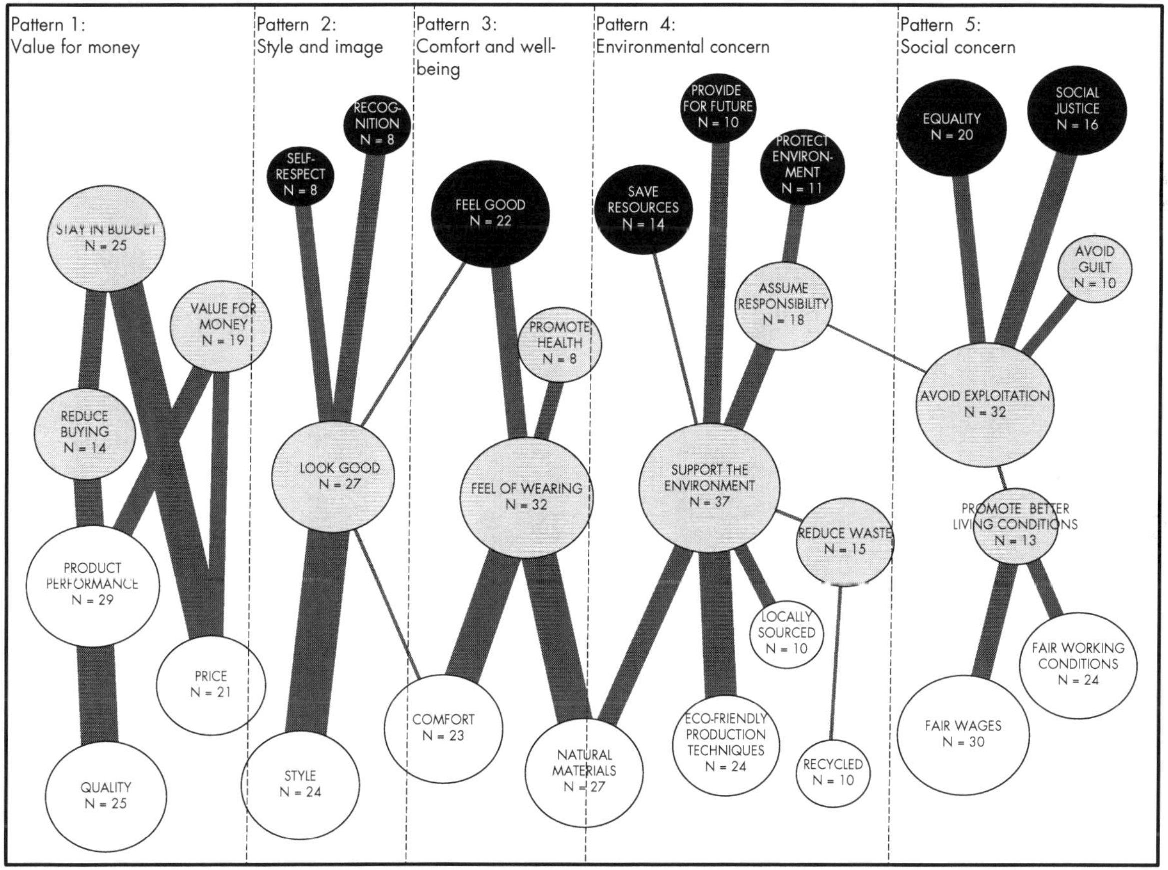

active focus that is further highlighted by its link to 'assuming responsibility'. Consumers who feel responsible are more likely to take pro-environmental action. The construct 'provide for future generations' (Bagozzi & Dabholkar, 1994) represents an environment-related value with a more anthropocentric focus. In this case, consumers' preference for environmental attributes is ultimately motivated by concern about humankind. However rich on attribute and value level, the pattern is still unified by a single and very pronounced mediating benefit: consumers want to 'support the environment' and reduce their own personal negative impact on it.

5. The fifth distinguishable perceptual pattern centres on aspects of consumers' social concern. By stressing fair wages and working conditions, respondents aim to help provide better living conditions for other people (Dickson, 2000). Nevertheless, 'avoid exploitation' is a more important motivating construct containing a societal and a psychological component. By avoiding involvement in exploitation of others, buyers of ethical clothing seek to avoid feelings of guilt, but more importantly consumers want to live up to their altruistic values of 'equality' and 'social justice'. In sum, this perceptual pattern concerns preferences ultimately rooted in enduring beliefs about equal opportunities and helping others.

It is noteworthy that these patterns are all of similar relevance in the HVM. Even though the environmentally centred pattern is the richest in numbers of concepts, it does not appear as a 'main' motivation in the HVM. This may be attributable to the sample composition with its widespread involvement with ethical clothing.

### Motivational incongruencies and value trade-offs

Looking at the dominant perceptual patterns and their relation to one another, there are two striking details. First, according to the Schwartz (1992) framework, patterns are rooted in supposedly opposing value orientations (egoistic vs. biospheric and altruistic). The end-states that consumers want to attain by buying ethical clothing are potentially conflicting. Second, there are few strong links between these patterns, with the exception of natural materials being solidly linked both to the 'comfort and well-being' as the 'environmental concern' pattern. This means that if consumers have to compromise on product features, they equally have to compromise on their opposing personal end-goals.

Grunert and Grunert (1995) describe both a motivational and structural view of the means-end approach from which meaning can be derived. From a motivational viewpoint, the distinct means-end chains help illuminate consumers' buying motives; from a cognitive structure view, they model consumption relevant cognitive structures (Reynolds & Gutman, 1988). Structurally, what is striking is the relative lack of links between patterns 1 and 5 with patterns 2, 3, and 4. Pattern 1 does not reach the value level, suggesting it is principally a utilitarian preference, whilst patterns 4 and 5 link back to principally moral values. Whilst it is true that the lack of links is a feature of the cut-off point used and some respondents may have expressed linkages, the numbers were so small (fewer than 4 of 98 respondents) that they did not appear. The lack of linkages suggests that pattern 1 is revealing a potential non-compensatory preference structure, that is, this preference must be fulfilled first before others (Edwards, 1986). Non-compensatory processes are widespread, especially when combining information from different demains. Etzioni (1986) argues that the qualitative differences between moral and utilitarian preferences may imply they cannot be traded off or substituted for each other. Thus, for some segments of customers, price can act as a decision heuristic, whose level (and indeed presence) may vary with changes in market characteristics. Thus we can explain why price is dominant for some consumers. If the price is too high, other preferences will have minimal effect. Conversely, for other consumers, strongly held moral values mean some products will not be bought, no matter how cheap they may be.

For patterns 2–5, through a combination of the structural and motivational aspects, we can conceive two configurations at work: one that seeks to satisfy values connected to the use of the clothing, which also seems to have links to the ego values, and another where the attraction of ethical clothing links back to environmental and altruistic values. This supposition is supported by Dickson and Littrell (1996) who also distinguished dual pathways leading to purchase: one attitude towards the behaviour of purchasing ethical clothing, and the other attitude towards the clothing itself. Thus, for many consumers, both a wider ethical attitude and narrower product attributes contribute to purchasing behaviour, a finding supported by the separation of the dominant pathways in the HVM. These distinctions and finding the dominant paths used by groups of consumers could greatly assist marketers enhance their targeting efforts.

We took this insight as a starting point for closer analysis of the laddering data to look for explicit consumer statements expressing such complexities, as these could not be captured during the coding procedure for constructing the HVM.

Indeed, we found evidence that requirements for 'value for money' and 'style and image', on the one hand, interfered with consumers' environmental and social concern (see Table 5 for sample quotes). Their financial limitations lead consumers to prioritise price, even though they want to ensure fair wages and (expensive) natural materials in order to live up to their altruistic and biospheric values. Furthermore, ethical clothing that is congruent with consumers' biospheric and altruistic values does not always fit with their style preferences that they need in their striving for (self-)respect.

Consequently, the ethical clothing consumer encounters complexities and needs to compromise (Szmigin et al., 2009), as s/he has to prioritise between self-enhancing and self-transcendent values. This results in 'value trade-offs' (Padel & Foster, 2005) that consumers need to make when buying ethical clothing (Dickson & Littrell, 1996).

Both these dimensions can be found within the HVM, as consumers not only have to balance between egoistic ('self-respect' and 'social recognition') and altruistic values, but also between presence ('feel good') and future ('provide for future generations'). The notion of 'balance' was explicitly addressed by some respondents. Respondents describe prioritising between competing motivations (see Table 5).

## Implications for theory and practice

Our laddering data results represented in the HVM contribute towards the body of knowledge first by reconciling the findings from other studies expounding a hierarchical system of effects (e.g. Dickson & Littrell, 1996) with those considering

**Table 5** Sample quotes expressing complexities and paradoxes.

|  | Price/value for money | Style and image |
|---|---|---|
| *Environmental concern* | It is important to me as a person to try and save money but also spend it on eco clothing<br><br>If the product is not able to wear well, then I would be forced to consider a less ecologically sound product due to financial necessities | I want to reuse old clothes but want myself and my children to look nice<br><br>Ethical/eco issues are important to me, but if the only choice is to look like a mad aura-therapist from darkest Glastonbury in acres of tie-dyed traily purple cotton, I'd rather find other ways than clothing to be a responsible human being |
| *Social concern* | On the one hand, my choice has to be cheap; on the other hand, if clothes are cheap they may result from unfair trade<br><br>We are living in difficult economic times, and it is a balance of doing good for the planet, others in countries where they depend on production of these goods, and being able to afford to buy 'luxury items' – it is sometimes cheaper to buy, for example, second-hand, which doesn't produce much money for those in need in developing countries, but does its bit for the planet. | I don't want to look bad, but I don't want others to suffer so I look better<br><br>Good styles so that it does not give a fuddy-duddy impression and so that I look good important because I want to support Fairtrade *and* look good |

|  | Need for balance | Willingness to pay |
|---|---|---|
| *Concern for effects on close family* | I have to put the needs of my family before the needs of the rest of society. The problem is that the one affects the other, and I have to be continually careful to maintain a balance.<br><br>I live on a budget but still care about the world – therefore, I need to find a way of maintaining a workable balance | I can afford to pay a little extra to support this issue – I cannot afford to erode the lifestyle of my whole family to the extent that they would resent these values<br><br>I need to be a realist – there is no point buying an ethically traded pair of jeans if it means that I can't put food on the table for my family or pay the bills |

the complexity of cognitive schema regarding ethical decisions (e.g. Whalen, Pitts, & Wong, 1991) and those discussing consumer trade-offs (e.g. Auger, Burke, Devinney, & Louviere, 2003; Dickson & Littrell, 1966). Second, the data augment previous findings, as meaning can be derived by examining data from both the motivational and structural viewpoint (Grunert & Grunert, 1995). Through examining the HVM alongside individual comments, researchers can better understand how specific attributes of products relate to the emotional and symbolic aspects and link back to consumer values. The study provides insight into how values in effect drive preference. By interpreting the links and their strength between concepts, we can identify clearly distinguishable motivational patterns centred on ethical concerns such as environmentalism or social consciousness, but also rather egoistic ones relating to value for money, image, or well-being. This helps to explain the complexities that consumers encounter in ethical consumption. It is also interesting that consumers place similar emphasis on environmental and social concern, confirming the image of an 'ethical' and not only 'green' consumer.

The study supports previous work on the width of consumer preferences, ranging from fair treatment of workers and an eco-friendly production mode to generic clothing requirements in terms of quality, price, and style and wide range of values such as biospheric, altruistic, but also egoistic, impacting on ethical clothing preference. This is consistent with findings from laddering studies in organic food (Baker et al., 2004; Padel & Foster, 2005). This potential for trade-offs between competing values in both food and clothing sectors suggests consumer internal conflicts can be expected across product categories.

The notion of 'balancing' links to research on consumer strategies in dealing with the complexities of ethical consumption (e.g. Newholm, 2005) and has analogies even outside of ethical consumer research, for example Mick and Fournier's (1999) balancing paradigm of consumer satisfaction. The respondent discourse about balancing and the distinct patterns in the HVM suggests that, at present, the 'ethical' component of clothing is seen as distinct to the product attributes and price/quality attributes. However, the HVM can also be understood as a potential network of interrelated concepts. It may be possible to encourage ethical clothing purchasing if 'ethical' aspects can become an intrinsic aspect of the product that are in balance with individual needs, style criteria, and so on. Respondents wanted a modern look, yet requirements of durability and ethical sustainability would not fit with styles that go out of fashion quickly. Marketers have to address consumer complexities and can deliver value with offerings that help consumers 'balance' their individual needs and desires and their ethical concerns. Based on our findings, we therefore suggest an approach of 'slow fashion' (Fletcher, 2007; Niinimäki, 2010) that combines high-quality materials with modern, yet timeless design. Critically, Fletcher (2007) describes slow fashion as about balance, that is, between 'change and symbolic expression as well as durability', so that clothes support identity and communication needs as well as utilitarian needs. Slow fashion provides opportunities for mutually beneficial relationships and interactions between makers, designers, buyers, retailers, and consumers in the production, design, and use of the garment. Consumers want a 'win–win' situation, in which all parties involved in and affected by the purchase profit. This includes the consumer getting good value for money. Especially in economically turbulent times, this approach creates promising marketing opportunities (Carrigan & de Pelsmacker, 2009).

Conceptually and methodologically, the application of a means-end approach indeed allows for capturing the whole range of relevant personal values and establishing clear and interpretable links between constructs at different levels of abstraction. It thereby proves a valuable approach in researching values in ethical consumption. This study represents the first means-end approach applied within the area of ethical clothing, and uses a significantly larger sample size than most laddering approaches within the area of ethical consumption research.

## Limitations and directions for further research

The study was mainly exploratory in nature; results remain tentative and require further substantiation. By using an existing representative panel and screening questions, we did our best to ensure a high sample quality of consumers engaging in ethical clothing consumption. Yet the sociodemographic profile of the sample still differs somewhat from Mintel's (2009) description of (potential) buyers of ethical clothing. Although a help function included probes to assist respondents reach their value level, the missing flexibility of soft laddering individual probing (Reynolds & Gutman, 1988) resulted in a lack of contextual cues to help code some borderline cases (Grunert et al., 2001). Furthermore, some of the detailed richness of the data cannot be displayed in the HVM (Velodu-de-Oliveira et al., 2006). We partly addressed this issue by looking closer into the data for reported complexities, yet had to neglect reporting here some potentially interesting phenomena due to their rarity within the data. So analysing the laddering data and constructing the HVM itself became a 'balancing' task (Gengler et al., 1995). Nevertheless, these remain as signposts for future research.

One major limitation lies in drawing conclusions to the single consumer based on the HVM, which represents an aggregated cognitive map of a relatively but not completely homogeneous consumer group. We can neither assume that all motivational patterns are relevant for all consumers nor that it is only one pattern per consumer. Indeed, our data suggest there are often conflicting multiple patterns for individuals. Further insight can therefore be gained by combining laddering data with a segmentation approach (see Botschen et al., 1999) to assess whether there are clearly distinguishable ethical consumer types. This way, we could add to what is already known about how consumers deal with competing values, and marketers could use this insight to refine their targeting efforts. There is already some evidence that distinct groups of ethical clothing purchasers and users exist (Auger et al., 2003; Dickson, 2005; Dickson & Littrell, 1996), and a tentative analysis that we conducted with this data set provided useful insight but lies beyond the scope of this paper and needs further substantiation with a larger sample size.

Similar to laddering studies within organic food (Baker et al., 2004; Padel & Foster, 2005), means-end approaches can be used further within the area of ethical clothing to provide more detailed insight. This could be done by comparing different consumer groups such as buyers and non-buyers of ethical clothing, different product categories (e.g. organic vs. fairly traded clothing), or adding an intercultural component. Means-end approaches can also be applied to yet other ethical product categories in which consumers pursue supposedly mixed values.

Based on our findings, we suggest an approach to researching ethical consumption that does not predetermine sets of values from the outset. Combining Schwartz's (1992) value framework with qualitative research techniques provides rich insights (e.g. G. Shaw et al., 2005). Personal values can rather be used to help explain consumer ambivalence and complexities in choice when it comes to ethical products. In sum, opportunities lie ahead not only rethinking the areas with which to do ethical consumer research, but also in the way to approach these.

# References

Auger, P., Burke, P., Devinney, T.M., & Louviere, J.J. (2003). What will consumers pay for social product features? *Journal of Business Ethics*, 42(3), 281–304.

Bagozzi, R.P., & Dabholkar, P.A. (1994). Consumer recycling goals and their effect on decisions to recycle: A means-end chain analysis. *Psychology and Marketing*, 11, 313–340.

Baker, S., Thompson, K.E., Egeiken, J., & Huntley, K. (2004). Mapping the values driving organic food choice: Germany vs. the UK. *European Journal of Marketing*, 38, 995–1012.

Botschen, G., Thelen, E.M., & Pieters, R. (1999). Using means-end structures for benefit segmentation. *European Journal of Marketing*, 33(1/2), 38–58.

Butler, S.M., & Francis, S. (1997). The effects of environmental attitudes on apparel purchasing behavior. *Clothing and Textiles Research Journal*, 15, 76–85.

Carrigan, M., & Attalla, A. (2001). The myth of the ethical consumer – Do ethics matter in purchase behaviour? *Journal of Consumer Marketing*, 18, 560–578.

Carrigan, M., & de Pelsmacker, P. (2009). Will ethical consumers sustain their values in the global credit crunch? *International Marketing Review*, 26, 674–687.

Christensen, G.L., & Olson, J.C. (2002). Mapping consumers' mental models with ZMET. *Psychology and Marketing*, 19(6), 477–501.

Claeys, C., & Abeele, P.V. (2001) Means-end chain theory and involvement: Potential research directions. In T.J. Reynolds & J.C. Olsen (Eds.), Understanding consumer decision making: The means-end approach to marketing and advertising strategy (pp. 359–387). Mahwah, NJ: Lawrence Erlbaum.

Co-operative Bank. (2009). *Ten years of ethical consumerism: 1999–2008*. Manchester: Co-operative Bank.

Co-operative Bank Ethical Consumerism Report (2010) Retrieved 12 February 2012 from http://www.goodwithmoney.co.uk/ethical-consumerism-report-2010.

Cova, B. (1999). From marketing to societing: When the link is more important than the thing. In D. Brownlie, M. Saren, R. Wensley, & R. Whittington (Eds.), *Rethinking marketing: Towards critical marketing accountings* (pp. 64–83). London: Sage.

Dickson, M.A. (2000). Personal values, beliefs, knowledge, and attitudes relating to intentions to purchase apparel from socially responsible businesses. *Clothing and Textiles Research Journal*, 18, 19–30.

Dickson, M.A. (2005). Identifying and profiling apparel label users. In R. Harrison, T. Newholm, & D. Shaw (Eds.), *The ethical consumer* (pp. 155–171). London: Sage.

Dickson, M.A., & Littrell, M.A. (1996). Socially responsible behaviour: Values and attitudes of the alternative trading organization consumer. *Journal of Fashion Marketing and Management*, 1(1), 50–69.

Dietz, T., Fitzgerald, A., & Shwom, R. (2005). Environmental values. *Annual Review of Environment and Resources*, 30, 335–372.

Doran, C. (2009). The role of personal values in Fairtrade consumption. *Journal of Business Ethics*, 84, 549–563.

Edwards, S.F. (1986). Ethical preferences and assessment of existence values: Does the neoclassical model fit? *Northeastern Journal of Agricultural and Resource Economics*, 15, 145–150.

Elliot, R. (1994). Exploring the symbolic meaning of brands. *British Journal of Management*, 5, S13–S19.

Etzioni, A. (1986). The case for a multiple utility conception. *Economics and Philosophy*, 2(2), 159–184.

Fletcher, K. (2007, June 1). Slow fashion. *The Ecologist*.

Gengler, C., & Reynolds, T. (1993). LADDERMAP: A software tool for analyzing laddering sata (Version 5.4) [Computer software].

Gengler, C.E., Klenosky, D.B., & Mulvey, M.S. (1995). Improving the graphic representation of means-end results. *International Journal of Research in Marketing*, 12, 245–256.

Gengler, C.E., & Reynolds, T. (1995). Consumer understanding and advertising strategy: Analysis and strategic translation of laddering data. *Journal of Advertising Research*, *35*, 19–32.

Gilg, B., & Ford, N. (2005). Green consumption or sustainable lifestyles? Identifiying the sustainable consumer. *Futures*, *37*, 481–504.

Grunert, K.G., Beckmann, S.C., & Sørensen, E. (2001). Means-end chains and laddering: An inventory of problems and an agenda for research. In T.J. Reynolds & J.C. Olsen (Eds.), *Understanding consumer decision making. The means-end approach to marketing and advertising strategy* (pp. 63–90). Mahwah, NJ: Lawrence Erlbaum.

Grunert, K.G., & Grunert, S. (1995). Measuring subjective meaning structures by the laddering method: Theoretical considerations and methodological problems. *International Journal of Research in Marketing*, *12*, 209–225.

Gutman, J. (1982). A means-end chain model based on consumer categorization processes. *Journal of Marketing*, *46*, 60–72.

Ha-Brookshire, J., & Hodges, N. (2009). Socially responsible consumer behavior?: Exploring used clothing donation behavior. *Clothing and Textiles Research Journal*, *27*, 179–196.

Harrison, R., Newholm, T., & Shaw, D. (2005). *The ethical consumer*. London: Sage.

Hartmann, P., Ibáñez, V.A., & Sainz, F.J. (2005). Green branding effects on attitude: Functional versus emotional positioning strategies. *Marketing Intelligence and Planning*, *23*(1), 9–29.

Hines, J., & O'Neill, G.S. (1995). Underlying determinants of clothing quality: The consumers' perspective. *Clothing and Textiles Resarch Journal*, *13*, 227–233.

Iwanow, H., McEachern, M.G., & Jeffrey, A. (2005). The influence of ethical trading policies on consumer apparel purchase decisions. A focus on The Gap Inc. *International Journal of Retail and Distribution Management*, *33*(5), 371–387.

Jackson, T. (2005). *Motivation sustainable consumption. A review of evidence on consumer behaviour and behavioural change*. Report to the Defra Sustainable Development Research Network. Retrieved 11 February 2012 from: https://www.c2p2online.com/documents/MotivatingSC.pdf

Joergens, C. (2006). Ethical fashion: Myth or future trend? *Journal of Fashion Marketing and Management*, *10*, 360–371.

Kilbourne, W.E., & Beckmann, S.C. (1998). Review and critical assessment of research on marketing and the environment. *Journal of Marketing Management*, *14*, 513–532.

Kim, H.E., & Damhorst, M.L. (1998). Environmental concern and apparel consumption. *Clothing and Textiles Research Journal*, *16*, 126–133.

Lin, S. (2009). Exploratory evaluation of potential and current consumers of organic cotton in Hawaii. *Asia Pacific Journal of Marketing and Logistics*, *21*, 489–506.

Mick, D., & Fournier, S. (1999). Rediscovering satisfaction. *Journal of Marketing*, *63*, 5–23.

Mintel. (2009). *Ethical clothing – UK 2009*. London: Mintel.

Newholm, T. (2005). Case studying ethical consumers' projects and strategies. In R. Harrison, T. Newholm, & D. Shaw (Eds.), *The ethical consumer* (pp. 107–124). London: Sage.

Niinimäki, K. (2010). Eco-clothing, consumer identity and ideology. *Sustainable Development*, *18*, 150–162.

Office for National Statistics. (2010). Retrieved 18 July 2011, from http://www.statistics.gov.uk/cci/nugget.asp?id=285.

Olsen, J.C., & Reynolds, T.J. (2001). The means-end approach to understanding consumer decision making. In T.J. Reynolds & J.C. Olsen (Eds.), *Understanding consumer decision making. The means-end approach to marketing and advertising strategy* (pp. 3–24). Mahwah, NJ: Lawrence Erlbaum.

Padel, S., & Foster, C. (2005). Exploring the gap between attitudes and behaviour. Understanding why consumers buy or do not buy organic food. *British Food Journal*, *107*, 606–624.

Pepper, M., Jackson, T., & Uzzell, D. (2009). An examination of the values that motivate socially conscious and frugal consumer behaviours. *International Journal of Consumer Studies*, *33*, 126–136.

Peter, J.P., Olson, J.C., & Grunert, K.G. (1999). *Consumer behaviour and marketing strategy* (European ed.). London: McGraw-Hill.

Philipps, J.M., & Reynolds, T. (2009). A hard look at hard laddering. A comparison of studies examining the hierarchical structure of means-end theory. *Qualitative Market Research: An International Journal, 12*, 83–99.

Reynolds, T.J. (2006). Methodologial and strategy development implications of decision segmentation. *Journal of Advertising Research, 46*(4), 445–461.

Reynolds, T.J., Dethloff, C., & Westberg, S.J. (2001). Advancements in laddering. In: Reynolds, Thomas J. and Olson, Jerry C. (Eds.), *Understanding consumer decision making - the means-end approach to marketing and advertising strategy*, Mahwah, NJ: Lawrence Erlbaum Associates, pp. 91–118.

Reynolds, T.J., & Gutman, J. (1988). Laddering theory, method, analyis and interpretation. *Journal of Advertising Research, 22*, 11–31.

Rokeach, M.J. (1973). *The nature of human values*. New York: Free Press.

Russell, C., Busson, A., Flight, I., Leppard, J., van Lawick van Pabst, J., & Cox, D.N. (2004). A comparison of paper-and-pencil and computerised methods of 'hard' laddering. *Food Quality and Preference, 15*, 279–291.

Schlegelmilch, B.B. (1996). The link between green purchasing decisions and measures of environmental consciousness. *European Journal of Marketing, 30*(5), 35–55.

Schwartz, S. (1992). Universals in the content and strcture of values: theoretical advances and empirical test in 20 countries. In M.C. Zanna (Ed.), *Advances in experimental psychology* (Vol. 25, pp. 1–65). Orlando, FL: Academic Press.

Schwartz, S. (1994). Are there universal aspects in the structure and content of values? *Journal of Social Issues, 50*(4), 19–45.

Shaw, D., Hogg, G., Wilson, E., Shiu, E., & Hassan, L. (2006). Fashion victim: The impact of Fairtrade concerns on clothing choice. *Journal of Strategic Marketing, 14*, 427–440.

Shaw, G., Grehan, E., Shiu, E., Hassan, L., & Thompson, J. (2005). An exploration of values in ethical consumer decision making. *Journal of Consumer Behaviour, 4*, 185–200.

Shim, S. (1995). Environmentalism and consumers' clothing disposal patterns. An exploratory study. *Clothing and Textiles Research Journal, 13*, 38–48.

Sneddon, J.N., Lee, J.A., Soutar. G.N. (2009). Ethical Issues That Impact On Wool Apparel Purchases. *Australia And New Zealand Marketing Academy Conference*, Melbourne, Australia, *1*, 1–8.

Stern, P., Dietz, T., & Kalof, L. (1993). Value orientations, gender, and environmental concern. *Environmental Behaviour, 25*. 322–348.

Szmigin, I., Carrigan, M., & McEachern, M.G. (2009). The conscious consumer: Taking a flexible approach to ethical behaviour. *International Journal of Consumer Studies, 33*, 224–231.

Thomas, S. (2008). From 'green blur to ecofashion': Fashioning an eco-lexicon. *Fashion Theory, 12*, 525–540.

Velodu-de-Oliveira, T.M., Ikeda, A.A., & Campomar, M.C. (2006). Laddering in the practice of marketing research: Barriers and solutions. *Qualitative Market Research: An International Journal, 9*, 297–306.

Whalen, J., Pitts, R.E., & Wong, J.K. (1991). Exploring the structure of ethical attributions as a component of the consumer decision model: The vicarious versus personal perspective. *Journal of Business Ethics, 10*(4), 285–293.

Zaichkowsky, J.L. (1994). The personal involvement inventory: Reduction, revision, and application to advertising. *Journal of Advertising, 23*(4), 59–70.

Zanoli, R., & Naspetti, S. (2002). Consumer motivations in the purchase of organic food. A means-end approach. *British Food Journal, 104*, 643–653.

# Barriers to downward carbon emission: Exploring sustainable consumption in the face of the glass floor

Hélène Cherrier, *Griffith University, Brisbane, Australia*
Mathilde Szuba, *University of Paris 1, Panthéon-Sorbonne, France*
Nil Özçağlar-Toulouse, *Univ Lille Nord de France - SKEMA Business School, France*

---

**Abstract** The present study explores the constraining forces to reducing greenhouse-gas emissions (GHG) via alternative and/or reduced consumption. The analysis of introspection, netnography, ethnographic work, and 18 interviews demonstrates that needs are not innate human requirements and that consumers are not free and autonomous agents able to incorporate reduce or alternative consumption within their lifestyles. Specifically, our analysis shows the existence of barriers to downward carbon emission. These barriers, which we combined under the concept of the *glass floor*, represent sociocultural standards preventing our informants from achieving their goal of reducing their carbon footprint. Our findings are presented around two main themes: the social construction of needs and the social imaginary.

---

## Introduction

In line with the Brundtland terminology of sustainable development (see Brundtland Commission, 1987, p. 1), environmentally and socially responsible consumption, that is, sustainable consumption, represents consuming in a manner that meets the needs of present generations without compromising the future ones (Heiskanen & Pantzar, 1997). It calls for consumers to 'consider ecological and social criteria in the purchase, use and post-use of products' (Belz & Peattie, 2009, p. 33). Within the green marketing field, sustainable consumption has been discussed in terms of 'alternative consumption', as well as 'reduced consumption' (Belz & Peattie, 2009; Fisk, 1973; Grant, 2007). In promoting alternative consumption, green marketers discuss sustainable consumption in terms of developing efficient supply, design, and production systems via technological innovation, and offering green products targeted to 'green consumers' or 'eco-consumers' (Dahlstrom, 2011). In addition to alternative consumption (getting more output out of less input), some green marketers endorse reduced consumption and sufficiency (having enough and acting with what we have) as a sustainable consumption practice. For example, Ottman (2011) supports 'energy conservation associated with using product' and encourages 'consumer to use only what is needed, and consciously reduce waste' (p. 154). Similarly, Grant (2007) identifies reduced consumption and consumption abstention as sustainable consumption practices.

Although distinctive in approach and practice, alternative and reduced consumption strategies both distribute consumers along the spectrum of autonomy, rationality, and need satisfaction. From the decision to purchase eco-friendly products to participation in anti-consumerist ethics, individuals are called to reflect on their idiosyncratic aspirations and socio-environmental concerns and accordingly to orient their lifestyles rationally. For example, alternative consumption practices satisfy consumers' needs for social esteem, identity, and political participation (Connolly, 2003; Heiskanen & Pantzar, 1997; Kilbourne, McDonald, & Prothero, 1997; Shaw, Newholm, & Dickinson, 2006), and reduced consumption satisfies consumers' needs for self-fulfilment, happiness, and good life (Elgin, 1981; Schumacher, 1974). Importantly, these approaches rest on the neo-liberal assumption that consumers are autonomous, free to choose alternative and/or reduced consumption to satisfy their self-interested needs, and respond to their socio-environmental concerns (Autio, Heiskanen, & Heinonen, 2009; Heiskanen, 2005). In this study, we argue that needs are not innate human requirements and that consumers are not free and autonomous agents able to incorporate reduce or alternative consumption into their lifestyles. Specifically, we show that accepting a neo-liberal approach to consumers as autonomous free agents in the domain of green marketing underestimates the powerful constraining forces embedded in the dominant system of codification, symbolic representations, and social norms. In the following discussion, we review the literature on alternative consumption and reduced consumption with an emphasis on the modernist axiom of autonomy, free choice, and need satisfaction. The analysis of introspection, netnography, ethnographic data, and 18 existential interviews collected from individuals who, through practices of alternative and/or reduced consumption, try to reduce their carbon footprint unveils the constraining social and cultural forces to sustainable consumption practices. Our findings are presented around two main themes: the social construction of needs and the social imaginary. Our discussion brings forward issues of the glass floor and the 'decolonisation of the social imaginary' to the green marketing debates.

## Green marketing and sustainable consumption: Alternative consumption

Consumer researchers often equate green marketing to 'the marketing of products that are presumed to be environmentally safe' (American Marketing Association).[1] Consequently, much attention in the green marketing literature has been placed on identifying 'green consumers' or 'eco-consumers', establishing relevant segmentation strategies, and developing eco-performance as a competitive advantage factor to

[1] http://www.marketingpower.com/_ayouts/Dictionary.aspx?dLetter=G

serve the green consumer (Belz & Peattie, 2009; Dahlstrom, 2011). This approach to green marketing is micro-situated and positions alternative consumption as an environmentally and socially responsible consumption – that is, sustainable consumption.

Within this stream of study, alternative consumption refers to a cut back in resource consumption per consumption unit (Fuchs & Lorek, 2005; Reisch, 2001; Sanne, 2000). The thrust of this perspective is questioning the quality, rather than the quantity, of consumption patterns in affluent societies. Proponents to alternative consumption argue that we 'mis-consume' and that consumers need to switch their consumption lifestyle to greener and more environmentally conscious consumption practices using eco-efficient product and services (Ottman, 1993). For the switch to occur, two components need to exist. First, improvements in production processes, eco-friendly designs, and environmental product innovations provide alternative eco-efficient means of consuming. This development is situated within the existing marketplace and rest on prevalent modernist notions of efficiency, measurement of ecological impact, technological rationality, and scientific objectivity (Kilbourne, 1998).

A second element of alternative consumption is the existence of rational and environmentally aware consumers who make decisions based on their deep values (Ottman, 1993). These consumers, known as 'environmentally conscious consumers' (Ottman, 1993) or 'green consumers' (Elkington, Hailes, & Makower, 1990; Tanner & Kast, 2003), are environmentally informed, care for the environment, and consume accordingly (Ottman, 1993). Green consumers rationally respond to their environmental concerns (Ottman, 1993) and use their purchasing power to construct green identities, uplift their self-esteem, or vote for sociopolitical changes (Connolly, 2003; Heiskanen & Pantzar, 1997; Kilbourne et al., 1997; Moisander & Pesonen, 2002; Nava, 1991; Shaw et al., 2006). Particular to this perspective is the emphasis on consumer power to bring about social change by considering the consequences of their purchase and usage on the environment and businesses. As Nava (1991) notes, people are 'able through their shopping to register political support or opposition' (p. 168). Here, the motivations for alternative consumption incorporate needs for functionality of the object/service, as well as needs for the meanings of consumption and needs for the values the meaning provides (Connolly, 2003).

The green claim in this spirit is that consumers are rational, goal-oriented individuals, attempting to satisfy their personal, social, and ecological needs via marketplace offerings. This perspective follows the prevalent ideology of progress and the marketplace in general (Belz & Peattie, 2009; Kilbourne et al., 1997), and is essentially based on the neo-liberal view that consumers are free and autonomous agents aiming at satisfying their needs. In other word, alternative consumption is positioned along the pervasive model of individual choice and agency, and consumers are empowered to switch their consumption patterns if that is what they choose.

Although the model of rational action, individual choice, autonomy, and agency is still prevalent in green marketing textbook (Ottman, 1993), many authors argue that the assumption of 'rationalization of lifestyles' (Hobson, 2002), 'individualistic conceptions of subjectivity and human agency' (Autio et al., 2009, p. 42), and autonomous agent (Heiskanen, 2005) is problematic, as it fails to consider the historical, political, and social constraining forces of daily lives. This discrepancy has prompted authors to call for conceptualisation of sustainable consumption, lifestyle, and behaviour outside of the dominant model of rational action and free choice (Black & Cherrier, 2010; Cherrier & Murray, 2007; Shove, 2005).

## Green marketing and sustainable consumption: Reduced consumption

According to recent literature, green marketing is shifting towards incorporating a macro-perspective by questioning the marketing ethos and consumerism (Kilbourne, 1998; Kilbourne & Beckmann, 1998). For example, Grant (2007) defines the new green marketing perspective by combining 'working with' to working 'against consumerism as we know it today' (p. IX). The new green marketing promotes conservation, sharing, reusing, recycling, slowing down, and treasuring, as well as a reduction of consumption and even an abstention from consumption (Grant, 2007). Compared to alternative consumption, which supports that continued economic growth is compatible with environmental preservation (Fisk, 1973), reduced consumption includes rethinking the predominant 'cycle of consumption' (Schor, 1999) and unlimited progress (Durning, 1992). The thrust of this perspective is questioning the quantity of our consumption patterns. Proponents to reducing consumption claim that consumers need to reconsider their needs and reflect on the relation between affluent consumption and life fulfilment. The concern is explicit in Arrow et al.'s (2004) paper entitled: 'Are we consuming too much?' and in Schor's (1999) book called *Why We Want What We Don't Need*.

In terms of the motivations to reduce consumption practices, studies show a combination of socio-environmental as well as self-interested concerns. For example, Sandıkçı and Ekici (2009) state:

consumer may refrain from using a particular product or brand as a reflection of their desire to influence business practices and promote what is good for the society overall, or as part of their desire to avoid social groups, roles, and identities that represent the negative self. (p. 3)

Another support for this perspective is found in Iyer and Muncy's (2009) distinction between societal anti-consumers and personal anti-consumers. While the former avoid practices of consumption for the benefit of society or the planet in general, the latter is dominantly concerned with being a healthy and happy self. From this perspective, reducing consumption is good for the environment and also good for the individuals. It is good for the environment, as reduced consumption leads to less production and waste, and it is good for consumers, as minimising consumption leads to financial freedom, less stress, personal integrity, and good life (Black & Cherrier, 2010; Cherrier & Murray, 2007; Schor, 1998, 1999, 2000). Here, consumers' personal interests constructed around socio-environmental concerns lead them to reduce the quantity of their consumption voluntarily by purchasing less, using less, and wasting less.

The model of reduced consumption is based on the consumers' interpretation of their environmental concerns and personal interests. This approach inevitably calls consumers to reflect and re-evaluate their personal needs in conjunction with their environmental concerns and self-interests. The task is to differentiate between paradigmatic/superfluous/false/non-sustainable needs versus focal/necessary/real/sustainable needs. For example, Reisch (2001) notes that individuals will change their lifestyle once they 'learn to identify those goods whose consumption adds little or nothing to welfare' (p. 369), and Borgmann (2000) urges consumers to break the spell of paradigmatic consumption in order to 'clear a central space in our lives for the engagement with focal things and practices' (p. 422). Ultimately, consumers who can identify their true needs will reduce their paradigmatic (Borgmann, 2000), superfluous (Schor, 1999), or non-sustainable (Pierce, 2000) consumption accordingly and 'be happier in the process' (Pierce, 2000).

However, following Dolan's (2002) argument, differentiating between types of needs raises questions on how to identify the 'real' from the 'false' needs and who can identify them. Furthermore, according to the social constructivists, needs are not absolute and mere representations of individual preferences (Slater, 1997). Rather, consumer needs are socially and culturally constructed. They emerge from evolving historical ways of life, constantly framed, constrained, and enabled by social interactions. As Dolan (2002) notes, 'needs are mediated by the prevailing symbolic order which is part and parcel of the cultural system' (p. 175). The social construction of needs creates cultural norms of how people should live and what needs have to be satisfied within society. Individual power to control and act upon their needs is consequently dependent on the historical, political, and social condition of daily life. Thus needs should only be conceptualised as part of the cultural system.

At its best, this brief review of the literature shows the emergence of a critical voice in discussions of alternative and reduced consumption. Broadly, this critical lens in the green marketing debate challenges the neo-liberal perspective per se by arguing for a re-conceptualisation of alternative and reduced consumption constrained by social and cultural forces, rather than located in the autonomous free agent aiming at satisfying its needs. Following this critical perspective, the present study explores the constraining forces to reducing greenhouse-gas emissions (GHG) via alternative and/or reduced consumption. The analysis reveals the existence of a minimum level of *socially required* GHG, which we explain using the analogy of a 'glass floor'. Under this threshold, an individual transgresses the socially dominant rules of the consumer society and faces risk of social exclusion and marginalisation. Our analysis shows two main strata to the glass floor: the social construction of needs and the social imaginary. Each stratum is discussed in the result section.

## The study

The study considers data collected during 2009 and 2010 from individuals who consciously aim at lowering their carbon footprint. These individuals are either self-proclaimed *objecteurs de croissance* living in France or belong to the Crag movement located in the UK. The choice of these groups is based on their commitment to lowering carbon emission. According to the 2008 census organised by the CRAG network, a CRAGger decreases its carbon footprint by 36% in the first year of participation in a CRAG, and an *objecteur de croissance*, whilst not taking a quantitative approach on their carbon footprint, consumes significantly less than what an average individual of the same social status consumes per year (Howell, 2009; Latouche, 2005). Personal contacts and snowball sampling offered access to each informant and fieldwork used for this study.

First, the *objecteurs de croissance* ('growth objectors', a play on conscientious objector/*objecteur de conscience* in French) were located in France and identify with degrowth economics. This movement first appeared in France around the year 2003 and is based, in particular, on the writings of the French economist Serge Latouche. He argues that seeking increased GDP and the tendency to assess everything in terms of economic growth is leading societies to their downfall. The movement aims to break with the ideology of growth (Latouche, 2005). Its environmental perspective leads to a strong desire to reduce carbon footprints (Boutaud & Gondran, 2009).

Second, the CRAGgers, members of Carbon Rationing Action Groups, were located in the UK. A CRAG is a group of around a dozen individuals who meet on a regular basis to calculate their GHG emissions together, set reduction goals, and exchange tips on how to reach them. Symbolic financial penalties are sometimes meted out if members exceed set targets. In 2008, while the average carbon footprint in the UK was 5.4 tons per capita per year, the average goal of CRAG members was to stay under 3.8 tons. Over the long term, they hope to reach a sustainable level of .5 tons.

The choice of these two groups is justified by their varied approaches to lowering carbon emission. Whilst the *objecteurs de croissance* are against the ideology of progress and mostly support reducing the quantity of our consumption in general, the CRAGgers seek to project a more efficient, alternative approach to sustainability (Howell, 2009). For example, CRAGgers set specific, scientifically measured goals and designate a 'carbon accountant' to calculate how much carbon emission is produced when using particular products, services, and brands. By contrast, the *objecteurs de croissance* do not keep a numerical tally of their emissions, preferring a general reduction of their consumption practices in order to reduce their carbon emission. Additionally, locating these two groups in different geographical contexts offered a richer view on ideological variances. For example, the *objecteurs de croissance* located in France express strong cultural contestations against progress, capitalism, or even American consumerism. In contrast, the CRAGgers located in the UK support progress, sustainable development, and technological innovations. Importantly, both groups of informants aimed at reducing their carbon emission and incorporated alternative and reduced consumption into their individual lifestyles.

This research is based on four types of data collection methodology: self-introspection, netnography, ethnographic, and existential interviews. The study started with the use of introspection methodology. Following Gould (1991) and Holbrook's (1995) conceptualisation of introspection, the process of researcher self-introspection offered records of the researcher's conscious awareness of past experiences. The authors, although located at different places around the globe, are trying to integrate sustainability into their consumption decisions and ultimately lower their carbon emission. With the use of social media and conference attendances, the authors discussed their engagement and disengagement with reduced and alternative consumption practices. Particularly, one author who self-identified as an *objecteur de croissance* offered clear notions of identity struggles, social stigmatisation, and societal constrains. This author discussed several experiences when maintaining an academic carrier and lowering carbon footprint were in conflict. The second method of data collection consisted of monitoring the CRAGs' and *objecteurs de croissance*'s blogosphere and forums, as well as reading activist works. The netnography provided insights into the similarity between the CRAGs and the *objecteurs de croissance* in their personal struggles to lower their carbon footprint. In order to understand the social meanings of lowering carbon footprint, the third step in data collection was ethnography. Through personal contacts and snowball sampling, one researcher was offered to spend time (one or two consecutive days) with 11 households (four CRAGgers and seven *objecteurs de croissance*). The researcher took the persona of a cultural anthropologist and lived with the informants, observing, discussing, as well as participating in their daily practices. The total data collection time resulted in 171 hours spent with the CRAGgers and 200 hours spent with the *objecteurs de croissance*. The ethnography allowed trustful relationships to be developed with informants and access to be gained to personal photos and artefacts (NGO brochures, tracts, energy consumption spreadsheets, letters promoting low-carbon practices, etc.) enriched by the participants' voices. This fieldwork helped unravel the multiple and complex meanings associated with lowering carbon footprint and the struggles associated with sustainable consumption practices. The forth step in data collection consisted of existential interviews of one to two hours with nine self-proclaimed *objecteurs de croissance* and nine members of the CRAGS' movement from various socio-professional categories aged between 27 and 73 (see Table 1). The interviews were performed at the interviewee's residence and/or during activists' gatherings, and followed the existential phenomenological process described by C.J. Thompson, Locander, and Pollio (1989).

In order to understand fully the lived experiences of individuals concerned with lowering their carbon emission, hermeneutic circle analysis (C.J. Thompson, 1997) was used to analyse the data. The method helps situate the practices of the respondents within a broader framework which includes their background (personal events, oppositions, and arguments). Following C.J. Thompson's (1997) approach, the first step of the analytical procedure was to read the entire text thoroughly. This gave a sense of the entire text as it related to lowering carbon emission. Next, intra-textual analysis helped identify the temporal sequencing and narrative framing of each story in relation to lowering carbon emission (C.J. Thompson, 1997). During the intertextual analysis, informants' story lines were compared and common themes emerged. In this phase, the analysis moved back and forth from the emic to etic interpretation, gradually providing insights in conceptualising lived experiences of lowering carbon emission via alternative and reduced consumption. The analysis provided 'the social construction of needs' and 'the social imaginary' as relevant themes to individuals' experience with lowering carbon emission. The triangulation technique combining nethnography, ethnographic observations, and existential interviews confirmed and enriched each theme under the concept of the glass floor. The following discussion provides details on each theme.

## Findings: The glass floor

No matter which practices are used (i.e. alternative or reduced consumption), all of our data depict personal efforts by informants to reduce their carbon footprint. Although variably committed and devoted, our informants' testimonials converge on the difficulties and struggles to reducing carbon emission. The difficulties are diverse, including financial constraints (purchase of more expensive or rarer products), time restraints (finding alternatives, culinary preparations, etc.), and social struggles (risks of exclusion, need to convince one's friends or family, social embarrassment).

**Table 1** Informants.

| Pseudonym | Group affiliation | Age | Gender | Family status | Occupation |
|---|---|---|---|---|---|
| Martin | *Objecteur de croissance* | 43 | Male | Married, 4 children | Architect |
| Kasia | *Objecteur de croissance* | 27 | Female | A partner, no child | Student |
| Juliette | *Objecteur de croissance* | 28 | Female | A partner, no child | Journalist |
| Violette | *Objecteur de croissance* | 32 | Female | Married, no child | University professor |
| Paulo | *Objecteur de croissance* | 41 | Male | Married, 2 children | University professor |
| Corentin | *Objecteur de croissance* | 31 | Male | A partner, 1 child | Unemployed ('working objector') |
| Alice | *Objecteur de croissance* | 29 | Female | A partner, 1 child | Unemployed ('working objector') |
| Audrey | *Objecteur de croissance* | 27 | Female | Single, no children | Employed environmental NGO |
| Annie | *Objecteur de croissance* | 49 | Female | A partner, no children | Language teacher |
| Jenny | CRAGger | 48 | Female | Married, 4 children | Doctor |
| Alistair | CRAGger | 55 | Male | Married, 2 children | Consultant |
| Jane | CRAGger | 29 | Female | Single, no children | Project manager on energy |
| Tim | CRAGger | 49 | Male | Single, no children | Employed environmental NGO |
| Simon | CRAGger | 60 | Male | Married, 1 child | Retired (bookseller) |
| Peter | CRAGger | 73 | Male | Married, 2 children | Retired (fireman) |
| Philip | CRAGger | 54 | Male | Married, 2 children | Green energy retailer |
| Ismael | CRAGger | 48 | Male | A partner, no children | Builder |
| William | CRAGger | 52 | Male | Single, 1 child | Farmer |

At times, the overwhelming difficulties and the tiresome struggles create barriers to carbon reduction. In these instances, switching or reducing consumption (both oriented towards a reduction in carbon footprint) is not an option. Clear to our analysis is the existence of societal barriers that limit downward carbon emission. The carbon emission threshold under which it is almost impossible to live without clashing with dominant social norms is referred to here as the glass floor.

The notion of glass floor is adapted from the concept of the glass ceiling, popularised in '70s and '80s American feminist literature. This image of an unexpected see-through obstruction developed in the context of corporate America represents the women facing the glass ceiling – a barrier that kept them from advancing past a certain point on the career ladder. Since then, the glass ceiling has been conceptualised to designate an imaginary yet very real barrier that prevents women or immigrants from achieving social and professional mobility, even though it is not visible, legal, or explicit (Baker & Lightle, 2001). In the same way that a glass ceiling represents a limitation blocking upward advancement, we conceptualise a glass floor as societal constrains to lowering one's carbon footprint emission. This bottom limit is a priori invisible, but it is an inevitable barrier for those who try to switch (alternative consumption) or cut their consumption (reduced consumption). The barrier can embody structural forces, sign values, or social imaginaries (Baudrillard, 1970; Castoriadis, 1987). Independent of what a glass floor is 'made of', it is a reflection of meanings that structure representations of the world in general, identify the purposes of actions and social norms, and establish different types of affects that characterise the consumer society. The glass floor is the expression of the consumer society as a constraint, or moral value, imposed on consumers (Baudrillard, 1970). It is an example of the imaginary institution of society, which determines what is real and what is not (Castoriadis, 1987). The analysis of 18 existential interviews and ethnographic work offers details on the different strata that make up the glass floor to lowering carbon footprint emission.

### *First stratum: The social construction of needs*

The glass floor is determined in relation to the definition of needs. Our analysis shows two levels of needs: the micro-individual level and the macro-individual level. The micro-individual level of need occurs when our informants focus on achieving efficiency – that is, consuming less energy and therefore reducing $CO_2$ emissions. An illustration of this would be travelling by car as usual, but using a hybrid car. In this case, the lifestyle change is minimal. The notion of need is hardly questioned. The gain in efficiency is generally brought about by a technical or social innovation that avoids rethinking or questioning the issue of mobility. Our respondents provided many examples of efficiency: weatherproofing the home, installing more efficient heating, and so on. The notion of need is defined on a micro-individual level and constraining forces are negligible.

In contrast, the macro-individual level of needs takes place when informants aimed towards sufficiency via a change in lifestyle, hence a reduction of consumption and $CO_2$ emissions. An example of this is not owning a car, even a 'clean' model, and therefore organising one's life accordingly. Here, the definition of need is operated on a macro-individual level and considerable constraining forces operate at this level. As Paulo explains, 'I don't know if you realise what it's like to work in research and refuse to fly, when everyone else is trying to get sent to international conferences!' (Paulo, 41). Paulo, like Jenny in the excerpt below, illustrates the constraining forces operating at a macro-social level of needs.

> Once, I was asked to examine a thesis in Aberdeen. Before, I would have agreed and flown there . . . But, instead I said, 'Sorry, I can't go because I belong to a CRAG and I don't fly. Could you consider organising videoconferences or something like that? Or maybe you should find someone locally?' . . . They thought I was nuts. They didn't even answer. They could have said, 'That's too bad, but we understand what you're trying to do and it's a good thing . . . '. But they didn't even bother to answer politely. Another time they asked me to do a conference in Vienna, and I said 'OK, if you book me a train ticket'. At first, they agreed, but a month later their accounting department rejected the idea, so finally they asked two of my colleagues to go . . . Of course, they said yes and took a plane! (Jenny, 48)

Jenny is one of our CRAGger informants. At 48 years old, Jenny struggles to incorporate green practices into her lifestyle. As Jenny explains, she belongs to a CRAG and does not want to fly. Whilst her determination to 'not flying' is strongly linked to her personal values and commitment to the CRAG movement, none of her colleagues appeared to understand or even 'answer politely'. Jenny's workplace and colleagues consider that the normal way of life is to fly to conferences and meetings. Resistance to flying represents a deviance from the norm and is therefore penalised. By refusing to fly, Jenny suffers being stigmatised as 'nuts' and excluded from participating in conferences and meetings. Clear to Jenny's excerpt is the societal need for physical mobility. Physical mobility is so embedded in individuals' routines and expectations that it is inscribed in our systems of social and cultural order (Shove, 2005). In order to participate in conferences and be part of the team, Jenny is pressured to fly. Jenny's excerpt brings to mind Reisch's (2001) study on time and sustainability in which he notes that in order to be part of what he calls 'the non-stop-society', individuals are forced to adopt unsustainable lifestyles (p. 374).

It is interesting to note that Jenny finds the strength to reject flying using her personal affiliation to a social group named the CRAG movement. Since being part of the CRAG, Jenny's determination towards reducing her carbon footprint has evolved. As she explained, 'before, I would have agreed and flown there'. Belonging to the CRAG movement changed the symbolic significance of flying. As a CRAGger, Jenny questions the normative standards of physical mobility and no longer expresses flying as a need. This example supports Slater's (1997) notion that needs are not absolute and mere representations of individual preferences. Jenny's need to fly has evolved along with her social interactions. As a member of the CRAG's movement, Jenny has learnt a new way of thinking about her personal consumption, lifestyles, and behaviour. In other words, Jenny's strength to address the normative standards of physical mobility underlines her commitment to the CRAG movement and its members. Here, incorporating green practices as a way of life does not necessarily depend upon environmental commitment but more upon social commitment.

Later in the interview, Jenny discusses a deeper and harder struggle associated with her commitment to lowering carbon emission. In the excerpt below, Jenny discusses how giving up her car created deep emotional conflicts with members of her family.

> When I decided to give up my car, my family put a lot of pressure on me . . . My children understood, but my brother, for example, was downright insulting. He couldn't understand; he was really harsh . . . When we had to meet somewhere, I told him I preferred to meet near a train station, and he would say 'why do you always need to make a fuss? I'm fed up!' Anyway, now he is more understanding, but that's because it's more mainstream. (Jenny, 48)

In order to reduce her carbon consumption, Jenny switched from using the car to using public transportation. In her determination to use public transportation, Jenny struggles with her brother who embraces the speed and convenience of modern life and 'couldn't understand'. It is interesting to note that Jenny does not use her affiliation to the CRAGs' movement when confronted with her brother. As she mentions, 'he couldn't understand'. The personal level of the relationship creates intense pressures for Jenny. In the interview, she hopes that, when lowering carbon emission becomes mainstream, her brother will accept her way of life. The need for social acceptance by close relatives and friends makes lowering carbon emission particularly challenging. At times, the pressure is bearable and our informants, like Jenny, persevere with lowering their carbon emission even if it means struggles and 'insults'. At other times, the social pressure is so intense that lowering carbon emission becomes impossible. As one could expect, our informants are individuals who are 'concerned with others' and have strong group ties, both in terms of the consequences of their consumption and responsibility for their behaviour (which can be perceived as marginal) (Moisander & Pesonen, 2002). Thus even if CRAGgers or *objecteurs* are very determined, they struggle to lower their carbon footprint and often 'give up' their efforts in order to 'live in peace' (Jenny).

In most cases, our informants expressed deep struggles and offered experiences of failure in their commitment to lowering carbon emission when confronted by or in conflicts with close friends and relatives. The case of air travel for international families offers an interesting example of this phenomenon.

> When my sister announced she was marrying an American, everyone was supposed to be happy, and I was the only one who was disappointed. For me, that meant I would never see her again, because I don't want to fly . . . But when I said that, obviously I was the villain. They started telling me I couldn't force my lifestyle on others, etc. . . . In the end I went to see her, a few months ago, because I wasn't feeling good and I really wanted to see her. And, one night, over there, she started saying, 'Anyway, thanks a lot for coming to see me. I know it was a difficult decision for you, so good for you'. And I said, 'No, no, don't congratulate me. I'm really not proud of what I did. For me it's really bad . . . I would have preferred being encouraged not to do it!' Once again, she didn't understand. For her, I was just annoying. (Juliette, 28)

In the excerpt above, Juliette expresses opposing forces. On the one hand, she does not want to fly and on the other she wants to see her sister who lives in America. Her strong commitment to low carbon emission creates tensions within her family and leads to internal struggles. For Juliette, disapprovals from family and friends are hard to accept. She does not feel 'good' being marginalised as the 'villain', the one who is not happy when 'everyone was supposed to be happy'. Juliette's family disapproval combined with the desire to see her sister led her, 'in the end', to give up reduced consumption and fly to America. This excerpt clearly shows the power of socially constructed needs. Although Juliette clearly expressed her refusal to fly, the general normative view around flying and visiting family members disempowered our informant. The need to be physically mobile is socially accepted and further re-enforced by close relatives, such as Juliette's sister, who congratulated the effort to fly and did not 'understand' its resistance. Juliette's struggles for acceptance and recognition reveal the inadequacy of autonomy and free choice in developing green marketing strategies. Juliette, like all of our informants, is not consuming alone. Our informants' consumption lifestyles are conditioned and mediated by the language of the marketplace, by social conventions and norms. Their aspiration to lower their carbon footprint has to be negotiated with socially constructed needs; needs that are nurtured by society in general and expressed by friends, family members, as well as colleagues. Examples of the societal pressure to drive and/or fly were offered in all narratives. In addition to the societal expectation for mobility, our informants experienced societal struggles in the consumption of food/eating. For further details, we now cite a young *objecteur* who chose not to eat meat in order to reduce her carbon footprint.

> Often, when I ate with my mother, she would start to cry because she thought I would suffer from deficiencies. And at family dinners there were always remarks and digs. My grandparents thought it was just a phase I was going through . . . In other words, they didn't understand. So, I started eating meat again, especially with them, but less than before. But recently I was in a bookstore with my mother and I was looking at a vegetarian cookbook and she said, 'Don't tell me you're a vegetarian again?' No, if you want to be left alone, it's easier to accept to eat meat. (Kasia, 27)

For Kasia's mother and grandparents, the 'normal' and acceptable practices and ways of life include eating meat. For them, the symbolic significance of not eating meat represents suffering from deficiencies. In a country where the most revered dish, foie gras, is produced using the rather cruel tradition of goose cramming, where there is still a relatively small number of vegetarians, and where supports for animal rights is relatively weak, considering vegetarianism as unhealthy is indeed a common perception (Sanches, 2005). In this context and faced with the familial pressure to eat meat, Kasia experiences a dilemma. Whilst she does not personally articulate a need to eat meat, she nevertheless feels obligated to fulfil such need when in the presence of her family members. As Kasia explains, the recurring 'remarks and digs' forced her to eat meat 'especially with them', her mother and grandparents. From this excerpt, we can see that green practices cannot emerge from an 'individual conceptions of subjectivity and human agency' (Autio et al., 2009, p. 42). The social construction of needs is embedded in the habits of individuals and is carried in modes of symbolic representation. Consumption practices such as eating meat or visiting exotic places respond to needs that have become naturalised and standardised and, in the process, have gained significant symbolic representation.

Talks reflecting the problems, struggles, and even failings to practice reduced or alternative consumption were also constructed around the area of housing/heating. In the domain of in-home, private consumption practices, informants discussed constraining forces to lowering carbon emission. For example, some of our informants complained about the French government imposing regulations on house heating. In France, the law on construction and habitation, code no. 69–256 developed on 14 June 1969 demands inhabitants to incorporate heating facilities capable of maintaining the house at 18°C. For our informants who attempt to re-evaluate these needs to lower their carbon footprint, they face legal penalties. Along heating the home, legal requirement exists around the construction of private properties. For example, one cannot insure a home built from straw.

Our analysis shows that by lowering carbon emission, our informants separate from our embedded societal norms of cleanliness (some *objecteurs de croissance* and CRAGgers wash quickly with cold water), of warmth and comfort (they use little heating), of mobility and speed (they travel on foot or by bike), and of freedom and choice (they refuse to travel by air). These societal norms confirm that we do not consume alone and that our needs for consumption are socially constructed and hence hard to renegotiate alone. In all the examples presented here, the individual must deal with external pressures against reduced carbon consumption. Those who manage to reduce their carbon emission continually and systematically to a minimum risk being singled out in various ways, from disapproval to conflict and marginalisation. In all cases, the social cost can be very high: permanent deterioration of family ties, professional disqualification, or social marginalisation. Faced with societal disapproval, individuals are forced either to reconsider their goals and lower their standards, for example by accepting to fly or eat meat, or to 'stand firm' and endure the consequences.

In the following discussion, we further explain the glass floor to low carbon emission offering the second stratum – the social imaginary.

### Second stratum: The social imaginary

In this manuscript, the notion of social imaginary refers to Castoriadis' (1987) conceptualisation of *l'imaginaire social*. For Castoriadis, the social imaginary represents the social world as a mediating collective life evolving along historical times. The social imaginary is made of first-person subjectivities that build upon implicit understandings that make possible common practices (Gaonkar, 2002).These implicit understanding are created and maintained by diverse institutions such as the laws or the media (Castoriadis, 1987). As such, the social imaginary is similar to a 'collective picture', which provides the means by which we understand our identities and our place in the world (Bouchet, 1994, p. 407). Castoriadis (1987) suggests the existence of different layers of the social imaginary: the external level imposed by the internal level which transforms 'psychic monads' into socialised individuals, the intrinsic level that represents individuals' need for coherence within the symbolic order, the natural and material environment, and the historical level and its reproductive inertia (Castoriadis, 1987). Each level, as we will discuss, is represented in our data.

The analysis of our informants' personal experience in lowering carbon emissions and the individual meanings they affiliate to alternative or reduced consumption unveils the four layers of the social imaginary presented by Castoriadis (1987). For example, in the excerpt below Audrey describes her sustainable practices along the line of social imaginary.

> I have made efforts in many areas. I gave up my car, for example, and that was a big deal . . . But never taking a plane is very difficult, because I need it to get away from it all and see the world . . . I allow myself a flight once in a while. (Audrey, 27)

Audrey, a 27 self-defined *objecteur de croissance* who works for an environmental not-for-profit organisation aims at resisting progress and reducing her $CO_2$ emissions to a bare minimum. Whilst strongly committed to the preservation of the natural environment within both her personal and professional spheres, Audrey admits that she enjoys seeing 'the world' and flying to exotic places. Situated within the social imaginary, the practice of flying engorges with symbolic representation. For Audrey, flying, unlike driving a car, represents a means 'to get away'. It symbolises an escape, a freedom to discover faraway places. Here, the symbolic representation of flying draws on a logic implicit to Audrey's social world and therefore cannot be reduced to a notion of rationality or reality. Rather, it responds to what Castoriadis calls la logique ensembliste-identitaire, a co-belonging of identification (J.B. Thompson, 1982). For Audrey, flying symbolises being part of the social world, it represents a co-belonging or a holding together as socialised individuals, the first layer of the social imaginary. Audrey, who again is extremely committed to reducing her carbon emission, accepts unsustainable practices as part of their daily life, or more precisely, as part of her identity. Later in her narrative, she explains that she 'wouldn't be the same if she gave up flying completely'. Here, reduced consumption is constrained by a need for coherence within the symbolic order, the second layer of the social imaginary.

Our fieldwork supports that alternative and reduced consumption practices are also constrained at the material level of the social imaginary. The CRAGgers and the *objecteurs de croissance* often face external difficulties when trying to reduce $CO_2$ emissions. For example, many of our informants' cannot find local food in a large city like Paris or London. Similarly, permaculture gardening requires land

**Figure 1** Permaculture allotment.

**Figure 2** Man-made chicken coop.

space, which some of our informants do not have access to (see Figures 1 and 2). In rural areas, the issue of transportation is more prominent, as it is difficult to manage without a car in areas where public transport is non-existent or not highly developed.

Finally, all of our informants faced constrained forces linked to the history and reproductive inertia level of the social imaginary. This constraining forth level of the social imaginary is exemplified in the following excerpt:

> My car runs on used cooking oil . . . Of course, that's illegal, but it's no big deal! I'm not hurting anyone; on the contrary, so I don't see why I shouldn't. (William, 52)

William, a 52-year-old CRAGger, is strongly committed to reducing his carbon emission. Towards this aim, William has developed several creative products that consume less energy, one of which is a car that runs on cooking oil. Whilst William is proud of his personal invention, he cannot communicate or share it with anyone as the product is 'illegal'. Similarly, in the area of eco-friendly architecture, one *objecteur de croissance* explained the loopholes he used to get around the historical inertia of rules and regulations in the insurance business:

> If you want to insure a straw house, most insurers refuse because they think that straw is an obvious fire hazard . . . It's stupid because compressed straw is less flammable than polystyrene, for example, but that's the way it is; they won't hear of it. So, I declared I had cellulose insulation. Technically, this is true because straw is a type of cellulose, but since it sounds more technical it's more easily accepted. (Martin, 43)

These illustrations show that, in their desire to reduce carbon emissions, our informants were confronted by the four different layers of the social imaginary described by Castoriadis (1987). Whilst these four layers of the social imaginary were most explicit in discussions of mobility and food consumption (perhaps due to their public consumption spaces), the social imaginary also played its role in the domain of house/heating consumption. For example, our informants' narratives offered representations of the social imaginary on domestic consumption and the ways in which consumer goods were used in the everyday life of the home when discussing issues of hospitality. For example, the ethnographic work reveals that, whilst all of our informants – whether CRAGgers or *objecteurs de croissance* – were most welcoming, they were also quite reluctant to invite the researcher to spend the night at their private home. One the one hand, our informants were willing to open their home and share their strong set of beliefs and values regarding carbon emissions. On the other hand, they were also required to respond to the societal norms of hospitality including providing comfort to guests. When the researcher was offered and ultimately spent the night, most informants repeatedly offered apologies and excuses for hosting the researcher without adequate heating, hot water, and comfort. These attempts to excuse their lower carbon consumption reveal the logic of the social imaginary and the powerful representations – 'the collective picture' we have of society imaginary, which operates as a fundamental principle within society (Bouchet, 1994, p. 407).

The recognition of constraining forces to alternative and reduced consumption gives us the capacity to think of sustainability outside of prescribed practices dictated by technical rationality or idealist philosophy. In all narratives, our informants' desire to lower their carbon emission does not fully respond to a prescribed idealist philosophy on how to live life nor does it fully respond to the technological rationality of eco-efficiency and/or sufficiency. Rather, our informants' reduced and alternative consumption practices primarily respond to practicality and are expressed through the medium of symbolic representation. As such, their practices are neither indifferent to nor wholly fixed by technological rationality. At the same times, these practices are neither accidental nor fully prescribed by idealistic philosophy. They are practical and symbolic. When reduced or alternative consumption are not practical, our informants opt for unsustainable options that they symbolically interpret as essential needs. These unsustainable options are situated within the social imaginary, which helps informants understand their identity and place in the world. The rationale observed here is very interesting and demonstrates that an unacceptable means of consumption in terms of the logic of sustainability is expressed as an acceptable need. How does an unsustainable practice become an acceptable need to our informants? If we follow the reasoning of Shove (2003) on the social construction of consumption standards, we can suppose that this subjective need, which appears to reflect individual preferences, corresponds to a social norm that contributes to determining the individual's preferences. Taking a trip to a faraway place (therefore by plane) offers the perfect illustration of an 'unsustainable' consumption standard that has been accepted and internalised by the interviewees as a necessary need. As Juliette explains below, flying, even for a vacation, is 'the way it is'.

I know, I shouldn't have gone, especially since it was just for a vacation . . . I'm not proud of myself, but that's the way it is. (Juliette, 28)

Juliette is a 28-year-old woman who identifies as an *objecteur de croissance*. Earlier in her narrative, Juliette expressed a firm resistance to flying. For Juliette, flying is particularly detrimental to the natural environment. Although well-rooted in her knowledge, the environmental impact of flying does not stop Juliette from flying. As presented earlier in the manuscript, Juliette flew to North America to visit her sister and, as she explains above, she also flies to go on vacation. Clear to this example is the notion that unacceptable consumption practices become internalised as essential needs. Furthermore, this excerpt challenges the modernist axiom of rationality and free choices when adopting sustainable practices. Above, Juliette explains that she is 'not proud' of herself and yet she flies because 'that's the way it is'. Here, Juliette is aware that flying is not sustainable and yet she flies. Her knowledge of the impact of flying on the environment does not lead to consequent action. In green marketing literature, this finding is not new. Many authors have discussed that knowledge does not translate to more sustainable consumption practices (Schaefer & Crane, 2005; Thøgersen, 2005). From our analysis, this knowledge–action gap may be due to the idea that consumers do not always have the choice to convey their knowledge into action. As Juliette explains, she 'shouldn't have gone'. Situated within the social imaginary, flying is for Juliette an internalised need that has to be satisfied. Consequently, Juliette's knowledge on environmental degradation is not absolute and definite. According to Castoriadis (1987), any action, including practicing reduced or alternative consumption, stands in relation to a knowledge that is fragmented and provisional. 'It is fragmented because there can be no exhaustive theory of humanity and of history; it is provisional because praxis itself constantly gives rise to new knowledge for it makes the world a language that is at once singular and universal' (Castoriadis, 1987, p. 77). Thus sustainable practices do not emerge from an absolute knowledge on environmental degradation leading to rational practices but rather from provisional knowledge that is adapted to individuals' first-person subjectivities and situated within the social imaginary.

To speak of fragmented and provisional knowledge is to raise again the ambiguity surrounding the definition of sustainability and its distinction from unsustainable practices (Black & Cherrier, 2010). Our analysis supports that sustainable consumption practices are situated within the social imaginary outside binary oppositions between right and wrong or, more particularly, between sustainable and unsustainable (Thompson, 1982). For our respondents, the dominant standard of consumption is a powerful source of temptation, even though it is often incompatible with their goal of sustainability. This incompatibility is accepted because it is part of the social imaginary. For example, most of our informants accept the norms of mobility and communication as a need. Our fieldwork reveals that both CRAGgers and *objecteurs de croissance* own a computer, and none of the narratives questioned the ownership and use of a computer even though it does consume energy. As such, alternative or reduced consumption cannot be reduced to a structure of oppositions between sustainable versus unsustainable; rather it refers to 'a meaning that can never be given independently of every sign but which is something other than the opposition of signs, and which is not unavoidably related to any particular signifying structure . . .' (Castoriadis, 1987, p. 137). The recognition of alternative and reduced consumption outside of oppositional structure gives us the capacity to think of sustainability outside of prescribed practices.

## Conclusion

Using the case of CRAGgers and *objecteurs de croissance*, we have tried to demonstrate the limits of reducing carbon emission as well as the constraining forces to sustainable practices. Clear to our analysis is that, today, alternative and reduced consumption remains a preoccupation limited to individual circles and a *terra incognita* for the collective social sphere.

Our analysis shows the existence of socio-cultural barriers to downward carbon emission. These barriers, that we combined under the concept of the *glass floor*, represents external as well as internalised sociocultural standards preventing our informants from achieving their goal of reducing carbon footprint to a bare minimum. With the risk of oversimplification, we can broadly perceive that external social standards are mostly linked to the social construction of needs and that internal social standards are mainly connected to the social imaginary.

The analysis identifies limits to reducing carbon emission in terms of socially constructed needs. Our informants do not have the autonomy to identify 'true' versus 'false' needs, nor do they have the capacity to satisfy the 'true' ones. Needs are relational; they are embedded in social relations and therefore cannot be re-evaluated at the individual level. When the interviewees do find the necessary willpower and self-confidence to reassess their needs and free themselves from external social standards, family and friends incarnate the dominant social norm and try to bring them back into the fold. What we have is something akin to humanity's collective unconscious (Campbell, 1991) where individuals unconsciously adhere to socially constructed needs. This findings stands in sharp contrast with commentators arguing that carbon emission is 'the one thing you have direct control over – your carbon footprint' and that 'our future is in our own hands' (Siegel, 2007).

In this respect, green marketing, the discipline of markets and marketers, builders of norms, has an important role to play. First, we suggest that green marketing approaches alternative and reduced consumption as social practices instead of individual choices performed by autonomous agents. Importantly, social practices are to be considered embedded in power relationships (Shove, 2005; Thøgersen, 2005; Wilhite & Lutzenhiser, 1998). Such consideration necessitates understanding how power relationships operate in the domain of sustainable practices and shift through individuals and institutions. According to Kilbourne et al. (1997), considering power relationships when promoting sustainable consumption calls for a paradigm shift. For Kilbourne et al. (1997), reframing consumption from a focus on acquisition to ways of living sustainably demands shifting away from the dominant social paradigm to integrate a 'new environmental paradigm' (Kilbourne, 1998). From policy initiatives, to educational program and the development of collaborative consumption support, the new environmental paradigm reflects a downstream approach to change and demands green marketers to work in close collaboration with structural powers. Second, our analysis points out that one big challenge in green marketing is to de-normalise needs for consumption beyond necessities and to normalise practices of conservation, sharing, reusing, recycling, slowing down, treasuring, and downshifting consumption. For Verplanken and Wood (2006), strategies aimed at countering the social and cultural barriers to downward consumption need to include an upstream approach that focuses on the individual desire for material acquisition. In this view, green marketing needs to embrace both a downstream as well as an upstream approach to societal change. This appears feasible via what Polonsky (2011) names transformative green marketing, which tackles simultaneously the inability of consumers, firms, and governments to integrate a macro-marketing perspective into their respective micro-decisions. Additionally, the glass floor is maintained and reinforced by the social imaginary. According to Castoriadis (1987), the social imaginary is necessary for society to articulate its identity and its relation to the world, as it 'contains a specific understanding of what human beings are to do in this world' (Bouchet, 1994, p. 420). To say that our informants' downward consumption faced the social imaginary is thus to indicate the power of institutions creating, supporting, and maintaining social and cultural barriers to lowering carbon footprint. As Castoriadis (1987) explains, the social imaginary is reinforced by institutions. These institutions are diverse. For example, money is an institution, that is, a collective tool organising societies and its people (Bouchet, 1994). Researchers have identified diverse institutions maintaining the social imaginary, including rituals, customs, festivals, ceremonies, norms, the media, or even magic, which inscribe individuals to cultural traditions (Arnould, Price, & Otnes, 1999; Baudrillard, 1997). Whilst our aim was not specifically to identify the institutions maintaining our informants' social imaginary, we argue, based on our data, that the media play a central role in maintaining consumption as the dominant norm and in marginalising downward consumption. For example, currently when sufficiency is covered in the media, the images or examples provided are often caricatures that highlight the exotic, even strange, aspects of these practices. Individuals who concentrate on reducing their carbon emission such as the CRAGgers or the *objecteurs de croissance* are sometimes referred to as 'carborexics' by moral entrepreneurs (Becker, 1963). In addition to the media, our study identifies academia as a powerful institution maintaining the social imaginary. For example, Shaw and Riach (2011) note that downshifters, voluntary simplifiers, or even ethical consumers are often studied along the notion of consumer resistance, rebellion, or counter-cultural movement. This, we believe, may have the powerful force to replicate our representations of voluntary simplicity as tree-huggers and downshifters as deviant and marginal individuals. To say that academia participate in reproducing the glass floor to downward consumption is thus a call for green marketing researchers to de-marginalise discussions on green practices.

The glass floor reflects the heteronomy of consumer societies where the notion of need is untouchable. Consumption practices have gradually become naturalised and standardised and are therefore non-negotiable even though they are unsustainable (Shove, 2003). This emphasises that we do not consume energy alone. The implication for green marketers is to understand consumption 'as a set of energy use behaviours deeply rooted in the social, cultural and symbolic presentation of the home' (Wilhite, Nakagami, Masuda, Yamaga, & Haneda, 2001, p. 166). As energy-use behaviours, consumption practices provide energy services including comfort, cleanliness, or speed that have an essential meaning within the social imaginary (Wilhite & Lutzenhiser, 1998). Such findings orient green practices close to tactics defined by de Certeau (1980). Tactics express a commitment to daily resistance, characterised by the immediacy of a struggle and the urgency of random actions. To change energy consumption habits, governments and NGOs have been devoting significant means to education, communication, and raising awareness among individuals, based on the principle that only the will was lacking (or what researchers refer to as 'attitude'). However, our research shows that an individual, although aware and highly motivated, must have a high capacity for resistance and even a willingness to make sacrifices, to bear the social cost of transgressing the collective consumption norms conveyed by the social imaginary. The changes our modern-day challenges require (global warming, limited resources, etc.) in terms of consumption should be the result of a strategy (e.g. de Certeau, 1980). It must consist in a quasi-methodical construction of a new balance of powers capable of producing a change in the social imaginary. This, we argue, is in part the role of green marketers.

## References

Arnould, E.J., Price, L.L., & Otnes, C. (1999). Making consumption magic: A study of white water river rafting. *Journal of Contemporary Ethnography, 28,* 33–68.

Arrow, K., Dasgupta, P., Goulder, L., Daily, G., Ehrlich, P., Heal, G., et al. (2004). Are we consuming too much? *Journal of Economic Perspectives, 18*(3), 147–172.

Autio, M., Heiskanen, E., & Heinonen, V. (2009). Narratives of 'green' consumers – The antihero, the environmental hero and the anarchist. *Journal of Consumer Behaviour, 8,* 40–53.

Baker, B., & Lightle, S.S. (2001). Cracks in the glass ceiling: An analysis of gender equity in the federal government auditing career field. *The Journal of Government Financial Management, 50*(3), 18–26.

Baudrillard, J. (1997/1970). *Consumer society: Myths and structures (theory, culture and society)*. London: Sage.

Becker, H.S. (1963). *Outsiders: Studies in the sociology of deviance*. New York: Free Press.

Belz, F.M., & Peattie, K. (2009). *Sustainability marketing, a global perspective*. London: Wiley-Blackwell.

Black, I., & Cherrier, H. (2010). Anti-consumption as part of living a sustainable lifestyle: Daily practices, contextual motivations and subjective values. *Journal of Consumer Behaviour, 9,* 437–453.

Borgmann, A. (2000). The moral complexion of consumption. *Journal of Consumer Research, 26,* 418–422.

Bouchet, D. (1994). Rails without tics: The social imaginary and postmodern culture. Can postmodern consumption replace modern questioning? *International Journal of Research in Marketing, 11,* 405–422.

Boutaud, A., & Gondran, N. (2009). *L'empreinte écologique*. Paris: La Découverte, Collection Repères.

Brundtland Commission. (1987). *Our common future*. Oxford: Oxford University Press.

Campbell, J. (1991). *The power of myth*. New York: Anchor Books.

Castoriadis, C. (1987). *The imaginary institution of society*. Cambridge, UK: Polity Press.

Cherrier, H., & Murray, J.B. (2007). Reflexive dispossession and the self: Constructing a processual theory of identity. *Consumption, Markets and Culture, 10,* 1–30.

Connolly, J. (2003). Sustainable consumption, consumption, consumers and the commodity discourse. *Consumption, Markets and Culture, 6,* 275–291.

Dahlstrom, R. (2011). *Green marketing management*. Mason, OH: South-Western Cengage Learning.

De Certeau, M. (1980). *L'invention du quotidien: Arts de faire* (Vol. 1). Paris: Folio.

Dolan, P. (2002). The sustainability of 'sustainable consumption'. *Journal of Macromarketing, 22,* 170–181.

Durning, A. (1992). *How much is enough? The consumer society and the future of the earth*. New York: Norton.

Elgin, D. (1981). *Voluntary simplicity: Toward a way of life that is outwardly simple, inwardly rich*. New York: Morrow.

Elkington, J., Hailes, J., & Makower, J. (1990). *The green consumer*. New York: Penguin Books.

Fisk, G. (1973). Criteria for a theory of responsible consumption. *Journal of Marketing, 37*(2), 24–31.

Fuchs, D.A., & Lorek, S. (2005). Sustainable consumption governance: A history of promises and failures. *Journal of Consumer Policy, 28*, 261–288.

Gaonkar, D.P. (2002). Toward new imaginaries: An introduction. *Public Culture, 14*, 1–19.

Gould, S.J. (1991). The self-manipulation of my pervasive, perceived vital energy through product use: An introspective-praxis perspective. *Journal of Consumer Research, 18*, 194–207.

Grant, J. (2007). *The green marketing manifesto*. Chichester, UK: John Wiley.

Heiskanen, E. (2005). The performative nature of consumer research: Consumers' environmental awareness as an example. *Journal of Consumer Policy, 28*, 179–201.

Heiskanen, E., & Pantzar, M. (1997). Toward sustainable consumption: Two new perspectives. *Journal of Consumer Policy, 20*, 409–442.

Hobson, K. (2002). Competing discourses of sustainable consumption: Does the rationalisation of lifestyles make sense? *Environmental Politics, 11*, 95–120.

Holbrook, M.B. (1995). *Consumer research: Introspective essays on the study of consumption*. Thousand Oaks, CA: Sage.

Howell, R. (2009). *The experience of carbon rationing action groups: Implications for a personal carbon allowances policy*. UKERC report. Retrieved from http://www.eci.ox.ac.uk/publications/downloads/howell09crags.pdf

Iyer, R., & Muncy, J.A. (2009). The purpose and object of anti-consumption. *Journal of Business Research, 62*, 160–168.

Kilbourne, W.E. (1998). Green marketing: A theoretical perspective. *Journal of Marketing Management, 14*, 641–655.

Kilbourne, W.E., & Beckmann, S. (1998). Review and critical assessment of research on marketing and the environment. *Journal of Marketing Management, 14*, 513–532.

Kilbourne, W.E., McDonald, P., & Prothero, A. (1997). Sustainable consumption and the quality of life: A macromarketing challenge to the dominant social paradigm. *Journal of Macromarketing, 17*, 4–23.

Latouche, S. (2005). *Décoloniser l'imaginaire*. Lyon, France: Parangon.

Moisander, J., & Pesonen, S. (2002). Narratives of sustainable ways of living: Constructing the self and the other as a green consumer. *Management Decision, 40*, 329–342.

Nava, M. (1991). Consumerism reconsidered: Buying and power. *Cultural Studies, 5*, 157–173.

Ottman, J.A. (1993). *Green marketing: Challenges and opportunities*. Lincolnwood, IL: NTC Business Books.

Ottman, J.A. (2011). *The New rule of green marketing: Strategies, tools, and inspiration for sustainable branding*. San Francisco: Berrett-Koehler.

Pierce, L.B. (2000). *Choosing simplicity, real people finding peace and fulfillment in a complex world*. Carmel, CA: Gallagher Press.

Polonsky, M.J. (2011). Transformative green marketing: Impediments and opportunities *Journal of Business Research, 64*, 1311–1319.

Reisch, L.A. (2001). Time and wealth: The role of time and temporalities for sustainable patterns of consumption. *Time and Society, 10*, 367–385.

Sanches, S. (2005). Sustainable consumption à la française? Conventional, innovative, and alternative approaches to sustainability and consumption in France. *Sustainability: Science, Practice, and Policy, 1*, 43–57

Sandıkcı, Ö., & Ekici, A. (2009). Politically motivated brand rejection. *Journal of Business Research, 62*(2), 208–217.

Sanne, C. (2000). Dealing with environmental saving in a dynamic economy: How to stop chasing our tail in the pursuit of sustainability. *Energy Policy, 28*, 487–495.

Schaefer, A., & Crane, A. (2005). Addressing sustainability and consumption. *Journal of Macromarketing, 25*, 76–92.

Schor, J. (1998). *The overspent American: Upscaling, downshifting, and the new consumer.* New York: Basic Books.

Schor, J. (1999). *The overspent American: Why we want what we don't need.* New York: HarperPerennial.

Schor, J. (2000). Toward a new politics of consumption. In J.B.S. & D.B. Holt (Eds.), *The consumer society reader* (pp. 446–462). New York: New Press.

Schumacher, E.F. (1974). *Small is beautiful: A study of economics as if people mattered.* London: Sphere Books.

Shaw, D., Newholm, T., & Dickinson, R. (2006). Consumption as voting: An exploration of consumer empowerment. *European Journal of Marketing, 40*, 1049–1067.

Shaw, D., & Riach, K. (2011). Embracing ethical fields: Constructing consumption in the margins. *European Journal of Marketing, 45*(7/8), 1051–1067.

Shove, E. (2003). *Comfort, cleanliness and convenience: The social organization of normality.* Oxford: Berg.

Shove, E. (2005). Changing human behaviour and lifestyle: A challenge for sustainable consumption? In I. Ropke & L. Reisch (Eds.), *Consumption – Perspectives from ecological economics* (pp. 111–132). Cheltenham, UK: Elgar.

Siegel, L. (2007, January 21). The low-carbon diet. *Observer Magazine.* Retrieved 27 June 2011, from http://www.guardian.co.uk/environment/2007/jan/21/observermagazine. ethicalliving

Slater, D. (1997). Consumer culture and the politics of needs. In M. Nava, A. Blake, I. MaRury, & B. Richards (Eds.), *Buy this book* (pp. 51–63). London: Routledge.

Tanner, C., & Kast, S.W. (2003). Promoting sustainable consumption: Determinants of green purchases by swiss consumers. *Psychology and Marketing, 20*, (pp. 883–903).

Thøgersen, J. (2005). How may consumer policy empower consumers for sustainable lifestyles? *Journal of Consumer Policy, 28*, 143–178.

Thompson, C.J. (1997). Interpreting consumers: A hermeneutical framework for deriving marketing insights from the texts of consumers' consumption stories. *Journal of Marketing Research, 34*(4), 438–456.

Thompson, C.J., Locander, W.B., & Pollio, H.R. (1989). Putting consumer experience back into consumer research: The philosophy and method of existential-phenomenology. *Journal of Consumer Research, 16*(4), 133–147.

Thompson, J.B. (1982). Ideology and the social imaginary: An appraisal of Castoriadis and Lefort. *Theory and Society, 11*, 659–681.

Verplanken, B., & Wood, W. (2006). Interventions to break and create consumer habits. *Journal of Public Policy and Marketing, 25*(1), 90–103.

Wilhite, H., & Lutzenhiser, L. (1998). Social loading and sustainable consumption. In E.J. Arnould & L.M. Scott (Eds.), *Advances in consumer research* Vol. 26, (pp. 281–287). Provo, UT: Association for Consumer Research.

Wilhite, H., Nakagami, H., Masuda, T., Yamaga, Y., & Haneda, H. (2001). A cross-cultural analysis of household energy-use behavior in Japan and Norway. In D. Miller (Ed.), *Consumption: Critical concepts in the social sciences* Vol. 4, (pp. 159–177). London: Routledge.

# Normalising green behaviours: A new approach to sustainability marketing

Ruth Rettie, *Kingston University, UK*
Kevin Burchell, *Kingston University, UK*
Debra Riley, *Kingston University, UK*

> **Abstract** This paper develops a new approach to sustainability marketing: repositioning activities as normal, or not normal, to encourage the adoption of more sustainable consumer practices. The paper is grounded in theories of social normalisation, conformity, and social practice theory. Previous qualitative work by the authors suggests that some sustainable behaviours are not adopted because they are perceived to be not normal, and that some unsustainable behaviours persist because they are seen as normal. This paper shows how consumer perceptions of the extent to which behaviours are normal or not normal can be identified and used in the design of sustainability marketing strategies. The research involved a survey of 1000 UK respondents' attitudes to 15 specific activities, and identifies marketing strategies for (re)positioning these activities as either normal or not normal, as appropriate. In addition, the paper provides guidance for targeting these normalisation strategies at specific demographic groups.

## Introduction

In recent years in the UK and elsewhere, interest in green marketing has grown among researchers, practitioners, commercial organisations, and policymakers. In particular, it is envisaged that consumer behaviour change will play an important role in the UK response to climate change and other sustainability issues (DECC, 2009, 2010; Defra, 2005, 2006a, 2006b, 2008; Defra & Collier, 2010; HM Government, 2009). This focus on sustainability challenges the discipline of marketing, which is accused of stimulating unsustainable levels of consumption (Abela, 2006; Sheth & Parvatiyar, 1995; Stearns, 2001; United Nations Environment Programme, 2005; Van Dam & Apeldoorn, 1996) and of responding to sustainability with misconceived marketing practices (Peattie & Crane, 2005) and illusory 'greenwash' (Brennan & Binney, 2008; Grant, 2007).

Peattie and Peattie (2009) argue that green marketing has been ineffective and claim that 'Creating meaningful progress towards sustainability requires more radical solutions than just the development of new products and product substitutions amongst consumers' (p. 261). This paper contributes to Peattie and Peattie's (2009) agenda by proposing and developing a new role for sustainability marketing: encouraging consumer adoption of sustainable behaviours, products, and services by positioning them as normal, and discouraging less sustainable ones by positioning them as not normal. The paper builds upon previous qualitative research by Rettie, Barnham, and Burchell (2011), which found that consumers assess green marketing initiatives, products, or behaviours in the context of what they understand to be normal, everyday, and mainstream. Further, consumer adoption and discontinuation of sustainability behaviours are influenced by their understandings of what is normal and not normal. Thus some sustainable behaviours are currently not adopted because they are seen as not normal, and relevant only to a niche group of 'green consumers'; similarly, some less sustainable behaviours are difficult to change because they are perceived as normal and as what everyone does. Further, Rettie et al.'s (2011) research shows that consumers understand that social conceptions of what is normal and not normal changes over time.

Drawing on these findings, Rettie et al. (2011) use the term 'social normalisation' to describe a social process in which activities and products gradually become accepted as mainstream, normal, and everyday, while other activities may be 'denormalised' and no longer regarded as normal. For example, some of their respondents remembered a period in the 1960s when taking shopping baskets or bags to the shops had been normal. Subsequently, this became less normal because shops provided plastic bags, but recently it has become normal again to take one's own bags. This reflects a cycle in which taking bags to shops has undergone a process of denormalisation, followed by a more recent process of social normalisation, accompanied by a corresponding denormalisation of plastic carrier bags. Similarly, respondents noted that recycling has become normal nowadays indicating that recycling has gone through a process of social normalisation. Importantly, processes of social normalisation are culturally specific; for example while waste recycling underwent social normalisation earlier in Canada than in the UK, it has yet to be normalised in Mexico. On the basis of their research, Rettie et al. (2011) propose that sustainability marketing can be used to support and drive processes of social normalisation and denormalisation, as appropriate. More specifically, they propose that marketing can, first, encourage consumer adoption of sustainable activities by repositioning them as mainstream, normal, and what everyone else does, and, second, encourage the consumer abandonment of unsustainable activities by repositioning them as no longer normal.

This study builds on this work, and develops an approach to sustainability marketing that influences behaviour by shaping consumer conceptions of what is normal. In particular, the paper provides guidance for the targeting of social normalisation marketing strategies on the basis of demographic groups. The paper reports quantitative research which explored consumer understandings of 15 sustainability-related activities in terms of the extent to which they were seen as normal and the extent to which they were seen as green. The research indicates that while there was general consensus among consumers about which activities were green or not green, conceptions about their normality were often polarised, demonstrating the potential for segmentation and targeting on the basis of conceptions of normality.

The paper is structured as follows. The next section reviews relevant green marketing studies. This is followed by a discussion of the theoretical foundations of the paper, a description of the research methodology, and the research findings. The final section includes discussion and conclusions, research limitations, and directions for future research.

## Green marketing

The term 'green marketing' is subject to a variety of definitions and near synonyms, and is typically used in the context of products and services. Mintu and Lozardo (1993) define green marketing as 'the application of marketing tools to facilitate exchanges that satisfy organisational and individual goals in such a way that the preservation, protection and conservation of the natural environment is upheld' (p. 2). Similar terms used interchangeably by most authors include 'sustainable marketing', 'environmental marketing', 'ecological marketing', 'eco-marketing', enviropreneurial marketing', and 'sustainable lifestyles marketing' (Chamorro, Rubio, & Miranda, 2009; Charter & Polonsky, 1999; Fuller, 1999; UNEP, 2005). In its concern for the environment, green marketing implies social responsibility (Peattie, 1995) with connotations of societal marketing (El-Ansary, 1974; Kotler, 1972; Prothero, 1990). This study focuses on sustainability marketing, which Belz and Peattie (2009) define as 'building and maintaining sustainable relationships with customers, the social environment and the natural environment' (p. 30); as used here, sustainability marketing includes *both* commercial marketing of green products and services, *and* social marketing of pro-environmental behaviours. Sustainability marketing can potentially play an important role in encouraging more sustainable behaviours (Jones, Clarke-Hill, Comfort, & Hillier, 2007; Peattie & Peattie, 2009; Sheth & Parvatiyar, 1995).

Peattie and Crane (2005) note the disappointing performance of green marketing. They attribute this failure to misconceived marketing practices which are ineffective and provoke consumer cynicism, and argue for green marketing strategies that adopt a holistic approach and a customer focus. Lee (2008) characterises the development of green marketing as encompassing three stages: introduction in the '80s, the consumer backlash of the '90s, and a third stage that commenced with the new millennium. She argues that increasing environmental concerns, technological innovation, and stricter regulation have created a new momentum that will move eco-friendly business into the mainstream. However, despite this resurgence of interest, research indicates that green marketing is still failing to engage consumers (Pickett-Baker & Ozaki, 2008).

Brennan and Binney (2008) claim that 'greenwash' has led to consumer scepticism and disillusionment. 'Greenwash' is defined as a superficial or insincere display of concern for the environment shown by an organisation (Collins English Dictionary, 2009). Escalation of greenwash in the UK is reflected in a sharp increase in complaints about environmental claims, which were up 470% in 2007 (Wilson, 2008). Global research (GfK Group, 2010) has also identified high levels of scepticism about green marketing. Scepticism about greenwash helps to explain the 'greenophobia' observed by Grant (2007, p. 200) who claims that consumers see green products as more expensive, less effective, and aimed at a small niche of green consumers.

A number of segmentation studies have attempted to profile the green consumer using geographic, cultural, psychographic, and demographic variables. Demographic variables are particularly suitable for targeting marketing activities, but research findings have been inconsistent or show little predictive value (Diamantopoulos, Schlegelmilch, Sinkovics, & Bohlen, 2003; Finisterra do Paço & Raposo, 2010). In their research, Diamantopoulos et al. (2003) found that although demographic variables predict, to some degree, environmental knowledge and attitude, they are less able to account for environmental behaviour. A number of studies use multivariate statistical analysis combining demographic and psychographic variables to identify segments of green consumers. For example, Finisterra do Paço and Raposo (2010) identify and profile three segments of Portuguese consumers: 'uncommitted' (36%), 'green activists' (35%), and 'undefined' (29%). Although the authors found some significant demographic differences between their segments (age, education, occupation, income), they conclude that Portuguese consumers rarely translate their environmental concerns into actions. A global commercial study (GfK Group, 2010), based on 36,000 consumers, identifies five consumer segments which they call: 'green in deed', 'carbon cultured', 'glamour greens', 'green in need', and 'jaded'. The Department for Environment, Food and Rural Affairs (2008) conducted its own segmentation study based on 3600 consumers, using attitudes and self-reported behaviours to identify seven clusters, ranging from the 'positive greens' to the 'honestly disengaged'. Whilst these segmentations studies are interesting, they do not readily lend themselves to strategies for green marketing or pro-environmental interventions because it is very difficult to target people on the basis of their attitudes and beliefs. Moreover, within these studies there are only limited correlations with claimed environmental behaviours, and none of the studies segment in terms of actual, rather than reported, behaviour. Underlying these approaches, there is an assumption that consumers are consistently green in their consumption, and that environmentally friendly buying behaviour in one market is related to green consumption and behaviour in other areas. However, as Finisterra do Paço and Raposo (2010) point out, some green behaviours such as saving electricity might be motivated by economic factors, rather than reflecting a general disposition for green consumption. The problem with trying to identify 'the green consumer' is that there are many different aspects of green behaviour and consumption; a consumer may adopt some green behaviours while rejecting others.

Young, Hwang, McDonald, and Oates (2010) note that there is an 'attitude–behaviour gap', so that although 30% of consumers claim to be very concerned about the environment, this does not translate into green purchase behaviour (see also Blake, 1999; Jackson, 2005). Research provides ample evidence of an attitude–behaviour gap. Studies in diverse countries report only modest correlations between environmental attitudes and self-reported ecological behaviours, including Spain (Fraj & Martinez, 2007), Portugal (Finisterra do Paço & Raposo, 2010), the UK (Schlegelmilch, Bohlen, & Diamantopoulos, 1996), Egypt (Mostafa, 2007), and Canada (Follows & Jobber, 2000). Bamberg and Moser's (2007) meta-analysis of 57 environmental studies shows there is also an intention–behaviour gap; intentions account for only 27% of the variance in self-reported pro-environmental behaviour. These studies measured self-reported behaviour; there may be a further gap between reported and actual behaviour. The complex relationship between attitudes and behaviour is also supported by qualitative research. Carrigan and Attalla (2001) report that despite consumer good intentions, actual purchase behaviour is often uninfluenced by ethical concerns, while Szmigin, Carrigan, and McEachern (2009) found that even ethically conscious consumers exhibit dissonance and flexibility in their purchase behaviour.

## Theoretical foundations

Previous research on green marketing has often used models such as Ajzen's (1985) Theory of Planned Behaviour (TPB), which explains behaviour in terms of complex relationships between knowledge, attitudes, perceptions of norms, intention, and behaviour. While compelling in some ways, these approaches are belied by the identification of 'attitude–behaviour' and 'intention–behaviour' gaps that were discussed earlier. Others, particularly in the health domain (such as Gregson et al., 2001), have drawn on variations of Bronfenbrenner's (1979) social ecological perspective on behaviour. Here, individual behaviour is understood in relation to social systems, which operate at macro-(cultural), exo-(community), meso-(organisational and institutional), and micro-(individual and interpersonal) levels. While this paper shares the emphasis on norms that is to be found in the TPB, and the emphasis on social systems that characterises the social ecological perspective, it employs these concepts within the sociological context of practice theory and social normalisation.

Psychologists have amassed extensive empirical evidence of conformity in group situations (e.g. Asch, 1956; Milgram, 1974); what other people do or say creates a normative social influence. This principle of conformity has been successfully used in social norm campaigns that shape behaviour by telling people about the *desirable* behaviour of the majority (Perkins, 2003). The social norm approach has also been successful in several sustainability contexts (Goldstein, Cialdini, & Griskevicius, 2008; Nolan, Schultz, Cialdini, Goldstein, & Griskevicius, 2008). Underlying the social norm approach is the idea that consumer behaviour is influenced by the behaviour of relevant reference groups, that is, by what is seen as normal within a particular social group.

Practice theory is characterised by a range of perspectives (Schatzki, 1996, 2005; Shove & Pantzar, 2005; Warde, 2005) that together represent a fundamental reassessment of the assumptions embodied in models such as the TPB and social ecological perspectives. Whereas these approaches emphasise individual behaviour, in practice theory the emphasis is on the practice or practices, for instance travel to work practices, which are understood as arrays of meanings, norms, material objects, and infrastructures, and might be undertaken in more or less sustainable ways. In addition, studies in practice theory often emphasise temporal change and the evolution of practices. For instance, Shove (2003) elegantly shows how practices of showering and laundering changed over the course of the twentieth century. This aspect of practice theory is important, because it reveals the mutability of practices and indicates how practices might be changed with sustainability objectives. Practice theory is also different from the TPB and social ecological perspectives in its emphasis – in addition to norms and social systems – on material things (often products, from a marketing perspective, but also material infrastructures), know-how (which also implies the importance of learning), and meanings. For example, a travel to work practice such as cycling requires particular arrangements of: cycling and geographical proficiency (know-how), bikes, helmets, safe cycle routes, and bike racks (materials), and social acceptability and safety (meanings). This emphasis on arrays is an important insight for marketers because it draws the mind towards a broad range of opportunities for change. For example, an absence of affordable bicycles, safe cycle routes, and secure bike racks clearly represent considerable practical barriers to cycling that can be addressed, but might not be relevant in the context of the TPB or social ecological perspectives alone. The practical potential of this for green marketers is discussed in greater detail in Rettie et al. (2011).

Within the context of this paper, the significance of meaning in practice theory is particularly strong. This facilitates the observation that the salient meaning of a product, service, or activity is often its positioning as normal or not normal, rather than as green or not green. Finally, in practice theory, behaviour is characterised as *taken-for-granted*, *habitual*, and *unreflective*, rather than *planned*, as in the TPB.

Returning to the example of recycling used to illustrate social normalisation, this can be recast in terms of practice theory. Thus one can argue that the *practice* of household waste disposal has changed over the past 20 years, with attendant changes in: material objects (from single bins to multiple bins), material infrastructures (from 'bank' systems to 'kerbside' systems), know-how and learning (from what day of the week the single collection takes place to cycles of different collections and rules about separating waste), external systems (from weaker to stronger pro-recycling regulatory and fiscal frameworks), and meanings (from unusual and green to mainstream and green).

## Methodology

The study explores whether consumer understanding, of what is normal and of what is green, can aid the selection of sustainability marketing strategies. The specific research questions were:

RQ1: *How do consumers assess common sustainability-related activities in terms of the extent to which they are normal, and the extent to which they are green?*

RQ2: *Is there consensus among consumers about whether an activity is normal or not normal, green or not green?*

RQ3: *Can one use conceptions of what is normal and what is green to segment and target consumers for sustainability marketing campaigns?*

RQ4: *Can research on conceptions of what is normal and what is green aid the selection of appropriate sustainability marketing strategies?*

A quantitative survey was developed with the objective of exploring three issues. First, respondents assessed 15 separate activities in terms of the extent to which they were perceived as 'normal' or 'not normal' behaviour. Second, respondents assessed the same 15 activities in terms of the extent to which they were perceived as 'green' or 'not green'. Third, the survey captured the extent to which respondents perceived themselves to be 'green'.

The 15 activities were selected from a longer list of 25 that were derived from Rettie et al.'s (2011) qualitative research (from photographs brought to the groups by participants, from stimulus materials used by the researchers, and from discussion within the groups). The 25 items were tested in an online pilot study that included

CONTEMPORARY ISSUES IN GREEN AND ETHICAL MARKETING

space for comments after every question and at the end of the survey. In addition, four individual interviews were conducted to understand respondents' interpretations of the survey questions. Overall, 30 respondents completed the pilot questionnaire and commented on the questions. From the initial 25 activities, 15 were selected for the final study on the basis that they were easily understood and covered a range of more and less sustainable behaviours.

The survey was administered by a professional market research agency, as part of a telephone omnibus survey, to a nationally representative sample of 1000 respondents in the UK. The study used a quota sample to match national proportions on gender, age, social class, and location. Respondents were asked 'To what extent do you think that these activities are normal (what people generally do)?' and were given a five-point Likert scale: 2 = 'very normal', 1 = 'normal', 0 = 'neither', −1 = 'not normal', −2 = 'not at all normal'. Later in the survey, a second question asked, 'To what extent do you think that these activities are green?' using the scale: 2 = 'very green', 1 = 'green', 0 = 'neither', −1 = 'not green', −2 = 'not at all green'. Finally, respondents were asked, 'To what extent do you think of yourself as green?' using the same Likert scale as in the second question. 'Don't know' options were given in all three cases. To reduce bias, the first two questions were separated in the omnibus and the order of each activity was rotated between, but not within, respondents. In addition to the three questions, the following demographic variables were collected in the survey: age, sex, marital status, working status, region, and social class.

## Results and analysis

This section presents the results of the research and addresses the four research questions, drawing on the conceptual and practical resources described earlier.

### Activity ratings on the normal and green scales

Respondents assessed a range of activities in terms of the extent to which they were normal, and the extent to which they were green. Table 1 shows the mean scores for each activity. Activities scoring highly on the normal scale include 'eating meat or fish' and 'recycling', while 'using patio heaters' and 'buying organic food' were seen as not normal. Activities scoring highly on the green scale include 'taking shopping bags to the shops' and 'using energy-saving light bulbs', while 'leaving the TV on standby' and 'drying clothes in a tumble drier' were seen as not green. The end column on Table 1 indicates the consensus within the public policy discourse, based on research of the websites both of activist organisations, such as Greenpeace and Friends of the Earth, and of government departments, such as Defra and DECC[1]. Table 1 shows that consumer conceptions of whether or not activities are green or not green generally concur with the expert view. This consistency indicates that untargeted informational marketing campaigns that aim to educate consumers about these green behaviours are of limited value, because most consumers already know which activities are green and which are not.

[1]http://www.greenpeace.org.uk/; http://www.foe.co.uk/; http://www.decc.gov.uk/; http://ww2.defra.gov.uk

## CONTEMPORARY ISSUES IN GREEN AND ETHICAL MARKETING

**Table 1** Activity mean scores.

| Activity | Normal scale (A) | Green scale (B) | Expert view |
|---|---|---|---|
| Monitoring electricity consumption | .39 | 1.03 | Green |
| Recycling | 1.14 | 1.40 | Green |
| Showering/bathing on alternate days | .15 | .77 | Green |
| Taking your own shopping bags to the shops | .91 | 1.26 | Green |
| Using energy-saving light bulbs | .96 | 1.28 | Green |
| Buying organic food | −.17 | .57 | Green |
| Using public transport whenever possible | .36 | 1.00 | Green |
| Driving a car | 1.07 | −.84 | Not green |
| Drying clothes in a tumble dryer | .31 | −.98 | Not green |
| Eating meat or fish | 1.17 | .20 | Not green |
| Flying overseas for holidays | .62 | −.85 | Not green |
| Leaving the TV on standby | .24 | −.06 | Not green |
| Buying bottled water | .10 | −.59 | Not green |
| Littering | −.22 | −1.24 | Not green |
| Using patio heaters at home | −.37 | −.78 | Not green |

Scales: A. 2 = 'very normal' to −2 = 'not at all normal'. B. 2 = 'very green to −2 = 'not at all green'.

Figure 1 displays the activity ratings along the two axes, 'very green' to 'not at all green', and 'normal' to 'not at all normal'. Depicting the activities on these scales shows how consumers currently understand these activities. More practically, and drawing on the conceptual resources discussed earlier, it facilitates the identification of marketing strategies to promote more sustainable behaviour. From quadrant 1, it is clear that a number of activities, such as recycling and using energy-saving light bulbs, are seen as green and as normal. Theories of conformity suggest that this supports the mainstream adoption of these sustainable behaviours. However, consumer assessment of some activities indicates scope for repositioning. For instance, respondents rated 'eating meat or fish' as green and normal, whereas most sustainability experts would argue that it is not green, emphasising the resource and land-hungry nature of meat production and the dangers of over-fishing. This indicates that there is potential for marketing campaigns designed to communicate these issues and to encourage meat-free meals. Second, although consumers rated 'showering/bathing on alternate days', 'using public transport', and 'monitoring electricity consumption' as green and normal, these ratings were rather low, indicating potential for reinforcement of these conceptions. Turning to quadrant 2, although buying organic food is seen as green, it is not seen as normal. Therefore, there is scope to normalise this activity. Conformity and social norm research suggest that more consumers are likely to buy organic food if it is positioned as normal, rather than a niche product (although premium pricing might preclude this strategy). Conversely, for activities in quadrant 3 ('using patio heaters at home', 'littering'), there is scope for marketing designed to reinforce and strengthen their status as not normal and not green.

There are a number of activities (quadrant 4) which consumers understand are not green, but nevertheless see as normal. The principle of conformity suggests that

**Figure 1** Graphical representation of activity ratings.

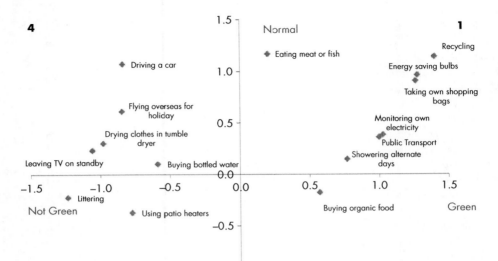

there is a normative social influence to conform to what is normal or what people generally do. Consequently, people are less likely to change behaviours that are seen as normal. Therefore, although consumers recognise that, for instance, flying overseas for holidays is not green, it is difficult to change their behaviour because they see it as normal and what people generally do. The conception that flying overseas for holidays is normal creates a positive feedback loop that reinforces the propensity to take holidays abroad. Rettie et al. (2011) suggest that, since flying is not green, the task for sustainability marketing is to try to reposition flying abroad for holidays as no longer normal. This could be done, for instance, by using celebrities and authority figures who choose to holiday in this country for sustainability reasons, or who choose to travel by train. Similar marketing strategies could be used for all the activities currently in quadrant 4 of Figure 1, challenging their status as normal, and attempting to move them towards quadrant 3, where they would be understood as neither green nor normal. At the same time, there is the opportunity to reposition alternative green behaviours as normal, for instance, taking holidays in this country, using public transport, line-drying, and so on.

## Consumer consensus?

This section reviews the frequency distributions within the data in order to determine whether or not there is broad consensus among respondents about whether an activity is normal or not normal, green or not green. Table 2 presents the frequency distributions as percentages, for the battery of activities, with respect to the extent

**Table 2** Consensus on whether activities are green.

| | Classification of activity by respondents (%) | | |
| Activity | Very green/green | Neither/don't know | Not green/not at all green |
| --- | --- | --- | --- |
| *Consensus that activities are green* | | | |
| Recycling | 95.7 | 1.8 | 2.6 |
| Taking your own shopping bags to the shops | 94.3 | 3.2 | 2.6 |
| Using energy-saving light bulbs | 93.5 | 2.5 | 3.9 |
| Monitoring electricity consumption | 85.6 | 7.3 | 8.1 |
| Using public transport whenever possible | 85.2 | 5.3 | 9.5 |
| Showering/bathing on alternate days | 74.5 | 13.4 | 14.4 |
| Buying organic food | 62.5 | 18.3 | 19.2 |
| *Consensus that activities are not green* | | | |
| Littering | 5.9 | 3.8 | 90.3 |
| Leaving the TV on standby | 7.7 | 4.5 | 87.7 |
| Drying clothes in a tumble dryer | 8.7 | 7.1 | 82.1 |
| Driving a car | 11.9 | 11.7 | 76.4 |
| Flying overseas for holidays | 10.4 | 14.6 | 75.0 |
| Buying bottled water | 21.8 | 13.4 | 64.8 |
| Using patio heaters at home | 17.9 | 13.8 | 68.2 |
| *No consensus* | | | |
| Eating meat or fish | 41.6 | 36.0 | 22.3 |

to which they are understood to be green or not green. Table 2 shows that there are high levels of agreement among consumers about what is green. The activities on which there was most agreement are recycling, taking one's own shopping bags, and using energy-saving light bulbs. These are all areas where there have been large-scale green initiatives. Table 2 also shows that, for some activities, there are some relatively strong minorities who disagree with the dominant view: 'eating organic food', 'using patio heaters at home', 'buying bottled water'. However, eating meat and fish emerges as the sole activity that is *not* subject to a dominant view among the respondents. Instead, eating meat and fish is characterised by an extremely high percentage of 'neither' (34%), and no dominant view as either green (41.6%) or not green (22.3%). Thus although Table 1 suggested a respondent view that eating meat and fish is green, examination of the frequency distributions reveals that consumers are polarised on this issue.

In contrast to the consensus about what was green or not green, there was much less consensus among respondents about which activities were normal. As shown in Table 3, the frequency distributions of only six activities indicate a consensus view (and in the case of 'flying for holidays', there is a relatively strong minority view). Most activities had bimodal frequency distributions, with two distinct frequency peaks indicating that respondents are polarised about whether these activities are normal. There is no precise definition of a bimodal distribution; the criterion used here is two frequency peaks with at least 25% of respondents. Bimodal distributions

# CONTEMPORARY ISSUES IN GREEN AND ETHICAL MARKETING

**Table 3** Consensus on whether activities are normal.

| Activity | Classification of activity by respondents (%) | | |
| --- | --- | --- | --- |
| | Very normal/normal | Neither/don't know | Not normal/not at all normal |
| *Consensus that activities are normal* | | | |
| Eating meat or fish | 93.0 | 2.8 | 4.1 |
| Driving a car | 87.3 | 3.2 | 9.5 |
| Recycling | 92.0 | 3.2 | 4.7 |
| Taking your own shopping bags to the shops | 93.1 | 4.5 | 12.4 |
| Using energy-saving light bulbs | 85.1 | 4.8 | 10.0 |
| Flying overseas for holidays | 70.6 | 8.0 | 21.3 |
| *No consensus* | | | |
| Monitoring electricity consumption | 63.7 | 7.6 | 28.8 |
| Using public transport whenever possible | 61.0 | 6.0 | 33.0 |
| Drying clothes in a tumble dryer | 58.1 | 10.6 | 31.3 |
| Leaving the TV on standby | 54.9 | 6.2 | 39.0 |
| Showering/bathing on alternate days | 52.0 | 8.6 | 39.3 |
| Buying bottled water | 50.8 | 8.4 | 40.8 |
| Littering | 39.0 | 5.9 | 55.2 |
| Buying organic food | 35.6 | 14.5 | 49.9 |
| Using patio heaters at home | 28.6 | 16.0 | 55.4 |

are interesting because they indicate that summary statistics, such as means, can be misleading. Bimodal distributions often indicate that a sample contains two distinct populations. This is important because the two modes may be associated with different demographic characteristics which can be used in profiling and targeting.

### Segmentation and profiling

Most consumers rated themselves as 'green' or 'very green' (73.5%) in response to the question, 'To what extent do you see yourself as green?' With only 8.1% claiming that they are not green, identifying oneself as green is of little value as a basis for segmenting green marketing campaigns. Females were more likely to see themselves as green or very green ($p < .001$), but no differences were found for age, social class, working status, marital status, or region.

Prompted by previous research on green consumer segmentation, segmentation analysis was undertaken to investigate whether there were identifiable groups of consumers who shared a common view in terms of (a) the normality or (b) the greenness of specific activities. A two-step clustering approach was employed, using both hierarchical and non-hierarchical methods, and a range of clusters were tested. The results suggested a three-segment solution. However, there were few differences

CONTEMPORARY ISSUES IN GREEN AND ETHICAL MARKETING

**Table 4** Significant ANOVA results by social class.

| Dependent variables | df | F | F sig. | Independent groups | Mean differences | Sig. |
|---|---|---|---|---|---|---|
| *Normal* | | | | | | |
| Driving a car | 3 | 7.368 | .000 | AB/DE | .245 | .010 |
| | | | | C1/DE | .245 | .010 |
| Eating meat or fish | 3 | 3.036 | .028 | AB/DE | .188 | .015 |
| Flying overseas for holidays | 3 | 5.547 | .001 | AB/DE | .390 | .001 |
| Leaving the TV on standby | 3 | 3.628 | .013 | AB/DE | .374 | .006 |
| Monitoring electricity consumption | 3 | 5.403 | .001 | C1/AB | .295 | .021 |
| | | | | DE/AB | .397 | .001 |
| Showering/bathing on alternate days | 3 | 4.554 | .004 | DE/AB | .446 | .000 |
| | | | | DE/C1 | .284 | .026 |
| Using patio heaters at home | 3 | 3.164 | .024 | DE/AB | .304 | .036 |
| Using public transport whenever possible | 3 | 4.360 | .005 | DE/AB | .370 | .003 |
| *Green* | | | | | | |
| Buying bottled water | 3 | 9.321 | .000 | C2/AB | .350 | .292 |
| Using a tumble drier to dry clothes | 3 | 3.125 | .025 | DE/AB | .229 | .026 |
| Eating meat and fish | 3 | 2.614 | .050 | DE/AB | .237 | .040 |
| Littering | 3 | 5.612 | .001 | C2/AB | .272 | .004 |
| | | | | DE/AB | .282 | .001 |

in demographics between the identified segments, which would make it difficult to target them effectively.

Ultimately, the use of cluster analysis was rejected in favour of individual analysis of each activity. This reveals important demographic differences between consumers that can potentially be used for segmentation and targeting of sustainability marketing. A one-way analysis of variance (ANOVA) was used to find out whether differences in consumer conceptions, of what is normal and of what is green, are related to demographic variables. Significant differences ($p < .05$) were identified and interpreted by examination of the post-hoc multiple comparisons of the means. Only the significant findings ($p < .05$) from these analyses are presented in Table 4 (social class), Table 5 (age), Table 6 (marital status), Table 7 (working status), Table 8 (region), and Table 9 (gender). In these tables, all of the mean differences are presented as positive figures, indicating that the first independent group understands the activity to be either *more* 'normal' or *more* 'green' than the second independent group.

Analysis and interpretation of the data in Tables 4 to 9 facilitates the identification of specific demographic groups that could be targeted in sustainability marketing campaigns. As an example, this analysis and the resulting targeting strategy is

**Table 5** Significant ANOVA results by age.

| Dependent variables | df | F | F sig. | Independent groups | Mean differences | Sig. |
|---|---|---|---|---|---|---|
| *Normal* | | | | | | |
| Buying bottled water | 5 | 6.395 | .000 | 16−24/65+ | .626 | .000 |
| | | | | 25−34/65+ | .534 | .001 |
| | | | | 35−44/65+ | .481 | .001 |
| Buying organic food | 5 | 6.368 | .000 | 16−24/35−44 | .413 | .010 |
| | | | | 16−24/45−54 | .444 | .006 |
| | | | | 16−24/65+ | .547 | .000 |
| Driving a car | 5 | 8.666 | .000 | 16−24/65+ | .558 | .000 |
| | | | | 25−34/65+ | .468 | .000 |
| | | | | 35−44/65+ | .458 | .000 |
| | | | | 55−64/65+ | .329 | .009 |
| Flying overseas for holidays | 5 | 4.814 | .000 | 16−24/65+ | .468 | .001 |
| | | | | 25−34/65+ | .338 | .036 |
| | | | | 35−44/65+ | .406 | .002 |
| | | | | 55−64/65+ | .394 | .006 |
| Leaving the TV on standby | 5 | 7.088 | .000 | 16−24/65+ | .606 | .000 |
| | | | | 25−34/65+ | .589 | .000 |
| | | | | 35−44/65+ | .597 | .000 |
| | | | | 45−54/65+ | .426 | .014 |
| | | | | 55−64/65+ | .520 | .000 |
| Shower/bath on alternate days | 5 | 3.470 | .004 | 65+/35−44 | .426 | .003 |
| Using energy-saving light bulbs | 5 | 3.729 | .002 | 25−34/65+ | .283 | .024 |
| | | | | 35−44/65+ | .262 | .024 |
| Using patio heaters at home | 5 | 4.106 | .001 | 16−24/45−65 | .442 | .014 |
| | | | | 65+/45−54 | .413 | .008 |
| Using public transport | 5 | 6.750 | .000 | 16−24/45−54 | .592 | .000 |
| | | | | 16−24/55−64 | .535 | .002 |
| | | | | 35−44/45−54 | .381 | .002 |
| | | | | 65+/55−64 | .436 | .004 |
| *Green* | | | | | | |
| Buying organic food | 5 | 9.074 | .000 | 16−24/65+ | .367 | .022 |
| | | | | 25−34/65+ | .484 | .000 |
| | | | | 35−44/65+ | .449 | .000 |
| | | | | 45−54/65+ | .323 | .033 |
| Using a tumble drier to dry clothes | 5 | 6.895 | .000 | 16−24/25−34 | .386 | .002 |
| | | | | 16−24/35−44 | .325 | .048 |

(*Continued*)

# CONTEMPORARY ISSUES IN GREEN AND ETHICAL MARKETING

**Table 5** (Continued).

| Dependent variables | df | F | F sig. | Independent groups | Mean differences | Sig. |
|---|---|---|---|---|---|---|
| | | | | 65+/35−44 | .295 | .021 |
| | | | | 65+/45−54 | .434 | .000 |
| | | | | 65+/55−64 | .372 | .002 |
| Leaving the tv on standby | 5 | 3.006 | .011 | 16−24/45−54 | .310 | .023 |
| | | | | 65+/45−54 | .256 | .037 |
| Monitoring electricity consumption | 5 | 4.352 | .001 | 16−24/65+ | .278 | .053 |
| | | | | 25−34/65+ | .418 | .000 |
| Recycling | 5 | 4.490 | .000 | 16−24/65+ | .259 | .012 |
| | | | | 25−34/65+ | .268 | .005 |
| | | | | 35−44/65+ | .199 | .049 |
| Using energy-saving light bulbs | 5 | 5.823 | .000 | 16−24/65+ | .244 | .031 |
| | | | | 25−34/65+ | .339 | .000 |
| | | | | 35−44/65+ | .339 | .000 |
| Using patio heaters at home | 5 | 13.362 | .000 | 16−24/65+ | .749 | .000 |
| | | | | 16−24/35−44 | .707 | .000 |
| | | | | 16−24/45−54 | .810 | .000 |
| | | | | 16−24/35−44 | .417 | .008 |
| | | | | 25−34/55−64 | .478 | .002 |
| | | | | 35−44/55−64 | .481 | .000 |
| | | | | 65+/45−54 | .439 | .002 |
| | | | | 65+/55−64 | .542 | .000 |
| Using public transport | 5 | 2.745 | .018 | 55−65/16−24 | .344 | .014 |

described in detail with respect to buying bottled water. The frequency distribution analysis (Tables 2 and 3) indicates that opinion is divided both about whether 'buying bottled water' is normal, and about whether it is green, indicating that there are different groups of consumers who could potentially be targeted. ANOVA analysis (Table 5) indicates that buying bottled water is more likely to be seen a normal behaviour among younger people. (In addition, Table 6 suggests buying bottled water is more likely to be considered normal among people who are single, married, or living as married, than those who are divorced, separated, or widowed, but this would be a difficult targeting criterion.) The analysis suggests that marketing communications that position buying bottled water as not normal should be targeted at younger people, for example using cinema, radio, or Internet media. The analysis (Table 4) also shows that social class groups C2DE and people who are not working are more likely to think that buying bottled water is green, suggesting that informational material should be targeted at these groups, for instance by sponsoring an appropriate daytime TV soap.

CONTEMPORARY ISSUES IN GREEN AND ETHICAL MARKETING

**Table 6** Significant ANOVA results by marital status.

| Dependent variables | df | F | F sig. | Independent groups | Mean differences | Sig. |
|---|---|---|---|---|---|---|
| *Normal* | | | | | | |
| Buying bottled water | 2 | 5.639 | .004 | Single1/Single2 | .116 | .005 |
| | | | | Married/Single2 | .289 | .010 |
| Buying organic food | 2 | 8.100 | .000 | Single1/Married | .299 | .001 |
| | | | | Single/Single2 | .376 | .001 |
| Driving a car | 2 | 7.605 | .001 | Married/Single2 | .299 | .003 |
| Eating meat or fish | 2 | 5.474 | .004 | Single1/Single2 | .180 | .006 |
| | | | | Married/Single2 | .182 | .006 |
| Recycling | 2 | 3.546 | .029 | Married/Single1 | .145 | .022 |
| Using public transport | 2 | 13.786 | .000 | Single1/Married | .440 | .000 |
| | | | | Single2/Married | .299 | .000 |
| *Green* | | | | | | |
| Drying clothes in a tumble drier | 2 | 4.765 | .009 | Single1/married | .165 | .046 |
| | | | | Single2/Married | .186 | .031 |
| Flying overseas on holiday | 2 | 4.608 | .010 | Single1/Married | .212 | .011 |
| Using energy-saving light bulbs | 2 | 5.488 | .004 | Married/Single2 | .199 | .003 |
| Using patio heaters at home | 2 | 11.179 | .000 | Single1/Married | .396 | .000 |
| | | | | Single2/Married | .247 | .047 |

*Note*: Single1 = never married; Single2 = widowed/divorced/separated.

### *Marketing strategies*

Positioning, reinforcing and targeting strategies for each activity researched are detailed in Table 10. There are two generic marketing strategies for mainstream sustainability-related behaviours: (1) position as green and normal or (2) position as not green and not normal. Thus sustainability marketing would generally encourage the adoption of green activities by positioning them as both normal and green, and discourage the adoption or encourage rejection of less green ones, by positioning them as not green and not normal. In some cases, this will involve supporting and maintaining current positioning; in others, repositioning is required. For example, Figure 1 shows that driving a car is understood to be not green and normal. The principle of conformity suggests that the fact that driving a car is understood to be normal increases the likelihood that people will conform to this way of doing things, despite their belief that it is not green. To put this another way, people's assessment of driving as normal provides a positive feedback loop that reinforces the propensity for people to do things in this way. From a social practice theory perspective, one of the meanings of the practice of driving (in this context, normal) itself serves to

## CONTEMPORARY ISSUES IN GREEN AND ETHICAL MARKETING

**Table 7** Significant ANOVA results by working status.

| Dependent variables | df | F | F sig. | Independent groups | Mean differences | Sig. |
|---|---|---|---|---|---|---|
| *Normal* | | | | | | |
| Driving a car | 2 | 4.614 | .010 | Part time/Not working | .254 | .013 |
| Flying overseas for holidays | 2 | 7.030 | .001 | Full time/Not working | .240 | .003 |
| | | | | Part time/Not working | .289 | .011 |
| Leaving the TV on standby | 2 | 9.414 | .000 | Full time/Not working | .338 | .000 |
| | | | | Part time/Not working | .355 | .003 |
| Shower/bath alternate days | 2 | 6.543 | .002 | Not working/Full time | .211 | .025 |
| | | | | Not working/Part time | .375 | .003 |
| Using patio heaters at home | 2 | 4.084 | .017 | Not working/Full time | .212 | .025 |
| Using public transport | 2 | 5.769 | .003 | Not working/Full time | .242 | .006 |
| | | | | Part time/Not working | .274 | .049 |
| *Green* | | | | | | |
| Buying bottled water | 2 | 5.068 | .006 | Not working/Full time | .241 | .004 |
| Buying organic food | 2 | 9.074 | .000 | Full time/Not working | .178 | .036 |
| | | | | Part time/Full time | .241 | .048 |
| | | | | Part time/Not working | .418 | .000 |
| Drying clothes in a tumble drier | 2 | 3.881 | .007 | Not working/Full time | .174 | .012 |
| | | | | Not working/Part time | .195 | .060 |
| Flying overseas on holiday | 2 | 4.073 | .017 | Not working/Full time | .173 | .016 |
| Monitoring electricity | 2 | 3.274 | .038 | Part time/Not working | .216 | .030 |
| Using patio heaters at home | 2 | 7.319 | .001 | Not working/Full time | .285 | .001 |
| | | | | Not working/Part time | .264 | .040 |

reinforce the habitual and taken-for-granted practice. Since driving a car is not green, the task for marketing is to reposition driving a car as not normal and to reinforce its current positioning as not green (see Table 10). This involves moving 'driving a car' from the 'normal-not green' quadrant to the 'not normal-not green' quadrant. At the

# CONTEMPORARY ISSUES IN GREEN AND ETHICAL MARKETING

**Table 8** Significant ANOVA results by region.

| Dependent variables | df | F | Sig. | Independent groups | Mean differences | Sig. |
|---|---|---|---|---|---|---|
| *Normal* | | | | | | |
| Buying organic food | 2 | 5.575 | .004 | South/North | .257 | .006 |
| | | | | South/Midlands | .220 | .021 |
| Taking your own shopping bags | 2 | 4.886 | .008 | South/North | .257 | .006 |
| *Green* | | | | | | |
| Driving a car | 2 | 4.244 | .015 | Midlands/North | .168 | .048 |
| | | | | Midlands/South | .189 | .019 |
| Flying overseas on holiday | 2 | 5.075 | .006 | South/North | .226 | .005 |
| Leaving the TV on standby | 2 | 3.303 | .037 | Midlands/North | .162 | .038 |
| Taking your own shopping bags | 2 | 3.809 | .023 | Midlands/South | .135 | .019 |
| Using public transport | 2 | 3.002 | .050 | North/Midlands | .161 | .047 |

**Table 9** Significant ANOVA results by gender.

| Dependent variables | df | F | Sig. | Mean differences |
|---|---|---|---|---|
| *Normal* | | | | |
| Eating meat or fish | 1 | 8.300 | .004 | .129 (F/M) |
| Littering | 1 | 8.592 | .003 | .235 (M/F) |
| Monitoring electricity | 1 | 5.606 | .018 | .167 (F/M) |
| Recycling | 1 | 8.663 | .003 | .129 (F/M) |
| Taking your own shopping bags | 1 | 9.838 | .002 | .180 (F/M) |
| *Green* | | | | |
| Drying clothes in a tumble drier | 1 | 8.895 | .004 | .161 (M/F) |
| Taking your own shopping bags | 1 | 8.961 | .003 | .125 (F/M) |
| Using public transport | 1 | 12.304 | .000 | .193 (F/M) |

same time, an associated task for marketing is to position more sustainable modes of transport as normal.

By contrast, Figure 1 also shows us that buying organic food is understood to be not normal and green. Here, the principle of conformity suggests that, despite the fact that buying organic food is understood to be green, the fact that it is also understood to be not normal provides an unhelpful feedback loop inhibiting practice change. In this instance, the task for marketing is to reposition buying organic food as normal and to reinforce its positioning as green, thus moving it from the 'not normal-green' quadrant to the 'normal-green' quadrant (see Table 10).

For most of the activities researched, undifferentiated, mass marketing is recommended because Tables 2 and 3 indicate that there is a broad consensus of

**Table 10** Marketing strategies.

| Activity | Strategy | Targeting (very normal-not at all normal) | Targeting (very green-not at all green) |
|---|---|---|---|
| Recycling | Maintain current positioning | Mass target | Mass target |
| Monitoring electricity consumption | Reinforce positioning as normal Maintain positioning as green | AB | Mass target |
| Showering/bathing on alternate days | Reinforce current positioning | ABC1, working | Mass target |
| Taking your own shopping bags to the shops | Maintain current positioning | Mass target | Mass target |
| Using energy-saving light bulbs | Maintain current positioning | Mass target | Mass target |
| Using public transport whenever possible | Reinforce positioning as normal Maintain positioning as green | ABC1, 45−65, working | Mass target |
| Buying organic food | Reposition as normal Reinforce green positioning | 25+, Midland, North, not single | Not working |
| Eating meat or fish | Reposition as no longer normal Reposition as not green | Mass target | C1DE |
| Driving a car | Reposition as no longer normal Reinforce not green positioning | Mass target | Mass target |
| Drying clothes in a tumble dryer | Reposition as no longer normal Maintain not green positioning | Mass target | Mass target |
| Flying overseas for holidays | Reposition as no longer normal Reinforce not green positioning | ABC1, working, >65 | Mass target |
| Leaving the TV on standby | Reposition as not normal Maintain not green positioning | Younger, working, ABC1 | Mass target |
| Buying bottled water | Reposition as not normal Reinforce not green positioning | Younger | C2DE, not working |
| Littering | Reinforce positioning as not normal Maintain not green positioning | Male | Mass target |
| Using patio heaters at home | Reinforce not normal positioning Reinforce not green positioning | 16−24, 65+, AB | Single, not working, 35−64 |

opinion between consumers. However, where the frequencies indicate that there are divergent views among consumers, relevant targeting variables identified in the ANOVA tests are shown. Note the analysis indicates that targets for changing conceptions about what is normal and about what is green may be different. For instance, the message that using patio heaters at home is not normal should be directed at those who are under 25 or over 65, and from AB social groups, while the message that it is not green should be directed at those who are 35–64, single, or not working.

# Discussion and conclusions

This study works on two levels. On one level, it is a study of 15 specific sustainability-related activities, but on another level, it tests a simple instrument for assessing (and, in longitudinal studies, tracking) the extent to which activities are thought to be green and normal. The low levels of 'don't know' responses indicate that respondents found the survey relatively easy to answer, and the generally low level of 'neither' responses indicates that in most cases they found it easy to categorise activities as either green or not green, normal or not normal. This suggests that the research instrument was effective despite its relative simplicity. In addition, the graphical representation of the research findings (Figure 1) is a useful tool for understanding consumer conceptions. This research method lends itself to extension to other activities but also to products and brands. Manufacturers could use a similar survey to identify the extent to which brands within specific markets are seen to be normal, and use data to inform their marketing strategies. The principle of conformity suggests that positioning a brand as normal should encourage adoption. This is particularly relevant for green products and brands which are often positioned as relevant only to a small niche of very green consumers.

An important finding of this research is that consumer conceptions of what is green are generally consistent and correspond with prevailing views on sustainability. This indicates that consumers already know what is green or not green, so that their failure to adopt green behaviours cannot just be ascribed to knowledge deficit and corrected by informational campaigns. It also supports the claim by Rettie et al. (2011) that consumers generally do not attempt to assess whether behaviours are green on a case-by-case basis, but instead rely on socially shared connotations. Three activities were rated highly on both the green and normal scales (Figure 1): 'recycling', 'taking one's own shopping bags', and 'using energy-saving light bulbs'. These are all areas in which there have been large-scale government and commercial initiatives. They are also activities where what other people do (or what is normal) is evidenced by material objects (recycling bins on neighbours' doorsteps, taking shopping bags to stores, the peculiar design of energy-saving bulbs). However, even for activity areas where there has been relatively little publicity such as showering on alternate days or using bottled water, consumers generally understand whether activities are green or not green. The exception was eating meat or fish, where polarised opinions and a high 'neither' response suggests that consumers do not see eating meat or fish as a green issue. This is one activity which could warrant an informational campaign.

In contrast to the consensus on green issues, for most of the activities tested, consumers were polarised about whether they were normal or not. This can be explained in terms of different reference groups. Research on the social norm approach indicates that people are more likely to be influenced by the behaviour of close reference groups (Lewis & Neighbors, 2006). The survey asked, 'To what extent do you think that these activities are normal (what people generally do)?', and in answering this question, it is likely that respondents related the question to their relevant reference groups. Thus one would expect younger people to report norms among young people, while older respondents reported norms within their own age group. This helps to explain why responses on the normal scale were frequently related to demographic characteristics. The survey used here had a limited number of demographic variables. In future research, these could be extended to include the presence of young/older children, ethnicity, and other factors which would help to define specific reference groups.

It is possible that research attempts to identify 'the green consumer' have been unsuccessful because there is no green consumer: consumers are green in relation to some activities and not others. The identification of demographic variables relevant to green consumption may have been confounded because the demographic factors relevant to one area of consumer green behaviour are not relevant to another. This research also indicates that segmenting in terms of self-perception as green is likely to be futile because most consumers think they are green. However, this research shows that where differentiated marketing is appropriate, profiling in terms of consumer conceptions of which activities are green and which are normal may offer an alternative basis for targeting sustainability marketing.

The paper suggests specific marketing strategies that could be used for the activities researched. Although these are summarised in a rather simplistic way, it is recognised that some of these strategies are very ambitious and present major problems. First, in many cases, the prevailing view of what is normal is correct: most people drive a car, tumble-dry clothes, and so on. Consequently, it would be impossible to reposition these activities instantly. Simply claiming that these activities are not normal would be dishonest and unbelievable. A more realistic objective would be to attempt to change the image of the activity gradually, moving conceptions towards the 'not normal' end of the scale, rather than an immediate repositioning. Marketing campaigns could focus on substitute activities (public transport, line-drying, holidays in the UK, tap water, etc.), emphasising their normality with celebrity and authority-figure endorsements. An alternative tactic is product placement ('behaviour placement'). This is increasingly recognised as an effective mechanic in the marketing of brands and was legalised in the UK Audiovisual Media Services (Product Placement) Regulations in 2010. This could involve, for instance, featuring more sustainable alternatives in the media whenever feasible: using buses and trains instead of cars, drinking tap water instead of bottled, taking local holidays, or, more ambitiously, storylines and discussion about sustainability-related behaviours. In the UK, radio and TV programmes such as *The Archers* and *Casualty* have in the past been used to promote social messages relating to agriculture and health. Many soaps lend themselves to sustainability themes and could endorse sustainable behaviours as normal or not normal as appropriate.

Equally, marketing could support social normalisation through the simple depiction of sustainable activities as normal. This approach is employed in a Royal Borough of Kingston campaign,[2] featuring simple messages such as 'We walk to school', 'We drink tap water', 'We buy things that last', and 'We give furniture a second life'. At the same time, a similar approach could be used to challenge concepts

[2] http://ww2.defra.gov.uk

CONTEMPORARY ISSUES IN GREEN AND ETHICAL MARKETING

of unsustainable activities as normal, recasting them as not normal or – to draw on the words of one of the participants in Rettie et al.'s (2011) research – 'offensive'.

Previous research (Rettie et al., 2011) suggests that thinking that an activity is normal or not normal may constrain sustainability-related behaviour change. This research provides a simple method for identifying the extent to which more and less sustainable activities have been normalised, so that consumer conceptions of normality can be mapped and tracked over time. The study also indicates that in many cases what is considered normal behaviour differs between different segments of the population, and it is therefore often possible to identify relevant demographic variables that can be used in targeted social marketing campaigns designed to change these conceptions

In particular, the research shows how a focus on consumer understandings of what is and what is not normal facilitates the selection of appropriate sustainability marketing strategies for particular consumer behaviours, and enables the identification of specific demographic targets for these marketing tasks.

## Limitations and suggestions for future research

This research has a number of limitations. Telephone surveys can incur mode and sample biases. The design of the survey may have created a framing cognitive bias (Tversky & Kahneman, 1981) or an order effect bias (Landon, 1971) by asking repeated questions about whether activities were normal or green. As the primary objective was to compare ratings, the scale used was consistent, with very normal/green as the first options for each question.

In this paper, activities have been categorised in a rather simplistic way as green or not green. It is recognised that this is an over-simplification; activities baldly described as 'driving a car' and as 'not green' cover a range of activities from car-pooling for essential journeys, using fuel efficient hybrid cars, to single occupants of $4 \times 4$ vehicles on leisure trips. These nuances and shades of green have inevitably been glossed in the approach taken here; this does not mean that they are considered irrelevant.

The research presented here offers many avenues for future research. The concept of social normalisation suggests that conceptions of what is normal will change over time, both overall and within specific demographic profiles. Consequently, the task for marketing will change over time too. The approach described here provides a means for tracking the positioning of activities over time, and the researchers plan to repeat the research on an annual basis. There are also opportunities for replication in other countries, enabling cross-cultural comparisons of the positions and trajectories of behaviours, products, and services. This research included a limited range of activities, but the technique could easily be extended to include other activities, or used to track the normalisation and green status of brands and products, with longitudinal tracking to gauge the success of marketing strategies.

More substantively, the research could be strengthened by incorporating into the survey questions about behaviour. In this way, relationships between understandings of activities as normal and behaviour could be analysed. There is also scope for qualitative research to illuminate further the ways in which conceptions of what is normal shape behaviour, and to explore how these conceptions can be shaped by the media and advertising campaigns.

## Acknowledgements

We are grateful to Chris Barnham for his contribution to the development of the survey instrument, and to everyone who participated in the pilot studies. We are also grateful to Kingston University for funding the research, and to GfK NoP for conducting the fieldwork.

## References

Abela, A.V. (2006). Marketing and consumerism: A response to O'Shaughnessy and O'Shaughnessy. *European Journal of Marketing*, 40(1/2), 5–16.

Ajzen, I. (1985). From intentions to actions: A Theory of Planned Behavior. In J. Kuhl & J. Beckmann (Eds.), *Action-control: From cognition to behavior* pp. 11–39. Heidelberg, Germany: Springer.

Asch, S.E. (1976). Studies of independence and conformity: A minority of one against a unanimous majority. *Psychological Monographs*, 70, 1–70.

Bamberg, S., & Moser, G. (2007). Twenty years after Hines, Hungerford, and Tomera: A new meta-analysis of psycho-social determinants of pro-environmental behavior. *Journal of Environmental Psychology*, 27(1), 14–25.

Belz, F., & Peattie, K. (2009). *Sustainability marketing a global perspective*. Chichester, UK: Wiley-Blackwell.

Blake, J. (1999). Overcoming the 'value–action gap' in environmental policy: Tensions between national policy and local experience. *Local Environment*, 4(3), 257–278.

Brennan, L. & Binney, W.M. (2008). Is it green marketing, greenwash or hogwash? We need to know if we want to change things. In S. Jones (Ed.), *Partnerships, proof and practice – International nonprofit and social marketing conference*. Wollongong, Australia: University of Wollongong.

Bronfenbrenner, U. (1979). *The ecology of human development*. Cambridge, MA: Harvard University Press.

Carrigan, M., & Attala, A. (2001). The myth of the ethical consumer: Do ethics matter in purchase behavior? *Journal of Consumer Marketing*, 18(7), 560–577.

Chamorro, A., Rubio, S., & Miranda, F.J. (2009). Characteristics of research on green marketing. *Business Strategy and the Environment*, 18(4), 223–239.

Charter, M., & Polonsky, M.J. (1999). *Green marketing: A global perspective on green marketing practices*. Sheffield, UK: Greenleaf Publications.

Collins English Dictionary. (2009). Greenwash. In *Collins English dictionary – Complete and unabridged* (10th ed.). London: Collins.

DECC. (2009, June 8). Minutes of the meeting of the Advisory Forum on the Quality Assurance Scheme for Carbon Offsetting. Retrieved 7 February 2012 from http://tinyurl.com/3439r8l

DECC. (2010, January 26). Minutes of the third meeting of the Advisory Forum on the Quality Assurance Scheme for Carbon Offsetting. Retrieved 7 February 2012 from http://tinyurl.com/2wy57tv

Defra. (2005). *Changing behaviour through policy making*. London: Defra.

Defra. (2006a). *Evidence based policy making*. London: Defra.

Defra. (2006b). An environmental behaviours strategy for Defra: A scoping report, December 2006. Retrieved from http://tinyurl.com/357cxwg

Defra. (2008). *A framework for pro-environmental behaviours*. London: Defra.

Defra, & Collier, A. (2010). Understanding and influencing behaviours: A review of social research, economics and policy making in Defra, February 2010. Retrieved 7 February 2012 from http://tinyurl.com/86uogzm

Diamantopoulos, A., Schlegelmilch, B.B., Sinkovics, R.R., & Bohlen, G.M. (2003). Can socio-demographics still play a role in profiling green consumers? A review of the evidence and an empirical investigation. *Journal of Business Research*, *56*(6), 465–480.

El-Ansary, A.I. (1974). Towards a definition of social and societal marketing. *Journal of the Academy of Marketing Science*, *2*(2), 316–321.

Finisterra do Paço, A.M., & Raposo, M.L.B. (2010). Green consumer market segmentation: Empirical findings from Portugal. *International Journal of Consumer Studies*, *34*(4), 429–436.

Follows, S.B., & Jobber, D. (2000). Environmentally responsible purchase behavior: A test of a consumer model. *European Journal of Marketing*, *34*(5/6), 723–746.

Fraj, E., & Martinez, E. (2007). Ecological consumer behavior: An empirical analysis. *International Journal of Consumer Studies*, *31*(1), 26–33.

Fuller, D.A. (1999). *Sustainable marketing: Managerial-ecological issues*. Thousand Oaks, CA: Sage.

GfK Group. (2010). Green gauge report. Retrieved 7 February 2012 from http://www.gfk.com

Grant, J. (2007). *The green marketing manifesto*. Chichester, UK: Wiley-Blackwell.

Gregson, J., Foerster, S., Orr, R., Jones, L., Benedict, J., Clarke, B., et al. (2001). System, environmental, and policy changes: Using the social-ecological model as a framework for evaluating nutrition education and social marketing programs with low-income audiences. *Journal of Nutrition Education*, *33*(1), 4–15.

Goldstein, N.J., Cialdini, R.B., & Griskevicius, V. (2008). A room with a viewpoint: Using social norms to motivate environmental conservation in hotels. *Journal of Consumer Research*, *35*(3), 472–483.

HM Government. (2009, July). *The UK low carbon transition plan: National strategy for climate and energy*. Retrieved 7 February 2012 from http://tinyurl.com/6z5p6yr

Jackson, T. (2005). *Motivating sustainable consumption: A review of evidence on consumer behavior and behavioural change*. London: Policy Studies Institute.

Jones, P., Clarke-Hill, C., Comfort, D., & Hillier, D. (2007). Marketing and sustainability. *Marketing Intelligence and Planning*, *26*(2), 123–130.

Kotler, P. (1972). What consumerism means for marketers. *Harvard Business School Review*, *50*(5), 54–57.

Landon, E.L., Jr. (1971). Order bias, the ideal rating, and the semantic differential. *Journal of Marketing Research*, *8*(3), 375–378.

Lee, K. (2008). Opportunities for green marketing: Young consumers. *Marketing Intelligence and Planning*, *26*(6), 573–586.

Lewis, M.A., & Neighbors, C. (2006). Social norms approaches using descriptive drinking norms education: A review of the research on personalised normative feedback. *Journal of American College Health*, *54*, 213–218.

Milgram, S. (1974). Obedience to Authority. New York, NY: Harper & Row.

Mintu, A.T., & Lozada, H.R. (1993). Green marketing education: A call for action. *Marketing Education Review*, *3*, 17–23.

Mostafa, M.M. (2007). A hierarchical analysis of the green consciousness of the Egyptian consumer. *Psychology and Marketing*, *24*(5), 445–473.

Nolan, J.M., Schultz, W.P., Cialdini, R.B., Goldstein, N.J., & Griskevicius, V. (2008). Normative social influence is underdetected. *Personal Social Psychology Bulletin*, *34*(7), 913–923.

Peattie, K. (1995). *Environmental marketing management: Meeting the green challenge*. London: Pitman.

Peattie, K., & Crane, A. (2005). Green marketing: Legend, myth, farce or prophesy? *Qualitative Marketing Research*, *8*(4), 357–370.

Peattie, K., & Peattie, S. (2009). Social marketing: A pathway to consumption reduction? *Journal of Business Research*, *62*(2), 260–268.

Perkins, H.W. (2003). *The social norms approach to preventing school and college age substance abuse*. San Francisco: Jossey-Bass.

Pickett-Baker, J., & Ozaki, R. (2008). Pro-environmental products: Marketing influence on consumer purchase decision. *Journal of Consumer Marketing*, 25(5), 281–293.

Prothero, A. (1990). Green consumerism and the societal marketing concept: Marketing strategies for the 1990s. *Journal of Marketing Management*, 6(2), 87–103.

Rettie, R., Barnham, C., & Burchell, K. (2011, July). *Social normalisation and consumer behaviour: Using marketing to make green normal* Working Research Paper 8. London: Kingston University Business School.

Schatzki, T.R. (1996). *Social practices: A Wittgensteinian approach to human activity and the social*. Cambridge, England: Cambridge University Press.

Schatzki, T.R. (2005). Peripheral vision: The sites of organizations. *Organization Studies*, 26(3), 465–484.

Schlegelmilch, B.B., Bohlen, G.M., & Diamantopoulos, A. (1996). The link between green purchasing decisions and measures of environmental consciousness. *European Journal of Marketing*, 30(5), 35–55.

Sheth, J., & Parvatiyar, A. (1995). Ecological imperatives and the role of marketing. In M.J. Polonsky & A.T. Mintu-Wimsatt (Eds.), *Environmental marketing: Strategies, practice, theory and research* pp. 3–20. New York: Haworth Press.

Shove, E. (2003). Comfort, Cleanliness and Convenience: The Social Organisation of Normality. Oxford: Berg.

Shove, E., & Pantzar, M. (2005). Consumers, producers and practices: Understanding the invention and reinvention of Nordic walking. *Journal of Consumer Culture*, 5(1), 43–64.

Stearns, P.N. (2001). *Consumerism in world history: The global transformation of desire*. New York: Routledge.

Szmigin, I., Carrigan, M., & McEachern M.G. (2009). The conscious consumer: Taking a flexible approach to ethical behavior. *International Journal of Consumer Studies*, 33(2), 224–231.

Tversky, A., & Kahneman, D. (1981). The framing of decisions and the psychology of choice. *Science*, 211(4481), 453–458

United Nations Environment Programme. (2005). *Talk the walk: Advancing sustainable lifestyles through marketing and communications. The global compact and utopies*. Paris: United Nations Environment Programme.

van Dam, Y.K., & Apeldoorn, P.A.C. (1996). Sustainable marketing. *Journal of Macromarketing*, 16(2), 45–56.

Warde, A. (2005). Consumption and theories of practice. *Journal of Consumer Culture*, 5(2), 131–150.

Wilson, M. (2008). Environmental claims in advertising: Is green a grey area? How the advertising standards authority rules on environmental marketing claims. World Advertising Research Centre Online Report. Retrieved 7 February 2012 from http://www.warc.com

Young, W., Hwang, K., McDonald, S., & Oates, C.J. (2010). Sustainable consumption: Green consumer behavior when purchasing products. *Sustainable Development*, 18(1), 21–31.

# Individual strategies for sustainable consumption

Seonaidh McDonald, *The Robert Gordon University, UK*
Caroline J. Oates, *Sheffield University, UK*
Panayiota J. Alevizou, *Sheffield University, UK*
C. William Young, *University of Leeds, UK*
Kumju Hwang, *Chung-Ang University, Korea*

---

**Abstract** Consumers have a key role to play in meeting government targets for reduced energy consumption, more sustainable waste management practices, and lifestyles with fewer environmental consequences. We discuss some of the assumptions underpinning academic debates about sustainable consumption and describe a research design which has helped us move beyond some of the less helpful conventions. We interviewed consumers in order to obtain a detailed understanding of several of their recent (non-)purchase processes. We identified three groups who have distinct strategies for greening their lifestyles: Translators, Exceptors, and Selectors. We illustrate these groups using empirical data. This detailed understanding of how individuals approach the problem of greening not only provides new insight into how the problem of consumption may be approached in conceptual and practical terms, but also explains some of the difficulties encountered by previous research. We revisit the literature to examine the challenges that this typology offers extant ways of thinking about 'the green consumer'. We identify ways in which we might influence the groups in our typology through marketing strategies and policy initiatives.

---

## Introduction

There are many approaches that governments and industry can take to reduce environmental degradation. However, one of the most difficult issues to address is how to change the day-to-day behaviour of individuals. Peattie (2001) notes that, 'the consumption undertaken by private households accounts for a large proportion of the economy's environmental impact' (p. 197), and some estimate that this proportion could be as high as 30–40% (Grunert, 1993). Although governments, NGOs, academics, and marketers are agreed that more people need to engage in a higher number of environmental activities (Defra, 2010; Dupré et al., 2005; Jackson, 2009; United States Environmental Protection Agency, 2010), research has failed to find straightforward ways to achieve this. More than 30 years ago, researchers began to address this problem by trying to identify the green consumer. Identification of groups of consumers who act in similar ways to each other is a cornerstone of marketing theory and practice (Piercy & Morgan, 1993), although it is not uncontested (Firat & Schultz, 1997). Segmentation of the public into well-defined groups whose behaviour or concerns can be predicted gives marketers and policymakers a basis on which to design interventions. However, there is considerable evidence that both identification and intervention strategies have failed to bring about the significant changes desired by green marketers and policymakers. In this paper, we will argue that by taking a grounded, qualitative research approach, we have found that, rather than demonstrating that one way of describing green consumers is better than all the others, what we need is a more complex conceptualisation of individuals working towards more sustainable consumption that combines many of the existing lines of enquiry and leads to a richer picture of the green consumer.

In the discussion that follows, we examine ideas from several social science literatures pertaining to individual responses to sustainable consumption. We begin our discussion by noting that individuals engaging in sustainable consumption behaviours are labelled using different terms depending on the norms of the literature of which the study is a part. For example, within the sustainable development literature, it is quite normal to refer to 'ethical consumers' and for this to mean consumers who prefer products or services which do least damage to the environment, as well as those which support forms of social justice (Harrison, Newholm, & Shaw, 2005). In the marketing literature, however, these same consumers would be termed 'green consumers', although this label would also carry an assumption that this description would include consumers who were interested in ethical issues such as Fairtrade (Solomon, Bamossy, Askegaard, 1999). In other words, although these discourses use different terms to signify individuals who embrace the ideals of sustainable consumption, we take these terms here to have the same broad meanings. For consumers who consistently do not engage with or have no interest in such issues, we use the term 'grey' consumers (Peattie, 2001; Wagner, 1997).

## Green consumers: Assumptions underpinning segmentation approaches

### Green is black and white

Previous research has tried to classify green and grey consumers as two separate groups of people. In the social psychology literature, for example, the notion of voluntary simplifiers has been used to distinguish between people who choose to reduce their 'expenditures on consumer goods and services, and to cultivate non-materialistic sources of satisfaction and meaning' (Etzioni, 1998, p. 620) and non-voluntary simplifiers who do not (Shaw & Newholm, 2002). In the recycling literature, a similar dichotomy has been set up. Many researchers have sought to categorise people as recyclers and non-recyclers (De Young, 1989; McDonald & Oates, 2003). There is also a significant amount of work in the marketing literature which characterises consumers as either grey or green (Wagner, 1997). Each of these strands of literature conceptualises these categories as mutually exclusive, black and white (even good and bad), and to a large extent homogenous. Even where researchers complexify this work by characterising multiple groups within the population (see below for further discussion of typologies), the individuals within these groups are discussed as if they are broadly similar. This is a quantitative research convention, but it does raise issues about how we currently conceptualise and research the problem of sustainable consumption.

## Green can be segmented

In both the marketing and recycling fields, the process of trying to populate these categories began by attempts to label them according to their demographic, socio-economic, or psychographic characteristics. More sophisticated work tries to combine a wide variety of these factors in order to build up a picture of the green or ethical consumer (see, e.g., Tiltman, 2007). This is an attractive strategy for both marketers and policymakers for a number of reasons. First, it is in line with many of the research norms around the promotion of goods and services. Second, these data (particularly demographics and socio-economic indicators) are easily obtained. Third, if, for example, recyclers can be shown to be female or better educated, this information would lend itself to clearer promotions strategies which target specific segments of the population. However, this segmentation approach did not produce clear evidence which allowed researchers to identify these groups consistently or reliably in practice (Peattie, 2001; Roberts, 1996; Straughan & Roberts, 1999; Teisl, Rubin, & Noblet, 2008; Van Liere & Dunlap, 1980; Wagner, 1997). There is resonance here with wider critiques of segmentation within the marketing literature (Firat & Schultz, 1997).

## Green can be typed

Another approach to investigating the problem of identifying green consumers is to type them. Here, we distinguish between what we are calling 'segmentation' which involves dividing the population (or in some cases, just green consumers) into groups according to characteristics which can be determined relatively objectively (such as age, gender, income, housing type, level of education), whereas what we are calling a typology means that groups are distinguished from each other using more subjective notions such as reported behaviour, intentions, and values. This is an important distinction because it means that the categories are no longer conceptually simple. Although these more complex ideas might help researchers understand the green consumer better, these insights will mean that they are harder to reach using traditional promotional tools and approaches. The development of typologies can be done statistically (e.g. Gilg, Barr, & Ford, 2005) or through more qualitative methods (e.g. Moisander, 2001, cited in Autio, Heiskanen, & Heinonen, 2009).

The problems associated with the simple either/or categories discussed above led some commentators to develop new, intermediate categories of green consumer, such as 'light' versus 'dark' green, or 'shallow' versus 'deep' green, or 'green' versus 'Green' (Dermody, 1999). Depending on how the membership of these intermediate groups is determined, these could be considered either more complex segmentation or simple typology approaches.

A wide range of bases for discriminating between different groups of green or ethical consumers can be found in the literature, and comprise two main types: behavioural and attitudinal. Some concepts, such as whether or not people act on their beliefs, offer bases for discriminating between groups that have both a behavioural and an attitudinal element. We will consider each of these ways of discriminating between groups of consumers in turn in the following sections, using studies drawn from across the social sciences for the purpose of illustration.

### Grouping individuals using behavioural constructs

The behavioural groupings consider issues such as the kinds of activities, amount of activities, and consistency of activities that are reported. These are considered here, rather than in the discussion about objective segmentation approaches above, because these studies rely on reported or hypothetical behaviour and so are considered to be subjective. In their study of 1600 households in Devon, UK, Gilg et al. (2005) found that people could be categorised by a combination of two behavioural considerations: the kinds of activities that they undertook, and how often (or consistently, see below) they performed these activities. Other studies centre on how often people undertake the same activity (Chan, 1999; Ozcaglar-Toulouse, Shiu, & Shaw, 2006), how consistently they behave (Neilssen & Scheepers, 1992; Peattie, 2001) or whether they undertake a few (different) activities or carry out a wide range of green or ethical activities (McDonald & Oates, 2006). Studies that assess a range of different kinds of activities or look at use and disposal as well as point of purchase offer a richer picture of green or ethical consumption than single-issue studies on the purchase of Fairtrade items, or recycling behaviour, for example, would allow. There is a tendency with much of the work related to examining behaviour to rely on self-reports.

### Grouping individuals using attitudinal constructs

The attitudinal bases for distinction include intentions, motivations, and beliefs or values. This category includes research that explores attitudes to social issues more generally, as well as research beliefs about specific green products or activities (Gold & Rubik, 2009).

There is a group of researchers concerned with distinguishing between consumers who feel that they can make a difference through their consumption choices (Peattie, 1999; The Roper Organization, 1992; Straughan & Roberts, 1999). There is also a number of studies that have sought to implement the ideas of Kahle (1983), Rokeach (1973), and Schwartz (1992) about consumer values in the arena of green or ethical consumption (see, e.g., Thørgersen & Ölander, 2003).

Researchers have also characterised individuals in terms of their intentions. Intentions towards sustainable consumption have been dealt with in these social science literatures in two main ways: they have been used as a proxy for action, and they have been examined in their own right. The studies which have used intentions as a proxy for actions include the many contributions to the marketing literature which, for example, asked consumers whether they would be prepared to pay a premium for green goods and services (Prothero, 1990; Rowlands, Scott, & Parker, 2003) or take part in recycling schemes (Hopper & Nielsen, 1991). Researchers were initially heartened by the overwhelmingly positive response to questions of this sort, and on the basis of this kind of work, they predicted a rise in various aspects of greener consumption (Davis, 1993; Elgin & Mitchell, 1976; Lawrence, 1993; Shama, 1985) which did not ultimately come to pass (Maniates, 2002), underlining the fact that although many aspects of sustainable consumption are endorsed by the general public, these attitudes will not necessarily translate into actions. In order to overcome the shortcomings of this methodological reliance on hypothetical behaviour (Rutherford, 1998), some researchers began to move their focus towards measuring concrete actions rather than reported or imagined future scenarios (Murphy, 2006; Tucker, 1999). Although this represents a positive step, researching actual sustainable consumption behaviours (or non-behaviours), as we shall see later from the findings discussed here, may still not be enough.

There is another strand of literature centred on intentions that uses intentions as a basis for distinguishing between different kinds of consumer and is perhaps of greater relevance. Here, rather than counting intentions to buy or not to buy green products or services, studies have sought to examine and classify different kinds of intentions; for example, McDonald, Oates, Young, and Hwang's, (2006) work on Beginner Voluntary Simplifiers or Kuijlen and van Raaij's (1979) classification of recyclers who are distinguished by their motivations.

### Single and multiple bases for distinguishing groups

Typologies may employ single or multiple bases for distinguishing between their consumer groups. The Ozcaglar-Toulouse et al. (2006) study of Fairtrade purchasing, or the Kuijlen and van Raaij (1979) typology of recycler motivations are both examples of studies which have employed a single dimension typology to group individuals. A famous example of a more complex typology from the marketing literature is the work undertaken by The Roper Organization (1992) into green consumers. This work, which has been widely adopted and in some cases adapted by others (e.g. Ottman, 1993), seeks to distinguish between five different kinds of green consumer, ranging from those who believe that individuals cannot make a difference (basic browns) through to actively green consumers (true blue greens). One of the most interesting things about this typology is that it blends behavioural and attitudinal elements, not only because it distinguishes between those who take action by making changes to their habits and routines (true blue greens) differently to those who support their environmentalist beliefs by spending money (greenback greens), but also because it distinguishes between those who act upon their beliefs and those who do not. In fact, the most complex typologies, often employing a range of behavioural and attitudinal constructs to distinguish between groups, tend to be found in market research rather than the academic literature. See, for example, Ferraro (2009), Rose, Dade, and Scott (2007), Simmons Market Research Bureau (1991), and Tiltman (2007) for interesting typologies developed or applied by marketers. One of the major drawbacks of this kind of work is that although it is potentially very powerful, commercial sensitivities sometimes deter the authors from sharing their methodologies, making it hard to determine how groups were arrived at in the first place and limiting their adoption by academic researchers.

### Green is all of these things – and none of them

The work on typologies is useful for identifying green consumers because it represents a move in the literature away from characterising green or ethical consumers as a homogenous group with uniform intentions. It has the potential to complexify our view of people working towards sustainable consumption. In fact, there is merit in each of these types of endeavour, and rather than arguing that one of these segmentation or typology approaches is better than the others, it might be that each of these ways of approaching the problem of identifying the green consumer needs to be layered together in order to present a richer, more realistic, and useful picture of sustainable consumption.

However, because the unit of analysis commonly used in studies of recycling or green purchases is the individual, this view of the green or ethical consumption still implicitly represents people as taking rational (Newholm & Shaw, 2007), coherent, deliberate positions through their consumption. Although this assumption is perhaps as natural as it is convenient, it should not go unexamined. It has been challenged by Peattie (1999) who depicts consumers as making a series of purchase decisions which are very much dependent on the context in which they are made and which are not necessarily related to each other or underpinned by a driving philosophy of consumption. This view suggests that it is not the individual that should be examined, but each act of consumption.

As well as focusing on the individual, much of the literature treats green or ethical purchases, recycling activities, and other decisions as if they were made by the individual examined ahistorically and without reference to others. On this issue, Burgess, Bedford, Hobson, Davies, and Harrison (2003) note that, ' . . . a tradition of environmental attitude-behaviour research, the primary focus has been the individual consumer...disassociated from their everyday lives. The challenge is to re-contextualise individuals . . . ' (p. 269). At the very least, we need to consider individuals as part of the immediate households and extended networks to which they belong and through which they negotiate their daily patterns of consumption, and examine each act or decision as part of an ongoing pattern of such acts and decisions.

In the marketing and recycling literatures, we have also been guilty of studying 'moments' in a product's or service's lifecycle, treating co-production, purchase, use, and disposal not just with separate studies, but studies embedded in different literatures. Many studies also examine single acts of purchase (e.g. Fairtrade coffee) or disposal (e.g. paper recycling) out of context of other purchase or disposal behaviour (Thørgersen & Ölander, 2003). There are a few examples, such as Dehab, Gentry, and Su (1995) in the recycling literature, of studies that employ a more holistic view of the elements of consumption that they examine, and it is this broad situated conceptualisation of the purchase act that we employ in this study.

To summarise, rather than conceptualising consumers as a series of individuals making a single purchase, in this study we have researched them as individuals who make multiple (possibly inconsistent) purchase, use, and disposal decisions as part of a household, within the context of a wide range of influences such as social norms, industry structures, and policy and regulatory frameworks, and in relation to other purchase, use, and disposal decisions.

These insights have been the starting point for the enquiry which is described below. Through extended empirical work, we have discovered that most consumers can be viewed as suspended in some kind of tension between grey and green purchasing. We see this position as an inevitable result of the trade-offs between green and ethical criteria and other, more conventional, issues such as price and availability. As well as competing with grey criteria, however, green and ethical factors are often incompatible with each other, meaning that as part of sustainable consumption, local outlets may have to be traded off against organic credentials, or food miles against Fairtrade. In this study, we have sought to understand the problematic of sustainable consumption more broadly by examining consumer decision making in context and, to some extent, over time, and product lifecycles in great detail. In the next part of the paper, we will describe our methodological approach. We will then present one of our most significant findings: a typology of approaches to sustainable consumption. Following a detailed discussion of each of the three approaches in our typology, we will revisit the literature set out above, showing how the ideas represented by this typology challenge and extend extant theory.

## Methods

The results discussed here are part of a wider study of green consumer behaviour. The typology presented in the following section was surfaced through the analysis of data from 81 semi-structured interviews with consumers who had some green or ethical aspect to their consumption. These ideas were further refined through three focus groups, which involved an additional 11 consumers. Following the qualitative rationale of the study, participants were selected through a process of purposive sampling. Initial participants were recruited through green and ethical networks in the UK, leaflets in green outlets, and adverts in green or ethical publications. The remainder of the participants was recruited through a process of snowballing outwards from the initial sample (Patton, 1990). The participants in this study have therefore identified themselves, to some extent, as green or ethical consumers.

The interviews themselves concentrated on recent purchases of technology-based products, such as small electrical goods (e.g. TVs, DVD players, cameras, stereos, and computers) or white goods (fridges, freezers, cookers, washing machines, clothes dryers, and dishwashers), and regular shopping for food and household products. We began each interview by asking participants to recall a list of their most recent purchases of technology-based products from the categories above. If (and only if) they struggled to think of an example from the past five years, we offered prompts about the product groups discussed. Where individuals had gone through a research and evaluation process but ultimately decided not to purchase a product in one of these groups, this was also eligible for inclusion in the next stage of the interview. From the list that was developed, we asked them to concentrate on the largest recent purchase and tell us about this process from the first decision to consider the purchase right through to post purchase in as much detail as they could. The emphasis on actual, recent purchases allowed us to avoid the pitfalls of considering hypothetical, idealised, or intended behaviour, as discussed above. The interview protocol[1] was designed to help the participants articulate their purchase experiences in as much detail as possible, including any research undertaken, the purchase itself, and the context for the purchase. Each interview discussed the purchase (or decision not to purchase) of one or more technology-based products, as well as their

---

[1] A copy of the full interview protocol is available from the corresponding author on request.

grocery shopping. Although our data-gathering strategy centres on purchase (or non-purchase) decisions, we have sought to include discussions of how issues relating to the production, use, and disposal of products are used to inform the decision-making process in order to introduce a consideration of the whole product lifecycle into our data.

In this way, we built up a data set which contains detailed, 'thick' descriptions (Blaikie, 2000) of more than 130 technology-based product purchase processes by consumers who are green in some aspect of their consumption. This process allowed strong theoretical saturation of the concepts outlined below. These findings were then further explored through focus groups, where the emphasis was on understanding the routes which have led to these different profiles of green and ethical consumption.

A grounded, inductive approach was used in both the data gathering and data analysis stages in order to make sense of the detailed pictures of individual acts of (non-)consumption. In practice, this meant stepping away from the ways in which others have tried to characterise or understand green consumers and surface an account of how specific decision-making processes built up a picture, first of how an individual approaches the greening of their lifestyle, and then how these approaches are similar and different to the approaches taken by others. In other words, in contrast to many of the approaches discussed above, our unit of analysis is the specific purchase (or non-purchase) decision process rather than the individual making that process. For each individual, we are then able to compare and contrast multiple purchases. This approach supports two forms of analysis: a comparison of the decision-making processes across product types (see McDonald, Oates, Thyne, Alevizou, & McMorland, 2009), and the patterns evident in the processes and strategies used by individuals to green their lifestyles when they are viewed as a series of (un)linked decision processes. This analysis is presented in the next section.

## Findings: Three strategies for moving towards more sustainable consumption

We began this study with Peattie's (1999) premise that there was no such thing as a green consumer. Our results certainly support this. We have discovered that, as predicted by McDonald et al. (2006), empirically, almost all of the self-selected green consumers in our study can be classified as 'greening' rather than 'green'. On the one hand, they all engaged in some form of green or ethical activity, and on the other hand, each of their lives contained at least some element of 'grey' consumption in product sectors where green alternatives clearly exist. This is not surprising given the social, economic, and technological infrastructures in the UK of which these consumers are a part.

Through this work, we have uncovered three distinct strategies for greening consumption. In the sections that follow, we will introduce each of the categories in our typology, using empirical data to illustrate each in turn. Following the description of each component of our typology, we will summarise the main ways in which these groups differ from each other. Our intention at this stage of enquiry is not to quantify these groups, but to characterise them with reference to our data, distinguish them

CONTEMPORARY ISSUES IN GREEN AND ETHICAL MARKETING

from each other, and to consider how their conceptualisation represents a departure from the work which has gone before.

### Translators

Translators are green in some aspects of their lives and grey in others. They do not necessarily think about sustainability in a holistic way. They are not motivated by a political agenda but by a sense of trying to do what they perceive to be the right thing. The consumers in this group are open to change, although they are not deliberately change seeking. So, for example, one Translator commented that, 'I'm not very good at making sure everything I do is environmentally friendly as I'd like it to be. If I'm prompted in some way to do it then I will do it' (Interview 7), demonstrating the basic tension within the Translator strategy: a willingness to make changes in the future, without the willingness to seek out that change. They are also prepared to make a certain amount of sacrifice if they can see a clear rationale for adopting a new routine or a slightly less convenient activity. One interviewee reflects, 'I think after I read that [newspaper article], I realised how much you could do on a daily basis and then armed with those little tips I started to do more' (Interview 46). We have termed them 'Translators' because if they are made aware of a concrete action that they can take and they can see a clear benefit from doing it, then they are apt to undertake it: Translators translate awareness into specific actions.

Translators are the consumers that the marketers of the '80s and '90s hoped to find. Their belief in being better citizens and their willingness to change means that if they know that an aspect of their consumption is problematic for the environment, or for others, then they are likely to change it. Unusually, there is a very small gap between awareness and action for this group (see Peattie, 2010, for a discussion of this issue). The problem here is not how to persuade them to change their behaviour, but how to communicate issues to them in the first place, as they are extremely passive in their information seeking. This means that word of mouth and opinion leaders are key sources of information about behaviour change for Translators. Once they have information, however, they tend to be much less critical of it than the other groups, and will treat it in a straightforward way, implementing behaviour changes where they can see the impact of their actions. When they have gone through a process of changing a particular behaviour, these consumers may also express guilt or regret about not changing earlier.

The outcome of these attitudes and behaviours tends to be a slightly fragmented collection of consumer behaviours which may appear to be inconsistent when judged from the outside. For example, it is possible that a Translator might be committed to composting (something which may be considered 'deep green') but does not use local recycling facilities (something which might be considered to be more mainstream) simply because they had never been presented with any convincing arguments or appropriate information. However, these activities may form a coherent set of activities when viewed from the Translator's own perspective, as they represent all the practices that they know about and can see a clear benefit from doing.

Due to this indiscriminate process of greening their consumption, Translators are also less likely to see the 'big picture' of sustainability. Although they may champion individual actions or products, they are unlikely to have a complex understanding of the interdependent nature of the elements of sustainability. Thus Translators may concentrate on the most tangible aspects of sustainability, such as reducing waste or lowering domestic energy or water use. They are therefore more likely to approach greening in an incremental, cumulative, product-by-product, process-by-process manner rather than beginning by articulating a principle and rearranging their lives accordingly.

### *Exceptors*

This group has the most sophisticated understanding of sustainability. In complete contrast to the Translators, this lifestyle is likely to be underpinned by, and designed to implement, a personal philosophy of consumption, such as, 'I don't believe in consumerism' (Interview 9), or 'I would place myself more in the ecological radical side but I am trying to reduce consumerism rather than make it greener. I don't want green . . . I don't want green capitalism . . . I don't want capitalism in a greener version. I want less capitalism, a more people-centred economy' (Interview 17). Sustainability is a priority for Exceptors in every aspect of their lives. Thus many seemingly unrelated consumption choices, such as where to live and what to eat, are seen as inextricably linked to the same issues and problems of living within a capitalist society and trying to achieve the least environmental impact coupled with the most social justice.

Exceptors are change seeking. They see individual change and personal sacrifice as key to safeguarding the planet for future generations. They see themselves as rejecting many of the tenets of mainstream society and are comfortable with alternative products and outlets. They tend to belong to networks, and will naturally seek out other Exceptors.

Although Exceptors are the most actively information seeking and information literate group, they cannot necessarily be reached by mainstream marketing. This is because they are highly critical (and even cynical) about most corporate and government communications. They favour and trust more specialist media, such as *The Ethical Consumer* magazine. They may engage in research about a product, and are likely to extend this to research about the company that produces it. This means that not only do the product's manufacturing processes come under scrutiny, but the totality of a company's (or parent company's or country of origin's) activities can be judged as part of this process.

However, despite being the greenest group in our typology, we have termed these consumers Exceptors because we have found that they all have at least one aspect of their lives in which they behave like grey consumers. This exception to their otherwise coherent sustainable lifestyles is likely to be a relatively small but conscious lapse into mainstream consumerism. Exceptions can take many forms, but in this study, centred as it was on technology-based products, we found a number of examples of small electrical appliances which you might have expected active green consumers like these to do without, such as a popcorn maker. We have found that during the purchase process for their 'exception' item, all of their normal information seeking routines and sustainability criteria will be suspended. The Exceptors will offer (themselves and others) a specific justification for this aberration in their approach to consumption that allows them to be happy with their purchase decision and not let it affect their idea of themselves as green consumers. This justification can be made strongly in terms of personal joy or quality of life, 'I am an American and I just think . . . I just love having a car' (Interview 47) or more simply in terms of grey criteria, 'Yes we bought a bad thing but very convenient' (Interview 60). Sometimes Exceptors have more than one exception to their otherwise green lifestyles.

### Selectors

The Selectors are an intriguing group. They are also likely to be the largest group in terms of numbers of the population, and therefore perhaps the most interesting to marketers. We term this group Selectors because they act as green or ethical consumers in one aspect of their lives, but as grey consumers in all other respects: Selectors select an aspect of sustainable consumption on which to focus. For example, they may be avid recyclers or pay a premium for green energy or sponsor a child in Africa but otherwise lead consumption-oriented lives. This group is attracted or motivated by a single issue but is not interested in sustainability in a holistic way. So, for example, one of our respondents was green in terms of their food shopping:

> I try to get organic where I can and there is another farmers' market only once a month which is mainly organic stuff and there are a couple of little organic shops in the town not far from here. So that is roughly where I shop . . . I am a Fairtrader. (Interview 71)

but grey in terms of their approach to purchasing white goods:

> ' . . . an American-type fridge-freezer with the ice dispenser, you know, a big one and I know they are terrible, I know they are, so we got one of those . . . because it had this ice-making facility and I liked the look of it, and we have got another smaller fridge we keep in the garage, but the one we have in our new formed kitchen, I just you know it was a lifestyle thing I suppose, we just liked it. We went out deliberately to buy it. We weren't seduced into it; we went into it with our eyes open (Interview 71)

Selectors do not see their own behaviour as contradictory. For the issue that they have selected to act on, they might mimic either the Translators or the Exceptors in terms of their information seeking and change orientations, but they ignore all other issues completely.

This is a maddening scenario for marketers, and may account for some of the inconsistent results found by marketers in the past. If a Selector is interested in the aspect of green or ethical behaviour that an organisation is trying to promote, then they may act as straightforward Translators and do as the marketing material provided suggests. S/he may even take up the cause actively like an Exceptor and get deeply involved in trying to make material changes to their own lives and perhaps even the lives of others. However, if the issue being promoted does not fall within their sphere of interest, they will simply ignore all marketing communications. Even if the aspect of sustainability a marketer wishes to influence does affect some Selectors, this success will have no benefit to others wishing to promote other, even seemingly comparable issues. For example, there is no reason to expect that someone who sponsors a child in Africa would donate their time to working in a charity shop. Nor would it necessarily be possible to persuade a consumer who went to great lengths to reduce their household energy consumption to take public transport or conserve water. In the same way that individuals can be multiple Exceptors, it is also possible that individuals could be multiple Selectors, favouring more than one (linked or unlinked) aspect of sustainable consumption.

### Summary of the typology

There is more than one way to be a green or ethical consumer. Every green or ethical consumer is locked in a balance between grey and green consumption, but different groups will choose different solutions to resolve this tension: Translators will change but not seek information; Selectors will compartmentalise and act or ignore; and Exceptors will offer justifications for what they see as their transgressions. Even the greenest consumer will have grey aspects of consumption in their lifestyle.

By undertaking detailed, qualitative research into real purchases, we have uncovered significant differences in the approaches that consumers take to green consumption. These differences cannot be predicted by the demographic, socio-economic, or psychographic characteristics of individuals, but rather by how they approach the problem of green or ethical consumption. These categories can be applied with confidence because our research process has led to strong theoretical saturation. Despite deliberately seeking out dissimilar consumer groups from a wide range of backgrounds and green and ethical perspectives, we have been able to incorporate the consumption behaviours of every one of our 81 participants into this typology.

Table 1 shows how Translators and Exceptors vary according to some key aspects of the purchase process. These aspects are somewhat different, and more difficult to research, than the constructs discussed above which centred on distinguishing individuals rather than their cumulative consumption strategies. However, they offer ways to identify these groups in practice. As Table 1 highlights, Selectors are not a distinct group per se. They can act as either Exceptors or Translators but only for their chosen focus. Therefore, Selectors will vary in any of these aspects, according to whether or not this issue is their chosen concern. If it is not their favoured issue, then they will operate as if they were grey consumers.

There is some previous evidence in the literature to support each of the three groups we have identified here. Exceptors and Translators, for example, share common features with some of the proposed 'sliding scales' presented in the past. For example, the kinship between our Exceptor group and notions such as 'deep greens' (Dermody, 1999) or 'true blue greens' (Ottman, 1993) is evident. Equally, aspects of the concept of a Translator can be found woven into the assumptions underpinning much of the environmental psychology literature on the role of information in increasing pro-environmental behaviours. Burgess et al. (2003) note that, 'cognitive approaches assume that increase in awareness will lead to more pro-environmental behaviour' (p. 270). Whilst this has clearly not been the case for the population as a whole, it may be true for Translators, again, perhaps explaining weak or contradictory results. Another literature relevant to Translators is the work that has been done on Perceived Consumer Effectiveness (PCE; Straughan & Roberts, 1999) which centres on whether people feel that they are able to make a difference through their individual actions. In these terms, Translators can be characterised as a group with high PCE.

Perhaps the idea of a Selector offers the most radical departure from extant thinking on green consumer behaviour, but here too we can find precedents for the reporting of Selector behaviour, although this has often been interpreted as a negative research result. A number of studies (see, e.g., Balderjahn, 1988; Pickett, Kangun, & Grove, 1993; Thørgersen & Ölander, 2003) have reported a lack of 'spillover' between different types of pro-environmental behaviour. Tracy and Oskamp (1983)

CONTEMPORARY ISSUES IN GREEN AND ETHICAL MARKETING

**Table 1** Identifying translators, exceptors, and selectors.

| Aspect of consumption | Translators | Exceptors | Selectors |
|---|---|---|---|
| Conception of sustainability | Fragmented | Holistic | Selectors may act as either Exceptors or Translators for their focus activity, but as grey consumers in all other aspects of their consumption |
| Orientation to information seeking | Passive | Active | |
| Treatment of sustainability information | Accepting and uncritical | Cynical | |
| Trusted information sources | Government info, product advertising, charity marketing campaigns | Specialist networks | |
| Information formats | Mainstream (television, direct mail) | Online searches for CSR. Specialist print media for product info | |
| Level of research focus | Products | Companies | |
| Compliance with information | High | Only if corroborated by research | |
| Motivation | Good citizen | Saving the planet | |
| Initiation of behaviour | External counsel | Internal values | |

found that, 'behaviours are not interchangeable, even within conceptual categories' (p. 121).

What is different here is that we have evidence of all of three approaches and conceptualise them as distinct, independent approaches to greening. In other words, we may have seen glimpses of these ideas before (although they may have been presented as aberrations or problems for environmental researchers) and each presents a faithful, but partial picture which has been helpful but necessarily limited in its application. This typology offers the opportunity to understand what all the different strategies for greening *are* (as opposed to what we thought or hoped they might be) and thus the ability to approach these groups in different ways.

It is not our intention here to suggest what proportions of green consumers use the three strategies we have identified. Our study was qualitative and the sampling strategy pursued was a theoretical one which does not allow us to make assertions about the population. In order to find out what proportion of consumers use each of these strategies, a stratified random, representative sample of a much greater size

**Figure 1** Proportions of strategies pursued by interviewees.

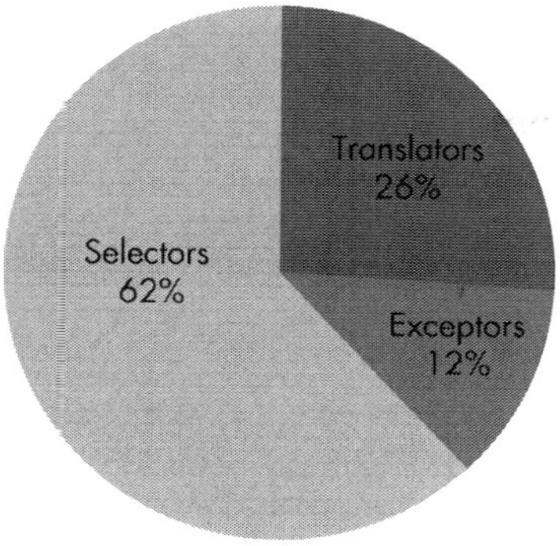

Selectors 62%
Translators 26%
Exceptors 12%

would be required. However, of the 81 respondents we did interview, Figure 1 shows the proportion of each found group in our data set.

### Complexifying the typology

There are a number of factors which affect the way that consumers play out their orientations to sustainable consumption in practice. This idea is not new, and there is considerable research in the marketing literature which shows that green or ethical aspirations may be tempered by other factors such as price (Harwood, 2005). Our data show that other criteria such as availability and brand also moderate the relationship between green intentions and purchase behaviour.

Another factor which our data show as having a direct effect on individuals is the orientation of the people with whom they live. Both people who form part of a single household and those who live independently in multiple households can be affected by the opinions of other household members. This can have a restricting effect on green consumption (such as when a housemate refuses to purchase recycled toilet tissue or Fairtrade coffee) or a facilitating effect (such as when a partner sets up a system to compost household waste; Scott, 2009). There are other, less direct ways in which other people can constrain the behaviour of individuals. For example, we have found a number of situations where landlords have either facilitated or blocked the purchase of green energy tariffs. In these situations, the green or ethical behaviour of the individual is not a direct consequence of their own orientation to sustainable consumption but a negotiated household outcome which may turn out to be more or less (or just differently) green or ethical than they would tend to be independently. This insight offers a significant critique of studies which examine individuals in isolation from their decision-making units, such as families or households (Burgess et al., 2003).

A further way in which the data suggest that we need to complexify this typology is by viewing these positions as dynamic and considering the possibility of movement between them. For example, with the identification of both multiple Selectors and multiple Exceptors within our data, it is possible to conceptualise distinct groups of consumers ranging from the 'lighter green' position of a Selector, through various manifestations of multiple Selectors, towards a situation best described as a multiple

Exceptor, and eventually to the 'darker green' position of the archetypal Exceptor. We suggest that it is probable that, although some green consumers may adopt a single strategy and continue to pursue that over many years, others may take different approaches to greening at different points of their lives. Understanding whether, how, and when individuals make such transitions is an important direction for further study.

This notion of movement between strategies is particularly important because it raises the question of how consumers get into each of these groups in the first place. Our focus group data suggest that changes in greening tend to be incremental. We also believe that different people may be more or less disposed to different categories depending on their personal orientations to change and to information seeking. There also appears to be a connection between the ways in which people deal with paradoxes and inconsistencies in their consumption practices and the likelihood of belonging to certain groups. These are important areas for new research.

As indicated above, our data also provide evidence of both Selectors who act as Translators and Selectors who act as Exceptors, and the study of Selectors is an important matter for further research. This is particularly pertinent given the expected size of this group within the population. These groups do not exist independently of each other, and our focus group data raise the issue of how they typically interact. For example, there is some evidence that Exceptors may have a role in informing the more passive Translators in their circles of friends and family. This finding would lend itself to a study informed by the work on 'opinion leaders' in marketing (Nisbet & Kotcher, 2009) and 'role modelling' in social psychology (Smith, Cowie, & Blades, 2003).

## Discussion: Grouping individuals by their strategy for greening

These findings offer a significant critique to the extant green marketing literature which has sought to characterise individuals as either grey or green consumers, as discussed above. What we see is not a group of consumers who are entirely grey, a group who are entirely green, and a third group which are neither one nor the other but that can be characterised as simply in transit between the two. Instead, we have uncovered three groups of individuals who are neither grey nor green but approach the greening of their lifestyles in distinct ways. Translators, Exceptors, and Selectors are all locked in a tension between grey and green consumption. For some of our respondents (mainly Exceptors), this tension is a real one, which is experienced by the individuals as disquiet about specific aspects of their current lifestyles. However, for others this tension is merely a conceptual one, seen by us as researchers and unnoticed by the individuals concerned. The three different strategies represent different ways to resolve this problem: adoption, compartmentalisation, and change.

First of all, this challenges the assumption in much of the marketing, recycling, and voluntary simplifier literatures that consumers are either green or not. Our data show that the traditional categories of grey and green consumer are not mutually exclusive and that, in line with Peattie (1999), purchases are both context and product dependent. Consequently, it also contests the notion of a homogenous green or ethical consumer.

The typology helps explain why studies focused on consumers' demographics, socioeconomic groups, and psychographics do not reveal consistent patterns. This is because a demographic profile, for example, is compiled at the level of an individual. However, if that individual is a Selector then that individual will choose to undertake some green or ethical activities but not others. For another Selector, the chosen activity might be different. Equally, one Translator may know about the activity under study, but another might not. Since individuals cannot be understood to act in uniform or coherent ways, it is unlikely that we can predict their behaviour from their personal, household, or social characteristics.

Another way that researchers have tried to classify individuals is by surveying their intentions and implying that these can be taken as a proxy for their actions. Aside from the problem already discussed in the literature that people exaggerate or idealise their intentions (Perrin & Barton, 2001), this is still problematic because, as the typology shows, an individual's values are not necessarily coherent. Examining intentions in order to classify them by motivation will also suffer from this problem. This is exacerbated by the fact that many intentions cannot be translated into real products and services because of the many constraints of the purchase process, the dampening effect of grey criteria such as time, money, and product availability, or the moderating effect of others in the household.

Lastly, the typology offers some insight into why categorising consumers in terms of their concrete actions does not offer a solution to the problem of relying on intentions as a proxy for actions. These data also show that even actions do not tell us enough about individuals to determine whether or not they are green or ethical consumers (Newholm, 2000). First, taking Peattie's (1999) insights to their logical conclusion makes us aware that even if a consumer makes a choice to buy a green or ethical product at one point in time, there is no guarantee that even this very same consumer will replicate this decision in the future. Second, even though three consumers buy exactly the same fridge or brand of coffee on the same day in the same shop for the same amount of money, they could each have taken a completely different set of values and research processes and implemented them in terms of different criteria and priorities in order to make that purchase. We have found evidence of different values, purchase criteria, and research processes leading to exactly the same purchase outcome: the same make and model of white good purchased from the same retailer for a similar price. In other words, a Translator, a Selector, and an Exceptor might all have the same concrete purchase outcome. So segmenting them according to their actions does not necessarily help us understand their behaviour or predict future purchases. Even if green or ethical consumers could be identified through examining their actions, this would not be sufficient to determine what kind of green or ethical consumer they are. In order to be able to place individuals in one of the three groups in the typology presented here, it is necessary to understand their orientations to research and purchase processes in some detail.

## Conclusions and implications

Our research shows that in order to understand an individual act of consumption, it has to be looked at as part of a stream of purchase and non-purchase decisions which should be contextualised in terms of research and purchasing heuristics, as well as lifestyle and philosophical approach. Looking at a large number of purchases in this way has allowed us to surface three distinct approaches to sustainable consumption. Rather than distinguishing between groups of consumers in terms of behavioural or attitudinal constructs, we have found that green consumers can be typed according to the strategies they employ for greening their lives. This typology can help explain why contemporary approaches to segmentation do not work in practice.

This work offers new challenges to marketers and policymakers hoping to promote different aspects of sustainable consumption. However, it also offers new insights which raise a number of practical implications. In the past, marketers, and to some extent marketing researchers, have conceptualised all consumers as if they are Translators or potential Translators. This is the consumer group that marketers hoped to 'find'. They are attractive to marketers and policymakers because a simple process of imparting information can lead to concrete actions. The passive relationship with information does make this group slightly harder to deal with in marketing terms, but these problems are not insurmountable. However, Translators may not be the correct target for marketing and policy initiatives, as they are unlikely to be either the largest or the most influential group.

Some marketing research has made allowances for the existence of a 'deeper green' position which is more akin to our Exceptor. For example, literature on voluntary simplicity in the social psychology literature (see McDonald et al., 2006, for a summary of this work) centres on active, committed individuals with a sophisticated understanding of sustainability that they attempt to operationalise through their consumption. Likewise, the action-oriented, information- and solution-seeking nature of the Exceptor has much in common with some of the literature on early adopters in the innovation literature (Venkatraman, 1989). However, our data suggest that both the Translator and Exceptor groups may in fact be more straightforward to address than the potentially larger Selector group with their fragmented actions and discriminating focus.

By framing the 'green consumer' as if they are a homogenous group of consistent individuals, marketers have assumed that green or ethical behaviour displayed in one aspect of consumption can be reproduced for other products or services. However, as well as the 'disconnected' consumption patterns of Selectors, we have uncovered very different decision-making processes associated with different products and sectors (McDonald, Oates, Thyne, Alevizou, & McMorland, 2009), leaving marketers with no recourse to traditional ways of predicting future purchase acts from a previous purchase act.

The issue of how information is received and where it comes from is particularly pertinent (Oates et al., 2008): from the Translators' point of view, a green or ethical act explained to them and made achievable is likely to produce a change in behaviour, especially if associated marketing messages centre on the difference that their actions will make (Peattie, 1999; Wiser, 1998). Therefore, marketers can use traditional means of mass communication such as television advertising to inform this group of consumers. Recent multimedia campaigns in the UK, such as Act on CO2 (2010), aimed at reducing individual carbon footprints, and Recycle Now (Wrap, 2010) typify this approach, as do national television commercials aimed at persuading the American public to replace traditional light switches with energy-saving dimmer switches (Business Wire, 2010). However, our data suggest that perhaps the most effective information channel for the Translators is word of mouth, and this is much harder for marketers and policymakers to instigate, sustain, and control (Lam & Mizerski, 2005). For Exceptors, mainstream communications will be received critically, so marketers need to utilise specialist channels such as *The Ethical Consumer* or green networks to gain credibility and approval for their products and services. Opinion leaders and word of mouth are also crucial here. Many organisations will not be considered by Exceptors due to past or current perceived unethical activities, for example Nestlé or Shell (Friedman, 1999; Harrison et al., 2005; Smith, 1990). Selectors, as always, prove more difficult to reach due to their particularly focused behaviour on one or more activities which may not be obviously linked in any coherent way. A traditional marketing approach which attempts to segment green consumers as all those interested in green or ethical matters might view a consumer who purchases organic products to be receptive to direct communications from Greenpeace, for example. Whilst this approach might be successful with a Translator or Exceptor (for different reasons), it may not necessarily be appropriate for Selectors. Reaching this latter group is really a process of trial and error for marketers. However, we suggest that although our typology might not necessarily help the marketer who is dependent on the more traditional segmentation strategies, we certainly see how it fits with more contemporary approaches to marketing. The integrated, holistic model (Kliatchko, 2009) which puts customers firmly at the core of any marketing activity becomes essential to establish meaningful communications and relations. Aligned with a shift in emphasis towards nurturing customer communities which trust peer recommendations over advertising campaigns, marketers can use our typology to facilitate engagement with consumers based on a thorough understanding of their approach to sustainability, using real-time data, insight, and social media (Mulhern, 2009). Our typology complements the current academic thinking in marketing which seeks to understand the consumer at an individual level rather than at the homogenous level of, for example, the 'green consumer'.

Given these issues, the best way to address the promotion of sustainable consumption may not be through marketing alone, but through a combination of marketing and policy initiatives. For example, limiting the choice of products available through legislation will guarantee greener or more ethical choices by all three of these groups, as well as the grey consumer. In the UK, recent joint industry and government action will see the phasing out of standard filament light bulbs altogether (Energy Saving Trust, 2010). This means that all consumers will be obliged to purchase low-energy products, reducing the energy consumption and $CO2$ output of domestic lighting in the UK. However, these measures are only really possible where the scientific (and economic) case is compelling and unambiguous, which is not the case for many products or technologies.

One key aspect that distinguishes Exceptors from the other groups is their holistic and sophisticated understanding of sustainability. As noted above, each of the groups views its own patterns of consumption as if they have an internal coherence, which may not be apparent to others. However, Exceptors, because of their conscious strategy of greening, can also be viewed as making (mainly) coherent, consistent decisions from an external point of view. It was noted above that Translators are what marketers *hoped* to find. In many ways, Exceptors are the group of consumers that marketers *expected* to find, in that they undertake a series of actions that can be viewed as consistent and are underpinned by specific beliefs and values.

Looked at another way, we argue that if an individual does not have a sophisticated understanding of sustainability then they can only take Translator or Selector approaches to greening their lifestyles or not green them at all (grey consumers). We stress that whilst having a thorough understanding of sustainability will not automatically imply an Exceptor approach, an individual cannot be (or become) an

Exceptor without this kind of knowledge. Thus we argue that education has a key role to play in the development or socialisation of individuals with more active, holistic approaches to greening their lifestyles. This leads us to suggest a twofold strategy: first, policymakers need to embed sustainability in the school curriculum in order to give the next generation access to the kind of knowledge that will give some of them the foundation for action (Duvall & Zint, 2007; Evans, Gill, & Marchant, 1996; Uzzell, 1994); and second, having identified this aspect of Exceptor make-up, we argue that traditional marketing techniques could be used to identify members of this relatively small group and use their natural predilection for networks and active orientation for greening to help policymakers and social marketers promote green behaviours amongst the other groups. In other words, educate them to educate others. Within the communications literature, this effect is known as a two-step flow where, 'ideas often flow from radio and print to opinion leaders and from these to the less active sections of the population' (Lazarfield, Berelson, & Gaudet, 1948, cited in Katz, 1957, p. 61). Following this idea, subscribers to *The Ethical Consumer* or members of specific networks could be invited to seminars about how best to inform others. Education rather than marketing approaches are likely to have more success with this critical group, especially if they were sponsored by relevant NGOs, although Nisbet and Kotcher (2009) note that, 'opinion leaders should be trained not as educators disseminating information about climate change, but as communications strategists initiating conversations with friends and acquaintances, deliberately framing messages in ways that make them more meaningful and persuasive to their recipients' (p. 339). Again, we see consistency here with our proposed strategies and the ideas that are developing in marketing communication studies which centre on a coherent, narrative approach involving new opinion formers such as bloggers, rather than simply an advertising-based model of message dissemination (Dahlen, Lange, & Smith, 2010).

In conclusion, much of the work that has been undertaken by social scientists has focused on one of a number of fragments of the complex picture that is presented here. By building up these many insights and using the typology as a sense-making framework, a less partial picture has been developed. Increasing green consumption has been understood as a consumer behaviour issue (or problem), but researched in a different way it is revealed to be a more complex problem than marketing alone can tackle. This will require a qualitative research approach which moves away from reductionism and simplification towards embracing complexity.

## Further research

As indicated above, more research is needed to establish how people get into the three groups described in our typology. Our view of consumption accepts it as a socially constructed process. This raises the question of whether people could effectively be brought up, or otherwise socialised, as grey consumers, or as Translators, Selectors, or Exceptors. We also need to research the possibility that people could move between groups. In depth, qualitative analysis will be required to identify any trigger points which facilitate this kind of movement. Our focus group data suggest that, for many, this movement will be an incremental, gradual assimilation over a long period of consumption history. We also need to know more about the potential inter-relationships between these groups. Narrative research methods could be employed to study whether there are any common routes between groups. Further work will also be required to uncover the roles of the more active Exceptors as information brokers and practical advocates in the Translator and grey consumer groups.

Further research into why Exceptors remain grey in one (or more) respect could also be undertaken. Infrastructure alone does not offer an explanation for a non-essential purchase such as a popcorn maker, and it would be very interesting to know whether identity issues are at the root of these decisions.

In order for this work to be useful to marketers and policymakers, it will also be important for us to establish the proportions of these three groups within the wider population. A larger scale, quantitative study is planned to test the existence of these groups and to provide data about the prevalence of these strategies in a representative sample of the population.

## Acknowledgements

The authors are grateful to the UK Economic and Social Research Council (ESRC) Sustainable Technologies Programme for funding the project 'Trade-offs in decision-making for sustainable technologies' (award RES-388-25-0001), of which this paper is an output.

## References

Act on CO2. (2010). Campaign homepage. Retrieved December 2010 from http://actonco2.direct.gov.uk/home.html

Autio, M., Heiskanen, E., & Heinonen, V. (2009). Narratives of 'green' consumers – The antihero, the environmental hero and the anarchist. *Journal of Consumer Behaviour, 8*, 40–53.

Balderjahn, I. (1988). Personality variables and environmental attitudes as predictors of ecologically responsible consumption patterns. *Journal of Business Research, 17*(1), 51–56.

Blaikie, N. (2000). *Designing social research*. Cambridge, UK: Polity Press.

Burgess, J., Bedford, T., Hobson, K., Davies, G., & Harrison, C. (2003). (Un)sustainable consumption. In F. Berkhout, M. Leach, & I. Scoones (Eds.), *Negotiating environmental change: New perspectives from social science*. Cheltenham, UK: Edward Elgar.

Business Wire. (2010). Lutron kicks off energy-saving awareness campaign with national TV commercials. Retrieved December 2010 from http://www.businesswire.com/news/home/20101101007329/en/Lutron-Kicks-Energy-Saving-Awareness-Campaign-National-TV

Chan, K. (1999). Market segmentation of green consumers in Hong Kong. *Journal of International Consumer Marketing, 11*(6), 7–23.

Dahlen, M., Lange, F., & Smith, T. (2010). *Marketing communications. A brand narrative approach*. Chichester, UK: Wiley-Blackwell.

Davis, J.L. (1993). Strategies for environmental advertising. *Journal of Consumer Marketing, 10*(2), 19–36.

De Young, R. (1989). Exploring the difference between recyclers and non-recyclers: The role of information. *Journal of Environmental Systems, 18*(4), 341–351.

Dehab, D.J., Gentry, J.W., & Su, W. (1995). New ways to reach non-recyclers: An extension of the model of reasoned action to recycling behaviors. *Advances in Consumer Research, 22*(1), 251–256.

Department for Environment, Food and Rural Affairs (Defra) (2010). *An invitation to shape the nature of England: A discussion document*. London: Defra.

Dermody, J. (1999). Environmental issues in marketing communications. In P.J. Kitchen (Ed.), *Marketing communications: Principles and practice*. London: Thomson.

Dupré, S., Sauvage, J., Dupal, T., Laville, E., Deveaux, R., Marchand, A.L., et al. (2005). *Talk the walk: Advancing sustainable lifestyles through marketing and communications*. Paris: UNEP, UN Global Compact Office and Utopies.

Duvall, J., & Zint, M. (2007). A review of research on the effectiveness of environmental education in promoting intergenerational learning. *Journal of Environmental Education*, *38*(4), 14–24.

Elgin, D., & Mitchell, A. (1976). *Voluntary simplicity*. Business Intelligence Program, SRI International. Reprinted in Elgin, D., & Mitchell, A. (1977). Voluntary simplicity (3). *The Co-Evolution Quarterly*, *3*, 4–19.

Energy Saving Trust. (2010). Energy saving light bulbs take over. Retrieved December 2010, from http://www.energysavingtrust.org.uk/Resources/Features/Features-archive/Energy-saving-light-bulbs-take-over

Etzioni, A. (1998). Voluntary simplicity: Characterization, select psychological implications, and societal consequences. *Journal of Economic Psychology*, *19*(5), 619–643.

Evans, S.M., Gill, M.E., & Marchant, J. (1996). Schoolchildren as educators: The indirect influence of environmental education in schools on parents' attitudes towards the environment. *Journal of Biological Education*, *30*(4), 423–248.

Ferraro, C. (2009). *The green consumer*. Victoria, Australia: Australian Centre for Retail Studies, Monash University.

Firat, A.F., & Schultz, C.J. (1997). From segmentation to fragmentation. *European Marketing Journal*, *31*(3), 183–207.

Friedman, M. (1999). *Consumer boycotts*. London: Routledge.

Gilg, A., Barr, S., & Ford, N. (2005). Green consumption or sustainable lifestyles? Identifying the sustainable consumer. *Futures*, *37*, 481–504.

Gold, S., & Rubik, F. (2009). Consumer affinity to wooden framehouses: A typology of German consumers. *International Journal of Sustainable Development*, *8*(1), 78–93.

Grunert, S.C. (1993). Green consumerism in Denmark: Some evidence from the OKO Foods Project. *Der Markt*, *3*, 140–151.

Harrison, R., Newholm, T., & Shaw, D. (2005). *The ethical consumer*. London: Sage.

Harwood, J. (2005). Travel operators on green alert. *Marketing Week*, *28*(49), 9.

Hopper, J.R., & Nielsen, J. McCarl (1991). Recycling as altruistic behaviour: Normative and behavioural strategies to expand participation in a community recycling program. *Environment and Behavior*, *23*(2), 195–220.

Jackson, T. (2009). *Prosperity without growth: Economics for a finite planet*. London: Earthscan.

Kahle, L. (1983). *Social values and social change: Adaptation to life in America*. New York: Praeger.

Katz, E. (1957). The two-step flow of communication: An up-to-date report on an hypothesis. *Public Opinion Quarterly*, *21*(1), 61–78.

Kliatchko, J.G. (2009). The primacy of the consumer in IMC: Espousing a personalist view and ethical implications. *Journal of Marketing Communications*, *15* (2–3), 157–178.

Kuijlen, A.A.A., & van Raaij, W.F. (1979). *Consumer participation in a glass recycling programme*. Paper presented at the Fourth European Colloquium on Economic Psychology, Stockholm, pp. 29–31.

Lam, D., & Mizerski, D. (2005). The effects of locus of control on word-of-mouth communication, *Journal of Marketing Communications*, *11*(3), 215–228.

Lawrence, J. (1993). Green products sprouting again: More focused efforts avoid controversy. *Advertising Age*, *64*(20), 12.

Maniates, M. (2002). In search of consumptive resistance: The voluntary simplicity movement. In T. Princen, M. Maniates, & K. Conca (Eds.), *Confronting consumption*. Cambridge, MA: MIT Press.

McDonald, S., & Oates, C.J. (2003). Reasons for non-participation in a kerbside recycling scheme. *Resources, Conservation and Recycling*, *39*(4), 369–385.

McDonald, S., & Oates, C.J. (2006). Sustainability: Consumer Perceptions and Marketing Strategies, *Business Strategy and the Environment Special Issue on Marketing Sustainability*, 15(3), 157–170.

McDonald, S., Oates, C.J., Thyne, M., Alevizou, P.J., & McMorland, L.-A. (2009). Comparing sustainable consumption patterns across product sectors. *International Journal of Consumer Studies*, 33(2), 137–145.

McDonald, S., Oates, C.J., Young, C.W., & Hwang, K. (2006). Towards sustainable consumption: Researching voluntary simplifiers. *Psychology and Marketing*, 23(6), 515–534.

Mulhern, F. (2009). Integrated marketing communications: From media channels to digital connectivity. *Journal of Marketing Communications*, 15(2–3), 85–102.

Murphy, C. (2006, February 22) Ethical investment. *Marketing*, p. 18.

Neilssen, N., & Scheepers, P. (1992). Business strategy and the environment: The need for information about environmental consciousness and behaviour. *Business Strategy and the Environment*, 1(2), 13–23.

Newholm, T. (2000). Consumer exit, voice and loyalty: Indicative, legitimation and regulatory role in agricultural and food economics. *Journal of Agricultural and Environmental Ethics*, 12, 153–164.

Newholm, T., & Shaw, D. (2007). Editorial: Studying the ethical consumer: A review of research. *Journal of Consumer Behaviour*, 6, 253–270.

Nisbet, M.C., & Kotcher, J.E. (2009). A two-step flow of influence? Opinion-leader campaigns on climate change. *Science Communication*, 30(3), 328–354.

Oates, C.J., McDonald, S., Alevizou, P.J., Hwang, K., Young, C.W., & McMorland, L.-A. (2008). Marketing sustainability: Use of information sources and degrees of voluntary simplicity. *Journal of Marketing Communications*, 14(5), 351–365.

Ottman, J.A. (1993). *Green marketing: Challenges and opportunities for the new marketing age*. Lincolnwood, IL: NTC Business Books.

Ozcaglar-Toulouse, N., Shiu, E., & Shaw, D. (2006). In search of fair trade: Ethical consumer decision making in France. *International Journal of Consumer Studies*, 30(5), 502–514.

Patton, M.Q. (1990). *Qualitative evaluation and research methods*. Newbury Park, CA: Sage.

Peattie, K. (1999). Trappings versus substance in the greening of marketing planning. *Journal of Strategic Marketing*, 7, 131–148.

Peattie, K. (2001). Golden goose or wild goose? The hunt for the green consumer. *Business Strategy and the Environment*, 10, 187–199.

Peattie, K. (2010). Green consumption: Behavior and norms. *Annual Review of Environment and Resources*, 35(8), 8.1–8.24.

Perrin, D., & Barton, J. (2001). Issues associated with transforming household attitudes and opinions into materials recovery: A review of two kerbside recycling schemes. *Resources Conservation and Recycling*, 33(1), 61–74.

Pickett, G.M., Kangun, N., & Grove, S.J. (1993). Is there a general conserving consumer? A public policy concern. *Journal of Public Policy and Marketing*, 12(2), 234–243.

Piercy, N.F., & Morgan, N.A. (1993). Strategic and operational market segmentation: A managerial analysis. *Journal of Strategic Marketing*, 1(2), 123–140.

Prothero, A. (1990). Green consumerism and the societal marketing concept: Marketing strategies for the 1990s. *Journal of Marketing Management*, 6(2), 87–103.

Roberts, J.A. (1996). Green consumers in the 1990s: Profile and implications for advertising. *Journal of Business Research*, 36(3), 217–231.

Rokeach, M. (1973). *The nature of human values*. London: Free Press.

The Roper Organization. (1992). *Environmental behavior, North America: Canada, Mexico, United States*. A report commissioned by S.C. Johnson and Son Inc., New York.

Rose, C., Dade, P., & Scott, J. (2007). *Research into motivating prospectors, settlers and pioneers to change behaviours that affect climate emissions*. Norfolk: Campaign Strategy.

Rowlands, I.H., Scott, D., & Parker, P. (2003). Consumers and green electricity: Profiling potential purchasers. *Business Strategy and the Environment*, *12*, 36–48.

Rutherford, C. (1998). *Individual participation in environmental actions and schemes.* Research Report for Centre for Interdisciplinary Environmental Studies, University of Cambridge.

Schwartz, S.H. (1992). Universals in the content and structures of values. *Advances in Experimental Social Psychology*, *25*, 1–61.

Scott, A.K. (2009). *Towards sustainable consumption: Understanding the adoption and practice of environmental actions in households.* Unpublished PhD thesis, University of Sheffield, UK.

Shama, A. (1985). The voluntary simplicity consumer. *The Journal of Consumer Marketing*, *2*(4), 57–63.

Shaw, D., & Newholm, T. (2002). Voluntary simplicity and the ethics of consumption. *Psychology and Marketing*, *19*(2), 167–185.

Simmons Market Research Bureau. (1991). *Earth calling: Is America listening?* New York: Simmons Market Research Bureau.

Smith, N.C. (1990). *Morality and the market: Consumer pressure for corporate accountability.* London: Routledge.

Smith, P.K., Cowie, H., & Blades, M. (2003). *Understanding children's development* (4th ed.). Oxford: Blackwell.

Solomon, M., Bamossy, G., Askegaard, S., & Hogg, M.K. (1999). *Consumer behavior: A European perspective.* Upper Saddle River, NJ: Prentice Hall.

Straughan, R.D., & Roberts, J.A. (1999). Environmental segmentation alternatives: A look at green consumer behaviour in the new millennium. *Journal of Consumer Marketing*, *16*(6), 558–575.

Teisl, M.F., Rubin, J., & Noblet, C.L. (2008). Non-dirty dancing? Interactions between eco-labels and consumers. *Journal of Economic Psychology*, *29*, 140–159.

Thørgersen, J., & Ölander, F. (2003). Spillover of environment-friendly consumer behaviour. *Journal of Environmental Psychology*, *23*, 225–236.

Tiltman, D. (2007, July 11). Who is the ethical consumer? *Marketing*, pp. 28–30.

Tracy, A.P., & Oskamp, S. (1983). Relationships among ecologically responsible behaviours. *Journal of Environmental Systems*, *13*(2), 115–126.

Tucker, P. (1999). Normative influences in household recycling. *Journal of Environmental Planning and Management*, *42*(1), 63–82.

United States Environmental Protection Agency. (2010). Preserve the environment: Act locally. Retrieved December 2010 from http://www.epa.gov/epahome/acting.htm#united

Uzzell, D. (1994). *Children as catalysts of environmental change (Final Report).* London: European Commission Directorate General for Science Research and Development Joint Research Centre.

Van Liere, K.D., & Dunlap, R.E. (1980). The social bases of environmental concern: A review of hypotheses, explanations and empirical evidence. *Public Opinion Quarterly*, *44*(2), 181–197.

Venkatraman, M.P. (1989). Opinion leaders, adopters, and communicative adopters: A role analysis. *Psychology and Marketing*, *6*(1), 51–68.

Wagner, S.A. (1997). *Understanding green consumer behaviour.* London: Routledge.

Wiser, R.H. (1998). Green power marketing: Increasing customer demand for renewable energy. *Utilities Policy*, *7*, 107–119.

Wrap. (2010). Recycle Now homepage. Retrieved December 2010 from http://www.recyclenow.com/

# Environmentally responsible behaviour in the workplace: An internal social marketing approach

Anne M. Smith, *The Open University Business School, UK*
Terry O'Sullivan, *The Open University Business School, UK*

---

**Abstract** The role of social marketing in encouraging environmentally responsible consumer behaviour is recognised. However, organisations account for a greater negative environmental impact. This study aims to identify how social marketers and organisations can reduce that impact by harnessing a valuable resource, that of employees' environmentally responsible organisational citizenship behaviours (EROCBs). Findings from focus group interviews with employees of five large UK organisations show that individual personal factors such as environmental concern, values, beliefs, norms, and habits formed from domestic behaviour are fundamental to EROCBs. An important role for internal social marketing (ISM) is highlighted in identifying environmentally concerned employees, or 'internal customers', creating incentives and removing barriers to pro-environmental behaviour. The need to increase employees' self-efficacy with respect to EROCBs is emphasised.

---

## Introduction

There is growing awareness of the potential to utilise marketing concepts and techniques for the achievement of social goals. In particular, the role of social marketing in achieving environmentally responsible behavioural (ERB) change has been emphasised (McKenzie-Mohr, 2000; Peattie & Peattie, 2009). Organisations, not individuals, however, are the main cause of many environmental problems (Nilsson, von Borgstede, & Biel, 2004; Senge, Smith, Kruschwitz, Laur, & Schley, 2008; Stern, 2000). Yet employees represent a 'captive audience' who can be more easily targeted and potentially more susceptible to normative influence than when in a domestic environment (Carrico & Riemer, 2011). Internal marketing (IM) (Berry, Hensel, & Burke, 1976; Wieseke, Ahearne, Lam, & van Dick, 2009) involves the adoption of marketing concepts and techniques to influence the attitudes and behaviour of employees or 'internal customers'. This paper examines the potential role of internal social marketing (ISM) in increasing ERB within organisations. ISM involves the application of IM for the achievement of

**Figure 1** Employee initiated change: A classification of environmentally responsible workplace behaviour.

|  | **DIRECTION** | |
|---|---|---|
|  | **Direct** | **Indirect** |
| **Impact** **Local** | *Adapting/ Extending Domestic Behaviour* | *Influencing Colleagues: Behavioural Change Within Teams* |
| **Wide** | *Creating New Behaviours* | *Influencing Management: Behavioural Change Across the Organisation* |

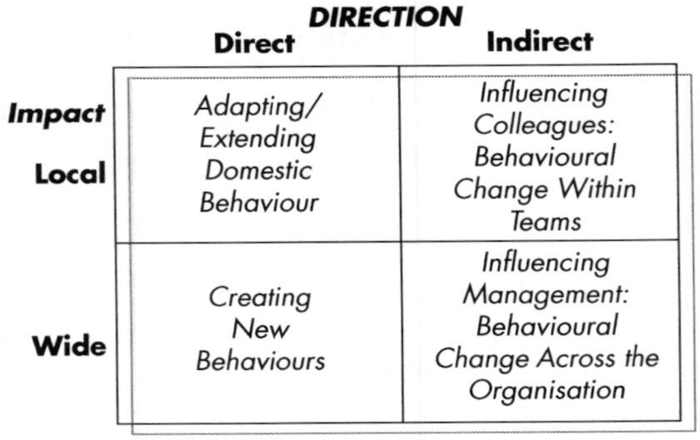

social rather than commercial objectives and is an approach which has so far been neglected in the marketing literature (Smith, 2011). ISM can potentially achieve ERB change within organisations by securing employee commitment to the organisation's environmental values and objectives and providing a working environment where employees voluntarily engage in environmentally responsible organisational citizenship behaviours (EROCBs), that is, behaviour that is beneficial for an organisation but falls outside formal role requirements (Organ, Podsakoff, & MacKenzie, 2006; Podsakoff, MacKenzie, Paine, & Bachrach, 2000). Such behaviours are likely to derive from the environmental concerns of employees and be related to domestic behaviour.

The aims of this research are, first, to explore the nature and determinants of OCBs relating to environmentally responsible workplace behaviour (ERWB), and, second, to assess the potential role of ISM in encouraging such behaviour. Findings from focus group interviews with employees of five large UK organisations are analysed within a social cognitive theoretical framework (Bandura, 1986) describing the relationships between environmentally responsible domestic behaviours, OCBs, individual, and organisational factors.

The paper is structured as follows. First, the literature review outlines the nature of ERWB and OCBs, suggesting a four-factor classification for the former (see Figure 1). Second, individual (personal), individual (employee), and organisational behavioural determinants are discussed and summarised in Figure 2. Third, the potential role of ISM in influencing ERWB is explored. The research methodology is then outlined followed by a discussion of the findings. Next, conclusions, together with both theoretical and managerial implications, are presented. Finally, study limitations and suggestions for further research are highlighted.

## Environmentally responsible workplace behaviours

Organisations are responding to the need to reduce their environmental impact by implementing policies and targets, employing specialist staff, investing in new technologies and working methods, and encouraging employees to change their behaviour through the provision of facilities and training. Environmentally

**Figure 2** Determinants of environmentally responsible organisational citizenship behaviours (EROCBs).

responsible workplace behaviours (ERWBs) may therefore result from organisational policy and formal job roles. A further source is from employees voluntarily engaging in OCBs, that is, behaviour that is beneficial for an organisation but falls outside formal role requirements (Podsakoff et al., 2000). However, while there is a substantial amount of research focussing on the behaviour of individuals and households, there is little evidence as to how household and workplace behaviour are related or how organisations can harness employees' environmental concerns as a resource to achieve environmental objectives. Additionally, the determinants of individual behaviour within organisations are likely to be different from those of household behaviours (Stern, 2000).

OCBs have been examined within the marketing literature, primarily with respect to service quality delivery (Bettencourt & Brown, 2003; Netemeyer & Maxham, 2007; Yi & Gong, 2008). Direct links have been established between OCBs and the achievement of organisational objectives such as customer satisfaction, retention, and profitability. Within the above context, OCBs typically relate to 'helping behaviours' where employees voluntarily help others with, or prevent the occurrence of, work-related problems. However, as organisations pursue their environmental goals and responsibilities, they need to encourage environmental entrepreneurship (Keogh & Polonsky, 1998) and worker participation (Rothenberg, 2003). Consequently, 'individual initiative', a form of OCB which involves 'voluntary acts of creativity and innovation,' 'volunteering to take on extra responsibilities', and 'encouraging others in the organisation to do the same', seems particularly relevant to a discussion of ERWB. A summary of the seven types of OCB identified by Podsakoff et al. (2000) is shown in Appendix 1.

Stern (2000) classifies environmentally significant behaviours as: 'environmental activism'; 'non-activist behaviours in the public sphere', for example acceptance and support of pro-environmental public policies; 'private-sphere environmentalism', that is, the purchase, use, and disposal of personal and household products that have environmental impact; and 'other environmentally significant behaviours' which include individuals influencing the actions of organisations to which they belong.

Kilbourne and Pickett (2008) distinguish between direct and indirect behaviours. The former includes purchase decisions and waste reduction and the latter includes petition signing and joining environmental organisations. Figure 1 adapts this approach to the workplace and classifies employee initiated ERWBs as direct, involving the individual's own behaviour, and indirect, in influencing the behaviours of others.

An individual's environmental concern has been described as a major determinant of behaviour (Dunlap & Jones, 2002) including workplace behaviour (Keogh & Polonsky, 1998). Environmental concern has been defined as:

> the degree to which people are aware of environmental problems and support efforts to solve them and/or indicate a willingness to contribute personally to their solution. (Dunlap & Jones, 2002, p. 485)

Consequently, a relationship between domestic and workplace behaviour can be expected. By extending, or adapting, their domestic behaviour to the workplace, for example switching off lights and computers, individuals will reduce environmental impact at the local level. Indirect behaviours which aim to influence others, for example to engage in recycling schemes, may also have a local impact on the team or workgroup but, depending on the level of influence of the individual, may have a wider impact across the organisation or supply chain. Finally, individuals may create new working practices by initiating new ideas or projects within the organisational context.

Antecedents of OCB can be classified as individual (personal or employee) or organisational. The latter includes task and organisational characteristics and leadership behaviours (Podsakoff et al., 2000). A similar distinction is made by social cognitive theory (SCT) (Bandura, 1986), one of the most commonly used theories in social marketing (Lefebvre, 2000) and described as the best theory for understanding organisational behaviour (Arnold et al., 2005). Consequently, SCT offers a promising framework for embedding social marketing within an organisational context, thus providing the conceptual base for an ISM approach. Bandura (1986) describes SCT as based on a model of 'triadic reciprocal determinism' where 'behaviour, cognitive and other personal factors, and environmental influences all operate interactively as determinants of each other' (p. 23). For this study, environmental factors are largely confined to those factors relating to the organisational context which determine the nature of EROCBs. Some of the main elements are shown in Figure 2 which recognises that the organisation and its employees comprise an open system. The permeable boundary highlights how wider environmental factors, including legislation, biospheric change, and societal norms and values (the dominant social paradigm; Kilbourne & Beckmann, 1998), will impact on the organisational context.

## Individual (personal) factors as determinants of environmentally responsible behaviours

In addition to personal factors such as age and gender, a number of individual cognitive factors have been identified as determinants of ERB in the home (see Bamberg & Moser, 2007, for a meta-analysis). Additionally, antecedents of individual ERBs are likely to vary (De Young, 2000). Pro-environmental personal norms have been described as the main basis for the individual's general predisposition to pro-environmental action (Stern, 2000) and an important predictor of behavioural intention (Bamberg & Moser. 2007). Thøgersen (2006) distinguishes between two types of personal, or internalised, norms: 'integrated' (based on conscious reflection on and evaluation of behaviour outcome) and 'introjected' (those which are only superficially internalised and which are enforced by anticipated guilt or pride). He also argues that different norms are activated for different ERBs, for example, purchasing energy-saving light bulbs, recycling behaviour, and transport choice. The role of personal norms is emphasised in the value-belief -norm (VBN) theory of environmentally significant individual behaviour (Stern, 2000). Here, personal values determine beliefs, which in turn determine personal norms and behaviour.

Beliefs play a major role in understanding environmental concern. Dunlap, Van Liere, Mertig, and Jones (2000) originally identified three beliefs fundamental to 'the new ecological paradigm', that is, 'balance of nature', 'limits to growth', and 'anti-anthropocentrism'. They later added 'human exemptionalism' and 'eco-crisis' (Dunlap & Jones, 2002). The VBN model, however, argues that pro-environmental beliefs alone will not necessarily lead to pro-environmental behaviours. Other beliefs, that is, the belief that environmental issues create adverse consequences for valued objects (where values relate to the biosphere, altruism, and egoism), and the perceived ability to reduce threat are fundamental to behaviour change (de Groot & Steg, 2010; Stern, 2000). Similarly, with respect to the latter, SCT emphasises the role of self-efficacy as a pivotal concept in determining behaviour (i.e. 'beliefs in one's capabilities to organize and execute the courses of action required to produce given attainments', Bandura, 1997, p. 3). Social marketing, together with environmental psychology, studies often invokes the Theory of Planned Behaviour (TPB) (Ajzen, 1985) as a framework for understanding pro-social behaviours. Here, beliefs that certain outcomes derive from particular behaviours will influence attitudes towards the behaviour, behavioural intentions, and thus the behaviour itself. It has also been suggested that attitudinal (affective) emotions, as opposed to attitudinal (cognitive) beliefs, may dominate ERBs (Costarelli & Colloca, 2004).

Other authors emphasise the role of motivation in determining ERBs. McKenzie-Mohr (2000) argues that there is strong support for the fact that ERB increases with the internalisation and integration of motivation to act in an environmentally responsible way. Attitude models such as the TPB are based on a value expectancy framework where motivation has its roots in the various beliefs, attitudes, and norms included in the model (Thøgersen, 1994). Perugini and Bagozzi (2001) suggest that their motivation–goal–behaviour (MGB) model is more appropriate than the TPB when actions are means to end state goals. Lindenberg and Steg (2007) describe three 'inclusive' goals, that is, goals which govern whole areas of sub-goals, knowledge, and attitudes, which seem highly relevant for environmental behaviour: the 'hedonic goal (to feel better right now), the gain goal (to guard and improve one's resources), and the normative goal (to act appropriately).

SCT (Bandura, 1986) describes a reciprocal relationship between personal characteristics and behaviour. Habits and past behaviour influence the belief component of attitude models for high frequency behaviours such as recycling and are important predictors of future behaviour (Knussen, Yule, MacKenzie, & Wells, 2004; Thøgersen, 1994). Perugini and Bagozzi (2001) highlight, however, that the relationship between frequency of past behaviour and future behaviour is often observed within a specific and stable context. Additionally, while the individual's environmental values, norms, and beliefs are likely to impact on their workplace behaviour, there will be a range of other determinants within the organisational context, as discussed in the next section.

## Individual (employee) factors as determinants of environmentally responsible behaviours

There is some evidence that domestic behaviours, such as recycling and materials conservation, are transferred to the work context (Lee, De Young, & Marans, 1995). Conversely, experience of work-based recycling can influence domestic behaviour (Fusco, 1991). Other studies focus on the employees' willingness to suggest and implement pro-environmental ideas (Hostager, Neil, Decker, & Lorentz, 1998). Andersson and Bateman (2000) emphasise the power of individual initiative in creating action on environmental issues and define champions as: 'individuals who, through formal organisational roles *and/or personal activism,* attempt to introduce or create change in a product, process or method within an organisation' (p. 549; emphasis added).

Important determinants of such innovation at the individual level are motivation and self-efficacy (Hostager et al., 1998). Motivation is determined by a range of intrinsic and extrinsic incentives and disincentives (De Young, 2000; Hostager et al., 1998). Research supports the view that self-efficacy beliefs mediate the effect of skills or other self-beliefs on subsequent performance (Pajares, 1997). Bandura (1997) states that employees who are assured in their efficacy to produce ideas and are proactively oriented will generate and submit ideas to improve work processes. Efficacy beliefs are closely related to perceived control and autonomy (Bell & Menguc, 2002). The level of perceived control can also have important direct effects on role conflict (Hartline, Maxham, & McKee, 2000). Role conflict (an incongruity within the expectations associated with a role; Singh, 2000) generally has a negative impact on the propensity to engage in OCBs (Podsakoff et al., 2000). De Ruyter, de Jong, and Wetzels (2009) highlight how organisational actors aim to balance their obligations to multiple stakeholders while upholding moral norms with respect to the environment.

Podsakoff et al. (2000) describe two major underlying antecedents of OCB as dispositional factors, such as positive and negative affectivity, which predispose people to certain orientations and a general affective 'morale' factor including organisational commitment and trust in the leader. The role of the leader and other organisational factors which impact on the individual's propensity to engage in pro-environmental OCBs are discussed in the next section.

## Organisational factors as determinants of environmentally responsible behaviours

Leadership behaviour plays a major role as a determinant of both OCBs (Schneider, Ehrhart, Mayer, & Saltz, 2005; Wieseke et al., 2009) and employees' willingness to adopt and create ERWB (Egri & Herman, 2000; Keogh & Polonsky, 1998).

Egri and Herman (2000) found that environmental leaders (those with the ability to influence individuals and mobilise organisations to realise a vision of long-term ecological sustainability) engaged in high levels of both transformational practices (such as collaboration, empowerment, two-way communication, change orientation, charisma, creating trust, and individualised consideration) and transactional practices (instrumental, contingent reward, and one-way communication). Supportive leader behaviour was found to be positively related to every form of OCB identified by Podsakoff et al. (2000) including 'individual initiative'. Leadership behaviour is the key mechanism by which culture is embedded in organisations (Schein, 1992). Organisations' environmental values, typically articulated in vision and/or mission statements, shape responses to natural environmental issues by influencing which issues are identified, which appear on the organisational agenda, and which are associated with organisational responses (Bansal, 2003). Further, Bansal argues, organisational responses to natural environmental issues are determined by an alignment of organisational values and individual concerns.

Organisational characteristics influencing OCBs include organisational formalisation and flexibility, spatial distance from leader, advisory/staff support, cohesive group, and the nature of rewards (Podsakoff et al., 2000). Similar factors, often described as 'organisational support', are frequently described in studies focussing on ERB and innovation. These include supervisory support behaviours and management of goals and responsibilities which have an impact on employee willingness to promote eco-initiatives. In particular, managerial behaviours that lead to feelings of self-efficacy contribute to higher levels of employee creativity (Ramus & Steger, 2000). Management support, resources, organisational structure, and other contextual factors are also highlighted as influential in promoting environmental intrapreneurship (Hostager et al., 1998). Effective communication, including feedback, and the quality of information play a number of important roles including reducing uncertainty about innovation (Lievens & Moenaert, 2000), building trust relationships (Rothenberg, 2003), and encouraging employee involvement in eco-initiatives (Bansal, 2003; Russo & Harrison, 2005). Rewards and incentives are key factors. Hostager et al. (1998) suggest that individuals should be able to select their own incentives from a smorgasbord of intrinsic and extrinsic motivators, for example through providing a stake in the ownership, development, and outcomes of their new idea. One challenge which has been highlighted, however, is that of how to encourage OCBs that are outside formal roles such that it is difficult to specify formally or reward them (Morrison, 1996; Yi & Gong, 2008).

Finally, task characteristics have been identified as important determinants of OCBs. Task feedback and intrinsically satisfying tasks are positively related while task routinisation is negatively related (Podsakoff et al., 2000). Task structure is an important determinant of the commitment and entrepreneurialism which fosters environmental concern within organisations (Keogh & Polonsky, 1998). A match between an organisation's design and its work tasks can boost environmental performance (Russo & Harrison, 2005). The nature of employees' tasks together with the organisational characteristics and leadership behaviours discussed earlier will determine the potential for changes in processes, procedures, and routines and hence employee behaviour. The next section describes how an ISM approach can potentially create an organisational environment for the creation and adoption of environmentally responsible OCBs.

## Integrating social and internal marketing to encourage environmentally responsible organisational citizenship behaviour

Social marketing adopts the concepts and techniques of commercial marketing to influence target audiences to adopt or sustain behaviour, for example pro-environmental behaviour, in pursuit of social goals. However, to date, social marketing studies have generally paid little attention to the organisational context of human behaviour and none have addressed the potential role of ISM in achieving social marketing objectives. The concept of IM originally developed in the services marketing literature as an approach to achieving attitudinal and behavioural change within organisations. A causal 'chain' was established between the services, such as rewards and training, provided to employees, their behaviour, and the achievement of organisational objectives such as customer loyalty and profitability (Heskett, Sasser, & Schlesinger, 1997). IM has been described as a philosophy for managing the organisation's human resources based on a marketing perspective (George, 1990) and has become accepted terminology in all types of organisations (Gummesson, 2002). Although a major focus of IM studies remains on achieving external customer service satisfaction, a number of authors have emphasised wider, and complementary, roles. These include the creation and communication of corporate values (Hogg & Carter, 2000), learning and competence building (Chaston, 2000), a role in strategy implementation and diffusion of innovations (Varey & Lewis, 1999), the implementation of any functional strategy (Rafiq & Ahmed, 1993), and a marketing perspective to build internal competencies for external success (Ahmed, Rafiq, & Saad, 2003). Varey and Lewis (2000) describe IM as 'a management framework, and not merely a marketing practice' (p. 293).

Within the context of an ISM approach to encouraging ERWB two inter-related roles can be proposed. First, ISM can aim to encourage employees to adopt and implement the organisation's formal environmental policy and objectives. Second, and the main emphasis of this discussion, is that of encouraging employees' voluntary participation in environmentally responsible OCBs. The organisational factors described in the previous section as essential to OCB also form the basis for IM programmes. The role of leadership and the need for senior management support is constantly emphasised as crucial to the success of an IM approach (Ahmed et al., 2003; George, 1990). Wieseke et al. (2009) highlight the indispensable role of leaders in instilling into employees company culture, values, and vision and continuously communicating by deeds. Further, they add that it is the role of leaders, especially middle managers, in building organisational identification (a sense of belonging to an organisation) that lays the foundation for IM. Authors have also emphasised the role of trust in internal relationship building (Bowen & Lawler, 1992), as an important antecedent of employee co-operation and commitment (Chenet, Tynan, & Money, 1999), and as a determinant of the propensity to engage in OCBs (Morrison, 1996).

Organisational vision and values play a central role in IM theory (Ahmed & Rafiq, 2002; Gummesson, 1987; Varey & Lewis, 1999) and practice (Foreman & Money, 1995). Organisational identification is based on positive feelings and a shared vision and values reflecting organisational culture. The previous section highlighted the need for an alignment of the organisation's environmental policy and employees' environmental concerns to encourage worker participation in environmental initiatives. Additionally, organisational identification has been identified as a key factor in encouraging behaviours that fall outside formal role requirements and therefore OCBs (Bell & Menguc, 2002; Wieseke et al., 2009).

IM programmes highlight the need for effective job design, performance feedback, training, and rewards. Task characteristics that increase employee perceived control through enhanced job autonomy increase job satisfaction and positive employee behaviour (Bowen & Lawler, 1992; Hartline et al., 2000; Morrison, 1996; Wieseke et al., 2009). Finally, the roles of communication, information gathering, and responding to employee feedback have been highlighted as key elements of an IM approach (Lings & Greenley, 2005). Communication is essential in clarifying organisational values, goals, and policies (Mukherjee & Malhotra, 2006). Two-way communication, between managers and employees, builds trust and is a key determinant of OI and the propensity to engage in OCBs (Wieseke et al., 2009). ISM programmes therefore which aim to encourage EROCBs amongst employees must be developed from a clear understanding of the individual's values, beliefs, norms, and motivations for engaging in such behaviour, as well as the organisational factors which can provide barriers or drivers to change. The following study aimed to achieve that understanding through discussions with groups of employees from private and public sector organisations in the UK.

## Methodology

The research had two main aims. The first was to explore the prevalence and nature of OCBs related to ERWB. The second aim was to examine the individual and organisational factors that influence employees' involvement in such behaviour. In view of the lack of prior research focussing on these issues, an exploratory, qualitative design was selected as the most appropriate methodology. Exploratory research aims to identify and clarify the nature of problems involving new insights and greater understanding of the issues involved (McGivern, 2009) while creating a general mental picture of the unfamiliar (Neuman, 2006). Steyaert and Bouwen (2004) argue that group contexts, for example focus groups created by the researcher, are the most natural method for exploration and gathering knowledge, especially in an organisational context. Focus groups also avoid the reductionism of more structured techniques allowing normally unarticulated normative assumptions to be expressed (Bloor, Frankland, Thomas, & Robson, 2001). They create a forum where participants can provide both previously shared and unshared information (Fern, 2001).

Fourteen groups of employees from five organisations were involved in discussions. A purposive non-probability sampling approach was adopted at both the organisational and group participant level. Since Nilsson et al. (2004) observe sectoral differences in values and norms related to ERB, organisations were selected so as to include both private (one service and one manufacturing), public (one local authority and one education), and 'third sector' (one charity), thus representing major sectors of the UK economy. A further sampling criterion was the requirement for a minimum level of organisational carbon emissions of 3000 tonnes per year (assessed by an independent carbon measurement consultant). This complied with the Carbon Reduction Commitment scheme on which the UK's Defra was consulting at the time of the research (see Carbon Trust, 2011). Key senior management contacts in a number of large UK organisations were identified, either through previous/existing relationships (unrelated to the current research) with the research team or other colleagues. A total of 18 organisations were sequentially approached until one participant from each sector was recruited.

Voluntary participation was considered the optimum approach to achieving the research aims in that participants would be more likely to have been involved in EROCBs and/or aware of others who had. Key contacts in the five organisations were asked to recruit participants by circulating a general invitation to discuss environmental issues. However, there was no attempt to preclude the self-selection of those who might have negative opinions (see Appendix 2 for details of the group composition for each organisation).

Group discussions were between 75 and 100 minutes in duration involving between 6 and 10 participants. They were conducted within the work environment and audio recorded. The majority of groups involved both male and female participants (one involved only female and another only male participants) but varied according to age and status characteristics, reflecting the nature of the organisations. Groups were first asked about their domestic behaviour and personal factors, for example their environmental values and beliefs. They were then asked to describe ERBs initiated by themselves (or others) as employees and the nature of the organisational context, for example their perceptions of the organisation's commitment to environmental issues (see Appendix 3 for the interview schedule). Procedures contributing to the reliability and validity of the method and findings (Fern, 2001) were adhered to, for example all were conducted by the same experienced moderator, with the same schedule of questions. Summaries of issues discussed were consistently 'fed back' to groups for comment.

Interviews were transcribed then coded and analysed using the software package NVivo. An iterative process followed involving further analysis and interpretation by two independent judges. Computer-aided qualitative data analysis (CAQDAS) organises and analyses unstructured data. It provides an overview of emerging themes while maintaining close contact with the detail of individual groups. It thus promotes the exploratory function of the research (Bazeley, 2007). The efficiency, accuracy, and transparency of the data analysis process is enhanced, while the researcher's interpretive analysis increases the validity of the findings (Mason, 1996). OCBs were identified and categorised according to whether they involved adapting domestic behaviours, creating new behaviours, or influencing colleagues or management (see Figure1), and their nature according to Podsakoff et al.'s (2000) schema (see Appendix 1). A final classification related to the type of ERB categorised according to the UK's Defra's (2006) priority groups for domestic behaviours, that is, transport, energy usage, water usage, purchasing, and waste reduction (e.g. recycling; see Table 1 for a summary of behaviours). A process of inductive, thematic analysis then identified the nature of inter-related factors (individual and organisational) involved in OCBs. Thematic analysis involves finding patterns within the data which can describe, organise, and even interpret aspects of the phenomena (Boyatzis, 1998). For example, a number of reciprocal relationships were identified, as described by SCT (Bandura, 1986). Consensus between the two judges for the categorisation of OCBs, identification of individual and organisational factors, and of consistent themes indicated a high level of inter-rater reliability (Boyatzis, 1998; Rust & Cooil, 1994). These are discussed in the next section.

**Table 1** Employee-generated environmentally responsible[1] OCBs[2].

| Adapting/extending domestic behaviour (7) | Influencing colleagues (7) |
|---|---|
| **Type of OCB** | **Type of OCB** |
| individual initiative (7) | sportsmanship (3); civic virtue (2); helping behaviour (1); individual initiative (1) |
| **Type of ERB** | **Type of ERB** |
| Energy usage (4); waste reduction (3) | Energy usage (3); waste reduction (3); transport (1) |
| **Description** | **Description** |
| Taking waste home to recycle | Cancelling unsolicited 'junk mail' from within the organisation |
| Reusing food packaging | Challenging colleagues on energy use |
| Customising light fittings | Campaigning to enforce printer sharing |
| Turning down heating in own office | Reducing frequency of printed reports |
| Turning off lights on behalf of others | Encouraging colleagues to recycle |
| Turning off electrical appliances on behalf of others | Turning off colleagues computers at night |
| Correctly reallocating recycling materials on behalf of others | Including environmental issues when mentoring trainees |
| **Creating new behaviours (8)** | **Influencing management (4)** |
| **Type of OCB** | **Type of OCB** |
| Individual initiative (7); helping behaviour (1) | Civic virtue (3); individual initiative (1). |
| **Type of ERB** | **Type of ERB** |
| Energy usage (2); waste reduction (4); transport (2) | Energy usage (2); waste reduction (1); transport (1) |
| **Description** | **Description** |
| Developing a car-sharing scheme | Lobbying for unit-level recycling facilities |
| Sharing mobile phone chargers | Lobbying for home working |
| Using excess printing as scrap paper | Resisting non-essential meetings |
| Voluntarily changing a system to reduce journeys made by empty lorries | Negotiating official sanction for a switch-off initiative |
| Sharing bins to save bin liners | |
| Unofficial recycling scheme | |
| Organising work around domiciling | |
| Toner recycling scheme involving users | |

[1] Defra (2006) – transport, energy usage, water usage, purchasing, and waste reduction.
[2] See Appendix 1 for Podsakoff et al.'s (2000) classification of OCBs.


## Findings and discussion

Twenty-six examples of employee generated EROCBs were extracted from the transcriptions. Behaviours which directly resulted from the organisation's environmental policy and initiatives (categorised as 'organisational compliance'; Podsakoff et al., 2000), for example complying with recycling directives, are excluded from the analysis. The following discussion focuses on the often neglected resource of employee-originated initiatives illustrated as the four types of behaviour in Table 1. The personal and organisational factors determining employees' propensity to engage in EROCBs are discussed and illustrated in Figure 3.

**Figure 3** Personal drivers and organisational constraints to environmentally responsible organisational citizenship behaviours.

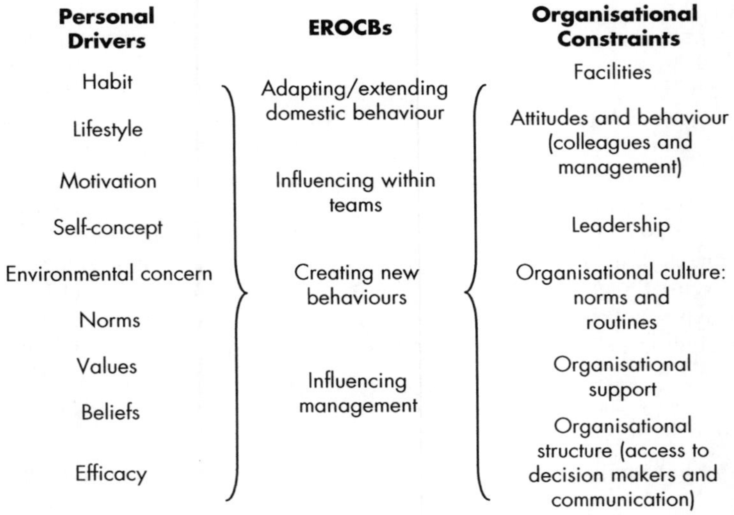

| Personal Drivers | EROCBs | Organisational Constraints |
|---|---|---|
| Habit | Adapting/extending domestic behaviour | Facilities |
| Lifestyle | | Attitudes and behaviour (colleagues and management) |
| Motivation | Influencing within teams | |
| Self-concept | | Leadership |
| Environmental concern | Creating new behaviours | Organisational culture: norms and routines |
| Norms | | |
| Values | Influencing management | Organisational support |
| Beliefs | | Organisational structure (access to decision makers and communication) |
| Efficacy | | |

### *Adapting/extending domestic behaviour*

Seven EROCBs were categorised as adapting behaviours, that is, those that participants voluntarily transferred from the home to the work context. All resulted from 'individual initiative' (Podsakoff et al., 2000). Participants described their domestic and work selves as a continuum in terms of environmental attitudes and behaviour, reflected in the nature of activities reported (saving power, recycling, and reusing material). Seamless transfer between work and home behaviour is illustrated by stories of taking recyclables home because of the lack of workplace facilities, or reusing packaging for food prepared at home to eat at work. Indeed, recycling, the most pervasive of the activities reported, epitomised this kind of integrated, ingrained behaviour, as implied in the following exchange:

> It becomes second habit, doesn't it?
>
> . . . because you do it automatically. (PS1)

The expected relationship between home and work behaviours (Lee et al., 1995) and the role of habit in pro-environmental behaviour (Knussen et al., 2004) was observed consistently across all groups. Many expressed their commitment to the environment as part of a holistic lifestyle essential to their self-concept:

> I just don't see the need for all this stuff, and that's where I see it, so just the simple life. Return to simple. (PR1)

Environmental concern (Dunlap & Jones, 2002) was a key theme manifest in all discussions. Concern was grounded in personal norms, values, beliefs providing a general predisposition towards ERB:

> I'm going to do this because I think it's the right thing to do. (PS1)
>
> Obviously there is an issue so why not take that into account in the way that you live and try and live responsibly? (PS3)

In particular, groups highlighted the need to consider the legacy left to future generations and the finite nature of the earth's resources. Participants gave less credence to the contradictory 'scientific' accounts of global warming available in contemporary news media (exasperation with this was a consistent theme across groups). By contrast, discussions consistently highlighted the level of perceived self and group efficacy required for behavioural change (Bandura, 1997):

> I personally feel that if we, if everybody does their little bit and there's billions of us on this planet, we will surely do something to try and stop it getting worse. (PR2)

Many also engaged in domestic behaviours aimed at persuading family and friends to reduce energy consumption or recycle waste. This too was extended into the organisational context as discussed below.

### Influencing within teams

A further seven EROCBs aimed to influence the behaviour of colleagues. Some attempts to influence resulted in ridicule and other unpleasant responses and are categorised as 'sportsmanship' (Podsakoff et al., 2000). Others represented 'civic virtue', by sharing ideas, combating groupthink, and challenging established norms and routines, for example by reducing the frequency of reports and the number of printers available. It was often emphasised that such changes could go unnoticed, whereas consultation could create resistance. Motivational factors typically included participants' environmental concerns and a desire for less waste. A reciprocal reinforcing relationship between work and domestic behaviour as a result of influencing others was also suggested:

> I think the more you encourage it in the workplace it'll probably rub off on them, so when they get home they start picking up those sorts of practices. (PR2)

A sense of such activities contributing to the influencer's self-concept was also in evidence:

> Well, I was renowned for turning people's monitors off at night and leaving little messages saying the pixies had been. (PS1)

However, many were frustrated by the attitudes and behaviour of colleagues who resisted change and emphasised the lack of financial incentive which often influenced domestic behaviour. Participants blamed senior managers who ought to lead on this important issue for a number of reasons, including the need for resource allocation and the enforcement of sanctions for non-compliance:

> The small people . . . are actually pulling their weight. It's the bigger fish that really need to lead the way. (PR1)
>
> That needs a directive from higher up to say if you're not going to be at your desk, you've got to turn this and that off. (PR2)

Although task structures could often accommodate change, participants often felt that they were battling against an organisational culture where waste and misuse of resources were acceptable behaviours. Norms and routines, for example with respect to travelling long distances to meetings, were rarely questioned, or alternatives, such as video conferencing, considered.

> We have a culture of attending meetings . . . of printing out lots and lots of paper. (PS1)

### Creating new behaviours

Creating new behaviours involved, with one exception, 'individual initiative' (Podsakoff et al., 2000). Whereas 'adapting' involves work initiatives extended from a domestic context, 'creating' involves new workplace initiatives with no direct domestic equivalent. For example, members of a College IT team initiated a toner cartridge recycling scheme which required users to return cartridges in person. A replacement was then issued and installed by the user. In addition to environmental benefits, users always received the correct replacement, the IT team could concentrate on 'more important work' and, ultimately, the scheme led to a rationalisation of equipment purchasing with additional environmental and cost benefits.

Although individual in origin, the majority of 'creating' behaviours were developed and implemented through teams. They typically required that others in the organisation should participate in order to be effective. Individuals saw opportunities and were intrinsically motivated. Groups continued to highlight their personal values, beliefs, and norms, and expressed their emotions as a basis for behaviour:

> It just annoys me because it is so wasteful. (PS1)
>
> I feel sad that we live in a throw-away society. (PR2)

Participants highlighted the lack of autonomy and control in the workplace as opposed to the domestic context. This impacted to some extent on all four types of EROCB illustrated in Table 1, but the implementation of 'creating behaviours' often had to be sanctioned by management. A reduction in the level of perceived self-efficacy often resulted, as illustrated in the final section.

### Influencing management

Four illustrations of EROCBs involved employees in 'influencing management' by lobbying for change in policy towards 'greener' working practices at the organisational level. Two of these, establishing a 'work from home' scheme and gaining support for a 'switch-off' initiative, had been successful. However, two others, involving reducing meeting attendance and increasing recycling facilities, had not gained support. 'Influencing management' behaviours are driven by similar personal factors as other forms of EROCB reflecting the personal norms, beliefs, and environmental concern of employees. Participants' accounts, however, emphasised the crucial role of organisational characteristics, and leadership in particular, in creating a climate where such influence seemed feasible. Many had ideas for environmentally focussed change, for example reducing printing, recycling, saving energy, and changing transport modes, but lacked the time or motivation to do so, usually because of anticipated barriers. Participants again emphasised the lack of control over the work environment:

> I think also, like at home, you have control of that environment, so if you have a problem with something, you can take the correct action. However, in a work environment, like you say, this admin person, they might have a problem printing 1000 pages, but they might not have any power to change. They could say to their manager, this is stupid, why are we doing that? And they'll just get told, we need it, do it. (PR2)

Employees typically saw senior management as unreceptive to their ideas and concerned with short-term financial or operational priorities rather than the environment:

> It's a nineteenth-century mill owner culture . . . we'd even have companies come to say if you put in different efficiency engine systems . . . But then the budget holder says, what's the return on investment . . . and you say five or six years. They say, not a chance. (PR2)

Any official support for environmentally responsible working practices tended to be seen as opportunistic, image-related, and slow rather than central to the organisation's mission. This often conflicted with employees' environmental concern:

> They might be planning five years in advance whereas we want to do something quickly. (PS2)

Many were unaware of their organisation's environmental policy, values, or objectives. Even where information concerning environmental policy and targets was effectively disseminated, for example through the organisational intranet and dedicated newsletters, there was often scepticism as to the motives involved. Many felt this was lip service rather than a genuine concern and willingness to commit resources.

Access to decision makers and anticipated management responses to employee ideas, however, varied between the groups, according to the level of seniority of participants and the organisational structure. One participant described a Catch 22-like situation whereby her employer had a well-established environmental policy at corporate level (playing a leading role in a local consortium) but a policy vacuum at the departmental level which impacted on her. Her attempts to prevent large amounts of unsolicited promotional material had been unsuccessful, and there were no channels in place whereby she could garner management support for her efforts. In the absence of either recycling facilities or access to decision makers, the individual concerned is subject to a weekly reminder of organisational indifference. However, where local managers had the autonomy to express their own environmental concern at the local level, there was a degree of management support for employees:

> Do you know what I think it comes down to? The actual person that's running the centre . . . I think he personally was pushing towards energy saving. And I don't think that was being pushed on by the chief exec or anything. (PS3)

Finally, many participants highlighted a sense of role conflict between that of an environmentally responsible citizen and that of an organisational employee. Consequently, there was little organisational identification in the key area of environmental policy, potentially jeopardising their continued willingness to engage in EROCBs. In addition, previous organisational responses had served to reduce efficacy with respect to ERB initiatives. Some individuals and teams now lacked the motivation or predisposition to become actively involved:

Even X, he's mad about the environment, but he's nearly given up. (PR1)

## Conclusions and implications

Organisations and social marketers are failing to harness a valuable resource in the pursuit of their environmental objectives. Discussions highlighted a high level of environmental concern amongst employees of five large UK organisations. Motivated by intrinsic factors, derived from their personal values, beliefs, and integrated norms, individuals are transferring their environmentally responsible domestic behaviours to the workplace. Typically participants failed to distinguish between the two contexts and highlighted the role of habit and previous behaviour as behavioural determinants. Consequently, the vast majority of behaviours focussed on those identified as most prevalent in the domestic context involving recycling and reducing energy consumption (Defra, 2006). Employees generally had the flexibility and autonomy to adapt their domestic behaviour to the workplace, although a lack of facilities could be an issue. Many tried to influence others at the local level to adopt ERB despite the potential for resistance and ridicule. There were also instances where individuals or teams had created new ways of working which potentially had a far wider impact on the organisation and had lobbied management to introduce and support change.

In view of the considerable stakeholder pressures to reduce environmental impact, including those from external customers, such employees provide a valuable resource to organisations. However, the main themes reflected many factors identified as detrimental to OCB (Organ et al., 2006; Podsakoff et al., 2000). These included a general lack of organisational support including lack of environmental leadership or access to decision makers; organisational cultures and norms where waste is considered to be acceptable; lack of priority of environmental issues; and failure to communicate the organisation's policy and objectives. Employees perceive that they are doing what they can, but this is not reflected by either organisational policy or leadership from senior management. In particular, they highlight the need for cultural change as a top-down priority to influence the behaviour of colleagues and the allocation of resources. Where there was awareness of environmental policy, there was also distrust of both the underlying motives and the likelihood of management action. As organisational actors, therefore, aiming to balance their obligations to multiple stakeholders (de Ruyter et al., 2009), participants often experienced tension or conflict between their role as an employee and that of a citizen in a wider society.

Employees often lacked the autonomy and control over their tasks and working environment which would be necessary to make more creative changes. Consequently, as predicted by both social cognitive and OCB theory, factors in the organisational environment resulted in role conflict, lower levels of efficacy, and reduced predisposition and motivation for future involvement in eco-initiatives. Bandura (1986) highlights how self-efficacy beliefs may not perform their influential, predictive, or mediational role in prejudicially structured systems which include lack of incentives, inadequate resources, and social constraints. However, he also highlights how role conflict can have a positive effect as people search for, and find, successful ways to cope. There were examples where individuals or teams had engaged in OCB, creating and implementing new working practices and thus achieving behavioural change at both the local and occasionally wider organisational level.

The findings suggest an important role for IM, and thus ISM, in achieving ERB change. IM has the potential to (a) create organisational identification (Wieseke et al., 2009) based on a closer alignment between individuals' environmental concerns and the organisation's values, for example through improved communication and information sharing, and (b) enhance employee self-efficacy with respect to pro-environmental OCBs, for example through increasing employee perceived control through job autonomy, supported by training and performance feedback. Effective internal customer segmentation based on individual personal factors such as environmental concern, beliefs, and motivation will identify those with a high level of willingness and ability to act with respect to both direct and indirect OCBs. For example, the effectiveness of peer education schemes in reducing energy consumption in organisations has also been highlighted (Carrico & Riemer, 2011). Barriers can then be removed and incentives/drivers created based on an in-depth understanding of the individual and organisational factors determining internal customer behaviour. In particular, Keogh and Polonsky (1998) describe how the creation of eco-initiatives requires support from all levels of management who encourage employees to feel empowered by the opportunities they see (as opposed to constrained by the restrictions they see).

### Theoretical implications

The vast majority of social marketing studies and theoretical development focus on the individual consumer or household. This study has provided a social cognitive theoretical framework for analysing ERB within the organisational context. Reciprocal relationships between behaviour, individual, and organisational factors have been identified, and the role of efficacy has been highlighted. The nature and determinants of OCBs have previously been examined in marketing literature as a means to achieving the organisation's service quality objectives. This study provides an alternative perspective by adapting the OCB framework to the context of the organisation's environmental policy and objectives. By classifying behaviours in this way, social marketing theory can draw on the extensive body of knowledge which examines OCB in other contexts including the antecedents of the various behavioural types. Similarly, the role of ISM in achieving pro-social behavioural change has not previously been examined. The focus group discussions have identified a substantial role for the concepts and techniques of IM within this context.

### Managerial implications

Organisations are under increasing pressure to reduce their environmental impact. People want to work for organisations which implement a sustainability and corporate social responsibility agenda (Bhattacharya, Sen, & Korschum, 2008; Senge et al., 2008). Yet many are failing to harness the considerable resource available to them in their employees' willingness and ability to become involved in environmental initiatives. Additionally, organisations are failing to communicate their environmental values and policies to employees. By adopting an ISM approach (as described above) and focussing on important determinants such as positive leadership behaviours and organisational support, managers can gain a number of benefits. These can include not only the achievement of environmental targets but also improved reputation, employee motivation, and cost reduction.

## Limitations and further research

Limitations of the study primarily relate to the nature of qualitative research and the focus group method in particular. While generating deeper insight into phenomena, the findings are restricted to small numbers of employees within five large organisations. Consequently, the nature and prevalence of OCBs and determinants cannot be generalised across populations. Additionally, the research aimed, through the voluntary nature of the recruitment process, to elicit the experiences and opinions of those employees who were more positively predisposed towards pro-environmental behaviours and therefore the potential targets of ISM programmes. Future research would aim to assess the barriers to EROCBs as perceived by a more diverse sample of employees.

The validity of the focus group approach has also been questioned, for example the potential for subjective interpretation of findings. However, close adherence to published guidelines, for example for reliability (Rust & Cooil, 1994) and validity assessment (Fern, 2001), encouraged rigour throughout the research process, increasing the credibility of the findings.

One assumption, which has not previously been addressed, is that of whether the behaviours highlighted can truly be considered as OCBs – that is, that they are 'beneficial for the organisation'. It could be suggested that since managers generally did not seem to be encouraging or supporting such behaviours, there is a misalignment between employee and management actions and goals. A dyadic approach to examine the apparent gaps between employee and management perceptions and expectations is therefore required. The service quality literature again provides useful models and frameworks to examine such gaps (Chenet et al., 1999; Zeithaml, Berry, & Parasuraman, 1988). Further research is also needed to assess the impact of high-profile, widely publicised organisational environmental policies on both OCBs and the relationship between internal and external customers. Finally, organisational life influences many of the choices which individual consumers make, for example with respect to health (such as exercise, eating patterns, work/life balance). The role of ISM in achieving other social marketing objectives should be examined.

## References

Ahmed, P.K., & Rafiq, M. (2002). *Internal marketing: Tools and concepts for customer-focused management*. Oxford: Butterworth-Heinemann.

Ahmed, P.K., Rafiq, M., & Saad, M. (2003). Internal marketing and the mediating role of organisational competencies. *European Journal of Marketing*, 37, 1221–1241.

Ajzen, I. (1985). From intentions to actions: A theory of planned behavior. In J. Kuhi & J. Beckmann (Eds.), *Action control: From cognition to behavior* (pp. 11–39). Heidelberg, Germany: Springer.

Andersson, L.M., & Bateman, T.S. (2000). Individual environmental initiative: Championing natural environmental issues in US business organisations. *Academy of Management Journal*, *43*, 548–570.

Arnold, J., Silvester, J., Patterson, F., Robertson, I., Cooper, C., & Burnes, B. (2005). *Work psychology: Understanding human behaviour in the workplace* (4th ed.). Harlow, UK: Financial Times/Prentice Hall

Bamberg, S., & Moser, G. (2007). Twenty years after Hines, Hungerford and Tomera: A new meta-analysis of psycho-social determinants of pro-environmental behaviour. *Journal of Environmental Psychology*, *27*, 214–225.

Bandura, A. (1986). *Social foundations of thought and action: A social cognitive approach.* Englewood Cliffs, NJ: Prentice Hall.

Bandura, A. (1997). *Self-efficacy: The exercise of control.* New York: W.H. Freeman.

Bansal, P. (2003). From issues to actions: The importance of individual concerns and organisational values in responding to natural environmental issues. *Organization Science*, *14*, 510–527.

Bazeley, P. (2007). *Qualitative data analysis* (2nd ed.). London: Sage.

Bell, S.J., & Menguc, B. (2002). The employee–organization relationship, organisational citizenship behaviors, and superior quality. *Journal of Retailing*, *78*(2), 31–46.

Berry, L.L., Hensel, J.S., & Burke, M.C. (1976). Improving retailer rapability for effective consumerism response. *Journal of Retailing*, *52*(3), 3–14.

Bettencourt, L.A., & Brown, S.W. (2003). Role stressors and customer-oriented boundary spanning behaviors in service organizations. *Journal of the Academy of Marketing Science*, *31*, 394–408.

Bhattacharya, C.B., Sen, S., & Korschum, D. (2008). Using corporate social responsibility to win the war for talent. *Sloan Management Review*, *49*(2), 37–44

Bloor, M., Frankland, J., Thomas, M., & Robson, K. (2001). *Focus groups in social research: Introducing qualitative methods.* London: Sage.

Bowen, D.E. & Lawler, E.E. (1992). The empowerment of service workers: What, why, how and when. *Sloan Management Review*, *33*(3), 31–39.

Boyatzis, R.E. (1998). *Transforming qualitative information: Thematic analysis and code development.* Thousand Oaks, CA: Sage.

Carbon Trust. (2011). Carbon Reduction Commitment Energy Efficiency Scheme (CRC) [online]. London: Carbon Trust. Retrieved 29 June 2011, from http://www.carbontrust. co.uk/policy-legislation/business-public-sector/pages/carbon-reduction-commitment.aspx

Carrico, A.R., & Riemer, M. (2011). Motivating energy conservation in the workplace: An evaluation of the use of group-level feedback and peer education. *Journal of Environmental Psychology*, *31*, 1–11.

Chaston, I. (2000). Internal marketing in small manufacturing firms: Extending the concept to encompass organisational learning. In R.J. Varey & B.R. Lewis (Eds.), *Internal marketing: Directions for management* (pp. 93–108). London: Routledge.

Chenet, P., Tynan, C., & Money, A. (1999). Service performance gap: Re-evaluation and re-development. *Journal of Business Research*, *46*(2), 133–147.

Costarelli, S., & Colloca, P. (2004). The effects of attitudinal ambivalence on pro-environmental behavioural intentions. *Journal of Environmental Psychology*, *24*, 279–288.

de Groot, J.I.M., & Steg, L. (2010). Relationships between value orientations, self-determined motivational types and pro-environmental behavioural intentions. *Journal of Environmental Psychology*, *30*, 368–378.

de Ruyter, K., de Jong, A., & Wetzels, M. (2009). Antecedents and consequences of environmental stewardship in boundary-spanning B2B teams. *Journal of the Academy of Marketing Science*, *37*, 470–487.

de Young, R. (2000). Expanding and evaluating motives for environmentally responsible behaviour. *Journal of Social Issues*, *56*, 509–526.

# CONTEMPORARY ISSUES IN GREEN AND ETHICAL MARKETING

Department for Environment, Food and Rural Affairs (Defra). (2006). *An environmental behaviours strategy for DEFRA: Scoping report*. London: Defra/HMSO. Retrieved 28 February 2011 from http://www.defra.gov.uk/evidence/social/behaviour/documents/behaviours-1206-scoping.pdf

Dunlap, R.E., & Jones, R.E. (2002). Environmental concern: Conceptual and measurement issues. In R.E. Dunlap & W. Michelson (Eds.), *Handbook of environmental sociology* (pp. 482–524). Westport, CT: Greenwood.

Dunlap, R.E., Van Liere, K.D., Mertig, A.G., & Jones, R.E. (2000). Measuring endorsement of the New Ecological Paradigm: A revised NEP Scale. *Journal of Social Issues, 56*, 425–442.

Egri, C.P., & Herman, S. (2000). Leadership in the North American environmental sector: Values, leadership styles, and contexts of environmental leaders and their organisations. *The Academy of Management Journal, 43*, 571–604.

Fern, E.F. (2001). *Advanced focus group research*. Thousand Oaks, CA: Sage.

Foreman, S.K., & Money, A.H. (1995). Internal marketing: Concepts, measurement and application. *Journal of Marketing Management, 11*, 755–768.

Fusco, M.A.C. (1991). Recycling in the office initially may be motivated by altruism but ultimately such efforts continue because they are cost effective. *Employment Relations Today, 17*, 333–335.

George, W.R. (1990). Internal marketing and organisational behaviour: A partnership in developing customer-conscious employees at every level. *Journal of Business Research, 20*(1), 63–70.

Gummesson, E. (1987). Using internal marketing to develop a new culture: The case of Ericsson quality. *Journal of Business and Industrial Marketing, 2*(3), 23–28.

Gummesson, E. (2002). *Total relationship marketing* (2nd ed.). Oxford: Butterworth-Heinemann.

Hartline, M.D., Maxham, J.G., & McKee, D.O. (2000). Corridors of influence in the dissemination of customer-oriented strategy to consumer contact service employees. *Journal of Marketing, 64*(2), 35–50.

Heskett, J.L., Sasser, W.E., & Schlesinger, L.A. (1997). *The service profit chain*. New York: Free Press.

Hogg, G., & Carter, S. (2000). Employee attitudes and responses to internal marketing. In R.J. Varey & B.R. Lewis (Eds.), *Internal marketing: Directions for management* (pp. 109–124). London: Routledge.

Hostager, T.J., Neil, T.C., Decker, R.L., & Lorentz, R.D. (1998). Seeing environmental opportunities: effects of intrapreneurial ability, efficacy, motivation and desirability. *Journal of Organisational Change Management, 11*(1), 11–25.

Keogh, P.D., & Polonsky, M.J. (1998). Environmental commitment: A basis for environmental entrepreneurship? *Journal of Organisational Change Management, 11*(1), 38–49.

Kilbourne, W.E., & Beckmann, S.C. (1998). Review and critical assessment of research on marketing and the environment. *Journal of Marketing Management, 14*, 513–532.

Kilbourne, W.E., & Pickett, G. (2008). How materialism affects environmental beliefs, concern, and environmentally responsible behaviour. *Journal of Business Research, 61*, 885–893.

Knussen, C., Yule, F., MacKenzie, J., & Wells, M. (2004). An analysis of intentions to recycle household waste: The roles of past behaviour, perceived habit and perceived lack of facilities. *Journal of Environmental Psychology, 24*, 237–246.

Lee, Y., De Young, R., & Marans, R.W. (1995). Factors influencing individual recycling behaviour in office settings: A study of office workers in Taiwan. *Environment and Behaviour, 27*, 380–403.

Lefebvre, R.C. (2000). Theories and models in social marketing. In P.N. Bloom & G.T. Gundlach (Eds.), *Handbook of marketing and society* (pp. 506–518). Newbury Park, CA: Sage.

Lievens, A., & Moenaert, R.K. (2000). Communication flows during financial service innovation. *European Journal of Marketing, 34*, 1078–1110.

Lindenberg, S., & Steg, L. (2007). Normative, gain and hedonic goal frames guiding environmental behaviour. *Journal of Social Issues, 63*, 117–137.

Lings, I.N., & Greenley, G.E. (2005). Measuring internal marketing orientation. *Journal of Service Research, 7*, 290–305.

Mason, J. (1996). *Qualitative researching.* London: Sage.

McGivern, Y. (2009). *The practice of market research* (3rd ed.). Essex, UK: Prentice Hall/Financial Times.

McKenzie-Mohr, D. (2000). Promoting sustainable behaviour: An introduction to community-based social marketing. *Journal of Social Issues, 56*, 543–554.

Morrison, E.W. (1996). Organisational citizenship behavior as a critical link between HRM practices and service quality. *Human Resource Management, 35*, 493–512.

Mukherjee, A., & Malhotra, N. (2006). Does role clarity explain employee-perceived service quality? *International Journal of Service Industry Management, 17*, 444–473.

Netemeyer, R.G., & Maxham, J.G. III, (2007). Employee versus supervisor ratings of performance in the retail customer service sector: Differences in predictive validity for customer outcomes. *Journal of Retailing, 83*, 131–145.

Neuman, W.L. (2006). *Social research methods: Qualitative and quantitative approaches* (6th ed.). Boston: Pearson/Allyn and Bacon.

Nilsson, A., von Borgstede, C., & Biel, A. (2004). Willingness to accept climate change strategies: The effect of values and norms. *Journal of Environmental Psychology, 24*, 267–277.

Organ, D.W., Podsakoff, P.M., & MacKenzie, S.B. (2006). *Organisational citizenship behavior: Its nature, antecedents, and consequences.* Thousand Oaks, CA: Sage.

Pajares, F. (1997). Current directions in self-efficacy research. In M. Maehr & P.R. Pintrich (Eds.), *Advances in motivation and achievement* Vol. 10, (pp. 1–49). Greenwich, CT: JAI Press.

Peattie, K., & Peattie, S. (2009). Social marketing: A pathway to consumption reduction? *Journal of Business Research, 62*, 260–268.

Perugini, M., & Bagozzi, R.P. (2001). The role of desires and anticipated emotions in goal-directed behaviours: Broadening and deepening the Theory of Planned Behaviour. *British Journal of Social Psychology, 40*, 79–98.

Podsakoff, P.M., MacKenzie, S.B., Paine, J.B., & Bachrach, D.G. (2000). Organisational citizenship behaviors: A critical review of the theoretical and empirical literature and suggestions for future research. *Journal of Management, 26*, 513–563.

Rafiq, M., & Ahmed, P.K. (1993). The scope of internal marketing: Defining the boundary between marketing and human resource management. *Journal of Marketing Management, 9*(3), 219–232.

Ramus, C.A., & Steger, U. (2000). The roles of supervisory support behaviours and environmental policy in employee 'ecoinitiatives' at leading-edge European companies. *Academy of Management Journal, 43*, 605–626.

Rothenberg, S. (2003). Knowledge content and worker participation in environmental management at NUMMI. *Journal of Management Studies, 40*, 1783–1802.

Russo, M.V., & Harrison, N.S. (2005). Organisational design and environmental performance: Clues from the electronics industry. *Academy of Management Journal, 48*, 582–593.

Rust, R.T., & Cooil, B. (1994). Reliability measures for qualitative data: Theory and implications. *Journal of Marketing Research, 31*, 1–13.

Schein, E.H. (1992). *Organisational culture and leadership* (2nd ed.). San Francisco: Jossey-Bass.

Schneider, B., Ehrhart, M.G., Mayer, D.M., & Saltz, J.L. (2005). Understanding organisation – Customer links in service settings. *Academy of Management Journal, 48*, 1017–1032.

Senge, P., Smith, B., Kruschwitz, N., Laur, J., & Schley, S. (2008). *The necessary revolution: How individuals and organisations are working together to create a sustainable world.* London: Nicholas Brealey.

Singh, J. (2000). Performance productivity and quality of frontline employees in service organisations. *Journal of Marketing, 64*(2), 15–34.

Smith, A.M. (2011). Internal social marketing: Lessons from the field of services marketing. In G. Hastings, K. Angus, & C. Bryant, *The SAGE handbook of social marketing* (chap. 20, pp. 298–316). London: Sage.

Stern, P.C. (2000). Toward a coherent theory of environmentally significant behaviour. *Journal of Social Issues, 56,* 407–424.

Steyaert, C., & Bouwen, R. (2004). Group methods of organizational analysis. In C. Cassell & G. Symon (Eds.), *Essential guide to qualitative methods in organizational research* chap.12, (pp. 140–153). London: Sage.

Thøgersen, J. (1994). A model of recycling behaviour, with evidence from Danish source separation programmes. *International Journal of Research in Marketing, 11,* 145–163.

Thøgersen, J. (2006). Norms for environmentally responsible behaviour: An extended taxonomy. *Journal of Environmental Psychology, 26,* 247–261.

Varey, R.J., & Lewis, B.R. (1999). A broadened conception of internal marketing. *European Journal of Marketing, 33,* 926–944.

Varey, R.J., & Lewis, B.R. (2000). End-view: Directions for management. In R.J. Varey & B.R. Lewis (Eds.), *Internal marketing: Directions for management* (pp. 293–301). London: Routledge.

Wieseke, J., Ahearne, M., Lam, S.K., & van Dick, R. (2009). The role of leaders in internal marketing. *Journal of Marketing, 73,* 23–145.

Yi, Y., & Gong, T. (2008). If employees 'go the extra mile', do customers reciprocate with similar behavior? *Psychology and Marketing, 25,* 961–986.

Zeithaml, V.A., Berry, L.L., & Parasuraman, A. (1988). Communication and control processes in the delivery of service quality.*Journal of Marketing, 52*(2), 35–48.

## Appendix 1. Types of organisational citizenship behaviour (Podsakoff et al., 2000)

| | |
|---|---|
| *Helping behaviour* | Helping with or preventing the occurrence of problems. Helping includes altruism, peacemaking, and cheerleading. Prevention includes courtesy. |
| *Sportsmanship* | Are not offended when others do not follow their suggestions, and do not take the rejection of their ideas personally. |
| *Organisational loyalty* | Endorsing, supporting, and defending organisational objectives. |
| *Organisational compliance* | Internalisation and acceptance of organisation's rules and procedures. |
| *Individual initiative* | Voluntary acts of creativity and innovation, volunteering to take on extra responsibilities, and encouraging others in the organisation to do the same. |
| *Civic virtue* | A commitment to 'organisational citizenship', for example sharing ideas, combating groupthink, identifying problems. |
| *Self-development* | Improving own knowledge and skills to be a better member of the organisation. |

# Appendix 2. Organisation descriptions and focus group composition

| Organisation | Participants and roles |
|---|---|
| PR1 – private sector service organisation; An internal (emergency) services department of a major transport facility | Group 1 ($n = 7$)<br>Senior administrator; Administrator; Emergency service team leader; 3 × Emergency service operatives; Maintenance engineer<br>Group 2 ($n = 6$)<br>5 × Emergency service operatives; Emergency service team leader<br>Group 3 ($n = 6$)<br>4 × Emergency service operatives; Administrator; Receptionist |
| PR2 – private sector manufacturing organisation A commercial manufacturer and installer of home and garden improvements | Group 1 ($n = 6$)<br>Purchasing Manager; Data Maintenance Officer: 2 × Network Support Officers; IT Director; Service Manager<br>Group 2 ($n = 6$)<br>IT Helpdesk Supervisor; Communications Technician; Project Accountant; Credit Control Supervisor; Stores Supervisor; Purchasing Scheduler |
| PS1 – public sector local authority Responsible for services to an area with a population of 300,000 | Group 1 ($n = 6$)<br>2 × Planning Officers; Road Safety Officer; Community Partnership Officer; Housing Policy Officer; Maintenance Engineer<br>Group 2 ($n = 6$)<br>2 × Professional Specialists; Head of Service; Senior Administrator; 2 × Administrative Assistants<br>Group 3 ($n = 6$)<br>2 × Principal Surveyors; 2 × Senior Surveyors; 2 × Surveyors |
| PS2 – public sector educational institution A multi-site Further Education College serving a large metropolitan area | Group 1 ($n = 6$)<br>IT Manager; 5 × IT Officers<br>Group 2 ($n = 9$)<br>3 × Site Heads of Security; College Caretaker; Head of Site Services; Site Services Officer; 2 × Maintenance Officers; Health and Safety Officer<br>Group 3 ($n = 6$)<br>IT Director; 2 × IT Helpdesk Officers; 2 × Executive Support Workers; Database Officer |
| PS3 – public sector leisure facility A non-profit organisation which runs sports and leisure facilities on behalf of local authorities | Group 1 ($n = 10$)<br>3 × Duty Managers; 2 × Life Guards; 2 × Maintenance Officers; IT Technician; Receptionist; Clerical Officer<br>Group 2 ($n = 6$)<br>3 × Duty Managers; Trust Secretary; Receptionist; Lifeguard<br>Group 3 ($n = 10$)<br>Active Health Co-ordinator; 2 × Duty Managers; Recreation Manager; Recreation Assistant; Centre Manager; Membership Manager; 2 × Lifeguards; Receptionist |

# Appendix 3. Focus group interview schedule

**Introductions, ethical statement, and 'icebreaker': How did you travel to work this morning?**

**Section 1 – General opinions about global warming/climate change - beliefs/efficacy and nature of domestic behaviours**
1. How important to you are environmental issues, for example, global warming? Prompt re impact of carbon emissions
2. How do you feel about these issues?
3. Do you think that individuals can make a difference?
4. What sort of things do you do at home to address these problems?Prompt to include influencing others.

**Section 2 – Work-related attitudes and behaviours**
5. Is it easier to be green at work or at home? Why? Prompt re relative drivers and constraints in each context
6. What sort of things do you do/have you done at work to address environmental issues?Prompt for drivers and constraints for these behaviours
7. What about other people (colleagues) – what do they do/have they done?Prompt for drivers and constraints for these behaviours
8. Can an individual (and/or team) in the workplace really make a difference to the environment? Prompt – If not, why not? If yes, how?
9. Who do you feel is responsible for environmental issues in organisations?
10. Have you (or other people) had ideas for environmental improvements which have (a) not been successful or (b) not been taken forward?Prompt for drivers and constraints for these behaviours

**Section 3 – Organisational policy and initiatives**
11. Does your organisation do much to help the environment/in what way?
12. Do you feel that the organisation really cares about its impact on the environment?
13. Is there an environmental policy and/or organisational environmental initiatives? Prompt for explanations/examples.
14. Are management receptive to/do they encourage ideas from employees about environmental issues? Prompt for examples and reasons.

**Concluding remarks**: Does anyone have anything else they would like to say about the issues discussed today?
Thank you for your participation

# Heterotopian space and the utopics of ethical and green consumption

Andreas Chatzidakis, *Royal Holloway University of London, UK*
Pauline Maclaran, *Royal Holloway University of London, UK*
Alan Bradshaw, *Royal Holloway University of London, UK*

---

**Abstract** In this article, we illustrate how Exarcheia, an Athenian neighbourhood that is renowned for its capacity for revolt and anti-capitalist ethos, provides a rich site for utopian praxis, particularly in relation to a range of green and ethical marketplace behaviours. Arguing that space and place are essential to questions of ethics, ecology, and politics, we explore Exarcheia as a heterotopian space that fosters critique and experimentation, generating new ways of thinking and doing green/ethical behaviours. Drawing on data from a two-year ethnography, our findings not only challenge individualised and de-contextualised notions of the consumer, but also expose moralistic and post-political assumptions that often go unnoticed in ethical and green consumer research. We point to the need for a counter-strand in the literature that reviews instances that we recognise as ethical or green consumerism not in terms of identity projects or given ideas of ethics but rather with reference to the particularity of the spatial contexts in which they occur and their political implications.

---

## Introduction

Exarcheia is an Athenian neighbourhood internationally renowned for its capacity for revolt and anti-capitalist ethos. Among others, this has been the birthplace of the Athens Polytechnic uprising (November 1973), the 2008 Greek riots and more recent protests against neo-liberal reforms posed by the EU/IMF and the (related) demise of the Greek welfare state. Graffiti-covered walls, bearing lurid anarchistic slogans, border restaurants and bars with names like 'Molotof', 'Kalashnikov Garden', and 'Necropolis', and the riot police that stand guard around the clock at main entrance points make Exarcheia a place that you cannot stray into accidentally. You are acutely aware that you have reached Exarcheia. Not only watchful policemen, splattered walls, and provocative names proclaim Exarcheia to be radically different from the rest of Athens, but also the ambience and ambiguity of its environs that create an overriding sense of (dis)place. This 'Exarcheian' identity stands in stark contrast to the rest of Athens, and is lauded alike by the many bohemians, anarchists, and other diverse groups of intellectuals and activists that dwell there.

Our research illustrates how this turbulent area provides a rich site for utopian praxis, particularly in relation to a range of green and ethical marketplace behaviours that reconstitute the radical political nature of the area itself as part of broader sociospatial dialectics (Lefebvre, 1991; Soja, 1980). These collective initiatives made us question and rethink many contemporary green/ethical practices that are often circumscribed by a neoliberal logic. Arguing that space and place are important and essential to questions of ethics, ecology, and politics, we explore Exarcheia as a heterotopian space that fosters critique and experimentation, generating new ways of thinking and doing green/ethical behaviours. First, we problematise the individualistic and decontextualised nature of much research into ethical/green consumerism and look at how space and place have been treated to date. Then we discuss the concepts of heterotopia and utopics before applying them to analyse our data, which were gathered during an ethnographic study of Exarcheia. Using three categories of difference by which a site can be identified as heterotopian (Hetherington, 1997) – built environment, social practices, and events contained therein – our findings reveal how Exarcheia acts as an agent for transformation in the urban environment.

## Problematising ethical/green marketing and consumption movements

Research into ethical/green consumerism, broadly defined to include any 'conscious and deliberate decision to make certain consumption choices due to personal moral beliefs and values' (Crane & Matten, 2004, p. 290), has grown substantially since *JMM*'s special issue on ethical/green marketing in the late 1990s. However, most of the existing studies continue to reflect the assumption that ethical/green consumption is a wholly depoliticised, individualistic, rational, and free-choice context, evident, for instance, in the large number of (inconclusive) attempts to profile the sociodemographic characteristics of the 'ethical' and 'green' consumer (e.g. Diamantapoulos, Schlegelmilch, Sinkovics, & Bohlen, 2003) or studies that persistently try to model the attitudinal and psychological variables of consumers' ethical decision making, despite the widespread observation of 'attitude–behaviour' gaps (e.g. Bray, Johns, & Kilburn, 2010; Carrington, Neville, & Whitwell, 2010; Chatzidakis, Hibbert, & Smith, 2007). This disproportionate emphasis on the individual decision maker is increasingly challenged by an emerging stream of – mainly interpretivist – studies that call for a more nuanced understanding of how ethical consumer discourses, micro-cultures, and identities are constructed in the marketplace and beyond (e.g. Barnett, Clarke, Cloke, & Malpass, 2005; Caruana & Crane, 2008; Cherrier, 2009; Moraes, Szmigin, & Carrigan, 2010). For example, in the context of ethical tourism, Caruana and Crane (2008) illustrate how corporate communications restrict the nature and meaning of 'responsible travel', ultimately rendering tourism an ethically non-conflicting market choice. Thus, despite the relative delay and in line with advancements in disciplines such as politics, sociology, and geography, there is a new wave of marketing theory building and inquiry that moves away from individualised notions of ethical consumerism to consider the intersection of ethical/green consumer culture(s) with civic life, and mass and micro culture(s) (see Shah, McLeod, Friedland, & Nelson, 2007). Our study contributes to this understanding by exploring the relationship of (ethical and green) consumption activities with space/place and a broader nexus of politics.

A common theme within interpretivist treatments of ethical/green consumerism is the acknowledgment of identity formation as central rather than peripheral to the understanding of ethical/green consumerism. For instance, in relation to anti-consumerist and sustainable consumer discourses, Cherrier (2009) identifies two key identity types, that is a 'hero identity' and 'project identities'. Furthermore, more recent research (e.g. Black & Cherrier, 2010; Eckhardt, Belk, & Devinney, 2010) challenges the notion of a 'green' or 'ethical consumer' identity or at least its prominence as a theme in people's narratives vis-à-vis thicker identity themes and projects such as parent, responsible citizen, worker, and so on. Black (2010, p. 406) notes that, in line with Arnould and Thompson's (2007) position that a 'consumer' identity does not exist, current theorising points to how '. . . instead we are sons, daughters, mothers, fathers, friends and workers who consume and do not consume as required'. Similarly, Barnett, Cloke, Clarke, and Malpass (2011) note that ordinary people engage with Fairtrade, environmental issues, and so on primarily as citizens, not as consumers. Seeing a real basis with which to problematise further the 'myth of the ethical consumer' (Devinney, Auger, & Eckhardt, 2010), our study counter-proposes that ethical and ecological practices are essentially spatialised and political. Indeed, although the importance of space/place has been acknowledged to some extent in marketing and consumer research studies that have focused on topics such as new consumption communities (e.g. Moraes et al., 2010; Szmigin, Carrigan, & Bekin, 2007), anti-market festivals (Kozinets, 2002), community-supported agriculture (Thompson & Coskuner-Balli, 2007), and local farmers' markets (e.g. McEachern, Warnaby, Carringan, & Szmigin, 2010), themes relating to space and its dialogical relationship with social relations and political cultivation have not been extensively considered. Within our data, we observe that being an 'Exarcheia resident and activist' (e.g. Kakissis, 2010) is a prevailing politics and collective identity that comes with its own requirements and challenges, defining and restricting what constitutes ethical/green consumption and non-consumption choices within a much wider nexus.

Furthermore, the way that Exarcheia frames ethical/green consumer decisions contributes to understanding how individuals consume (or choose not to) within broader networks of socially embedded relations and cultural codes (e.g. Barnett et al., 2005) and how these are ultimately spatio-temporally bound. From this perspective, Exarcheia facilitates the emergence of a particular type of 'social capital', which, similar to the case of different cultural contexts, such as urban versus rural centres (Neilson & Paxton, 2010) or physical spaces hosting specific consumption movements (e.g. Moraes et al., 2010), encapsulates all the social interactions between Exarcheia residents and the anti-capitalist, anti-materialist, and anti-consumerist 'cultivation' that takes place therein. Exarcheia residents' responses to the dilemmas characterising modern (non-)consumption environments are at the same time framed as Exarcheian responses to these dilemmas and vice-versa. We attempt to understand these practices by drawing on Foucault's (1967) concept of heterotopias and related tools of analysis. First, we investigate the heterotopic nature of Exarcheia and illustrate how this translates into alternative ways of doing politics and day-to-day community living. Subsequently, we illustrate how forms of consumer-oriented ethical and green activism are constituted by the radical nature of the area and how the area is in turn constituted by them as part of a broader sociospatial dialectic (Lefebvre, 1991; Soja, 1980).

## Heterotopia and utopic spatial play

Heterotopias, according to Foucault (1967), are collective or shared spaces of 'otherness' where alternative forms of social organisation take place, forms that stand in stark contrast to their surrounding environment. Often important institutions of the city, Foucault highlights a variety of sites that disrupt our taken-for-granted notions about the ordering of space, for example, prisons, retirement homes, mental institutions, theatres, brothels, gardens, and so forth. Since Foucault's introduction of the concept into the social sciences (it was originally a medical term), it has become popular with cultural geographers and urban studies theorists, particularly in relation to understanding life at the margins and sites of transgression. Theorists such as Hetherington (1997) and Soja (1996) have developed Foucault's original concept to reflect social changes since the 1960s and, in particular, the changing nature of heterotopian spaces (Cenzatti, 2008). In doing so, they have moved beyond Foucault's structuralist arguments of normality/deviance to include the notion of 'difference' that has permeated social science thinking in more recent years. Heterotopias are thus 'spaces of representation' (Lefebvre, 1968) produced by different social relations (Cenzatti, 2008).

Scholars have identified many contemporary consumer heterotopias: gated communities, theme parks, shopping malls, holiday resorts, wellness hotels, jazz clubs, and dance halls to name but a few (see Dehaene & De Cauter, 2008). Whilst acknowledging such sites as heterotopian, Kohn (2003) argues that they are limited in terms of their criticality because they seek to perfect rather than undermine contemporary forms of consumption and, as such, pose no threat to the status quo. In a similar vein, Murtola (2010, p. 50) argues that commodified utopias (such as shopping malls, gated communities, etc.) are limited in their potential for change because their commercial interests frame and shape whatever utopian imaginings occur: 'within a capitalist context, utopia is put to particular ends'. By contrast, Kohn (2003) conceives of 'heterotopia of resistance', whose function is to bring about some type of social transformation. Rather than generating escapist fantasies that reinforce the existing social order, these challenge the ruling norms and are thus important sites of difference and rebellion. Importantly, such sites offer a refuge from dominant discourses as illustrated in Campo and Ryan's (2008) study of unplanned entertainment zones in cities that encourage social inhibitions to be cast aside and ruling norms of behaviour to be questioned, negotiated, and ultimately reconfigured. Kohn concludes that the power of place is that it makes an intuitive, corporeal impact as well as a more intellectual, cognitive one. Thus sharing the same space deepens connections between people and can also lead to more radical political action.

In considering the critical potential of heterotopia, it is important to distinguish the concept from that of utopia, as there is sometimes confusion in the literature. Whereas the concept of utopia envisages a future state of perfection, heterotopia is in the here and now, facilitating what Marin (1984) terms 'utopic spatial play', the function or process of utopian thinking rather than its ultimate realisation (see Maclaran & Brown, 2005). Marin conceives the negating 'u' of utopia (between eu-topia, a good place, and ou-topia, a no place, i.e. nowhere being a good place) as signifying a space that is between affirmation and negation, a space that is neither yes or no, true or false, neither one nor the other (Jameson, 1977). Within this neutral space, the logic of antithesis is suspended and contradictions are allowed to play against one another rather than being resolved or hidden in the text (Bann, 1993; Jameson, 1977). Likewise, Hetherington sees heterotopia as existing in these spaces-in-between, spaces of 'deferral', which, like laboratories, can provide sites of experimentation where different social orderings can be tested. Indeed, heterotopic sites (i.e. the theatre) often juxtapose different social orderings that may be incompatible with each other (Foucault, 1967) but that co-exist without seeking resolution, 'playing' against each other in Marin's terms in the way that two taut ropes intertwine in perpetual tension. This perpetual tension is what gives such sites their creative and radical potential. Heterotopia are sites where we can witness engagements with difference as they take place and as new social orderings emerge to challenge the dominant social order. Hetherington argues that heterotopia come into existence 'when utopian ideals emerge from forms of difference which offer alternative ideas about the organisation of society' (p. 54).

This view of heterotopia is in line with Bloch's (1995) distinction between *abstract and concrete* utopias. Whereas abstract utopias are disconnected from the conditions of the present, concrete utopias are clearly based on the material possibilities of a historical present, with 'path, compass, order' (p. 1053). Browning and McDonald (2007) note that the conceptualisation of concrete utopias emphasises emancipation as procedural or work-in-progress and therefore avoids accusations of objectivism and association with the grand meta-narratives of modernity (Jameson, 1977, 1982). In summary, as space becomes place, it produces webs of meanings and connections between people, thereby bringing a sense of community and identity, which in turn paves the way for collective action. In a heterotopian space, these webs are about radical difference to the norms of the dominant society, a difference that generates 'utopic spatial play' as a crucial part of this meaning creation process. Importantly, utopic dynamics are not just about thinking but also about *doing* and thus a form of utopian praxis.

Given that green/ethical marketing and consumer movements are inherently about environmental and societal change, it is indeed surprising how the role of utopian imagination therein has not been (explicitly) acknowledged, and yet such movements are equally susceptible to commercial appropriations within a capitalist context. In attempting to illustrate this empirically, we focus on Exarcheia, a radical Athenian neighbourhood that is now (thanks to the 2008 riots) globally renowned for its capacity for revolt, resistance, and an explicit anti-capitalist, anti-commercial ethos. By illustrating Exarcheia residents' fights against the forces of globalisation and commodification and how these have translated into more radical and problematised versions of ethical/green activism, we provide a theoretical and empirical counterpoint to current readings of ethical/green marketing and consumerism.

## Methodology

The present research is based on an ethnographic study of Exarcheia that was carried out over a two-year period (see Table 1). During this time, one or more of the researchers spent a total of 16 weeks in the field to record observations, participate in local events, and interview informants. The main questions driving the research were how does this area generate new ways of thinking about consumption practices, and in which ways do its inhabitants resist a neo-liberal market ideology?

The study commenced with an initial exploratory phase of two weeks during which the lead researcher lived in another part of Athens but visited Exarcheia every day, spending long periods strolling the neighbourhood and absorbing the atmosphere in shops, bars, and cafes. At this time, the researcher (a native Greek) had many ad hoc conversations that led to more formalised interviews at later stages of the research. These visits resulted in field notes describing initial impressions and feelings about the consumer experience there. In keeping with Sanders' (1987) recommendations, these notes systematically recorded descriptions about the setting, the social behaviours, and the interactions and relationships taking place. The exploratory visit was followed by the researcher spending two weeks for more systematic data collection, including in-depth interviews with seven residents, additional ad hoc conservations, photographic records of many posters, slogans, and protest graffiti that abound everywhere in Exarcheia, as well as analysis of journal articles about Exarcheia and related websites. Subsequently, the entire research team spent five days there to share observations and undertake additional interviews. After the team visit, the lead researcher returned on two different occasions (phase 3 and 4) to spend 10 weeks living in Exarcheia, immersing himself in local events, volunteering assistance with various projects, and conducting further interviews.

**Table 1** Research phases and methods.

| Time period | Research phase | Research methods |
|---|---|---|
| April 2009 | Exploratory phase (lead researcher) | • Observation studies (14 days)<br>• Ad hoc conversations/interviews (50+)<br>• Field notes |
| November 2009 | Phase 1 (lead researcher) | • In-depth interviews with residents (7)<br>• Ongoing observations and photographic recording<br>• Field notes<br>• Documentation of posters, slogans, graffiti, journal articles, and websites |
| March 2010 | Phase 2 (research team) | • 11 interviews with residents<br>• Tours of the area (2): with graffiti artist and art historian<br>• Ongoing observations and photographic recording |
| October 2010– November 2010 | Phase 3 (lead researcher) | • In-depth interviews with retailers<br>• Working as volunteer<br>• Attending community events<br>• Ongoing observations and photographic recording |
| April 2011 | Phase 4 (lead researcher) | • 16 in-depth interviews with members of various Exarcheia-based collectives<br>• Ongoing observations and photographic recording |

The final data set includes transcripts from 34 interviews, copious field notes from participant observations and more than 50 ad hoc conversations and interviews, more than 200 photographs, and community literature and activist group pamphlets, including more than 20 posters. Comparison processes guided the data collection. This is sometimes referred to as 'purposive sampling' (Lincoln & Guba, 1985) or 'theoretical sampling' (Glaser & Strauss, 1967; Strauss & Corbin, 1990). This means that as the researchers identified initial categories, constructs, and conceptual linkages, they defined subsequent individuals or groups to sample that maximised or minimised differences between them across various dimensions (Spiggle, 1994). In keeping with the sampling method, we collected data during several phases, simultaneously conducting analysis and interpretation. This sensitised us to emerging concepts, and we moved back and forth between data sets and the literature, as recommended by Spiggle (1994) and others (Arnould & Wallendorf, 1994; Strauss & Corbin, 1990).

## Findings

Hetherington identifies three core categories of difference against which heterotopic spaces can be assessed: the built environment (or materiality), social practices, and events contained therein. Using these as the basis for our analysis, we explore how Exarcheia challenges and resists the dominant social ordering, of which consumer society and culture are very much a part. In doing so, we seek to illustrate the power of heterotopian place (Kohn, 2003) and the various ways in which it impacts on ethical and green consumer behaviours.

### Built environment and material elements

> Staying clear of affluent consumer stereotypes and Hollywood-like entertainment. (Papadopoulou, 2010)

The anti-consumerist, anti-materialist, and (overall) anti-capitalist ethos of Exarcheia becomes manifest in many tangible features of its environs. First, it is in the signs that communicate entrance to the neighbourhood, such as the presence of riot police at main entrance points and the use of every wall as canvas for artistic and political expression. These, according to many of our informants, generate a sense of 'tension and urgency', a feeling that 'something is about to or could happen at any point in time' (see also Dimitriou, 2011). This common embodied response to the Exarcheian ambience resonates with Kohn's (2003) argument about the corporeal, intuitive impact of heteropotian places. Concurrently, the widespread use of graffiti is a reminder that, in the lack of adequate public spaces, the impersonal shell of private buildings is reclaimed and transformed 'into a dynamic living organism that constantly beats, yells, makes a multitude of noises, falls in love and quarrels' (Makrygianni & Tsavdaroglou, 2011, p. 35).

A walk around Exarcheia's 50-odd blocks unveils further material objects and artefacts that communicate difference from other Athenian districts. For instance, there is an implicit preference for gifted, second-hand, and 'natural', unprocessed materials (e.g. cob), visible in places such as a guerrilla park (described below) and various squatted areas. Encounters of objects that are inserted by local residents and which are more often associated with the private rather than public sphere, such as handcrafted wood benches and free-to-use table games along pedestrian streets and squares, remind visitors of Exarcheiots' commitment to aesthetically improving and promoting usage of their public space (field notes, October 2010). In turn, Exarcheiots' sense of common history and solidarity is evident in unexpected encounters of places, such as a shrine dedicated to Alexandros Grigoropoulos (Figure 1), the 15-year-old whose shooting by a policeman on 6 December 2008 sparked 'the worst riots Greece has seen since the restoration of democracy in 1974' (Kat, 2008). Finally, additional physical and geometrical characteristics of the area, such as streets intersecting every 45 metres (as opposed to 220 metres in more affluent Athenian areas) can explain how the murder was instantly communicated and riots were spread so quickly (Makrygianni & Tsavdaroglou, 2011). Such geographical characteristics are silent facilitators of most social activity and communication in Exarcheia:

> (Exarcheia) is dense, very dense . . . not dense in the sense of population density per square meter but dense in, how do I say this, culturally . . . It is not just the people that live here but also the people that visit, it is a reference point, this is where people meet easily and so are ideas, things are tried out . . . it is a laboratory. (Male, member of Exarcheia-based collective)

Concurrently, such observations reiterate not only how social life and interrelations produce space and place but also how it is space and place that create social life and interrelations (Soja, 1980, 1996).

Notwithstanding, it is perhaps those material objects that are conspicuous in their absence that are more revealing of Exarcheia's heterogeneous character. At least for some of its residents, it is 'by staying clear of affluent consumer stereotypes and Hollywood-like entertainment' that the authenticity of the neighbourhood and immunity to culturally imported notions of lifestyle and entertainment (mainly from North America) is maintained. For instance, those wearing business attire may feel at times that Exarcheia is a no-go area or in their words, an 'abaton', an almost elusive and inaccessible place (e.g. Chouliara, 2010). Likewise, conspicuous signs of wealth such as SUVs often become targets of vandalism in Exarcheia, and it is a well-kept secret among the more affluent residents that these are either to be avoided or to be kept at more secluded, private car parks (female, residents' committee meeting). According to one of our informants, such behaviours are so pervasive and consistent that parking such cars around Exarcheia may create suspicion:

> . . . So my friend said, wait a moment, who would have parked his car outside the Polytechnic during riots? Why would you do that? So we were sort of thinking, it's a bit odd. So we looked at the cars, they were all big BMWs and Mercedes and Porsches, and they were parked here to be burnt. This was an insurance thing. (Male, Exarcheia resident)

### The Exarcheian marketplace

The profile of Exarcheia's commercial zone and its consumptionscapes (Ger & Belk, 1996) also reflect its heterogeneous character. For instance, a highly disproportionate amount of bookstores and print shops (approximately 1 per 60 residents) stands as testament to the intense political and intellectual activity in the area and its

**Figure 1** The shrine dedicated to Alexandros Grigoropoulos.

strong student population. Equally disproportionate is the amount of record shops, alternative small businesses, and various organic and local food stores. For some of the more traditionally left-wing residents, these signify a 'happier' generation of outlets, starting in the early 2000s, to cater for newer forms of lifestyle-based activism There is a particular aesthetic to many Exarcheian bars, cafes, and restaurants, and this is often further expressed in names such as Decadence, Molotof, Kalashnikov Garden, and Necropolis. As one of our informants said, Exarcheia residents wouldn't like their bars and restaurants to look like the ones in neighbouring areas '. . . which are very fancy and without a character. In this area you'll find taverns or bars that have a strong sense of character . . .' (female, Exarcheia resident).This sense of being separate and adrift of the mainstream marketplace is reinforced via a variety of artefacts, such as a disposable tablecloth that depicts Exarheia as an island (see Figure 2).

Concurrently, the relatively rundown character of some parts of Exarcheia, along with cheap rental prices and a laissez-faire attitude by residents, have allowed the proliferation of various 'here and now' experimentations with performing the economy differently, from informal alternative exchange networks, occupied public spaces, and gifting bazaars to more formalised spaces such as Sporos, a popular collective that promotes solidarity trading with the Zapatistas, and Skoros, an anti-consumerist collective where people can come and give, or take, or give and take several goods and services. Again, however, it is also those (retail) spaces that are

**Figure 2** A disposable tablecloth, found in some low-budget restaurants, which depicts Exarcheia as an island (reproduced with permission).

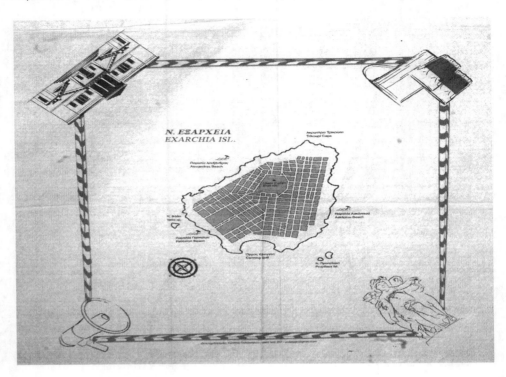

conspicuously absent that mark Exarcheia's anti-establishment character and distaste for any symbols of global capitalism. Among others, names such as Starbucks and Apple have taken the decision to locate away from Exarcheia after having their shops burned down or vandalised. Boycotting principles (e.g. Smith, 1990) in Exarcheia have been taken to a somewhat different level by often 'demanding' market exit for targeted brands: 'We do not want to be one of those neighbourhoods where Starbucks moves in . . . along with its security guards' (female, residents' committee meeting).

## Social practices

### *Need for autonomy*

Consistent with the heterotopian notion of different social orderings existing in the same space, there are many social groups that co-exist in Exarcheia, including left-wing intellectuals, anarchists, Maoists, urban professionals, students, artists, artisans, immigrants, homeless people, and numerous social movements. It is not surprising, therefore, that Exarcheia hosts a wide array of social practices that reflect the diversity of these groups. These practices 'play' against each other in the Marinian sense of not seeking resolution, engaging with each other's differences rather than seeking to oppress or eradicate them. This is also reflected in the politics of day-to-day consumption:

> ... Sporos has met a lot of criticism from a large part of the antagonist movement because it does solidarity 'trading' and yet these same people consume products produced by big multinationals and don't even bother to think about that, they are more concerned about how you do trade and you shouldn't do trade ... Such things are part of the Exarcheian melting pot. (Female, member of Exarcheia-based collective)

Concurrently, they relate to a strong quest for autonomy through self-organisation. Many posters promote the values of 'self-organisation', urging people not to vote for any of the mainstream political parties and critiquing the principles of neoliberalism. Key themes on posters are 'self-managed squats', 'occupied public spaces', 'anti-authoritarianism', 'anti-commercialisation', and 'community-based projects' (field notes, October 2010). There is an overriding preference for mobilisation of the immediate community rather than seeking outside help: 'We don't need the police here at all. We are open enough and conscious enough to deal with such things ourselves' (female, Exarcheia resident).

### Inclusivity/exclusivity

The above example serves to illustrate that there are certain identifiable practices that cut across the different social groupings and that give Exarcheia its special ethos, an identity of place that differentiates it strongly from other Athenian neighbourhoods. Exarcheiots' quest for autonomy goes hand in hand with an overriding tolerance and inclusivity that informants displayed with pride and that certainly facilitate the development of 'utopian spatial play'. As one female member of the residents' association put it, 'there is an openness to different ideas and to tendencies, most of the time left ideas. Conservative people are not very welcome'. Likewise, as noted earlier, conspicuous consumption practices are equally frowned upon and unwelcomed. Thus we can see that despite inclusion there is also exclusion; mainstream society and figures of authority are unwelcome:

> ... And then he said that he works in an arms-trading company and we all froze, we were left with our mouths open ... He had come from work and he was wearing a suit and he was going on about how he feels stupid wearing a tie in Exarcheia, as this is not the kind of place to dress like this ... (Female, member of Exarcheia-based collective)

The theme of inclusivity/exclusivity resonates with Foucault's (1986) idea of heterotopias as sites where individuals are placed whose behaviours challenges to societal norms. Furthermore, being a heterotopia of resistance, the politics of inclusivity/exclusivity in Exarcheia work in reverse to welcome symbols of anti-establishment and express solidarity to the excluded. For instance, in places like Skoros (described below) there are frequent encounters of less affluent and marginalised individuals who, being excluded from conventional marketplace settings, use it as a final resort for 'over-consumption' (such as visitors quickly grabbing as many items as possible or items that are clearly not needed, such as an Internet router by a young kid; field notes, October 2011):

> Anti-consumerism is a pertinent need but so is solidarity. Skoros is an oasis for everyone, and this means everyone. The illegal immigrant is member of our society too. (Female, member of Exarcheia-based collective)

Finally, the theme of inclusivity/exclusivity encapsulates one of the most obvious ways in which place makes an impact to social relations and strengthens existing networks, that is, it act as a destination that appeals to like-minded people (and alienates not-so-like-minded ones):

> It seemed the perfect neighbourhood to me ... here you can do many of the things you generally do but from within 'the movement': you can have your coffee in a collective, you can buy some food stuff from Skoros, you can hang around and have a good debate in the park, you can get your clothes from Skoros. Not as if that includes literally everything you do – I wish – but slowly there is a tendency towards this direction and I do not think you can find this anywhere else ... much of your daily life is politicised. (Male, member of Exarcheia-based collective)

### *Solidarity*

Another related theme crossing a variety of social practices in Exarcheia is solidarity towards other radical movements, spaces of resistance, and vulnerable groups, among others. For instance, there is a variety of events such as talks and protests in support of radical movements in Palestine and Latin America, as well as exhibitions of solidarity towards resident movements in other parts of Athens and beyond. Concurrently, Exarcheia itself is receiving solidarity in the form of transnational activism (Leontidou, 2010); for instance, activists from across the world come to Exarcheia in December every year to join the protests in memory of the 2008 riots. Furthermore, a variety of educational seminars, legal services, collective cooking events, and help appeals are organised to support vulnerable groups such as the homeless and illegal immigrants, the *flâneurs par excellence* (Leontidou, 2010), making Exarcheia a stark contrast to more conservative and rather less hospitable parts of the city (see, e.g., Vradis & Dalakoglou, 2010).

More specific forms of consumer-oriented activism are also utilised as a way of expressing solidarity to like-minded movements across the globe. Sporos, for example, is a popular collective that seeks to promote alternative and solidarity trading mainly with the Zapatistas – themselves a revolutionary movement from Chiapas – but also, more recently, with various other organic and ethical producers. This cooperative critiques and problematises the global nature of the Fairtrade movement, seeing this as having sold out to the marketing system. Solidarity trading for Sporos volunteers meant scrutinising more closely the whole distribution chain, what is a 'fair price', and what model of consumer is assumed behind more mainstream Fairtrade movements.

> ... the problem is the way that Fairtrade has been developed in Europe and now you can find Fairtrade products in supermarkets and even in Starbucks. So we don't agree with that ... (Female, member of Exarcheia-based collective)

Similar networks of solidarity trading are organised by other collectives such as Nosostros and Autonomous Social Centre, which also promote solidarity trading through their own 'ethical baskets' and 'cupboards' respectively (similar to networks of community-supported agriculture; e.g. Thompson & Coskuner-Balli, 2007) but also theatrical plays, lectures, free music/photography/painting/language lessons, and community cooking events, among others. In addition, there is a variety of less formalised forms of solidarity-driven market exchanges. For instance, there is a network of retailers that has opted for a scheme in which various forms of discount and benefits are given to financial supporters of a left-wing radio station labelled 'in the red'. Less formally still, several participants mentioned that they would often buy only from those shops in which the political views of their owners aligned with theirs.

### Gifting, sharing, co-producing, and caring

Equally prevalent is an underlying logic of gifting, sharing, and co-producing various goods and services. For example, there are regular collective or community cooking events that run by the various Exarcheian movements on a weekly basis, as well as several ad hoc ones in relation to particular events and causes. The logic of gifting and caring for the community is also evident in the various examples of artwork and other installations that form part of the Exarcheian public space, such as benches and table games noted above In addition, a more explicit anti-consumerist ethos is noted in movements such as Skoros, a permanent gifting bazaar that is housed in a space that is co-rented by its members and where people can come and give goods, or take goods, or give and take goods. The explicit aim of Skoros is to promote anti-consumption and cultivate an ethos of gifting and sharing not only goods and services (e.g. hairdressing and furniture fixing) but also skills and knowledge (e.g. there are free weekly seminars on knitting and creative writing). Volunteers are committed to an alternative lifestyle that questions the 'restless dissatisfaction' that drives consumer culture (Campbell, 1987). As one informant elaborated:

> There is a saying that time is money and there is a thought that you have to work more to get more money to have goods, to buy things. And if you start to think that you can use your time in the way you want as an alternative to making money. If you don't get money but you have more time. This time is somehow like money because you do things you like and you can be creative and productive in another way. You can learn things, you exchange things and somehow this moves away from needing money for everything. (Female, member of Exarcheia-based collective)

Concurrently, as noted above, Skoros functions as a form of solidarity for the less affluent segments of the population (e.g. illegal immigrants), acknowledging that anti-consumerist and anti-materialistic ideals may not resonate with population segments that still struggle to meet basic material needs. Once again, we found informants challenging and moving away from the conventional logic of mainstream charity shops when they identified problems with both people that 'give' as a way to alleviate their guilt at overconsumption and those regular visitors that 'take' in order to become 'overconsumers' (field notes, October 2010). Volunteers sometimes expressed a wish to actively change behaviours in this respect and saw talking and discussion with visitors to their premises as a way to bring this about:

> There are things, clothes, that come here exactly as they were bought from the shop that are never worn, with the price on them, never touched. It's really something and you have to talk sometimes with these people to ask why you have to buy so many things and then give them away? And you give this away to go and buy again . . . Why is this happening, do I need all this stuff? I mean it's not only don't bring the stuff and go and buy more new. It's also don't bring stuff and don't take so much because maybe you don't need so much anyway. Try to reduce your need for stuff. (Female, member of Exarcheia-based collective)

In this way, Skoros, like so many sites in Exarcheia, becomes a place for the exchange and cultivation of ideas as much as any physical goods. Visitors learn to question their everyday assumptions and think in different ways. Concurrently, talks on related issues such as 'de-growth' (Latouche, 2009) and capitalist cracks (Holloway, 2010) are frequently organised and this helps contextualise these everyday struggles. 'I think it works like a stimulation, something happens here' (female, member of Exarcheia-based collective) was how one informant expressed it. This points to the power of heterotopian place in creating an intellectual, cognitive, (and political) impact in addition to a more corporeal one (Kohn, 2003).

Throughout these practices, there is also an underlying ethic of care not only for people and the community but also for the planet and the extent to which this can be accomplished in a neoliberal milieu. One of the most striking manifestations of this is residents' ongoing struggle to promote recycling in Exarcheia. Upon the introduction of new recycling bins across the neighbourhood, the issues for the 'Exarcheia Residents Committee' stretched way beyond the (individual) decision to recycle or not (e.g. Davies, Foxall, & Pallister, 2002), to include requests that the recycling is done by the council (rather than being outsourced to private companies) and that more information is provided on the methods of material separation.

## Events

One of the most striking manifestations of utopic imagination in Exarcheia is its 'park' or 'parko Navarinou' (Figure 1), a public place created as an act of civil disobedience in the aftermath of the Athens riots (March 2009) in what used to be a deserted parking lot earmarked for (commercial) redevelopment by the mayor and city planners. Tired of living in a city renowned for its grey spaces and lack of greenery (Ioannou & Serraois, 2007), the residents met overnight to break the asphalt with their own drills and cutters. They brought trucks carrying soil, plants, and seeds, and in the end transformed the parking lot into a very impressive park and public place. Trees and flowers have been planted throughout, along with several displays of artwork, a children's playground, benches, and a stage for music, talks, and theatrical performances.

The park is now a legitimate part of the Exarcheia public sphere, acclaimed by various politicians, journalists, and intellectuals as a successful example of 'here and now' social experimentation with horizontal structuring and self-management. An eclectic variety of groups co-exists within its borders, as documented in the following field notes (April, 2009):

> Mothers are visiting with children in the playground area and elderly folk resting on the many wooden benches mingle alongside politically motivated anarchists, left-wing residents and students. For older visitors I've chatted with, the park reminds them of a past era: people of all ages hanging around the same square, playing and interacting with each other.

Anyone can come to the weekly gatherings and request permission to use the park for events such as theatrical performances, talks, gigs, movie and poetry nights, anti-consumerism seminars, gifting bazaars, and so on, provided there is no entrance fee. Many local organisations, artists, and movements, otherwise disconnected from each other, use the park for special events. The park thus becomes a focal point to draw them together as the utopian heart of Exarcheian idealism. Any commercial venture is kept away, and the park relies on volunteers and donations for its support. Another requirement is that all events are not explicitly affiliated with any political parties, addressing another utopic aim: people of different ideological and political backgrounds creating new forums for dialogue in the will of creating and 'sharing out' a collective good (in addition to 'sharing in' private goods; Belk, 2010). A poster relating to a lecture on reclaiming public space by Andrea Papi (anarchist intellectual) encapsulates this notion of a space for utopian praxis:

> We should not be afraid to experiment, we have to, however, be non-flexible about our ideals. We have to create spaces of free creativity, where we will be able to live and try out different models of self-governing and social solidarity, saying no to the dominance of one model over the others. Multi-centres and non-centres, without hierarchies and bureaucracies within their core, capable of generating cultural innovations. A society within a society, a society ultimately capable of overturning the existing models and the collective subconscious. If, as it spreads, this society gets attacked by powerful institutional actors, then it will defend itself and will rebel in order to maintain its right for free choice, free will, free experimentation. Such a society is possible!

As such, the park represents one amongst several emerging Exarcheian 'agoras', where residents meet to debate and take decisions on a variety of issues that concern their right to the city (Harvey, 2003; Lefebvre, 1968) from drug trafficking to antisocial behaviour and educational initiatives. For instance, another relatively recent Exarcheian agora has been the pedestrian street in which the police shooting of a 15-year-old sparked the December 2008 riots. Troubled by the ongoing occurrence of antisocial behaviour, the Exarcheia residents have organised successful public talks in exactly the same space with a view to communicate to potential vandals what Exarcheia is and what is not: 'Not in the park, not in Exarcheia, not anywhere else' read one of the posters regarding zero tolerance to antisocial and bullying behaviours. Interestingly, although at the time of writing antisocial behaviour still represents a key problem in Exarcheia, a variety of solutions have been proposed, sharing in common a logic that is against any form of police intervention or involvement by other institutional actors and in favour of reviving the community ethos of that particular area through 'cultural interventions', including live music events, theatrical plays, wall painting activities, and so on. Paralleling the original twin function of 'agoras' in ancient Greece as political and commercial spaces, it is interesting that one of the most popular ideas concerned the establishment of a weekly market by organic food producers. Civic and commercial lives are once again tightly intertwined.

## Discussion

> . . . an urban exclave, surrendered not as much by the police as by the rest of the city, in which it feels like an alien object . . . an ugly facial spot that needs to be squeezed, otherwise its pus – urbane culture and political consciousness – threatens to infect the rest of the city . . . (Paraskevopoulos, 2009)

Exarcheia is everywhere. (newspaper headline during the Greek 2008 riots) Unlike other contemporary heterotopias such as gated communities, shopping

**Figure 3** The guerrilla park.

malls, and holiday resorts (see, e.g., Dehaene & De Cauter, 2008) or even anti-market festivals (Kozinets, 2002) and alternative consumption communities (e.g. Moraes et al., 2010; Szmigin et al., 2007), Exarcheia aims to confront directly rather than celebrate or escape the symbols of global capitalism and neoliberalism. It is a 'heterotopia of resistance' (Kohn, 2003), identified as such in a variety of 'antis' – for example, anti-commercial, anti-establishment, anti-authoritarian, anti-capitalist, and anti-consumerist – and yet it aspires to be an agent of urban and social transformation. For instance, it is widely acknowledged that the scale of the 2008 riots would not have been the same had the police shooting of a 15-year-old taken place in any other neighbourhood of Athens (e.g. Makrygianni & Tsavdaroglou, 2011). Perhaps less visible still but of equal importance is Exarcheia's role as a site that symbolises resistance and capacity for revolt against any neoliberal or conservative reforms in Greek politics and beyond.

Despite the wealth of social movements operating in Exarcheia and their diversity in ideological aims and objectives, they remain essentially spatialised and their interests often converge when it comes to broader political threads. Our findings corroborate Kohn's (2003) thesis that living in the same place makes an intuitive, corporeal, and a more intellectual impact. In addition, space/place acts as a destination and as a form of supportive environment or 'social capital' (Neilson & Paxton, 2010) that allows similar initiatives and movements to emerge. Indeed, a common view expressed in the interviews was that although there is nothing 'truly unique' about the area and similar collectives and initiatives have started in

CONTEMPORARY ISSUES IN GREEN AND ETHICAL MARKETING

other neighbourhoods, on the whole they are not as 'enthusiastically welcomed' and supported by residents as they are in Exarcheia. Living in Exarcheia deepens connections between people and leads to political cultivation. According to several informants from various groups and collectives, a sense of operating in the same area and having a related place identity feels in many cases all-they have in common.

This sense of Exarcheian community and identity often paved the way for various forms of collective action. For instance, the widespread use of graffiti, insertions of artwork and table games in public spaces, and the creation of guerrilla parks are not only acts of civil disobedience that encapsulate residents' actions against the commodification and private appropriation of public space, but also their ongoing attempt to live more communal and anti-consumerist lifestyles. As a participant in a resident committee meeting mentioned, 'public space is not as public as it appears to be' and most people continue to associate it with 'the arena for wearing trendy clothes, ordering frapuccinos and engaging in celebrity gossip'. This seemed to be far away from the utopian ideals of Exarcheia residents. Such findings corroborate calls for more research into the (anti-)consumption of public space/place and a deeper understanding of the dialogical relationship between space/place and various public and private consumption settings (e.g. Visconti, Sherry, Borghini, & Anderson, 2010). There is need to reconsider both the (ethical and green) consumption *of* space and place (e.g. guerrilla parks, spaces of solidarity trading) and (ethical and green) consumption *in* space and place (e.g. Exarcheia, Athens; see Goodman, Goodman, & Redclift, 2010).

Furthermore, as a heterotopia of resistance, Exarcheia's intellectual impact translates in radicalisation and can be viewed in the context of a broader social antagonist movement (Vradis & Dalakoglou, 2011). The agent behind most forms of ethical and green consumerism firmly remains the political activist and/or the Exarcheia resident rather than the consumer. To contrast this with debates in consumer research, this is not about a temporary escape from the symbols of capitalism, as in Kozinet's (2002) *Burning Man* or micro-emancipatory practices such as frequenting anti-Starbucks coffee establishments (Thompson & Arsel, 2004) and boycotting (Smith, 1990). Instead, Exarcheia emerges as a permanent site of antagonism (rather than escapism) that allows the inherent contradictions of doing so in a capitalist city to play against each other in a Marinian sense (e.g. debates about solidarity trading while consuming products of big multinationals). Whether this form of resistance allows true emancipation from the influences of consumer culture and commodification remains unresolved, but at a more practical level, it is a matter addressed by ensuring that even the most mundane forms of (consumer) resistance 'have a political rationale and are seen in the context of broader social and class struggles . . .', as one of our informants claimed.

Despite the fact that 'thicker' identity themes related to the political activist and/or Exarcheia resident rather than 'the consumer' (Barnett et al., 2011), our informants' commitment to taking responsibility, expressing solidarity, and exercising autonomy translated in various forms of consumer-oriented activism (cf. Micheletti, Follesdal, & Stolle, 2004). The overall heterotopic nature of Exarcheia paved the way for 'alternative ways of doing things' (Hetherington, 1997), and these included consumption-related action. For instance, concerns about trading relationships with the developing South can be addressed by visiting Sporos, a collective in support of Zapatistas, where people can go and read books on exploitative global trading systems (among other subjects), meet like-minded people, and enjoy a free cup of tea or coffee. Although Zapatistas coffee and other ethical and organic products are sold in Sporos, its members eschewed the category 'shop', in a similar vein to Dobscha and Ozanne's (2001) study of a group of ecofenimists that refused the category 'consumer'. Clearly, as a model of Fairtrade activism, this is fundamentally different from the occasion of an individual who walks around the aisles of a big supermarket chain (e.g. in London) and chooses to buy branded Fairtrade coffee upon weighting all available information. Likewise, recycling in Exarcheia is much more than the final stage of the consumption process: it is, for example, about questioning the role of institutional actors and finding out more about what happens to litter upon collection. Boycotting practices (e.g. Smith, 1990) in Exarcheia, as noted above, have also been taken to a somewhat different level by often vandalising and in effect 'demanding' market exit for retailer brands that are associated with global capitalism. Clearly, although in many other respects Exarcheia remains a typical Athenian neighbourhood and its residents have not escaped the influences of the global capitalist system (cf. Kozinets, 2002), they have a greater say in the nature and composition of both their public place and marketplace.

Exarcheia residents' examples of confronting consumer culture not only challenge individualised notions of the consumer, but also expose moralistic and post-political assumptions that often go unnoticed in ethical and green consumer research. For instance, an apparent lack of adequate 'ethical' behaviour on behalf of consumers is often documented by citing the rather low demand for ethical and green products and comparing this with concurrent high levels of demand for illegal and counterfeit goods (Devinney et al., 2010). In contrast, many of our informants challenged marketplace ideologies that equate illegal transgressions with (un)ethical ones (e.g. Vitell, 2003). For them, sharing intellectual properties and stealing from big corporations was essentially a political act, and they endorsed movements such as 'Sid', a collective for the promotion of freeware and sharing of intellectual properties that promote citizen emancipation on the web, and 'Robins of the Supermarkets', a group of people that organises robberies of supermarkets and then gives everything away to the poor. Clearly, such findings provide a real basis with which to problematise further what Devinney et al. (2010) refer to as the 'myth of the ethical consumer'.

Within consumer culture theory, a spirit of post-politics prevails with the subjective consequences of ideology finding outlets via consumption practices, performed mythologies and identity projects (Arnould & Thompson, 2007; Kozinets & Handelman, 2004; Luedicke, Giesler & Thompson 2010). In other words, a condition of neoliberal capitalism is understood to prevail within which all that is left is a playing out of an impotent consumer culture and a condition of post-politics with activism reduced to a series of alternative purchase decisions or naive political viewpoints and moralistic dismissals of consumers. By contrast, we submit that any transformation of consumer behaviour towards notionally green or ethical practices must be viewed in a more macro context of unsustainable capital expansion (Harvey, 2010) and an unchallenged paradigm of growth (Latouche, 2009). Therefore, we submit that if there is to be a consideration of a possibility of sustainability in real terms – that is, that we might not destroy the ecology on which we depend – then it must take place within a context of more radicalised politics. Whether or not Exarcheia is such a place remains unresolved, but it certainly is a context that at least pressurises existing assumptions of post-politics and decontextualised notions of ethical and green consumerism. Exarcheia may not be 'everywhere' – an actual newspaper headline during the 2008 riots, encapsulating that the turbulence of Exarcheia had already spread to Athens and beyond – but reminds us that all (ethical and green) consumption activity is essentially spatialised and has political implications.

## References

Arnould, E., & Thompson, C. (2007). Consumer culture theory (and we really mean theoretics): Dilemmas and opportunities posed by an academic branding strategy. In R. Belk & J. Sherry (Eds.), *Research in consumer behaviour*. Oxford: Elsevier.

Arnould, E., & Wallendorf, M. (1994). Market-oriented ethnography: Interpretation building and marketing strategy formulation. *Journal of Marketing Research*, 31, 484–504.

Bann, S. (1993). Introduction. In K. Kumar & S. Bann (Eds.), *Utopias and the millennium* (pp. 1–6). London: Reaktion Books.

Barnett, C., Clarke, N., Cloke, P., & Malpass, A. (2005). The political ethics of consumerism. *Consumer Policy Review*, 15(2), 45–51.

Barnett, C., Cloke, P., Clarke, N., & Malpass, A. (2011). *Globalising responsibility: The political rationalities of ethical consumption*. Oxford: Wiley-Blackwell.

Belk, R.W. (2010). Sharing. *Journal of Consumer Research*, 36(5), 715–734.

Black, I. (2010). Sustainability through anti-consumption. *Journal of Consumer Behaviour*, 9, 403–411.

Black, I.R., & Cherrier, H. (2010). Anti-consumption as part of living a sustainable lifestyle: Daily practices, contextual motivations and subjective values. *Journal of Consumer Behaviour*, 9, 437–453.

Bloch, E. (1995). *The principle of hope*. Cambridge: MIT Press.

Bray, J., Johns, N., & Kilburn, D. (2010). An exploratory study into the factors impeding ethical consumption. *Journal of Business Ethics*, 98(4), 597–608.

Browning, C., & McDonald, M. (2007). *Securitisation and emancipation: Towards a middle ground?* Paper presented at the annual meeting of the International Studies Association 48th Annual Convention, Chicago, IL.

Campbell, C. (1987). *The romantic ethic and the spirit of modern consumerism*. Oxford: Basil Blackwell.

Campo, D., & Ryan B. (2008). The entertainment zone: Unplanned nightlife and the revitalization of the American downtown. *Journal of Urban Design*, 13(3), 291–315.

Carrington, M.J., Neville, B.A., & Whitwell, G.J. (2010). Why ethical consumers don't walk their talk: Towards a framework for understanding the gap between the ethical purchase intentions and actual buying behaviour of ethically minded consumers. *Journal of Business Ethics*, 97(1), 139–158.

Caruana, R., & Crane, A. (2008). Constructing consumer responsibility: Exploring the role of corporate communications. *Organization Studies*, 29(12), 1495–1519.

Cenzatti, M. (2008). Heterotopias of difference. In M. Dehaene & L. De Cauter (Eds.), *Heterotopia and the city: Public space in a postcivil society* (pp. 75–86). London: Routledge.

Chatzidakis, A., Hibbert, S., & Smith, A. (2007). Why people don't take their concerns about Fair Trade to the supermarket: The role of neutralisation. *Journal of Business Ethics*, 74, 89–100.

Cherrier, H. (2009). Anti-consumption discourses and consumer-resistant identities. *Journal of Business Research*, 62(2), 181–190.

Chouliara, A. (2010). The 'abaton' of Exarcheia. Retrieved 5 September 2011 from http://www.newstime.gr/?i=nt.el.article&id=19540

Crane, A., & Matten, D. (2004). *Business ethics: A European perspective*. Oxford: Oxford University Press.

# CONTEMPORARY ISSUES IN GREEN AND ETHICAL MARKETING

Davies, J.D., Foxall, G.R., & Pallister, J. (2002). Beyond the intention–behaviour mythology: An integrated model of recycling. *Marketing Theory*, 2(1), 29–113.

Dehaene, M., & De Cauter, L. (2008). *Heterotopia and the city: Public space in a postcivil society*. London: Routledge.

Devinney, T.M., Auger, P., & Eckhardt, G. (2010). *The myth of the ethical consumer*. Cambridge: Cambridge University Press.

Diamantapoulos, A., Schlegelmilch, B.B., Sinkovics, R.R., & Bohlen, G.M. (2003). Can socio-demographics still play a role in profiling green consumers? A review of the evidence and an empirical investigation. *Journal of Business Research*, 56(4), 465–480.

Dimitriou, O. (2011). Avaton, 13th Thessaloniki Documentary Festival, 11–20th March.

Dobscha, S., & Ozanne, J.L. (2001). An ecofeminist analysis of environmentally friendly women using qualitative methodology: The emancipatory potential of an ecological life. *Journal of Public Policy and Marketing*, 20(2), 201–214.

Eckhardt, G.M., Belk, R., & Devinney, T. (2010). Why don't consumers consume ethically? *Journal of Consumer Behaviour*, 9, 426–436.

Foucault, M. (1986). Of other spaces. *Diacritics*, 16(1), 22–27.

Foucault, M. (2008 [1967]). Of other spaces. In M. Dehaene & L. De Cauter (Eds.), *Heterotopia and the city: Public space in a postcivil society* (pp. 13–30). London: Routledge.

Ger, G., & Belk, R.W. (1996). I'd like to buy the world a Coke: Consumptionscapes of the 'less affluent world'. *Journal of Consumer Policy*, 19(3), 271–304.

Glaser, B., & Strauss, A. (1967). *The discovery of grounded theory*. Chicago: Aldine.

Goodman, M.K., Goodman, D., & Redclift, M. (2010). *Consuming space – Placing consumption in perspective*. Farnham, England: Ashgate.

Harvey, D. (2003). The right to the city. *International Journal of Urban and Regional Research*, 27(4), 939–941.

Harvey, D. (2010). *The enigma of capital and the crises of capital*. London: Profile Books.

Hetherington, K. (1997). *The badlands of modernity: Heterotopia and social ordering*. New York: Routledge.

Holloway, J. (2010). *Crack capitalism*. London: Pluto Press.

Ioannou, B., & Serraos, K. (2007). The new 'faces' of the European metropolis and their Greek version. *International Journal of Sustainable Development and Planning*, 2(2), 205–221.

Jameson, F. (1977). Of islands and trenches: Naturalization and the production of utopian discourse. *Diacritics*, 7(2), 2–21.

Jameson, F. (1982). Progress versus utopia; Or, can we imagine the future. *Science Fiction Studies*, 9, 147–166.

Kakissis, J. (2010). Rebels hope new austerity rekindles spirit of Greece's activist heart. *New York Times*. Retrieved 20 May 2010 from: http://www.nytimes.com/2010/05/20/world/europe/20iht-greece.html?_r=1

Kat, C. (2008). Athenian democracy in ruins. *The Guardian*. Retrieved 8 December 2008 from http://www.guardian.co.uk/commentisfree/2008/dec/08/greece

Kohn, M. (2003). *Radical spaces: Building the house of the people*. Ithaca, NY: Cornell University Press.

Kozinets, R.V. (2002). Can consumers escape the market? Emancipatory illuminations from burning man. *Journal of Consumer Research*, 29, 20–38.

Kozinets, R.V., & Handelman, J. (2004). Adversaries of consumption: Consumer, movements, activism and ideology. *Journal of Consumer Research*, 31, 691–704.

Latouche, S. (2009). *Farewell to growth*. Cambridge: Polity Press.

Lefebvre, H. (1968). *Le droit à la ville*. Paris: Anthropos.

Lefebvre, H. (1991). *The production of space*. Oxford: Blackwell.

Leontidou, L. (2010). Urban social movements in 'weak' civil societies: The right to the city and cosmopolitan activism in Southern Europe. *Urban Studies*, 47(6), 1179–1203.

Lincoln, Y.S., & Guba, E.G. (1985). *Naturalistic inquiry*. Newbury Park, CA: Sage.

Luedicke, M.K., Thompson, C.J., & Giesler, M. (2010). Consumer identity work as moral protagonism: How myth and ideology animate a brand-mediated moral conflict. *Journal of Consumer Research*, 36(6), 1016–1032.

Maclaran, P., & Brown. S. (2005). The centre cannot hold: Consuming the utopian marketplace. *Journal of Consumer Research*, 32, 311–323.

Makrygianni, V. and Tsadvaroglou, H. (2011). Urban planning and revolt: A spatial analysis of the December 2008 uprising in Athens. In Vradis, A., & Dalakoglou, D. (Eds). Revolt and crisis in Greece – Between a present yet to pass and a future yet to come. London: AK Press. (pp. 29–57).

Marin, L. (1984). *Utopics: The semiological play of textual spaces* (R.A. Vollrath, Trans.). Atlantic Highlands, NJ: Humanities Press.

McEachern, M.G., Warnaby, G., Carringan, M., & Szmigin, I. (2010). Thinking locally, acting locally? Conscious consumers and farmers' markets, *Journal of Marketing Management*, 26, 395–412.

Micheletti, M., Follesdal, A., & Stolle, D. (2004). *Politics, products and markets: Exploring political consumerism past and present*. London: Transportation.

Moraes, C., Szmigin, I., & Carrigan, M. (2010). Living production-engaged alternatives: An examination of new consumption communities. *Consumption, Markets and Culture*, 13(3), 273–298.

Murtola, A.-M. (2010). Commodification of utopia: The lotus eaters revisited. *Culture and Organisation*, 15, 37–54.

Neilson, L.A., & Paxton, S. (2010). Social capital and political consumerism: A multi-level analysis. *Social Problems*, 57, 5–24.

Papadopoulou, C. (2010). The other Exarcheia. *Athens News*. Retrieved 5 September 2011 from: http://www.athensnews gr/issue/13373/20999

Paraskevopoulos, Y. (2009). Exarcheiosis of values. *Eleftherotypia*. Retrieved 5 September 2011 from: http://www.enet.gr/?i=arthra-sthles.el.home&id=97088

Sanders, C.R. (1987). Consuming as social action: Ethnographic methods in consumer research. In M. Wallendorf & P. Anderson (Eds.), *Advances in consumer research* (Vol. 14, pp. 71–75). Provo, UT: Association for Consumer Research.

Shah, D.V., McLeod, D.M., Friedland, L., & Nelson, M.R. (2007). The politics of consumption/the consumption of politics. *The Annals of the American Academy of Political and Social Science*, 611, 6–15.

Smith, N.C. (1990). *Morality and the market: Consumer pressure for corporate accountability*. London: Routledge.

Soja, E.W. (1980). The socio-spatial dialectic. *Annals of the Association of American Geographers*, 70, 207–225.

Soja, E.W. (1996). *Thirdspace: Journeys to Los Angeles and other real – and – imagined places*. Cambridge, MA: Blackwell.

Spiggle, S. (1994). Analysis and interpretation of qualitative data in consumer research. *Journal of Consumer Research*, 21, 491–503.

Strauss, A., & Corbin, J. (1990). *Basics of qualitative research*. Thousand Oaks, CA: Sage.

Szmigin, I., Carrigan, M., & Bekin, C. (2007). New consumption communities and the re-enabling of 21st century consumers. In B. Cova, R.V. Kozinets, & A. Shankar (Ed.), *Consumer tribes* (pp. 296–311). Oxford: Elsevier/Butterworth-Heinemann.

Thompson, C.J., & Arsel, Z. (2004). The Starbucks brandscape and consumers' (anticorporate) experiences of glocalisation. *Journal of Consumer Research*, 31, 631–642.

Thompson, C.J., & Coskuner-Balli, G. (2007). Countervailing market responses to corporate co-optation and the ideological recruitment of consumption communities. *Journal of Consumer Research*, 34, 135–152.

Visconti, L.M., Sherry, J.F., Borghini, S., & Anderson, L. (2010). Street art, sweet art? Reclaiming the 'public' in public space. *Journal of Consumer Research*, 37(3), 511–529.

Vitell, S.J. (2003). Consumer ethics research: Review, synthesis and suggestions for the future. *Journal of Business Ethics*, 43, 33–47.

Vradis, A., & Dalakoglou, D. (2010). After December: Spatial legacies of the 2008 Athens uprising. *Upping the Anti*, 10, 123–135.

Vradis, A., & Dalakoglou, D. (2011). *Revolt and crisis in Greece – Between a present yet to pass and a future yet to come*. London: AK Press.

# Index

Note:
Page numbers in **bold** type refer to figures
Page numbers in *italic* type refer to tables
Page numbers followed by 'a' or 'n' refer to
appendices or notes respectively

Abdul-Muhmin, A.G. 51
Act on CO2 266
activism: Fairtrade 183, 308, 314
ageing 103–6
air travel 213, 214–15, 217, 219–20, 234
Alevizou, P.J.: et al 4, 250–69
Allport, G. 53
alternative consumption 204–6
altruism 194
altruistic values 184
Alzate, M.: et al 13
American Marketing Association (AMA) 205
Andersson, L.M.: and Bateman, T.S. 278
Angell, R.J.: Megicks, G. and Memery, J. 2–3, 74–93
Arnould, E.: and Thompson, C. 299
Athens 312
Attalla, A.: and Carrigan, M. 229–30
attitudes: consumer towards food production sustainability 143–80; environmental 52, 53; formation 133; to pig meat production 148–9; towards buying organic food 131, 133–7, *133*
attitudinal constructs 253–4
Autonomous Social Centre 308
autonomy: need 306–7

Bae, H-S. 12
Bagozzi, R.P.: and Perugini, M. 11, 13, 277–8
balancing paradigm of customer satisfaction (Mick and Fournier) 199
Bamberg, S. 55; and Moser, C. 229
Bandura, A. 276, 288
Bang, H.K.: et al 52
Bansal, P. 279
Barber, N.: et al 54
Barcellos, M. de: et al 3, 143–63
Bateman, T.S. 278; and Andersson, L.M. 278
Bedford, T.: et al 255
behaviour 230; citizenship 278–9; creating new 286; electric car drivers 9; environmental 16, 55–7; environmentally responsible (ERB) in workplace 273–96; ethical consumer 101–3; generalised environmental behaviours (GEB)

55; leadership 278–9; normalising green 226–46; organisational citizenship behaviour (OCB) 280–1, 294a, 295a, 296a; pro-environmental consumer 100–16; Theory of Planned Behaviour (TPB) 11–12, 230
behavioural groupings 253
Belgians: electric car use study 7–33
beliefs 277
Belz, F.: and Peattie, K. 228
Binney, W.M.: and Brennan, L. 228
biospheric values 184
Black, I. 299
Bloch, E. 301
Borgmann, A. 208
Bouwen, R.: and Steyaert, C. 281
Bradshaw, A.: Chatzidakis, A. and Maclaran, P. 5, 297–318
Brazil 146, 157; citizen types and sustainability *160–1*; cluster profiles 166–80a; conjoint factors *149*; food production 143–80; sociodemographic characteristics *152*
Brennan, L.: and Binney, W.M. 228
Bronfenbrenner, U. 230
Browning, C.: and McDonald, M. 301
Burchell, K.: Riley, D.L. and Rettie, R. 4, 226–46
Burgess, J.: et al 255, 261
*Burning Man* (Kozinet) 313
buying: socially responsible 76–7

Campo, D.: and Ryan, B. 300
Campomar, M.C.: Velodu-de-Oliveira, T.M. and Ikeda, A.A. 186
carbon emissions 49; reduction study 208–20
carbon footprints 54–5, 209, 210, 212–16, 221–2, 266
Carbon Rationing Action Groups 209
Carbon Reduction Commitment Scheme 281
caring 309–10
Carrigan, M.: and Attalla, A. 229–30
cars 212, 213–14; electric 7–33
Caruana, R.: and Crane, A. 298
Castoriadis, C. 216–20

# INDEX

Certeau, M. de 222
Chang, C-M.: *et al* 12
change: employee initiated 274
Chatzidakis, A.: Maclaran, P. and Bradshaw, A. 5, 297–318
Cherrier, H. 299; Szuba, M.; and Özçağlar-Toulouse, N. 4, 204–23
chicken coop **218**
China 157–8; citizen types and sustainability *160-1*; cluster profiles 166–80a; conjoint factors *149*; consumers and organic food 122–42; food production 143–63; organic food attitudes **133**; study sociodemographic characteristics *152*
Chiu, C-M.: *et al* 12
citizen types: EU *160-1*; and sustainability *160-1*
citizenship 115; behaviour 278–9
clothing *see* ethical clothing
co-producing 309–10
$CO_2$ gas emission 50
cognitive approaches 261
comfort and fit 194
computer ownership 220
computer-aided qualitative data analysis (CAQDAS) 282
concern *198*; environmental 16, 194–6, 284–5; social 196
consumers: attitudes towards food production sustainability 143–80; cars 16; Chinese and organic food 122–42; electric car usage 15–17; environmental behaviour 16; environmental concern 16; environmentally conscious 206; ethical 251; ethical behaviour 101–3; green 206, 251, 251–65; grey 251; personal values 16; Portuguese 229; pro-environmental behaviour 100–16; senior 100–21; US and environmental knowledge 49–68
consumption 250; alternative 204–6; ethical 183–4; ethical clothing 181–200; green 297–315; movements 298–300; reduced 207–8; sustainable 250–69; sustainable and greenhouse-gas (GHG) reduction 204–25; sustainable individual strategies 250–69
CRAGgers 208–21
Crane, A.: and Caruana, R. 298; and Peattie, K. 228
customer satisfaction 199
cycling 230–1

Damhorst, M.L.: and Kim, H.E. 194
Davenport, E.: and Low, W. 101
Davies, G.: *et al* 255
Department for Environment, Food and Rural Affairs (DEFRA) 229
Devinney, T.M.: *et al* 314
Devon (UK) 253
Diamantopoulos, A.: *et al* 229
Dickson, M.A. 183; and Littrell, M.A. 183, 197

Dietz, T.: Kalof, L. and Stern, P. 184
Dobscha, S.: and Ozanne, J.L. 314
Dolan, P. 208
Dunlap, R.F.: *et al* 277
Duran, M.: *et al* 136

Ecologically Conscious Consumer Behaviour (ECCB) scale 3, 107, **110**
education 268
egoistic values 184
Egri, C.P.: and Herman, S. 279
Ehrenfeld, J.R. 7
Ekici, A.: and Sandıkçı, Ö. 207
electric car use 7–33; emotions items 45–6a; emotions role 7–9, 10–14; intention for different consumers 15–17; models of new product and behaviour adoption 9; opinion leadership 16; sociodemographic characteristics and usage intention 14–15; study 17–29; study behavioural control 43–4a; study full sample regression analysis *20-2*; study personal values items *47–8a*; study regression analyses *19*; study results 18–24; study use intention *23, 25, 26, 27-8*; study variables 38–42a; usage intention 14–15
emotions: consumer decision making 10–11; and electric car use 7–33; and TPB 11–14
employee initiated change 274
environmental attitudes 53; hypothesised model **52**
environmental behaviour 16, 55–7
environmental concern 16, 194–6, 284–5
environmental knowledge 49–68; scales 73a
environmentally conscious consumers 206
environmentally responsible behaviour (ERB): workplace 273–96
environmentally responsible organisational citizenship behaviours (EROCBs) 273–90, **274, 275**; individual determinants 276–8; individual factors 278; organisational factors 278–9; personal drives **284**
ethical clothing: consumption 181–200; consumption value map *193*; environmental concern 194–6; quality 194; social concern 196; study 186–99; study attributes table *190*; study consequences table *192*; study patterns 194–6; study values table *192*; style 194; value map patterns **195**; wearing 194
ethical consumer behaviour 101–3
*Ethical Consumer, The* 259, 268
ethical consumers 251
ethical consumption: values driver 183–4
ethical tourism 298–9
ethnographic study: Exarcheia (Athens, Greece) 301–11
Etzioni, A. 197

# INDEX

European Union (EU) 156–7; citizen types *160-1*; cluster profiles 166–180a; conjoint factors *149*; food production 143–63; study sociodemographic characteristics *152*
events 310–11
Exarcheia (Athens, Greece) 297–318; boycotting practices 314; caring 309–10; co-producing 309–10; disposable tablecloth **306**; ethnographic study 301–11; events 310–11; exclusivity 307–8; gifting 309–10; guerrilla park **312**; inclusivity 307–8; marketplace 304–6; movements 309; research phases and methods *302*; sharing 309–10; social practices 306–10; solidarity 308–9
Exceptors 259, 261–9, *262*, **263**
exclusivity 307–8

Fairtrade activism 183, 308, 314
farms: pig *150–1*, 157, 159, 162
fashion: slow 199
Ferdous, A.S.: *et al* 2, 49–68
Finisterra do Paço, A.M.: and Raposo M.L.B. 229
Flamm, B. 54
Fletcher, K. 199
flying 213, 214–15, 217, 219–20, 234
food: safety 146n *see also* local food; organic food
food production (pork): Brazil, China, EU 143–80; sustainability aspects 143–63
Foucault, M. 299, 300, 307
Fournier, S.: and Mick, D. 199
France: *objecteur de croissance* 208–21
Friends of the Earth 232

Gärling, A.: and Thøgersen, J. 13
Garma, R.: *et al* 2, 49–68
generalised environmental behaviours (GEB) 55
Germany: senior consumers 100–21
gifting 309–10
Gilg, A.: *et al* 253
glass floor: concept 204–25; study findings 210–20
global warming 49, 285
Gould, S.J. 209
graffiti 303
Grant, 205, 207, 228
Grau, S.L.: *et al* 2, 49–68
green behaviour: normalising 226–45
green consumers 206, 251–65; Exceptors 259; identifying Exceptors *262*; identifying Selectors *262*; identifying Translators *262*; interviewees strategies **263**; Selectors 260; study 256–65; Translators 258–9
green consumption 297–315
green marketing 205–7, 228–30, 298–300; age ANOVA results *238-9*; gender ANOVA results *242*; marital status ANOVA results *240*; regional ANOVA results *242*; social class

ANOVA results *237*; strategies *243–4*; study 231–46; study activity consensus 235, *236*; study activity ratings **234**; working status ANOVA results *241*
green segmentation 252
greenhouse-gas (GHG): emissions reduction 204–25
greenophobia 228
Greenpeace 232
greenwash 228
grey consumers 251
Grigoropoulos, A.: shrine 304, **305**
group contexts 281
groups: distinguishing 254
Gruber, T.: *et al* 3–4, 181–200
Grunert, K.G.: *et al* 3, 143–63; and Grunert, S. 187
Guangzhou (China): organic food buying study 122–42

Harrison, C.: *et al* 255
Herman, S.: and Egri, C.P. 279
heterotopian space *see* Exarcheia (Athens, Greece)
heterotopias 301, 307; of resistance 300, 307, 312, 313; and utopic social play 300–1
Hetherington, K. 300, 301
hierarchical value map (HVM) 185, 196, 197–9, 200; ethical clothing **193**
Hines, J.: and O'Neill, G.S. 184
Hobson, K.: *et al* 255
Hofmeister, A.: Kohlbacher, F. and Riley, L.S. 3, 100–16
Hofstede, G. 127
Holbrook, M.B. 209
holistic model 267
Hostager, T.J.: *et al* 279
house heating 215–16
Howell, R.A. 53
Hsu, M-H.: *et al* 12
human values 184
Hungary: senior consumers 100–21
Hynie, M.: MacDonald, T.K. and Marques, S. 12–13

Ikeda, A.A.: Campomar, M.C. and Velodu-de-Oliveira, T.M. 186
imaginary: social 216–23
inclusivity 307–8
innovation adoption model 123–5, *124*
Institute of Grocery Distribution (IGD): report (2008) 76
internal marketing (IM) 280–1, 289
internal social marketing (ISM) 273–96
introspection 209
Iwanow, H.: *et al* 183
Iyer, R.: and Muncy, J.A. 207

# INDEX

Jägel, T.: *et al* 3–4, 181–200
Jansson, J. 14
Japan: senior consumers 100–21
Joergens, C. 183
Joireman, J.A.: Van Lange, P.A.M. and Van Vugt, M. 13
Jones, R.E.: *et al* 277
Jong, A. de: Wetzels, M.; and de Ruyter, L. 278
*Journal of Marketing Management* 1

Kalof, L.: Stern, P. and Dietz, T. 184
Katz-Gerro, T.: and Oreg, S. 55–6
Keeling, K.: *et al* 3–4, 181–200
Kilbourne, W.E.: *et al* 221; and Pickett, G. 276
Kim, H.E.: and Damhorst, M.L. 194
knowledge: environmental 49–68
Kohlbacher, F.: Riley, L.S. and Hofmeister, A. 3, 100–16
Kohn, M. 300, 303, 312
Kotcher, J.E.: and Nisbet, M.C. 28
Kozinet, R.V. 313
Krystallis, A.: *et al* 3, 143–63
Kuijlen, A.A.A.: and van Raaij, W.F. 254
Kumju Hwang, C-A.: *et al* 4, 229, 250–69
Kvasova, O.: Leounidou, L.C. and Leonidou, C.N. 8
Kwortnik, R.J.: and Ross, W.T. 13

laddering technique 184–5, 186
LADDERMAP 189
Latouche, S. 209
leadership behaviour 278–9
Lee, K. 228
Leonidou, L.C.: Leonidu, C.N. and Kvasova, O. 8
Lewis, B.R.: and Varey, R.J. 280
light bulbs 267
Lindenberg, S.: and Steg, L. 277
Littrell, M.A.: and Dickson, M.A. 183, 197
local food: definition 75–6; development 75–6; factor analysis 83; influence studies 78–9; items 96–9a; post-hoc tests 86; qualitative investigation 79–89, 79; quantitative investigation 80–9, 81; regression analysis 88; shopping 74–93; as shopping experience 77; socially responsible buying 76–7
Loewenstein, G.F. 8
Lopez, W.: *et al* 13
Low, W.: and Davenport, E. 101
Lozada, H.R.: and Mintu, A.T. 228

McDonald, M.: and Browning, C. 301
McDonald, S.: *et al* 4, 229, 250–69
MacDonald, T.K.: Marques, S. and Hynie, M. 12–13
McEachern, M.G.: and Schröder, M.J.A. 102
McKenzie-Mohr, D. 277
McKercher, B.: *et al* 55

Maclaran, P.: Bradshaw, A. and Chatzidakis, A. 5, 297–318
management: influencing 286–8
Manzini, E. 7
Marin, L. 300–1
marketing: laddering 186; social 273–90; strategies 240–4, 245; sustainability 226–46
marketplace: Exarcheia (Athens, Greece) 304–6
Marques, S.: Hynie, M. and MacDonald, T.K. 12–13
means-end chain theory 184–5, 200
meat eating 215
media 126, 245
Megicks, P.: Memery, J. and Angell, R.J. 2–3, 74–93
Mertig, A.C.: *et al* 277
Mick, D.: and Fournier, S. 199
Miller, D. 77
Mintel 75, 183, 186, 187–8
Mintu, A.T.: and Lozada, H.R. 228
Moons, I.: and de Pelsmacker, P. 2, 7–33
Moreau, C.P.: and Wood, S.L. 13
Moser, C.: and Bamberg, S. 229
motivation 278
Muncy, J.A.: and Iyer, R. 207
Murtola, A-M. 300

Nava, M. 206
needs 208; autonomy 306–7; social construction 212–16
Ness, M.: and Tregear, A. 78
new product adoption: models 9
Niinimäki, K 190, 194
Nilsson, A.: *et al* 281
Nisbet, M.C.: and Kotcher, J.E. 28
Norm Activation Theory (Schwartz) 56
normalising green behaviours 226–46
Norman, D.A. 18
norms 277; social 227, 230, 231, 245–6; societal 216
Nosotros 308

Oates, C.J.: *et al* 4, 229, 250–69
*objecteur de croissance* 208–21
Ölander, F.: and Thøgersen, J. 55
older (senior) consumers: study 100–21
Oliver, J.D.: and Rosen, D.E. 14
O'Neill, G.S.: and Hines, J. 184
opinion leadership: cars 16
Oreg, S.: and Katz-Gerro, T. 55–6
organic food: attitudes towards buying 131, 133–7, 133; buying motives 125–6; Chinese attitudes 133; and Chinese consumers 122–42; innovation adaption model 123–5, 124; intentions 135; motives research 125–36
organisational citizenship behaviour (OCB): descriptions 295a; focus group interview

# INDEX

schedule 296a; social marketing 280–1; types 294a
organisational factors 298–9
Oskamp, S.: and Tracy, A.P. 261–2
O'Sullivan, T.: and Smith, A.M. 4–5, 273–90
Ottman, J.A. 205
Ozanne, J.L.: and Dobscha, S. 314
Özçağlar-Toulouse, N.: Cherrier, H. and Szuba, M. 4, 204–23; *et al* 254

Papadopoulou, C. 303
Papi, A. 311
Paraskevopouos, Y. 311
Peattie, K. 250, 255, 257, 264–5; and Belz, F. 228; and Crane, A. 227, 228; and Peattie, S. 227
Pelsmacker, P. de: and Moons, I. 2, 7–33
Perceived Consumer Effectiveness (PCE) 261
permaculture gardening 217–18; allotment 217
Perrea, T.: *et al* 3, 143–63
personal values 16
Perugini, M.: and Bagozzi, R.P. 11, 13, 277–8
Philipps, J.M.: *et al* 187; and Reynolds, T. 186
Pickett, G.: and Kilbourne, W.E. 276
pig meat production: attitudes to 148–9
pig production 145–6
Podsakoff, P.M.: *et al* 278, 279, 282
Polonsky, M.J. 222; *et al* 2, 49–68
Portrait Value Questionnaire (PVQ) 131
Portuguese consumers 229
practice theory 230–1
pro-environmental consumer behaviour 100–16
products: sustainable 7–9
Prothero, A. 1

quality 194

Raaij, W.F. van: and Kuijlen, A.A.A. 254
Raposo, M.L.B.: and Finisterra do Paço, A.M. 229
Recycle Now 266
reduced consumption 207–8
Reisch, L.A. 208, 213
Reppel, A.: *et al* 3–4, 81–101
resistance: heterotopia 300, 307, 312, 313
Rettie, R.: Burchell, K. and Riley, D.L. 4, 226–46; *et al* 227
Reynolds, T. 187; and Philipps, J.M 186
Riach, K.: and Shaw, D. 222
Riley, L.S.: Hofmeister, A. and Kohlbacher, F. 3, 100–16
Rokka, J.: and Uusitalo, L. 55
role conflict 278
Roper Organization 254
Rosen, D.E.: and Oliver, J.D. 14
Ross, W.T.: and Kwortnik, R.J. 13
Ruyter, L. de: de Jong, A. and Wetzels, M. 278
Ryan, B.: and Campo, D. 300

Sabucedo, M.: *et al* 13
Sanders, C.R. 302
Sandıkçı, Ö.: and Ekici, A. 207
Schlegelmilch, B.B. 182
Schor, J. 207
Schröder, M.J.A.: and McEachern, M.G. 102
Schwartz, S.H. 127, 196; 15-item value scale 18; human values 184; Norm Activation Theory 56; Portrait Value Questionnaire (PVQ) 131
segmentation 236–40; approach assumptions 251–6; green 252 studies 229
Selectors 260, 261–9, *262*, **263**
SEM (structural equation modelling) 51, 57, 131
senior consumers 100–21; ethical behaviour 106
sharing 309–10
Shaw, D.: and Riach, K. 222
shopping: local food 74–93
Shove, E. 219, 230
Skoros (gifting bazaar) 305, 307, 308, 309, 310
slow fashion 199
Smith, A.M.: and O'Sullivan, T. 4–5, 273–90
social cognitive therapy (SCT) 276
social concern 196
social imaginary 216–23
social marketing approach: internal 273–96
social normalisation 227, 230, 231, 245–6
social practices 306–10
socially responsible buying 76–7
societal norms 216
Socio-Economic Research and Intelligence Observatory (SERIO) investigation (2008) 76
Soja, E.W. 300
solidarity 308–9
Steg, L.: and Lindenberg, S. 277; and Vleka, C. 55
Stern, P.: Dietz, T. and Kalof, L. 184
Stern, S. 275; *et al* 145
Steyaert, C.: and Bouwen, R. 281
style 194
Sun, H.: and Zhang, P. 8
sustainability: and citizen types *160-1*; food production aspects 143–63; marketing 226–46; pig production 145–6
sustainable consumption: and greenhouse-gas (GHG) reduction 204–25; individual strategies 250–69
sustainable products: emotions 7–9
Szuba, M.: Özçağlar-Toulouse, N. and Cherrier, H. 4, 204–23

tablecloth: disposable **306**
teams 285–6
Technology Acceptance Model (TAM) 8
Theory of Planned Behaviour (TPB) 11–12, 230; and emotions 11–14
Theory of Reasoned Action (TRA) 49, 51–2, 54–6

323

# INDEX

Thøgersen, J. 3, 277; and Gärling, A. 13; and
 Ölander, F. 55; and Yanfeng, Z. 3, 122–39
Thompson, C.J. 210; and Arnould, E. 299
toner cartridge recycling 286
tourism: ethical 298–9
Tracy, A.P.: and Oskamp, S. 261–2
Translators 258–9, 261–9, *262*, **263**
Tregear, A.: and Ness, M. 78
two-step flow 268

United Kingdom (UK): CRAGgers 208–21;
 Defra 282; Devon study 253; senior consumers
 100–21
United Nations (UN): Environment Programme
 (EP) 226
United States of America (USA): $CO_2$ gas
 emissions 50
United States consumers: and environmental
 knowledge 49–68, *73a*; study 57–65; study
 convergent validity assessment *62*; study data
 analysis 59–65; study descriptive statistics *60–
 1*; study discriminant validity assessment *63*;
 study factors' correlations matrix *64*; study
 respondents *58*; study structural coefficients *64*
universalism values (Schwartz) 126, 127
utopias 309–10; commodified 300
utopic social play: and heterotopias 300–1
Uusitalo, L.: and Rokka, J. 55

values: 15-item scale (Schwartz) 18; as drivers of
 ethical consumption 183–4; personal 16;
 universalism 126, 127
Van Lange, P.A.M.: Van Vugt, M.; and Joireman,
 J.A. 13
Van Liere, K.D.: *et al* 277
Varey, R.J.: and Lewis, B.R. 280

VBN model 277
vegetarianism 215
Velodu-de-Oliveira, T.M.: Ikeda, A.A. and
 Campomar, M.C. 186
Verbeke, W.: *et al* 3, 143–63
Vermeir, I.: and Verbeke, W. 78
Verplanken, B.: and Wood, W. 221
Vleka, C.: and Steg, L. 55
Vocino, A.: *et al* 2, 49–68

Wang, X. 12
waste recycling 227
Weatherell, C.: *et al* 78
Wetzels, M.: de Ruyter, L.; and de Jong, A. 278
*Why We Want What We Don't Need* (Schor) 207
Wieseke, J.: *et al* 280
Wood, S.L.: and Moreau, C.P. 13
Wood, W.: and Verplanken, B. 221
workplace: environmentally responsible behaviour
 (ERB) 273–96

Yanfeng, Z.: and Thøgersen, J. 3, 122–39
Yen, C-H.: *et al* 12
Young, C.W.: *et al* 4, 250–69
Young, W.: *et al* 229

Zapatistas 313–14
Zhang, P.: and Sun, H. 8

# Journal of Marketing Management

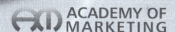 

**Editors: Mark Tadajewski,** *University of Strathclyde, UK* and **Paul Hewer,** *University of Strathclyde, UK*

**Founding Editor: Michael J Baker,**
*University of Strathclyde, UK*

The *Journal of Marketing Management* (*JMM*) is the official Journal of the Academy of Marketing and is a double-blind peer-reviewed periodical with an international reputation for publishing influential and original contributions.

*JMM* is concerned with all aspects of the management of marketing and is intended to provide a forum for the exchange of the latest research ideas and best practice in the field of marketing as a whole. *JMM* seeks to meet the needs of a wide but sophisticated audience comprising senior marketing executives and their advisors, senior line managers, teachers and researchers in marketing and undergraduate and postgraduate students of the subject.

Visit the *Journal of Marketing Management* website to:

- subscribe
- view an online sample copy
- view free articles, news and offers
- register to receive quarterly eUpdates
- register to receive table of contents alerts
- submit your research

# www.tandfonline.com/rjmm

www.routledge.com/9780415628891

## Key Issues in Marketing Management

# New Horizons in Arts, Heritage, Nonprofit and Social Marketing

Edited by Roger Bennett, Finola Kerrigan and Daragh O'Reilly

Arts, heritage, non-profit and social marketing today comprise key components of the contemporary marketing management scene. Governments, charities and voluntary sector organisations throughout the world are increasingly involved in the development of marketing campaigns, and more and more of these organisations are likely to utilise the latest marketing methods. Research in the arts, heritage, non-profit and social marketing fields is intellectually rigorous, relevant for user communities, and has a great deal to offer to marketing theory as well as to promotional practice.

This book presents a collection of stimulating articles that report some of the freshest and most innovative empirical and conceptual research in arts, heritage, non-profit and social marketing. They explore new ideas, challenge pre-existing orthodoxies, develop knowledge, and demonstrate the epistemological importance of current research in these critical areas.

This book was originally published as a special issue of the *Journal of Marketing Management*.

June 2012: 246 x 174: 192pp
Hb: 978-0-415-62889-1
£85 / $135

For more information and to order a copy visit
www.routledge.com/9780415628891

Available from all good bookshops